HANDBOOK OF COMMONLY USED AMERICAN IDIOMS

Third Edition

Adam Makkai, Ph. D.
Maxine T. Boatner, Ph. D.
John E. Gates , Ph. D.

Revised and Updated
by Adam Makkai
Professor of Linguistics
University of Illinois at Chicago

BARRON'S

This book is based on *A Dictionary of American Idioms* (Barron's © 1975) by Maxine Tull Boatner, Ph.D., John Edward Gates, Ph.D., Professor of English, Indiana State University, and Adam Makkai, Ph.D., Professor of Linguistics, University of Illinois at Chicago.

All inquiries should be addressed to:
Barron's Educational Series, Inc.
250 Wireless Boulevard
Hauppauge, New York 11788

International Standard Book Number 0-8120-9239-2

Library of Congress Catalog Card Number 95-78494

PRINTED IN THE UNITED STATES OF AMERICA

5678   5500   987

Table of Contents

Acknowledgments

This handbook is the result of the work of many hands. It is based on *A Dictionary of American Idioms*, first published by Barron's Educational Series 1975, which, in turn, had its source in *A Dictionary of Idioms for the Deaf*, edited by Maxine Tull Boatner, project director, aided by chief linguistic advisor, J. Edward Gates, published in 1969 and copyrighted by the American School for the Deaf. The consulting committee consisted of Dr. Edmund E. Boatner, Dr. William J. McClure, Dr. Clarence D. O'Connor, Dr. George T. Pratt, Jack Brady, M.A., Richard K. Lane, and Professor H. A. Gleason, Jr., of the Hartford Seminary Foundation. Special editors for various subcategories, such as usage, sport terms, etc., were Elizabeth Meltzer and E. Ward Gilman; Loy E. Golladay helped as language consultant with reviewing and editing. Definers were Edmund Casetti, Philip H. Cummings, Anne M. Driscoll, Harold J. Flavin, Dr. Frank Fletcher, E. Ward Gilman, Loy E. Golladay, Dr. Philip H. Goepp, Dr. Beatrice Hart, Dr. Benjamin Keen, Kendall Litchfield, Harold E. Niergarth, Ruth Gill Price, Thomas H. B. Robertson, Jess Smith, Rhea Talley Stewart, Harriet Smith, Elizabeth D. Spellman, John F. Spellman, George M. Swanson, Barbara Ann Kipfer, and Justyn Moulds. The following have cooperated as simplifiers: Linda Braun, Dr. G. C. Farquhar, Carey S. Lane, Wesley Lauritsen, Nellie MacDonald, Ruth S. McQueen, and Donald Moores.

For the second edition, Dr. Adam Makkai of the University of Illinois at Chicago, a well-known expert on idioms, added several hundred contemporary idiomatic phrases to the collection and edited the entire text for ease and convenience of reference. Many of the new entries were of the slang character, originating within recent cultural movements, while others reflected the popular usage of terms coined in various technological fields.

Preparing the third edition, Dr. Makkai eliminated dated idioms and added a large number of modern idiomatic phrases. This new edition capitalizes on its astounding past success and brings brand-new idioms from all areas of human endeavor.

Introduction

WHAT IS AN IDIOM?

If you understand every word in a text and still fail to grasp what the text is all about, chances are you are having trouble with the idioms. For example, suppose you read (or hear) the following:

> *Sam is a real cool cat. He never blows his stack and hardly ever flies off the handle. What's more, he knows how to get away with things . . . Well, of course, he is getting on, too. His hair is pepper and salt, but he knows how to make up for lost time by taking it easy. He gets up early, works out, and turns in early. He takes care of the hot dog stand like a breeze until he gets time off. Sam's got it made; this is it for him.*

Needless to say, this is not great literary style, but most Americans, especially when they converse among themselves, will use expressions of this sort. Now if you are a foreigner in this country and have learned the words *cool* 'not very warm,' *cat* 'the familiar domestic animal,' *blow* 'exhale air with force,' *stack* 'a pile of something, or material heaped up,' *fly* 'propel oneself in the air by means of wings,' *handle* 'the part of an object designed to hold by hand'—and so forth you will still not understand the above sample of conversational American English, because this basic dictionary information alone will not give you the meaning of the forms involved. An idiom—as it follows from these observations—is the assigning of a new meaning to a group of words which already have their own meaning. Below you will find a 'translation' of this highly idiomatic, colloquial American English text, into a more formal, and relatively idiom free variety of English:

> *Sam is really a calm person. He never loses control of himself and hardly ever becomes too angry. Furthermore, he knows how to manage his business financially by using a few tricks . . . Needless to say, he, too, is getting older. His hair is beginning to turn gray, but he knows how to compensate for wasted time by relax-*

v

ing. He rises early, exercises, and goes to bed early. He manages his frankfurter stand without visible effort, until it is someone else's turn to work there. Sam is successful; he has reached his life's goal.

Now if you were to explain how the units are organized in this text, you would have to make a little idiom dictionary. It would look like this:

to be a (real) cool cat	to be a really calm person
to blow one's stack	to lose control over oneself, to become mad
to fly off the handle	to become excessively angry
what's more	furthermore, besides, additionally
to get away with something	to perpetrate an illegitimate or tricky act without repercussion or harm
of course	naturally
to be getting on	to age, to get older
pepper and salt	black or dark hair mixed with streaks of gray
to make up for something	to compensate for something
lost time	time wasted, time spent at fruitless labor
to take it easy	to relax, to rest, not to worry
to get up	to rise from bed in the morning or at other times
to work out	to exercise, ʻo do gymnastics
to turn in	to go to bed at night
like a breeze	without effort, elegantly, easily
time off	period in one's job or place of employment during which one is not performing one's services
to have got it made	to be successful, to have arrived
this is it	to be in a position or in a place, or to have possession of an object, beyond which more of the same is unnecessary

Many of the idioms in this little sample list can be found in this dictionary itself. The interesting fact about most of these idioms is that they can easily be identified with the familiar parts of speech. Thus some idioms are clearly verbal in nature, such as *get away with*, *get up*, *work out*, and *turn in*. An equally large number are nominal in nature. Thus *hot dog* and *cool cat* are nouns. Many are adjectives, as in our example *pepper and salt* meaning '*black hair mixed with gray.*' Many are adverbial, as the examples *like the breeze* 'easily, without effort,' *hammer and tongs* 'violently' (as in *she ran after him hammer and tongs*), and so forth. These idioms which correlate with the familiar parts of speech can be called *lexemic idioms*.

The other most important group of idioms are of larger size. Often they are an entire clause in length, as our examples to *fly off the handle*, 'lose control over oneself,' and to *blow one's stack*, 'to become very angry.' There are a great many of these in American English. Some of the most famous ones are: to *kick the bucket* 'die,' *to be up the creek* 'to be in a predicament or a dangerous position,' to *be caught between the devil and deep blue sea* 'to have to choose between two equally unpleasant alternatives,' to *seize the bull by the horns* 'to face a problem and deal with it squarely,' and so on. Idioms of this sort have been called *tournures* (from the French), meaning 'turns of phrase,' or simply *phraseological idioms*. What they have in common is that they do not readily correlate with a given grammatical part of speech and require a paraphrase longer than a word.

Their form is set and only a limited number of them can be said or written in any other way without destroying the meaning of the idiom. Many of them are completely rigid and cannot show up in any other form whatever. Consider the idiom *kick the bucket*, for example. In the passive voice, you get an unacceptable form such as *the bucket has been kicked by the cowboy*, which no longer means that the 'cowboy died.' Rather it means that he struck a pail with his foot. Idioms of this type are regarded as *completely frozen forms*. Notice, however, that even this idiom can be inflected for tense, e.g., it is all right to say *the cowboy kicked the bucket*, *the cowboy will kick the bucket*, *he has kicked the bucket*, etc. Speakers disagree as much as do grammarians whether or not, for example, it is all right to use this idiom in the gerund form (a gerund being a noun derived from a verb by adding *-ing* to it, e.g., *singing* from *sing*, *eating* from *eat*, etc.) in *His kicking the bucket surprised us all*. It is best to avoid this form.

The next largest class of idioms is that of well established sayings and proverbs. These include the famous types of *don't count your chickens before they're hatched* (meaning 'do not celebrate the outcome of an undertaking prematurely because it is possible that you will fail in which case you will look ridiculous'); *don't wash your dirty linen in public* (meaning 'do not complain of your domestic affairs before strangers as it is none of their business'), and so forth.

Many of these originate from some well known literary source or come to us from the earliest English speakers of the North American Continent.

Lack of predictability of meaning (or precise meaning) is not the only criterion of idiomaticity. Set phrases or phraseo- logical units are also idiomatic, even though their meanings may be transparent. What is idiomatic (unpredictable) about them is their construction. Examples include *How about a drink? What do you say, Joe?* (as a greeting); *as a matter of fact, just in case, just to be on the safe side,* and many more.

Another important case of idiomaticity is the one-word idiom that occurs when a word is used in a surprisingly different meaning from the original one. Examples include *lemon,* said of bad watches, cars, or machines in general; and *dog,* said of a bad date or a bad exam. *(My car is a lemon, my math exam was a dog.)*

Why is English, and especially American English, so heavily idiomatic? The most probable reason is that as we develop new concepts, we need new expressions for them, but instead of creating a brand new word from the sounds of the language, we use some already existent words and put them together in a new sense. This, however, appears to be true of all known languages. There are, in fact, no known languages that do not have some idioms. Consider the Chinese expression for 'quickly,' and translated literally it means 'horse- back.' Why should the concept of 'quick' be associated with the back of a horse? The answer reveals itself upon a moment's speculation. In the old days, before the train, the automobile, and the airplane, the fastest way of getting from one place to the other was by riding a horse, i.e., on horseback. Thus Chinese *mǎ shāng* is as if we said in English *hurry up! We must go 'on horseback,'* i.e., 'Hurry up! We must go quickly.' Such a form would not be unintelligible in English at all, though the speaker would have to realize that it is an idiom, and the foreigner would have to learn it. However, in learning idioms a person may make an incorrect guess. Consider the English idiom *Oh well, the die is cast!* What would you guess this means—in case you don't know it? Perhaps you may guess that the speaker you heard is acquiescing in something because of the *Oh well* part. The expression means 'I made an irreversible decision and must live with it.' You can now try to reconstruct how this idiom came into being: the image of the die that was cast in gambling cannot be thrown again; that would be illegal; whether you have a one, a three, or a six, you must face the consequences of your throw, that is, win or lose, as the case may be. (Some people may know that the phrase was used by Caesar when he crossed the Rubicon, an event that lead to war.)

How, then, having just learned it, will you use this idiom correctly? First of all, wait until you hear it from a native speaker in a natural context; do not experiment yourself with using an idiom until you have mastered the basics of English grammar. Once you have heard the idiom being used more than once, and fully understand its meaning, you can try using it yourself. Imagine that you have two job offers, one sure, but lower paying, and one that pays more, but is only tentative. Because of nervousness and fear of having no job at all, you accept the lower paying job, at which moment the better offer comes through and naturally you feel frustrated. You can then say *Oh well, the die is cast* . . . If you try this on a native speaker and he looks at you with sympathy and does not ask 'what do you mean?'— you have achieved your first successful placement of a newly learned idiom in an appropriate context. This can be a rewarding experience. Americans usually react to foreigners more politely than do people of other nations, but they can definitely tell how fluent you are. If a person always uses a bookish, stilted expression and never uses an idiom in the right place, he might develop the reputation of being a dry, unimaginative speaker, or one who is trying to be too serious and too official. *The use of idioms is, therefore, extremely important. It can strike a chord of solidarity with the listener.* The more idioms you use in the right context, the more at ease Americans will feel with you and the more they will think to themselves 'this is a nice and friendly person—look at how well he expresses himself!'

We will now take a look at some practical considerations regarding the use of *Handbook of Commonly Used American Idioms*.

HOW TO USE THIS DICTIONARY

This handbook can be used successfully by nonnative speakers of English, students, workers, immigrants—in short, anybody who wants to make his English more fluent, more idiomatic. It contains phrases of the types mentioned above, lexemic idioms, phrase idioms, and proverbial idioms, that have a special meaning. When a phrase has a special meaning that you cannot decode properly by looking up and understanding the individual words of which it is composed, then you know you are dealing with an idiom. You may already know some of these idioms or may be able to imagine what they mean. Look in the book for any of the following idioms that you may already know well; this will help you to understand how you should use this book: *boyfriend, girlfriend, outer space, piggy bank, get even, give up, going to, keep on, keep your mouth shut, lead somebody by the nose, look after, show off, throw away, all over, in love, mixed-up, out of this world, throw away, I'll say, both X and Y.*

A dictionary is like any other tool: You must familiarize yourself with it and learn how to use it before it begins to work well for you. Study the directions carefully several times, and practice looking up idioms. That way, searching for an idiom and finding it will become second nature to you. If you hear an idiomatic expression that is not in this book, after using it for a while, you will develop the ability to track down its meaning and write it down for yourself. Keep your own idiom list at home, right beside your regular dictionary. If you read a technical text, or a novel or a newspaper article and do not understand an expression, look it up in your regular school dictionary first; if you do not find it, try this one.

How do you find out if this dictionary can help you understand a hard sentence? Sometimes you can easily see what the phrase is, as with *puppy love, fun house, dog-eat-dog, mixed-up*. If not, pick out an important word from the most difficult part and look for that. If it is the first word in the idiom, you will find the whole phrase, followed by an explanation. Thus the expression *bats in the belfry* is listed in this dictionary under *b*, the word *bats*. If the word you picked is not the first word, you will find a list of idioms that contain that word. For example the word *toe* will be found in entries such as *curl one's hair OR curl one's toes, on one's toes, step on the toes (of somebody)*. You may, of course, find that the reason why you do not understand a particular sentence is not because of any idioms in it; in that case your regular dictionary will be of help to you. Also, there are more idioms than listed in this book; only the most frequently occurring in *American English* are included. British English, for example, or the English spoken in Australia, certainly has many idiomatic expressions that are not a part of American English.

TYPES OF ENTRY

This dictionary contains four kinds of entry: *main entries, run-on entries, and index entries*. A main entry includes a full explanation of the idiom. A run-on entry is a phrase which is derived from another idiom but would be separated from it if it entered at its own alphabetical place. These derived idioms have been run on at the end of the main entry (e.g., *fence-sitter* at *sit on the fence*) with an illustration and a paraphrase; an extra explanation has been added when understanding the derivative from the main explanation seemed difficult. When an idiom has come to be used as more than one part of speech, a separate entry has been made for each usage.

An index entry directs you to all other entries containing the index word. Thus the word *chin* is followed by the phrases of which it is a part, e.g., *keep one's chin up, stick one's chin (or neck) out, take it on the chin, up to the chin in*.

PARTS OF SPEECH LABELS

Those idioms that correlate with a well-defined grammatical form class carry a part of speech label. Sometimes, as with many prepositional phrases, a double label had to be assigned because the given phrase has two grammatical uses, e.g., *in commission* can be either adverbial or adjectival. Many prepositional phrases are adverbial in their literal sense, but adjectival in their nonpredictable, idiomatic sense. *v.* stands for verb; it was assigned to phrases containing a verb and an adverb; verb and preposition; or verb, preposition, and adverb, *v. phr.* stands for 'verbal phrase'; these include verbs with an object, verbs with subject complement, and verbs with a prepositional phrase.

RESTRICTIVE USAGE LABELS

You must pay particular attention to whether it is appropriate for you to use a certain idiom in a certain setting. The label *slang* shows that the idiom is used only among very close friends who are quite familiar with one another. *Informal* indicates that the form is used in conversation but should be avoided in formal composition. *Formal* indicates the opposite, this is a form that people usually do not say, but they will write it in an essay or will state it in a speech or a university lecture. *Literary* alerts you to the fact that people are usually aware that the form is a quotation; it would be inappropriate for you to use these too often. *Vulgar* indicates that you should altogether avoid the form; recognizing it may, of course, be important to you as you can judge a person by the language he uses. *Substandard* labels a form as chiefly used by less educated people; *nonstandard* means that a phrase is felt to be awkward. *Archaic* (rarely used in this book) means that the form is heavily restricted to Biblical or Shakespearean English. *Dialect* means that the form is restricted to its geographical source; e.g., *chiefly British* means that Americans seldom use it, *Southern* means that the form is of much higher currency in the South of the United States than in the North.

Adam Makkai, Ph.D.
Professor of Linguistics
University of Illinois at Chicago
Executive Director and Director of
Publications, Linguistic Association of
Canada and the United States (LACUS), Inc.

A Handbook of
Commonly Used
American Idioms

abide by *v.* To accept and obey; be willing to follow. *A basketball player may know he did not foul, but he must abide by the referee's decision. The members agree to abide by the rules of the club.*

a bit *n., informal* A small amount; some. *There's no sugar in the sugar bowl, but you may find a bit in the bag. If the ball had hit the window a bit harder, it would have broken it.*—Often used like an adverb. *This sweater scratches a bit.*—Also used like an adjective before *less, more. Janet thought she could lose weight by eating a bit less. "Have some more cake?" "Thanks. A bit more won't hurt me."*—Often used adverbially after verbs in negative, interrogative, and conditional sentences, sometimes in the form *one bit. "Won't your father be angry?" "No, he won't care a bit." Helen feels like crying, but I'll be surprised if she shows it one bit.*—Sometimes used with *little* for emphasis, also in the emphatic form *the least bit. "Wasn't Bob even a little bit sorry he forgot his date?" "No, Bob wasn't the least bit sorry."*

about face *n.* A sudden change of course or a decision opposite to what was decided earlier. *Her decision to become an actress instead of a dentist was an about face from her original plans.*

about time *n. phr.* Finally, but later than it should have been; at last. *Mother said, "It's about time you got up, Mary." The basketball team won last night. About time.*

about to 1. Close to; ready to.—Used with an infinitive. *We were about to leave when the snow began. I haven't gone yet, but I'm about to.* **2.** *informal* Having a wish or plan to.—Used with an infinitive in negative sentences. *Freddy wasn't about to give me any of his ice-cream cone. "Will she come with us?" asked Bill. "She's not about to," answered Mary.*

above all *adv. phr.* Of first or highest importance; most especially. *Children need many things, but above all they need love.*

according to *prep.* **1.** So as to match or agree with; so as to be alike in. *Many words are pronounced according to the spelling but some are not. The boys were placed in three groups according to height.* **2.** On the word or authority of. *According to the Bible, Adam was the first man.*

ace in the hole *n. phr.* **1.** An ace given to a player face down so that other players in a card game cannot see it. *When the cowboy bet all his money in the poker game he did not know that the gambler had an ace in the hole and would win it from* him **2.** *informal* Someone or something important that is kept as a surprise until the right time so as to bring victory or success. *The football team has a new play that they are keeping as an ace in the hole for the big game. The lawyer's ace in the hole was a secret witness who saw the accident.*

across the board *adv. phr.* **1.** So that equal amounts of money are bet on the same horse to win a race, to place second, or third. *I bet $6 on the white horse across the board.*—Often used with hyphens as an adjective. *I made an across-the-board bet on the white horse.* **2.** *informal* Including everyone or all, so that all are included. *The President wanted taxes lowered across the board.*—Often used with hyphens as an adjective. *The workers at the store got an across-the-board pay raise.*

act of faith *n. phr.* An act or a deed that shows unquestioning belief in someone or something. *It was a real act of faith on Mary's part to entrust her jewelry to her younger sister's care.*

act of God *n.* An occurrence (usually some sort of catastrophe) for which the people affected are not responsible; said of earthquakes, floods, etc. *Hurricane Andrew destroyed many houses in Florida, but some types of insurance did not compensate the victims, claiming that the hurricane was an act of God.*

act up *v., informal* **1.** To behave badly; act rudely or impolitely. *The dog acted up as the postman came to the door.*

2. To work or run poorly (as a machine); skip; miss. *The car acted up because the spark plugs were dirty.*

add fuel to the flame *v. phr.* To make a bad matter worse by adding to its cause; spread trouble, increase anger or other strong feelings by talk or action. *By criticizing his son's girl, the father added fuel to the flame of his son's love. Bob was angry with Ted and Ted added fuel to the flame by laughing at him.*

add insult to injury *v. phr.* **1.** To hurt someone's feelings after doing him harm. *He added insult to injury when he called the man a rat after he had already beaten him up.* **2.** To make bad trouble worse. *We started on a picnic, and first it rained, then to add insult to injury, the car broke down.*

add up *v.* **1.** To come to the correct amount. *The numbers wouldn't add up.* **2.** *informal* To make sense; be understandable. *His story didn't add up.*

add up to *v.* **1.** To make a total of; amount to. *The bill added up to $12.95.* **2.** *informal* To mean; result in. *The rain, the mosquitoes, and the heat added up to a spoiled vacation.*

afraid of one's shadow *adj. phr., informal* Scared of small or imaginary things; very easily frightened; jumpy; nervous. *Mrs. Smith won't stay alone in her house at night; she is afraid of her own shadow. Johnny cries whenever he must say hello to an adult; he is afraid of his own shadow.*

after all *adv. phr.* **1.** As a

change in plans; anyway. Used with emphasis on *after*. *Bob thought he couldn't go to the party because he had too much homework, but he went after all.* **2.** For a good reason that you should remember.—Used with emphasis on *all*. *Why shouldn't Betsy eat the cake? After all, she baked it.*

after one's own heart *adj. phr., informal* Well liked because of agreeing with your own feelings, interests, and ideas; to your liking—agreeable. Used after *man* or some similar word. *He likes baseball and good food; he is a man after my own heart. Thanks for agreeing with me about the class party; you're a girl after my own heart.*

ahead of the game *adv. or adj. phr., informal* **1.** In a position of advantage; winning (as in a game or contest); ahead (as by making money or profit); making it easier to win or succeed. *The time you spend studying when you are in school will put you ahead of the game in college. After Tom sold his papers, he was $5 ahead of the game.* **2.** Early; too soon; beforehand. *When Ralph came to school an hour early, the janitor said, "You're ahead of the game." John studies his lessons only one day early; if he gets too far ahead of the game, he forgets what he read.*

a hell of a *or* **one hell of a** *adj., or adv. phr. informal* Extraordinary; very. *He made a hell of a shot during the basketball game. Max said seven months was a hell of a time to have to wait for a simple visa.*

The fall Max took left one hell of a bruise on his knee.

air one's dirty linen in public *or* **wash one's dirty linen in public** *v. phr.* To talk about your private quarrels or disgraces where others can hear; make public something embarrassing that should be kept secret. *Everyone in the school knew that the superintendent and the principal were angry with each other because they aired their dirty linen in public. No one knew that the boys' mother was a drug addict, because the family did not wash its dirty linen in public.*

a little bird told me To have learned something from a mysterious, unknown, or secret source. *"Who told you that Dean Smith was resigning?" Peter asked. "A little bird told me," Jim answered.*

a little knowledge is a dangerous thing *literary* A person who knows a little about something may think he knows it all and make bad mistakes.—A proverb. *John has read a book on driving a car and now he thinks he can drive. A little knowledge is a dangerous thing.*

all along *or* (*informal*) **right along** *adv. phr.* All the time; during the whole time. *I knew all along that we would win. I knew right along that Jane would come.*

all at once *adv. phr.* **1.** At the same time; together. *The teacher told the children to talk one at a time; if they all talked at one time, she could not understand them. Bill can play the piano, sing, and lead his orchestra all at once.* **2.** *or* **all of a**

sudden Without warning; abruptly; suddenly; unexpectedly. *All at once we heard a shot and the soldier fell to the ground. All of a sudden the ship struck a rock.*

all better *adj. phr.* Fully recovered; all well again; no longer painful.—Usually used to or by children. *"All better now," he kept repeating to the little girl.*

all but *adv. phr.* Very nearly; almost. *Crows all but destroyed a farmer's field of corn. The hikers were exhausted and all but frozen when they were found.*

all ears *adj. phr., informal* Very eager to hear; very attentive.—Used in the predicate. *Go ahead with your story; we are all ears. When John told about the circus, the boys were all ears.*

alley cat *n., slang* **1.** A stray cat. **2.** A person (usually a female) of rather easy-going, or actually loose sexual morals; a promiscuous person. *You'll have no problem dating her; she's a regular alley cat.*

all eyes *adj. phr., informal* Wide-eyed with surprise or curiosity; watching very closely.—Used in the predicate. *At the circus the children were all eyes.*

all gone *adj. phr.* Used up; exhausted (said of supplies); done with; over with. *We used to travel a lot, but, alas, those days are all gone.*

all out *adv. phr., informal* With all your strength, power, or determination; to the best of your ability; without holding back.—Usually used in the phrase *go all out. We went all out to win the game. John went all out to finish the job and was very tired afterwards.*

all over *adv. phr.* **1.** In every part; everywhere. *He has a fever and aches all over. I have looked all over for my glasses.* **2.** *informal* In every way; completely. *She is her mother all over.* **3.** *informal* Coming into very close physical contact, as during a violent fight; wrestling. *Before I noticed what happened, he was all over me.*

all right¹ *adv. phr.* **1.** Well enough. *The new machine is running all right.* **2.** *informal* I am willing; yes. *"Shall we watch television?" "All right."* **3.** *informal* Beyond question, certainly.—Used for emphasis and placed after the word it modifies. *It's time to leave, all right, but the bus hasn't come.*

all right² *adj. phr.* **1.** Good enough; correct; suitable. *His work is always all right.* **2.** In good health or spirits; well. *"How are you?" "I'm all right."* **3.** *slang* Good. *He's an all right guy.*

all right for you *interj.* I'm finished with you! That ends it between you and me!—Used by children. *All right for you! I'm not playing with you any more!*

all set *adj. phr.* Ready to start. *"Is the plane ready for take-off?" the bank president asked. "Yes, Sir," the pilot answered. "We're all set."*

all shook up *also* **shook up** *adj., slang* In a state of great emotional upheaval; disturbed; agitated. *What are you so shook up about?*

all systems go *Originally from space English, now general colloquial usage.* Everything is complete and ready for action; it is now all right to proceed. *After they wrote out the invitations, it was all systems go for the wedding.*

all the thing *or* **all the rage, the in thing** *n. phr.* The fashionable or popular thing to do, the fashionable or most popular artist or form of art at a given time. *After "The Graduate" Dustin Hoffman was all the rage in the movies. It was all the thing in the late sixties to smoke pot and demonstrate against the war in Vietnam.*

all the way *or* **the whole way** *adv. phr.* **1.** From start to finish during the whole distance or time. *Jack climbed all the way to the top of the tree. Joe has played the whole way in the football game and it's almost over.* **2.** In complete agreement; with complete willingness to satisfy.—Often used in the phrase *go all the way with. I go all the way with what George says about Bill. Mary said she was willing to kiss Bill, but that did not mean she was willing to go all the way with him. The bank was willing to lend Mr. Jones money to enlarge his factory but it wasn't willing to go all the way with his plans to build another in the next town.*

all wet *adj., slang* Entirely confused or wrong; mistaken. *When the Wright brothers said they could build a flying machine, people thought they were*

all wet. *If you think I like baseball, you're all wet.*

along for the ride *adv. phr., informal* Being in a group for the fun or the credit without doing any of the work. *He wants no members in his political party who are just along for the ride.*

along in years *or* **on in years** *adj. phr.* Elderly; growing old. *As Grandfather got on in years, he became quiet and thoughtful. Our dog isn't very playful because it is getting on in years.*

a lot *n., informal* A large number or amount; very many or very much; lots. *I learned a lot in Mr. Smith's class. A lot of our friends are going to the beach this summer.*—Often used like an adverb. *Ella is a jolly girl; she laughs a lot. Grandfather was very sick last week, but he's a lot better now. You'll have to study a lot harder if you want to pass.*—Also used as an adjective with *more, less,* and *fewer. There was a good crowd at the game today, but a lot more will come next week.*—Often used with *whole* for emphasis. *John has a whole lot of marbles. Jerry is a whole lot taller than he was a year ago.*

and how! *interj. informal* Yes, that is certainly right!—Used for emphatic agreement. *"Did you see the game?" "And how!" "Isn't Mary pretty?" "And how she is!"*

and then some And a lot more; and more too. *It would cost all the money he had and then some. Talking his way out of this trouble was going to take all his wits and then some.*

answer for *v.* **1.** To take responsibility for; assume charge or supervision of. *The secret service has to answer for the safety of the President and his family.* **2.** To say you are sure that (someone) has good character or ability; guarantee; sponsor. *When people thought Ray had stolen the money, the principal said, "Ray is no thief. I'll answer for him."* **3.** Take the blame or punishment for. *When Mother found out who ate the cake, Tom had to answer for his mischief.*

ante up *v., informal* To produce the required amount of money in order to close a transaction; to pay what one owes. *"I guess I'd better ante up if I want to stay an active member of the Association," Max said.*

ants in one's pants *n. phr., slang* Nervous over-activity; restlessness. *Jane can not sit still; she has ants in her pants. You have ants in your pants today. Is something wrong?*

apple of one's eye *n. phr.* Something or someone that is adored; a cherished person or object. *Charles is the apple of his mother's eye. John's first car was the apple of his eye. He was always polishing it.*

apple-pie order *n. phr., informal* Exact orderly arrangement, neatness; tidy arrangement. *The house was in apple-pie order. Like a good secretary, she kept the boss's desk in apple-pie order.*

arm and a leg *n., slang* An exorbitantly high price that must be paid for something that isn't really worth it. *It's true that to get a decent apartment these days in New York you have to pay an arm and a leg.*

arm in arm *adv. phr.* With your arm under or around another person's arm, especially in close comradeship or friendship. *Sally and Joan were laughing and joking together as they walked arm in arm down the street. When they arrived at the party, the partners walked arm in arm to meet the hosts.*

around the clock *also* **the clock around** *adv. phr.* For 24 hours a day continuously all day and all night. *The factory operated around the clock until the order was filled. He studied around the clock for his history exam.* **round-the-clock** *adj.*— *That filling station has round-the-clock service.*

around the corner *adv. phr.* Soon to come or happen; close by; near at hand. *The fortune teller told Jane that there was an adventure for her just around the corner.*

as a matter of fact *adv. phr.* Actually; really; in addition to what has been said; in reference to what was said.—Often used as an interjection. *It's not true that I cannot swim; as a matter of fact, I used to work as a lifeguard in Hawaii. Do you think this costs too much? As a matter of fact, I think it is rather cheap.*

as good as *adv. phr.* Nearly the same as; almost. *She claimed that he as good as promised to marry her. He as good as called me a liar. We'll get to school on time, we're as good as there now. The man* *who had been shot was as good as dead.*—Often used without the first *as* before adjectives. *When the car was repaired, it looked good as new.*

as hard as nails *adj. phr.* Very unfeeling; cruel, and unsympathetic. *Uncle Joe is as hard as nails; although he is a millionaire, he doesn't help his less fortunate relatives.*

as it were *adv. phr.* As it might be said to be; as if it really were; seemingly. Used with a statement that might seem silly or unreasonable, to show that it is just a way of saying it. *In many ways children live, as it were, in a different world from adults. The sunlight on the icy branches made, as it were, delicate lacy cobwebs from tree to tree.*

ask for *v., informal* To make (something, bad) likely to happen to you; bring (something bad) upon yourself. *Charles drives fast on worn-out tires; he is asking for trouble. The workman lost his job, but he asked for it by coming to work drunk several times.*

ask for the moon or **cry for the moon** *v. phr.* To want something that you cannot reach or have; try for the impossible. *John asked his mother for a hundred dollars today. He's always asking for the moon.*

asleep at the switch *adj. phr.*
1. Asleep when it is one's duty to move a railroad switch for cars to go on the right track. *The new man was asleep at the switch and the two trains crashed.* **2.** *informal* Failing to act promptly as expected; not alert to an opportunity. *When*

the ducks flew over, the boy was asleep at the switch and missed his shot.

as luck would have it *adv. clause* As it happened; by chance; luckily or unluckily. *As luck would have it, no one was in the building when the explosion occurred. As luck would have it, there was rain on the day of the picnic.*

as much *n.* The same; exactly that. *Don't thank me, I would do as much for anyone. Did you lose your way? I thought as much when you were late in coming.*

as soon as *conj.* Just after; when; immediately after. *As soon as the temperature falls to 70, the furnace is turned on. As soon as you finish your job let me know. He will see you as soon as he can.*

as the crow flies *adv. clause* By the most direct way; along a straight line between two places. *It is seven miles to the next town as the crow flies, but it is ten miles by the road, which goes around the mountain.*

as the story goes *adv. phr.* As the story is told; as one has heard through rumor. *As the story goes, Jonathan disappeared when he heard the police were after him.*

as well as *conj.* In addition to; and also; besides. *Hiking is good exercise as well as fun. He was my friend as well as my doctor. The book tells about the author's life as well as about his writings.*

as yet *adv. phr.* Up to the present time; so far; yet. *We know little as yet about the* *moon's surface. She has not come as yet.*

at all *adv. phr.* At any time or place, for any reason, or in any degree or manner.—Used for emphasis with certain kinds of words or sentences. **1.** Negative *It's not at all likely he will come.* **2.** Limited *I can hardly hear you at all.* **3.** Interrogative *Can it be done at all?* **4.** Conditional *She will walk with a limp, if she walks at all.*

at all costs *adv. phr.* At any expense of time, effort, or money. Regardless of the results. *Mr. Jackson intended to save his son's eyesight at all costs. Carl is determined to succeed in his new job at all costs.*

at a loss *adj. phr.* In a state of uncertainty; without any idea; puzzled. *A good salesman is never at a loss for words. When Don missed the last bus, he was at a loss to know what to do.*

at any rate *adv. phr.* In any case; anyhow. *It isn't much of a car, but any any rate it was not expensive.*

at bay *adv. or adj. phr.* In a place where you can no longer run away; unable to go back farther; forced to stand and fight, or face an enemy; cornered. *The dog ran the rat into a corner, and there the rat turned at bay. The police chased the thief to a roof, where they held him at bay until more policemen came to help.*

at best *or* **at the best** *adv. phr.* **1.** Under the best conditions; as the best possibility. *A coal miner's job is dirty and dangerous at best. We can't get to New York before ten o'clock at best.* **2.** In the most favorable way of

looking at something; even saying the best about the thing. *The treasurer had at best been careless with the club's money, but most people thought he had been dishonest.*

at cross purposes *adv. phr.* With opposing meanings or aims; with opposing effect or result; with aims which hinder or get in each other's way. *Tom's parents acted at cross purposes in advising him; his father wanted him to become a doctor; but his mother wanted him to become a minister.*

at death's door *adj. or adv. phr.* Very near death; dying. *He seemed to be at death's door from his illness.*

at ease *or* **at one's ease** *adj. or adv. phr.* **1.** In comfort; without pain or bother. *You can't feel at ease with a toothache.* **2.** *or* **at one's ease** Comfortable in one's mind; relaxed, not troubled.—Often used in the phrase *put at ease* or *put at one's ease. We put Mary at her ease during the thunderstorm by reading her stories.* **3.** Standing with your right foot in place and without talking in military ranks. *The sergeant gave his men the command "At ease!"*

at fault *adj. phr.* Responsible for an error or failure; to blame. *The driver who didn't stop at the red light was at fault in the accident. When the engine would not start, the mechanic looked at all the parts to find what was at fault.*

at first *adv. phr.* In the beginning; at the start. *The driver didn't see the danger a first. At first the job looked good to*

Bob, but later it became tiresome. There was a little trouble at first, but things soon were quiet.

at first blush *adv. phr.* When first seen; without careful study. *At first blush the offer looked good, but when we studied it, we found things we could not accept.*

at first glance *or* **at first sight** *adv. or adj. phr.* After a first quick look. *At first sight, his guess was that the whole trouble between the two men resulted from personalities that did not agree. Tom met Mary at a party, and it was love at first sight.*

at hand *also* **at close hand** *or* **near at hand** *adv. phr.* **1.** Easy to reach; nearby. *When he writes, he always keeps a dictionary at hand.* **2.** *formal* Coming soon; almost here. *Examinations are past and Commencement Day is at hand.*

at heart *adv. phr.* **1.** In spite of appearances; at bottom; in reality. *His manners are rough but he is a kind man at heart.* **2.** As a serious interest or concern; as an important aim or goal. *He has the welfare of the poor at heart.*

at large *adv. or adj. phr.* **1.** Not kept within walls, fences, or boundaries; free. *The killer remained at large for weeks. Cattle and sheep roamed at large on the big ranch.* **2.** In a broad, general way; at length; fully. *The superintendent talked at large for an hour about his hopes for a new school building.* **3.** As a group rather than as individuals; as a whole; taken together. *The junior*

class at large was not interested in a senior yearbook.* **4.** As a representative of a whole political unit or area rather than one of its parts; from a city rather than one of its wards, or a state rather than one of its districts. *He was elected congressman at large. Aldermen are voted for at large.*

at last *also* **at long last** *adv. phr.* After a long time; finally. *The war had been long and hard, but now there was peace at last. The boy saved his money until at last he had enough for a bicycle.*

at least *adv. phr.* **1.** *or* **at the least** At the smallest guess; no fewer than; no less than. *You should brush your teeth at least twice a day. At least three students are failing in mathematics. Mr. Johnson must weigh 200 pounds at least.* **2.** Whatever else you may say; anyhow; anyway. *It was a clumsy move, but at least it saved her from getting hit. She broke her arm, but at least it wasn't the arm she writes with. The Mortons had fun at their picnic yesterday—at least the children did—they played while their parents cooked the food. He's not coming—at least that's what he said.*

at leisure *adj. or adv. phr.* **1.** Not at work; not busy; with free time; at rest. *Come and visit us some evening when you're at leisure.* **2.** *or* **at one's leisure** When and how you wish at your convenience; without hurry. *John made the model plane at his leisure. You may read the book at your leisure.*

at length *adv. phr.* **1.** In detail; fully. *You must study the subject at length to understand it. The teacher explained the new lesson at length to the students.* **2.** In the end; at last; finally. *The movie became more and more exciting, until at length people were sitting on the edge of their chairs.*

at liberty *adv. or adj. phr.* Free to go somewhere or do something; not shut in or stopped. *The police promised to set the man at liberty if he told the names of the other robbers. I am sorry, but I am not at liberty to come to your party.*

at loggerheads *adj. or adv. phr.* In a quarrel; in a fight; opposing each other. *The two senators had long been at loggerheads on foreign aid. Because of their barking dog, the Morrises lived at loggerheads with their neighbors.*

at odds *adj. phr.* In conflict or disagreement; opposed. *The boy and girl were married a week after they met and soon found themselves at odds about religion.*

at once *adv. phr.* Without delay; right now or right then; immediately. *Put a burning match next to a piece of paper and it will begin burning at once. Mother called the children to lunch, and Paul came at once, but Brenda stayed in the sand pile a little longer.*

at one's beck and call *or* **at the beck and call of** *adj. phr.* Ready and willing to do whatever someone asks; ready to serve at a moment's notice. *A good parent isn't necessarily always at the child's beck and call.*

at one's best *prep. phr.* In best form; displaying one's best qualities. *Tim is at his best when he has had a long swim before a ballgame. Jane rested before the important meeting because she wanted to be at her best.*

at one's door *or* **at one's doorstep** *adv. phr.* Very close; very near where you live or work. *Johnny is very lucky because there's a swimming pool right at his doorstep. Mr. Green can get to work in only a few minutes because the subway is at his door.*

at one's fingertips *adv. phr.* **1.** Within easy reach; quickly touched; nearby. *Seated in the cockpit, the pilot of a plane has many controls at his fingertips.* **2.** Readily usable as knowledge or skill; familiar. *He had several languages at his fingertips. He had the whole design of the machine at his fingertips.*

at one's wit's end *or* **at wits end** *adj. phr.* Having no ideas as to how to meet a difficulty or solve a problem; feeling puzzled after having used up all of your ideas or resources; not knowing what to do; puzzled. *He had approached every friend and acquaintance for help in vain, and now he was at his wit's end. The designer was at his wit's end: he had tried out wings of many different kinds but none would fly.*

at pains *adj. phr.* Making a special effort. *At pains to make* a good impression, she was prompt for her appointment.

at sea[1] *adv. or adj. phr.* **1.** On an ocean voyage; on a journey by ship. *They had first met at sea.* **2.** Out on the ocean; away from land. *By the second day the ship was well out at sea. Charles had visited a ship in dock, but he had never been on a ship at sea.*

at sea[2] *adj. phr.* Not knowing what to do; bewildered; confused; lost. *The job was new to him, and for a few days he was at sea. When his friends talked about chemistry, Don was at sea, because he did not study chemistry.*

at sixes and sevens *adj. phr.* Not in order; in confusion; in a mess. *He apologized because his wife was away and the house was at sixes and sevens. Our teacher had just moved to a new classroom, and she was still at sixes and sevens. After the captain of the team broke his leg, the other players were at sixes and sevens.*

at —— stage of the game *adv. phr.* At (some) time during an activity; at (some) point. *At that stage of the game, our team was doing so poorly that we were ready to give up. It's hard to know what will happen at this stage of the game. At what stage of the game did the man leave?*

at stake *adj. phr.* Depending, like a bet, on the outcome of something uncertain; in a position to be lost or gained. *The team played hard because the championship of the state was*

at stake. *The farmers were more anxious for rain than the people in the city because they had more at stake.*

at swords' points *adj. phr.* Ready to start fighting; very much opposed to each; other hostile; quarreling. *The dog's barking kept the Browns at swords' points with their neighbors for months. The mayor and the reporter were always at swords' points.*

at the drop of a hat *adv. phr., informal* **1.** Without waiting; immediately; promptly. *If you need a babysitter quickly, call Mary, because she can come at the drop of a hat.* **2.** Whenever you have a chance; with very little cause or urging. *At the drop of a hat, he would tell the story of the canal he wanted to build. He was quarrelsome and ready to fight at the drop of a hat.*

at the eleventh hour *prep. phr.* At the last possible time. *Aunt Mathilda got married at the eleventh hour; after all, she was already 49 years old.*

at the ready *adj. phr.* Ready for use. *The sailor stood at the bow, harpoon at the ready, as the boat neared the whale.*

at the tip of one's tongue *or* **on the tip of one's tongue** *adv. phr. informal* **1.** Almost spoken; at the point of being said. *It was at the tip of my tongue to tell him, when the phone rang. John had a rude answer on the tip of his tongue, but he remembered his manners just in time.* **2.** Almost remembered; at the point where one can almost say it but cannot because it is forgotten. *I have his name on the tip of my tongue.*

at this rate *or* **at that rate** *adv. phr.* At a speed like this or that; with progress like this or that. *John's father said that if John kept going at that rate he would never finish cutting the grass. So Johnny has a whole dollar! At this rate he'll be a millionaire. "Three 100's in the last four tests! At this rate you'll soon be teaching the subject," Tom said to Mary.*

at times *adv. phr.* Not often; not regularly; not every day; not every week; occasionally; sometimes. *At times Tom's mother lets him hold the baby. You can certainly be exasperating, at times! We have pie for dinner at times.*

at will *adv. phr.* As you like; as you please or choose freely. *Little Bobby is allowed to wander at will in the neighborhood. With an air conditioner you can enjoy comfortable temperatures at will.*

ax to grind *n. phr. informal* Something to gain for yourself: a selfish reason. *In praising movies for classroom use he has an ax to grind; he sells motion picture equipment. When Charles told the teacher he saw Arthur copying his homework from Jim, he had an ax to grind; Arthur would not let Charles copy from him.*

babe in the woods *n. phr.* A person who is inexperienced or innocent in certain things. *He is a good driver, but as a mechanic he is just a babe in the woods.*

baby boom *n.* A sudden increase in the birth rate. *The universities were filled to capacity due to the baby boom that followed World War II.*

baby grand *n.* A small grand piano no longer than three feet, maximally four feet. *This apartment can't take a regular grand piano, so we'll have to buy a baby grand.*

back and forth *adv.* Backwards and forwards. *The chair is rocking back and forth. The tiger is pacing back and forth in his cage.*

back away *v.* To act to avoid or lessen one's involvement in something; draw or turn back; retreat. *The townspeople backed away from the building plan when they found out how much it would cost.*

back down or **back off** *v., informal* To give up a claim; not follow up a threat. *Bill said he could beat Ted, but when Ted put up his fists Bill backed down. Harry claimed Joe had taken his book, but backed down when the teacher talked with him.*

back out *v. phr.* **1.** To move backwards out of a place or enclosure. *Bob slowly backed his car out of the garage.* **2.** To

withdraw from an activity one has promised to carry out. *Jim tried to back out of the engagement with Jane, but she insisted that they get married.*

backseat driver *n., informal* A bossy person in a car who always tells the driver what to do. *The man who drove the car became angry with the back seat driver.*

back talk *n.* A sassy, impudent reply. *Such back talk will get you nowhere, young man!*

back the wrong horse *v. phr.* To support a loser. *In voting for George Bush, voters in 1992 were backing the wrong horse.*

back-to-back *adv.* **1.** Immediately following. *The health clinic had back-to-back appointments for the new students during the first week of school.* **2.** Very close to, as if touching. *Sardines are always packed in the can back-to-back. The bus was so full that people had to stand back-to-back.*

back to the salt mines *informal* Back to the job; back to work; back to work that is as hard or as unpleasant as working in a salt mine would be.—An overworked phrase, used humorously. *The lunch hour is over, boys. Back to the salt mines!—"Vacation is over," said Billy. "Back to the salt mines."*

back to the wall or **back against the wall** *adv. phr.* In a trap, with no way to escape; in bad trouble. *The soldiers had their* *backs to the wall. He was in debt and could not get any help; his back was against the wall. The team had their backs to the wall in the second half.*

back up *v.* **1.** To move backwards. *The train was backing up.* **2.** To help or be ready to help; stay behind to help; agree with and speak in support of. *Jim has joined the Boy Scouts and his father is backing him up. The principal backs up the faculty. Jim told us what had happened and Bob backed him up.* **3.** To move behind (another fielder) in order to catch the ball if he misses it.

bad blood *n., informal* Anger or misgivings due to bad relations in the past between individuals or groups. *There's a lot of bad blood between Max and Jack; I bet they'll never talk to each other again.*

bad egg *n., slang* A ne'er-do-well; good-for nothing; a habitual offender. *The judge sent the bad egg to prison at last.*

bad mouth (someone) *v., slang* To say uncomplimentary or libelous things about someone; deliberately to damage another's reputation. *It's not nice to bad mouth people.*

bad news *n., slang* An event, thing, or person which is disagreeable or an unpleasant surprise. *What's the new professor like?—He's all bad news to me.*

bad paper *n., slang* **1.** A check for which there are no funds in the bank. **2.** Counterfeit paper money. *Why are you so*

mad?—I was paid with some bad paper.

bad shit *n., vulgar, avoidable* An unpleasant event or situation, such as a long lasting and unsettled quarrel or recurring acts of vengeance preventing two people or two groups from reaching any kind of reconciliation. *There is so much bad shit between the two gangs that I bet there will be more killings this year.*

bad trip *n., slang, also used colloquially* A disturbing or frightening experience, such as terrifying hallucinations, while under the influence of drugs; hence, by colloquial extension any bad experience in general. *Why's John's face so distorted?—He had a bad trip. How was your math exam?—Don't mention it; it was a bad trip.*

bag and baggage *adv., informal* With all your clothes and other personal belongings, especially movable possessions; completely. *If they don't pay their hotel bill they will be put out bag and baggage.*

baker's dozen *n., informal* Thirteen. *"How many of the jelly doughnuts, Sir?" the salesclerk asked. "Oh, make it a baker's dozen."*

ball game *n., slang, also informal* The entire matter at hand; the whole situation; the entire contest. *You said we can get a second mortgage for the house?! Wow! That's a whole new ball game.*

ball of fire *n., informal* A person with great energy and ability; a person who can do something very well. *He did poorly in school but as a salesman he is a ball of fire. The new shortstop is a good fielder but certainly no ball of fire in batting.*

bang up *adj., informal* Very successful; very good; splendid; excellent. *The football coach has done a bang-up job this season. John did a bang-up job painting the house.*

bank on *v., informal* To depend on; put one's trust in; rely on. *He knew he could bank on public indignation to change things, if he could once prove the dirty work. The students were banking on the team to do its best in the championship game.*

bargain for or **bargain on** *v.* To be ready for; expect. *When John started a fight with the smaller boy he got more than he bargained for. The final cost of building the house was much more than they had bargained on.*

barge in *v. phr., informal* To appear uninvited at someone's house or apartment, or to interrupt a conversation. *I'm sorry for barging in like that, Sir, but my car died on me and there is no pay phone anywhere. I'm sorry for barging in while you two are having a discussion, but could you please tell me where the nearest exit is?*

bark up the wrong tree *v. phr., informal* To choose the wrong person to deal with or the wrong course of action; mistake an aim. *If he thinks he can fool me, he is barking up the wrong tree. He is barking up the wrong tree when he blames his troubles on bad luck. The police were looking for a tall thin man, but were barking up the wrong tree; the thief was short and fat.*

bark worse than one's bite *informal* Sound or speech more frightening or worse than your actions. *The small dog barks savagely, but his bark is worse than his bite. The boss sometimes talks roughly to the men, but they know that his bark is worse than his bite. She was always scolding her children, but they knew her bark was worse than her bite.*

basket case *n., slang, also informal* **1.** A person who has had both arms and both legs cut off as a result of war or other misfortune. **2.** A helpless person who is unable to take care of himself, as if carted around in a basket by others. *Stop drinking, or else you'll wind up a basket case!*

bat an eye or **bat an eyelash** *v. phr., informal* To show surprise, fear, or interest; show your feelings.—Used in negative sentences. *When I told him the price of the car he never batted an eye. Bill told his story without batting an eyelash, although not a word of it was true.*

bats in one's belfry or **bats in the belfry** *n. phr., slang* Wild ideas in his mind; disordered senses; great mental confusion. *When he talked about going to the moon he was thought to have bats in his belfry.*

batting average *n. phr.* Degree of accomplishment (originally used as a baseball term). *Dr. Grace has a great batting average with her heart transplant operations.*

battle of nerves *n. phr.* A contest of wills during which the parties do not fight physically but try to wear each other out. *It has been a regular battle of nerves to get the new program accepted at the local state university.*

bawl out *v., informal* To reprove in a loud or rough voice; rebuke sharply; scold. *The teacher bawled us out for not handing in our homework.*

beach bunny *n., slang* An attractive girl seen on beaches—mostly to show off her figure; one who doesn't get into the water and swim. *What kind of a girl is Susie?—She's a beach bunny; she always comes to the Queen's Surf on Waikiki but I've never seen her swim.*

be an item *v. phr.* To be a couple; belong to one another. *No one is surprised to see them together anymore; it is generally recognized that they are an item.*

bear a grudge *v. phr.* To persist in bearing ill feeling toward someone after a quarrel or period of hostility. *Come on, John, be a good sport and don't bear a grudge because I beat you at golf.*

bear down *v.* **1.** To press or push harder; work hard at; give full strength and attention. *She is bearing down in her studies to win a scholarship. The baseball pitcher is bearing down. The pitcher bore down on the star batter. Teachers of the deaf bear down on English. The sergeant bears down on lazy soldiers.* **2.** To move toward in an impressive or threatening way. —Often used with *on. While he was crossing the street a big truck bore down on him. The little ship tried to escape when the big pirate ship bore down. After the boys threw the snowballs they saw a large lady bearing down upon them from across the street.*

bear in the air *or* **bear in the sky** *n. phr., slang, citizen's band jargon* A police helicopter flying overhead watching for speeders. *Slow down, good buddy, there's a bear in the air.*

bear out *v.* To show to be right; prove; support. *Modern findings do not bear out the old belief that the earth is flat. Seward's faith in his purchase of Alaska was borne out, even though it was once called "Seward's Folly."*

bear up *v.* **1.** To hold up; carry; support; encourage. *The old bridge can hardly bear up its own weight any more. He was borne up by love of country.* **2.** To keep up one's courage or strength; last.—Often used with *up. This boat will bear up under hurricane winds. She bore up well at the funeral.*

bear watching *v. phr.* **1.** To be worth watching or paying attention to; have a promising future. *That young ball player will bear watching.* **2.** To be dangerous or untrustworthy. *Those tires look badly worn; they will bear watching.*

bear with *v., formal* To have patience with; not get angry with. *Your little sister is sick.*

Try to bear with her when she cries. It is hard to bear with criticism.

beat about the bush *or* **beat around the bush** *v. phr., slang* To talk about things without giving a clear answer; avoid the question or the point. *He would not answer yes or no, but beat about the bush. He beat about the bush for a half hour without coming to the point.*

beat all hollow *also* **beat hollow** *v. phr., slang* To do much better than; to beat very badly. *We beat their team all hollow. As a speaker, he beats us all hollow.*

beat a retreat *v. phr.* **1.** To give a signal, esp. by beating a drum, to go back. *The Redcoats' drums were beating a retreat.* **2.** To run away. *They beat a retreat when they saw that they were too few. The cat beat a hasty retreat when he saw the dog coming.*

beat into one's head *v. phr., informal* To teach by telling again and again; repeat often; drill, also, to be cross and punish often. *Tom is lazy and stubborn and his lessons have to be beaten into his head. I cannot beat it into his head that he should take off his hat in the house.*

beat it *v., slang* To go away in a hurry; get out quickly. *When he heard the crash he beat it as fast as he could.*— Often used as a command. *The big boy said, "Beat it, kid. We don't want you with us."*

beat one to it *v. phr.* To arrive or get ahead of another person. *I was about to call you, John,* *but you have beat me to it! Thanks for calling me.*

beat one's brains out *or* **beat one's brains** *v. phr., slang* To try very hard to understand or think out something difficult; tire yourself out by thinking. *It was too hard for him and he beat his brains out trying to get the answer. Some students are lazy, but others beat their brains and succeed.*

beat one's gums *v. phr., slang* To engage in idle talk, or meaningless chatter; generally to talk too much. *"Stop beating your gums, Jack," Joe cried. "I am falling asleep."*

beat one's head against a wall *v. phr.* To struggle uselessly against something that can't be beaten or helped; not succeed after trying very hard. *Trying to make him change his mind is just beating your head against a wall.*

beat the band *adv. phr., informal* At great speed; with much noise or commotion.— Used after *to*. *The fire engines were going down the road to beat the band. The audience cheered and stamped and clapped to beat the band.*

beat the bushes *also* **beat the brush** *v. phr., informal* To try very hard to find or get something. *The mayor was beating the bushes for funds to build the playground.*

beat the drum *v. phr.* To attract attention in order to advertise something or to promote someone, such as a political candidate. *Mrs. Smith has been beating the drum in her town in order to get her husband elected mayor.*

beat the rap v. phr. To escape the legal penalty one ought to receive. *In spite of the strong evidence against him, the prisoner beat the rap and went free.*

beat to v., informal To do something before someone else does it. *I was waiting to buy a ticket but only one ticket was left, and another man beat me to it. We were planning to send a rocket into space but the Russians beat us to it.*

beat to the punch or **beat to the draw** v. phr., slang To do something before another person has a chance to do it. *John was going to apply for the job, but Ted beat him to the draw. Lois bought the dress before Mary could beat her to the punch.*

beat up v., informal To give a hard beating to; hit hard and much; thrash; whip. *When the new boy first came, he had to beat up several neighborhood bullies before they would leave him alone.*—Used with *on* in substandard speech. *The tough boy said to Bill, "If you come around here again, I'll beat up on you."*

beauty sleep n. A nap or rest taken to improve the appearance. *She took her beauty sleep before the party. Many famous beauties take a beauty sleep every day.*

because of prep. On account of; by reason of; as a result of. *The train arrived late because of the snowstorm.*

bed of roses or **bowl of cherries** n. phr. A pleasant easy place, job, or position; an easy life. *A coal miner's job is not a bed of roses. After nine months of* school, summer camp seemed a bowl of cherries.

bed of thorns n. phr. A thoroughly unhappy time or difficult situation. *I'm sorry I changed jobs; my new one turned out to be a bed of thorns.*

beef up v., informal To make stronger by adding men or equipment; make more powerful; reinforce. *The general beefed up his army with more big guns and tanks. The university beefed up the football coaching staff by adding several good men.*

bee in one's bonnet n. phr., informal A fixed idea that seems fanciful, odd, or crazy. *Robert Fulton had a bee in his bonnet about a steamboat. Grandmother has some bee in her bonnet about going to the dance.*

be even-Steven v. phr. To be in a position of owing no favors or debt to someone. *Yesterday you paid for my lunch, so today I paid for yours; now we're even-Steven.*

before long adv. phr. In a short time; without much delay; in a little while; soon. *Class will be over before long. We were tired of waiting and hoped the bus would come before long.*

before one can say Jack Robinson adv. cl., informal Very quickly; suddenly.—An overused phrase. *Before I could say Jack Robinson, the boy was gone.*

beg off v. To ask to be excused. *Father told Tom to rake the yard, but Tom tried to beg off. Mrs. Crane accepted an in-*

vitation to a luncheon, but a headache made her beg off.

beg the question *v. phr., literary* To accept as true something that is still being argued about, before it is proved true; avoid or not answer a question or problem. *The girls asked Miss Smith if they should wear formal dresses to the party; Miss Smith said they were begging the question because they didn't know yet if they could get permission for a party. Laura told Tom that he must believe her argument because she was right. Father laughed and told Laura she was begging the question.*

be hard on *v. phr.* To be strict or critical with another; be severe. "*Don't be so hard on Jimmy,*" *Tom said.* "*He is bound to rebel as he gets older.*"

behind bars *adv. phr.* In jail; in prison. *He was a pickpocket and had spent many years behind bars. That boy is always in trouble and will end up behind bars.*

behind one's back *adv. phr.* When one is absent; without one's knowledge or consent; in a dishonest way; secretly; sneakily. *Say it to his face, not behind his back. It is not right to criticize a person behind his back.*

behind the eight-ball *adj. phr., slang* In a difficult position; in trouble. *Mr. Thompson is an older man, and when he lost his job, he found he was behind the eight-ball. Bill can't dance and has no car, so he is behind the eight-ball with the girls.*

behind the scenes *adv. phr.* Out of sight; unknown to most people; privately. *Much of the banquet committee's work was done behind the scenes. John was president of the club, but behind the scenes Lee told him what to do.*

behind the times *adj. phr.* Using things not in style; still following old ways; old-fashioned. *Johnson's store is behind the times. The science books of 30 years ago are behind the times now. Mary thinks her parents are behind the times because they still do the fox-trot and don't know any new dances.*

be-in *n., slang, hippie culture* A gathering or social occasion with or without a discernible purpose, often held in a public place like a park or under a large circus tent. *The youngsters really enjoyed the great springtime jazz be-in at the park.*

be in a stew *v. phr.* To be worried, harassed, upset. *Al has been in a stew ever since he got word that his sister was going to marry his worst enemy.*

be into something *v. phr., informal* To have taken something up partly as a hobby, partly as a serious interest of sorts (basically resulting from the new consciousness and self-realization movement that originated in the late Sixties). *Roger's wife is into women's liberation and women's consciousness. Did you know that Syd is seriously into transcendental meditation? Jack found out that his teenage son is into pot smoking and gave him a serious scolding.*

be itching to *v. phr.* To have a

very strong desire to do something. *Jack is itching to travel abroad.*

believe one's ears *v. phr.* **1.** To believe what one hears; trust one's hearing.—Used with a negative or limiter, or in an interrogative or conditional sentence. *He thought he heard a horn blowing in the distance, but he could not believe his ears.* **2.** To be made sure of (something). *Is he really coming? I can hardly believe my ears.*

believe one's eyes *v. phr.* **1.** To believe what one sees; trust one's eyesight.—Used with a negative or limiter or in an interrogative or conditional sentence. *Is that a plane? Can I believe my eyes?* **2.** To be made sure of seeing something. *She saw him there but she could hardly believe her eyes.*

belly up *adj., informal* Dead, bankrupt, or financially ruined. *Tom and Dick struggled on for months with their tiny computer shop, but last year they went belly up.*

belly up *v., informal* To go bankrupt, become afunctional; to die. *Uncompetitive small businesses must eventually all belly up.*

below the belt *adv. phr.* **1.** In the stomach; lower than is legal in boxing. *He struck the other boy below the belt.* **2.** *informal* In an unfair or cowardly way; against the rules of sportsmanship or justice; unsportingly; wrongly. *It was hitting below the belt for Mr. Jones's rival to tell people about a crime that Mr. Jones committed when he was a young boy. Pete told the*

students to vote against Harry because Harry was in a wheelchair and couldn't be a good class president, but the students thought Pete was hitting below the belt.*

be my guest *v. phr.* Feel free to use what I have; help yourself. *When Suzie asked if she could borrow John's bicycle, John said, "Be my guest."*

beneath one *adj. phr.* Below one's ideals or dignity. *Bob felt it would have been beneath him to work for such low wages.*

bend over backward or **lean over backward** *v. phr., informal* To try so hard to avoid a mistake that you make the opposite mistake instead; do the opposite of something that you know you should not do; do too much to avoid doing the wrong thing; also, make a great effort; try very hard. *Instead of punishing the boys for breaking a new rule, the principal bent over backward to explain why the rule was important. Mary was afraid the girls at her new school would be stuck up, but they leaned over backward to make her feel at home.*

bent on or **bent upon** Very decided, determined, or set. *The sailors were bent on having a good time. The policeman saw some boys near the school after dark and thought they were bent on mischief. The bus was late, and the driver was bent upon reaching the school on time.*

be nuts about *v. phr.* To be enthusiastic or very keen about someone or something; be greatly infatuated with someone. *Hermione is nuts about* modern music. "I am nuts about you, Helen," Jim said. "Please let's get married!"

be off v. phr. **1.** v. To be in error; miscalculate. *The estimator was off by at least 35% on the value of the house.* **2.** v. To leave. *Jack ate his supper in a hurry and was off without saying good-bye.* **3.** adj. Cancelled; terminated. *The weather was so bad that we were told that the trip was off.* **4.** adj. Crazy. *I'm sure Aunt Mathilda is a bit off; no one in her right mind would say such things.* **5.** adj. Free from work; having vacation time. *Although we were off for the rest of the day, we couldn't go to the beach because it started to rain.*

be on v. phr. **1.** To be in operation; be in the process of being presented. *The news is on now on Channel 2; it will be off in five minutes.* **2.** To be in the process of happening; to take place. *We cannot travel now to certain parts of Africa, as there is a civil war on there right now.*

be on the verge of v. phr. To be about to do something; be very close to. *We were on the verge of going bankrupt when, unexpectedly, my wife won the lottery and our business was saved.*

be over v. phr. To be ended; be finished. *The show was over by 11 p.m. The war will soon be over.*

be out v. phr. **1.** To not be at home or at one's place of work. *I tried to call but they told me that Al was out.* **2.** To be unacceptable; not be considered; impossible. *I suggested*

that we hire more salespeople but the boss replied that such a move was positively out. **3.** To be poorer by; suffer a loss of. *Unless more people came to the church picnic, we realized we would be out $500 at least.* **4.** To be in circulation, in print, published. *Jane said that her new novel won't be out for at least another month.* **5.** A baseball term indicating that a player has been declared either unfit to continue or punished by withdrawing him. *The spectators thought that John was safe at third base, but the umpire said he was out.*

be out to v. phr. To intend to do; to plan to commit. *The police felt that the gang may be out to rob another store.*

beside oneself adj. phr. Very much excited; somewhat crazy. *She was beside herself with fear. He was beside himself, he was so angry. When his wife heard of his death, she was beside herself.*

beside the point or **beside the question** adj. or adv. phr. Off the subject; about something different. *What you meant to do is beside the point; the fact is you didn't do it. The judge told the witness that his remarks were beside the point.*

best man n. The groom's aid (usually his best friend or a relative) at a wedding. *When Agnes and I got married, my brother Gordon was my best man.*

best seller n. An item (primarily said of books) that outsells other items of a similar sort. *Catherine Neville's novel The Eight has been a national* best seller for months. Among imported European cars, the Volkswagen is a best seller.

bet one's boots or **bet one's bottom dollar** or **bet one's shirt** v. phr., informal **1.** To bet all you have. This horse will win. I would bet my bottom dollar on it. Jim said he would bet his boots that he would pass the examination. **2.** or **bet one's life.** To feel very sure; have no doubt. Was I scared when I saw the bull running at me? You bet your life I was!

bet on the wrong horse v. phr., informal To base your plans on a wrong guess about the result of something; misread the future; misjudge a coming event. To count on the small family farm as an important thing in the American future now looks like betting on the wrong horse. He expected Bush to be elected President in 1992 but as it happened, he bet on the wrong horse.

better half n., informal One's marriage partner (mostly said by men about their wives.) "This is my better half, Mary," said Joe.

better late than never It is better to come or do something late than never. The firemen didn't arrive at the house until it was half burned, but it was better late than never. Grandfather is learning to drive a car. "Better late than never," he says.

between the devil and the deep blue sea or literary **between two fires** or **between a rock and a hard place** adv. phr. Between two dangers or difficulties, not knowing what to

do. The pirates had to fight and be killed or give up and be hanged; they were between the devil and the deep blue sea. The boy was between a rock and a hard place; he had to go home and be whipped or stay in town all night and be picked up by the police. When the man's wife and her mother got together, he was between two fires.

be up to no good v. phr., informal To be plotting and conniving to commit some illegal act or crime. "Let's hurry!" Susan said to her husband. "It's dark here and those hoodlums obviously are up to no good."

beyond measure adj. or adv. phr., formal So much that it can not be measured or figured without any limits. With her parents reunited and present at her graduation, she had happiness beyond measure. No one envied him for he was popular beyond measure.

beyond one's depth adj. or adv. phr. **1.** Over your head in water; in water too deep to touch bottom. Jack wasn't a good swimmer and nearly drowned when he drifted out beyond his depth. **2.** In or into something too difficult for you; beyond your understanding or ability. Bill decided that his big brother's geometry book was beyond his depth. Sam's father started to explain the atom bomb to Sam but he soon got beyond his depth. When Bill played checkers against the city champion, Bill was beyond his depth.

beyond one's means adj. phr. Too expensive, not affordable. Unfortunately, a new Mercedes

Benz is beyond my means right now.

beyond the pale *adv. or adj. phr.* In disgrace; with no chance of being accepted or respected by others; not approved by the members of a group. *After the outlaw killed a man he was beyond the pale and not even his old friends would talk to him. Tom's swearing is beyond the pale; no one invites him to dinner any more.*

bide one's time *v. phr.* To await an opportunity; wait patiently until your chance comes. *Refused work as an actor, Tom turned to other work and bided his time. Jack was hurt deeply, and he bided his time for revenge.*

big as life *or* **large as life** *adj. phr.* **1.** *or* **life-size** The same size as the living person or thing. *The statue of Jefferson was big as life. The characters on the screen were life-size.* **2.** *or* **big as life and twice as natural** *informal* In person; real and living. *I had not seen him for years, but there he was, big as life and twice as natural.*

big cheese *or* **big gun** *or* **big shot** *or* **big wheel** *or* **big wig** *n., slang* An important person; a leader; a high official; a person of high rank. *Bill had been a big shot in high school. John wanted to be the big cheese in his club.*

big daddy *n., slang, informal* The most important, largest thing, person or animal in a congregation of similar persons, animals, or objects. *The whale is the big daddy of everything that swims in the ocean.*

The H-bomb is the big daddy of all modern weapons. Al Capone was the big daddy of organized crime in Chicago during Prohibition.

big deal *interj., slang, informal* (loud stress on the word *deal*) Trifles; an unimportant, unimpressive thing or matter. *So you became college president— big deal!*

big frog in a small pond *n. phr., informal* An important person in a small place or position; someone who is respected and honored in a small company, school, or city; a leader in a small group. *As company president, he had been a big frog in a small pond, but he was not so important as a new congressman in Washington.*

big head *n., informal* Too high an opinion of your own ability or importance; conceit. *When Jack was elected captain of the team, it gave him a big head.*

big lie, the *n., informal* A major, deliberate misrepresentation of some important issue made on the assumption that a bold, gross lie is psychologically more believable than a timid, minor one. *We all heard the big lie during the Watergate months. The pretense of democracy by a totalitarian regime is part of the big lie about its government.*

big stink *n., slang* A major scandal; a big upheaval. *I'll raise a big stink if they fire me.*

big time *n., informal* **1.** A very enjoyable time at a party or other pleasurable gathering. *I certainly had a big time at the club last night.* **2.** The top group; the leading class; the best or most important company. *After his graduation from college, he soon made the big time in baseball. Many young actors go to Hollywood, but few of them reach the big time.*

big-time *adj.* Belonging to the top group; of the leading class; important. *Jean won a talent contest in her home town, and only a year later she began dancing on big-time television. Bob practices boxing in the gym every day; he wants to become a big time boxer.*—Often used in the phrase *big-time* operator. *Just because Bill has a new football uniform he thinks he is a big-time operator.*

big wheel *n., informal* An influential or important person who has the power to do things and has connections in high places. *Uncle Ferdinand is a big wheel in Washington; maybe he can help you with your problem.*

bird has flown *slang* The prisoner has escaped; the captive has got away. *When the sheriff returned to the jail, he discovered that the bird had flown.*

bird in the hand is worth two in the bush (a) Something we have, or can easily get, is more valuable than something we want that we may not be able to get; we shouldn't risk losing something sure by trying to get something that is not sure.—A proverb. *Johnny has a job as a paperboy, but he wants a job in a gas station. His father says that a bird in the hand is worth two in the bush.*

bird of a different feather *n. phr.* A person who is free thinking and independent. *Syd won't go along with recent trends in grammar; he created his own. He is a bird of a different feather.*

birds of a feather flock together People who are alike often become friends or are together; if you are often with certain people, you may be their friends or like them.—A proverb. *Don't be friends with bad boys. People think that birds of a feather flock together.*

birds and the bees (the) *n. phr., informal* The facts we should know about our birth. *At various ages, in response to questions, a child can be told about the birds and the bees.*

birthday suit *n.* The skin with no clothes on; complete nakedness. *The little boys were swimming in their birthday suits.*

bite off more than one can chew *v. phr., informal* To try to do more than you can; be too confident of your ability. *He bit off more than he could chew when he agreed to edit the paper alone. He started to repair his car himself, but realized that he had bitten off more than he could chew.*

bite one's head off *v. phr.* To answer someone in great anger; answer furiously. *I'm sorry to tell you that I lost my job, but that's no reason to bite my head off!*

bite one's lips *v. phr.* To force oneself to remain silent and not to reveal one's feelings. *I had to bite my lips when I*

heard my boss give the wrong
orders.

bite the dust v. phr., informal
1. To be killed in battle. Captain Jones discharged his gun
and another guerrilla bit the
dust. **2.** To fall in defeat; go
down before enemies; be overthrown; lose. Our team bit the
dust today.

bite the hand that feeds one v.
phr. To turn against or hurt a
helper or supporter; repay
kindness with wrong. He bit the
hand that fed him when he
complained against his employer.

bitter pill n. Something hard
to accept; disappointment. Jack
was not invited to the party and
it was a bitter pill for him.

black and blue adj. Badly
bruised. Poor Jim was black
and blue after he fell off the
apple tree.

black and white n. phr. **1.**
Print or writing; words on paper, not spoken; exact written
or printed form. He insisted on
having the agreement down in
black and white. Mrs. Jones
would not believe the news, so
Mr. Jones showed her the article in the newspaper and said,
"There it is in black and white."
2. The different shades of black
and white of a simple picture,
rather than other colors. He
showed us snapshots in black
and white.

black-and-white adj. Divided
into only two sides that are
either right or wrong or good
or bad, with nothing in between; thinking or judging
everything as either good or

bad. Everything is black-and-white to Bill; if you're not his
friend, you are his enemy. The
old man's religion shows his
black-and-white thinking; everything is either completely good
or completely bad.

black day n. A day of great
unhappiness; a disaster. It was
a black day when our business
venture collapsed.

black eye n. **1.** A dark area
around one's eye due to a hard
blow during a fight, such as
boxing. Mike Tyson sported a
black eye after the big fight. **2.**
Discredit. Bob's illegal actions
will give a black eye to the
popular movement he started.

blackout n. **1.** The darkening
of a city during an air raid by
pulling down all curtains and
putting out all street lights. The
city of London went through
numerous blackouts during
World War II. **2.** A cessation
of news by the mass media.
There was a total news blackout
about the kidnapping of the
prime minister.

black out v. **1.** To darken by
putting out or dimming lights.
In some plays the stage is
blacked out for a short time and
the actors speak in darkness. In
wartime, cities are blacked out
to protect against bombing
from planes. **2.** To prevent or
silence information or communication; refuse to give out
truthful news. In wartime, governments often black out all
news or give out false news.
Dictators usually black out all
criticism of the government.
Some big games are blacked

out on television to people who live nearby. **3.** *informal* To lose consciousness; faint. *It had been a hard and tiring day, and she suddenly blacked out.*

black sheep *n.* A person in a family or a community considered unsatisfactory or disgraceful. *My brother Ted is a high school dropout who joined a circus; he is the black sheep in our family.*

blast off *v.* **1.** To begin a rocket flight. *The astronaut will blast off into orbit at six o'clock.* **2.** *Also* **blast away** *informal* To scold or protest violently. *The coach blasted away at the team for poor playing.*

blaze a trail *v. phr.* **1.** To cut marks in trees in order to guide other people along a path or trail, especially through a wilderness. *Daniel Boone blazed a trail for other hunters to follow in Kentucky.* **2.** To lead the way; make a discovery; start something new. *Henry Ford blazed a trail in manufacturing automobiles. The building of rockets blazed a trail to outer space.*

blind alley *n.* **1.** A narrow street that has only one entrance and no exit. *The blind alley ended in a brick wall.* **2.** A way of acting that leads to no good results. *John did not take the job because it was a blind alley. Tom thought of a way to do the algebra problem, but he found it was a blind alley.*

blind as a bat/beetle/mole/owl *adj. phr.* Anyone who is blind or has difficulty in seeing; a person with very thick glasses.

Without my glasses I am blind as a bat.

blind date *n.* An engagement or date arranged by friends for people who have not previously known one another. *A blind date can be a huge success, or a big disappointment.*

blind leading the blind One or more people who do not know or understand something trying to explain it to others who do not know or understand. *Jimmy is trying to show Bill how to skate. The blind are leading the blind.*

blind spot *n.* **1.** A place on the road that a driver cannot see in the rearview mirror. *I couldn't see that truck behind me, Officer, because it was in my blind spot.* **2.** A matter or topic a person refuses to discuss or accept. *My uncle Ted has a real blind spot about religion.*

blood is thicker than water Persons of the same family are closer to one another than to others; relatives are favored or chosen over outsiders. *Mr. Jones hires his relatives to work in his store. Blood is thicker than water.*

blood runs cold *also* **blood freezes** *or* **blood turns to ice** You are chilled or shivering from great fright or horror; you are terrified or horrified. — Usually used with a possessive. *The horror movie made the children's blood run cold. Mary's blood froze when she had to walk through the cemetery at night. Oscar's blood turned to ice when he saw the* *shadow pass by outside the window.*

blot out *v. phr.* **1.** To obstruct; cover; obscure. *The high-rise building in front of our apartment house blots out the view of the ocean.* **2.** To wipe out of one's memory. *Jane can't remember the details when she was attacked in the streets; she blotted it out of her memory.*

blow a fuse *or* **blow a gasket** *or* **blow one's top** *or* **blow one's stack** *v. phr., slang* To become extremely angry; express rage in hot words. *When Mr. McCarthy's son got married against his wishes, he blew a fuse. When the umpire called Joe out at first, Joe blew his top and was sent to the showers.*

blow in *v., slang* To arrive unexpectedly or in a carefree way. *The house was already full of guests when Bill blew in.*

blow into *v., slang* To arrive at (a place) unexpectedly or in a carefree way. *Bill blows into college at the last minute after every vacation. Why Tom, when did you blow into town?*

blow one's brains out *v. phr.* **1.** To shoot yourself in the head. *Mr. Jones lost all his wealth, so he blew his brains out.* **2.** *slang* To work very hard; overwork yourself. *The boys blew their brains out to get the stage ready for the play. Mary is not one to blow her brains out.*

blow one's cool *v. phr., slang, informal* To lose your composure or self-control. *Whatever you say to the judge in court,*

make sure that you don't blow your cool.

blow one's lines *or* **fluff one's lines** *v. phr., informal* To forget the words you are supposed to speak while acting in a play. *The noise backstage scared Mary and she blew her lines.*

blow one's mind *v. phr., slang, informal*; originally from the drug culture **1.** To become wildly enthusiastic over something as if understanding it for the first time in an entirely new light. *Read Lyall Watson's book* Supernature, *it will simply blow your mind!* **2.** To lose one's ability to function, as if due to an overdose of drugs. *Joe is entirely incoherent—he seems to have blown his mind.*

blow one's own horn *or* **toot one's own horn** *v. phr., slang* To praise yourself; call attention to your own skill, intelligence, or successes; boast. *People get tired of a man who is always blowing his own horn. A person who does things well does not have to toot his own horn; his abilities will be noticed by others.*

blow one's top *v. phr.* To become very excited, angry, hysterical, or furious. *"No need to blow your top, Al," his wife said, "just because you lost a few dollars."*

blow out *v. phr.* **1.** To cease to function; fail; explode (said of tires and fuses). *The accident occurred when Jim's tire blew out on the highway. The new dishwasher blew out the fuses in the whole house.* **2.** To extinguish. *Jane blew out her* *birthday cake candles before offering pieces to the guests.*

blowout *n.* **1.** An explosion of a tire or a fuse. *Jim's van veered sharply to the right after his car had a blowout.* **2.** A big party. *After graduation from college, my son and his friends staged a huge blowout.*

blow over *v.* To come to an end; pass away with little or no bad effects. *The sky was black, as if a bad storm were coming, but it blew over and the sun came out. They were bitter enemies for a while, but the quarrel blew over. He was much criticized for the divorce, but it all blew over after a few years.*

blow the lid off *v. phr., informal* Suddenly to reveal the truth about a matter that has been kept as a secret either by private persons or by some governmental agency. *The clever journalists blew the lid off the Watergate cover-up.*

blow the whistle on *v. phr., slang* **1.** To inform against; betray. *The police caught one of the bank robbers, and he blew the whistle on two more.* **2.** To act against, stop, or tell people the secrets of (crime or lawlessness). *The mayor blew the whistle on gambling. The police blew the whistle on hot rodding.*

blow up *v.* **1a.** To break or destroy or to be destroyed by explosion. *He blew up the plane by means of a concealed bomb. The fireworks factory blew up when something went wrong in an electric switch.* **1b.** *informal* To explode with anger or strong feeling; lose control of

yourself. *When Father bent the nail for the third time, he blew up.* **1c.** To stop playing well in a game or contest, usually because you are in danger of losing or are tired; especially: To lose skill or control in pitching baseball. *The champion blew up and lost the tennis match. Our team was behind but the pitcher on the other team blew up and we got the winning runs.* **2.** *informal* To be ruined as if by explosion; be ended suddenly. *The whole scheme for a big party suddenly blew up.* **3a.** To pump full of air; inflate. *He blew his tires up at a filling station.* **3b.** To make (something) seem bigger or important. *It was a small thing to happen but the newspapers had blown it up until it seemed important.* **4.** To bring on bad weather; also, to come on as bad weather. *The wind had blown up a storm. A storm had blown up.* **5.** To copy in bigger form; enlarge. *He blew up the snapshot to a larger size.*

blow up in one's face *v. phr., informal* To fail completely and with unexpected force. *The thief's plan to rob the bank blew up in his face when a policeman stopped him.*

blue collar worker *n. phr.* A manual laborer who is probably a labor union member. *Because Jack's father is a blue collar worker, Jack was so anxious to become an intellectual.*

blue in the face *adj. phr., informal* Very angry or upset; excited and very emotional. *Tom argued with Bill until he was blue in the face. Mary scolded*

Jane until she was blue in the face, but Jane kept on using Mary's paints.

bog down *v. phr.* To be immobilized in mud, snow, etc.; slow down. *Our research got bogged down for a lack of appropriate funding. Don't get bogged down in too much detail when you write an action story.*

bog down, to get bogged down *v. phr.,* mostly intransitive or passive **1.** To stop progressing; to slow to a halt. *Work on the new building bogged down, because the contractor didn't deliver the needed concrete blocks.* **2.** To become entangled with a variety of obstacles making your efforts unproductive or unsatisfying. *The novelist wrote little last summer because she got bogged down in housework.*

boggle the mind *v. phr., informal* To stop the rational thinking process by virtue of being too fantastic or incredible. *It boggles the mind that John should have been inside a flying saucer!*

boil down *v.* **1.** To boil away some of the water from; make less by boiling. *She boiled down the maple sap to a thick syrup. The fruit juice boiled down until it was almost not good for jelly.* **2.** To reduce the length of; cut down; shorten. *The reporter boiled the story down to half the original length.* **3.** To reduce itself to; come down to; be briefly or basically. *The whole discussion boils down to the question of whether the government should fix prices.*

bonehead *n., slang* An unusually dense or stupid person. *John is such a bonehead—small wonder he flunks all of his courses.*

bone of contention *n. phr.* Something to fight over; a reason for quarrels; the subject of a fight. *The boundary line between the farms was a bone of contention between the two farmers. The use of the car was a bone of contention between Joe and his wife.*

bone to pick or **crow to pick** *n. phr., informal* A reason for dispute; something to complain of or argue about.—Often used jokingly. *"I have a bone to pick with you," he said. There was always a crow to pick about which one would shave first in the morning.*

bone up *v., informal* To fill with information; try to learn a lot about something in a short time; study quickly. *Carl was boning up for an examination. Jim had to make a class report the next day on juvenile delinquency, and he was in the library boning up on how the courts handle it.*

bore to tears *v. phr.* To fill with tired dislike; tire by dullness or the same old thing; bore. *The party was dull and Roger showed plainly that he was bored to tears. Mary loved cooking, but sewing bores her to tears.*

born with a silver spoon in one's mouth *adj. phr.* Born to wealth and comfort; provided from birth with everything wanted; born rich. *The stranger's conduct was that of a* *man who had been born with a silver spoon in his mouth.*

born yesterday *adj. phr.* Inexperienced and easily fooled; not alert to trickery; easily deceived or cheated.—Usually used in negative sentences. *When Bill started the new job, the other workers teased him a little, but he soon proved to everyone that he wasn't born yesterday. I won't give you the money till I see the bicycle you want to sell me. Do you think I was born yesterday?*

bosom friend *n. phr.* A very close friend; an old buddy with whom one has a confidential relationship. *Sue and Jane have been bosom friends since their college days.*

boss one around *v. phr.* To keep giving someone orders; to act overbearingly toward someone. *"If you keep bossing me around, darling," Tom said to Jane, "the days of our relationship are surely numbered."*

botch up *v. phr.* To ruin, spoil, or mess something up. *"I botched up my chemistry exam," Tim said, with a resigned sigh.*

bottleneck *n.* A heavy traffic congestion. *In Chicago the worst bottleneck is found where the Kennedy and the Eden's expressways separate on the way to the airport.*

bottle up *v.* **1.** To hide or hold back; control. *There was no understanding person to talk to, so Fred bottled up his unhappy feeling.* **2.** To hold in a place from which there is no escape; trap. *Our warships bottled up the enemy fleet in the harbor.*

bottom dollar *n., v. phr., informal* One's last penny; one's last dollar. *He was down to his bottom dollar when he suddenly got the job offer.*

bottom drop out or **bottom fall out** *v. phr. informal* **1.** To fall below an earlier lowest price. *The bottom dropped out of the price of peaches.* **2.** To lose all cheerful qualities; become very unhappy, cheerless, or unpleasant. *The bottom dropped out of the day for John when he saw his report card. The bottom fell out for us when the game ended with our team on the two-yard line and six points behind.*

bottom line *n., informal* (stress on *line*) **1.** The last word on a controversial issue; a final decision. *"Give me the bottom line on the proposed merger,"* said John. **2.** The naked truth without embellishments. *Look, the bottom line is that poor Max is an alcoholic.* **3.** The final dollar amount; for example, the lowest price two parties reach in bargaining about a sale. *"Five-hundred," said the used car dealer, "is the bottom line. Take it or leave it."*

bottom line *v., informal* (stress on *bottom*) To finish; to bring to a conclusion. *Okay, you guys, let's bottom line this project and break for coffee.*

bottom out *v. phr.* To reach the lowest point (said chiefly of economic cycles). *According to the leading economic indicators the recession will bottom out within the next two months.*

bound for *adj. phr.* On the way to; going to. *I am bound* for the country club. *The ship is bound for Liverpool.*

bow out *v., informal* **1.** To give up taking part; excuse yourself from doing any more; quit. *Mr. Black often quarreled with his partners, so finally he bowed out of the company. While the movie was being filmed, the star got sick and had to bow out.* **2.** To stop working after a long service; retire. *He bowed out as train engineer after forty years of railroading.*

box office *n., informal* **1.** The place at movies and theaters where tickets may be purchased just before the performance instead of having ordered them through the telephone or having bought them at a ticket agency. *No need to reserve the seats; we can pick them up at the box office.* **2.** A best selling movie, musical, or drama (where the tickets are all always sold out and people line up in front of the box office). *John Wayne's last movie was a regular box office.* **3.** Anything successful or well liked. *Betsie is no longer box office with me.*

boyfriend *n., informal* **1.** A male friend or companion. *"John and his boyfriends have gone to the ball game," said his mother.* **2.** A girl's steady date, a woman's favorite man friend; a male lover or sweetheart. *Jane's new boyfriend is a senior in high school.*

boys will be boys Boys are only children and must sometimes get into mischief or trouble or behave too roughly. *Boys will be boys and make a lot of*

noise, so John's mother told him and his friends to play in the park instead of the back yard.

brain bucket *n., slang* A motorcycle helmet. *If you want to share a ride with me, you've got to wear a brain bucket.*

brain drain *n., informal* **1.** The loss of the leading intellectuals and researchers of a country due to excessive emigration to other countries where conditions are better. *Britain suffered a considerable brain drain to the United States after World War II.* **2.** An activity requiring great mental concentration resulting in fatigue and exhaustion. *That math exam I took was a regular brain drain.*

brain-storm *v.* To have a discussion among fellow researchers or co-workers on a project in order to find the best solution to a given problem. *Dr. Watson and his research assistants are brain-storming in the conference room.*

brainstorm *n.* A sudden insight; a stroke of comprehension. *Listen to me, I've just had a major brainstorm, and I think I found the solution to our problem.*

brain trust *n.* A group of specially trained, highly intelligent experts in a given field. *Albert Einstein gathered a brain trust around himself at the Princeton Institute of Advanced Studies.*

branch off *v.* To go from something big or important to something smaller or less important; turn aside. *At the bridge a little road branches off from the highway and follows* the river. Martin was trying to study his lesson, but his mind kept branching off onto what girl he should ask to go with him to the dance.

branch out v. To add new interests or activities; begin doing other things also. *First Jane collected stamps; then she branched out and collected coins, too. John started a television repair shop; when he did well, he branched out and began selling television sets too.*

brand-new also **bran-new** adj. As new or fresh as when just made and sold by the manufacturer; showing no use or wear. *He had taken a brand-new car from the dealer's floor and wrecked it. In Uncle Tom's trunk, we found a wedding ring, still in its little satin-lined box, still brand-new.*

brazen it out v. phr. To pretend you did nothing wrong; be suspected, accused, or scolded without admitting you did wrong; act as if not guilty. *The teacher found a stolen pen that the girl had in her desk, but the girl brazened it out; she said someone else must have put it there.*

bread and butter[1] n. phr. The usual needs of life; food, shelter, and clothing. *Ed earned his bread and butter as a bookkeeper, but added a little jam by working with a dance band on weekends.*

bread and butter[2] adj. Thanking someone for entertainment or a nice visit; thank-you. *After spending the weekend as a guest in the Jones' home, Alice wrote the Joneses the usual bread-and-butter letter.*

break down v. (stress on *down*) **1.** To smash or hit (something) so that it falls; cause to fall by force. *The firemen broke down the door.* **2.** To reduce or destroy the strength or effect of; weaken; win over. *By helpful kindness the teacher broke down the new boy's shyness. Advertising breaks down a lot of stubbornness against change.* **3.** To separate into elements or parts; decay. *Water is readily broken down into hydrogen and oxygen. After many years, rocks break down into dirt.* **4.** To become unusable because of breakage or other failure; lose power to work or go. *The car broke down after half an hour's driving. His health broke down. When the coach was sick in bed, the training rules of the team broke down.*

break even v. phr., informal (stress on *even*) To end a series of gains and losses having the same amount you started with; have expenses equal to profits; have equal gain and loss. *The storekeeper made many sales, but his expenses were so high that he just broke even. If you gamble you are lucky when you break even.*

break-even n. The point of equilibrium in a business venture when one has made as much money as one had invested, but not more—that would be "profit." *"We've reached the break-even point at long last!" Max exclaimed with joy.*

break ground v. phr. To begin a construction project by digging for the foundation; especially, to turn the formal first spadeful of dirt. *City officials and industrial leaders were there as the company broke ground for its new building.*

break in v. (stress on *in*) **1a.** To break from outside. *The firemen broke in the door of the burning house.* **1b.** To enter by force or unlawfully. *Thieves broke in while the family was away.* **2.** To enter suddenly or interrupt. *A stranger broke in on the meeting without knocking. The secretary broke in to say that a telegram had arrived.* **3.** To make a start in a line of work or with a company or association; begin a new job. *He broke in as a baseball player with a minor league.* **4.** To teach the skills of a new job or activity to. *An assistant foreman broke in the new man as a machine operator.* **5.** To lessen the stiffness or newness of by use. *He broke in a new pair of shoes. Breaking in a new car requires careful driving at moderate speeds.*

break-in n. (stress on *break*) A robbery; a burglary. *We lost our jewelry during a break-in.*

break into v. **1.** To force an entrance into; make a rough or unlawful entrance into. *Thieves broke into the store at night.* **2.** *informal* To succeed in beginning (a career, business, or a social life). *He broke into television as an actor.* **3.** To interrupt. *He broke into the discussion with a shout of warning.* **4.** To begin suddenly. *He broke into a sweat. She broke into tears. The dog heard his master's whistle and broke into a run.*

break new ground v. phr. **1.** To start a new activity previously neglected by others; do pioneering work. *Albert Einstein broke new ground with his theory of relativity.* **2.** To begin something never done before. *The school broke new ground with reading lessons that taught students to guess the meaning of new words.*

break off v. **1.** To stop suddenly. *The speaker was interrupted so often that he broke off and sat down. When Bob came in, Jean broke off her talk with Linda and talked to Bob.* **2.** *informal* To end a friendship or love. *I hear that Tom and Alice have broken off. She broke off with her best friend.*

break one's balls v. phr., slang, vulgar, avoidable To do something with maximum effort; to do something very difficult or taxing. *I've been breaking my balls to buy you this new color TV set and you aren't the least bit appreciative!*

break one's heart v. phr. To discourage greatly; make very sad or hopeless. *His son's disgrace broke his heart. When Mr. White lost everything he had worked so hard for, it broke his heart.*

break one's neck v. phr., slang To do all you possibly can; try your hardest.—Usually used with a limiting adverb or negative. *John nearly broke his neck trying not to be late to school. Mother asked Mary to go to the store when she was free, but not to break her neck over it.*

break one's word v. phr. To renege on a promise. *When Jake broke his word that he* *would marry Sarah, she became very depressed.*

break out *v.* **1.** To begin showing a rash or other skin disorder.—Often used with *with. He broke out with scarlet fever.* **2.** To speak or act suddenly and violently. *He broke out laughing. She broke out, "That is not so!"* **3.** To begin and become noticeable. *Fire broke out after the earthquake. War broke out in 1812.* **4.** *informal* To bring out; open and show. *When word of the victory came, people began breaking out their flags. When Carson's first son was born, he broke out the cigars he had been saving.*

break the ice *v. phr., informal* **1.** To conquer the first difficulties in starting a conversation, getting a party going, or making an acquaintance. *To break the ice Ted spoke of his interest in mountain climbing, and they soon had a conversation going. Some people use an unusual thing, such as an unusual piece of jewelry, to break the ice.* **2.** To be the first person or team to score in a game. *The Wolves broke the ice with a touchdown.*

break the record *v. phr.* To set or to establish a new mark or record. *Algernon broke the record in both the pentathlon and the decathlon and took home two gold medals from the Olympics.*

break through *v.* To be successful after overcoming a difficulty or bar to success. *Dr. Salk failed many times but he finally broke through to find a successful polio vaccine. Jim studied very hard this semester*

in college, and he finally broke through onto the Dean's List for the first time.

breakthrough *n.* A point of sudden success after a long process of experimentation, trial and error. *The U.S. Space Program experienced a major breakthrough when Armstrong and Aldrin landed on the moon in June of 1969.*

break up *v. phr.* To end a romantic relationship, a marriage, or a business partnership. *Tom and Jane broke up because Tom played so much golf that he had no time for her.*

break up *v.* **1.** To break into pieces. *The workmen broke up the pavement to dig up the pipes under it. River ice breaks up in the spring.* **2.** *informal* To lose or destroy spirit or self-control.—Usually used in the passive. *Mrs. Lawrence was all broken up after her daughter's death, and did not go out of the house for two months.* **3.** To come or to put to an end, especially by separation; separate. *Some men kept interrupting the speakers, and finally broke up the meeting. The party broke up at midnight.*—Often used in the informal phrase *break it up. The boys were fighting, and a passing policeman ordered them to break it up.* **4.** *informal* To stop being friends. *Mary and June were good friends and did everything together, but then they had a quarrel and broke up.*

break-up *n.* The end of a relationship, personal or commercial. *The break-up finally occurred when Smith and*

Brown decided to sue each other for embezzlement.

break with v. To separate yourself from; end membership in; stop friendly association with. *He broke with the Democratic party on the question of civil rights. He had broken with some friends who had changed in their ideas.*

breathe down one's neck v. phr., informal To follow closely; threaten from behind; watch every action. *Too many creditors were breathing down his neck. The carpenter didn't like to work for Mr. Jones, who was always breathing down his neck.*

breathe easily or **breathe freely** v. To have relief from difficulty or worry; relax; feel that trouble is gone; stop worrying. *Now that the big bills are paid, he breathed more easily. His mother didn't breathe easily until he got home that night.*

breathe one's last v. phr. To die. *The wounded soldier fell back on the ground and breathed his last.*

breeze in v. phr., slang, informal To walk into a place casually (like a soft blowing wind). *Betsie breezed in and sat down at the bar.*

bright and early adj. phr. Prompt and alert; on time and ready; cheerful and on time or before time. *He came down bright and early to breakfast. She arrived bright and early for the appointment.*

bring about v. To cause; produce; lead to. *The war had brought about great changes in*

living. Drink brought about his downfall.

bring around or **bring round** v. **1.** informal To restore to health or consciousness cure. *He was quite ill, but good nursing brought him around.* **2.** To cause a change in thinking; persuade; convince; make willing. *After a good deal of discussion he brought her round to his way of thinking.*

bringdown n., slang, informal **1.** (from bring down, past brought down). A critical or cutting remark said sarcastically in order to deflate a braggard's ego. *John always utters the right bringdown when he encounters a braggard.* **2.** A person who depresses and saddens others by being a chronic complainer. *John is a regular bringdown.*

bring down v. phr., slang, informal **1.** To deflate (someone's ego). *John brought Ted down very cleverly with his remarks.* **2.** To depress (someone). *The funeral brought me down completely.*

bring down the house v. phr., informal To start an audience laughing or clapping enthusiastically. *The principal's story was funny in itself and also touched their loyalties, so it brought down the house. The President made a fine speech which brought down the house.*

bring home v. To show clearly; emphasize; make (someone) realize; demonstrate. *The accident caused a death in his family, and it brought home to him the evil of drinking while driving. A* *parent or teacher should bring home to children the value and pleasure of reading.*

bring home the bacon *v. phr., informal* **1.** To support your family; earn the family living. *He was a steady fellow, who always brought home the bacon.* **2.** To win a game or prize. *The football team brought home the bacon.*

bring in *v.* In baseball: To enable men on base to score, score. *Dick's hit brought in both base runners. A walk and a triple brought in a run in the third inning.*

bring into line *v. phr.* To make someone conform to the accepted standard. *Sam had to be brought into line when he refused to take his muddy shoes off the cocktail table.*

bring off *v.* To do (something difficult); perform successfully (an act of skill); accomplish (something requiring unusual ability). *By skillful discussion, Mr. White had brought off an agreement that had seemed impossible to get. He tried several times to break the high jump record, and finally he brought it off.*

bring on *v.* To result in; cause; produce. *The murder of Archduke Franz Ferdinand in the summer of 1914 brought on the First World War. Spinal meningitis brought on John's deafness when he was six years old. Reading in a poor light may bring on a headache.*

bring out *v.* **1.** To cause to appear; make clear. *His report brought out the foolishness of the plan. Brushing will bring out the beauty of your hair.* **2.**

To help (an ability or skill) grow or develop. *The teacher's coaching brought out a wonderful singing voice of great power and warmth.* **3.** To offer to the public by producing, publishing, or selling. *He brought out a new play. The company brought out a line of light personal airplanes.*

bring to *v.* (stress on *to*) **1.** To restore to consciousness; wake from sleep, anesthesia, hypnosis, or fainting. *Smelling salts will often bring a fainting person to* **2.** To bring a ship or boat to a stop. *Reaching the pier, he brought the boat smartly to.*

bring to light *v. phr.* To discover (something hidden); find out about; expose. *Many things left by the ancient Egyptians in tombs have been brought to light by scientists and explorers. His enemies brought to light some foolish things he had done while young, but he was elected anyway because people trusted him.*

bring to one's knees *v. phr.* To seriously weaken the power or impair the function of. *The fuel shortage brought the automobile industry to its knees.*

bring to pass *v. phr., informal* To make (something) happen; succeed in causing. *By much planning, the mother brought the marriage to pass. The change in the law was slow in coming, and it took a disaster to bring it to pass.*

bring to terms *v. phr.* To make (someone) agree or do; make surrender. *The two brothers were brought to terms by their father for riding the bi-*

cycle. The war won't end until we bring the enemy to terms.

bring up *v.* **1.** To take care of (a child); raise, train, educate. *He gave much attention and thought to bringing up his children. Joe was born in Texas but brought up in Oklahoma.* **2.** *informal* To stop; halt.— Usually used with *short. He brought the car up short when the light changed to red. Bill started to complain, I brought him up short.* **3.** To begin a discussion of; speak of; mention. *At the class meeting Bob brought up the idea of a picnic.*

bring up the rear *v. phr.* **1.** To come last in a march, parade, or procession; end a line. *The fire truck with Santa on it brought up the rear of the Christmas parade. The governor and his staff brought up the rear of the parade.* **2.** *informal* To do least well; do the most poorly of a group; be last. *In the race, John brought up the rear. In the basketball tournament, our team brought up the rear.*

brown-bagger *n., slang, informal* A person who does not go to the cafeteria or to a restaurant for lunch at work, but who brings his homemade lunch to work in order to save money. *John became a brown-bagger not because he can't afford the restaurant, but because he is too busy to go there.*

brown-nose *v., slang, avoidable, though gaining in acceptance* To curry favor in a subservient way, as by obviously exaggerated flattery. *Max brown-noses his teachers,*

that's why he gets all A's in his courses.

brush off *or* **give the brush off** *v. phr.* **1.** To refuse to hear or believe; quickly and impatiently; not take seriously or think important. *John brushed off Bill's warning that he might fall from the tree. I said that it might rain and to take the bus, but Joe gave my idea the brushoff. Father cut his finger but he brushed it off as not important and kept working.* **2.** *informal* To be unfriendly to; not talk or pay attention to (someone); get rid of. *Mary brushed off Bill at the dance. I said hello to Mr. Smith, but he gave me the brushoff.*

brush up *or* **brush up on** *v.* To refresh one's memory of or skill at by practice or review; improve; make perfect. *She spent the summer brushing up on her American History as she was to teach that in the fall. He brushed up his target shooting.*

bubble gum music *n., slang* The kind of rock'n'roll that appeals to young teenagers. *When will you learn to appreciate Mozart instead of that bubble gum music?*

buckle down *or* **knuckle down** *v.* To give complete attention (to an effort or job); attend. *They chatted idly for a few moments then each buckled down to work. Jim was fooling instead of studying; so his father told him to buckle down.*

bug-eyed *adj., slang* Wide-eyed with surprise. *He stood there bug-eyed when told that he had won the award.*

buggy-whip *n., slang* An unusually long, thin radio antenna on a car that bends back like a whip when the car moves fast. *He's very impressed with himself ever since he got a buggy whip.*

bughouse[1] *n., slang* An insane asylum. *They took Joe to the bughouse.*

bughouse[2] *adj., slang* Crazy, insane. *Joe's gone bughouse.*

bug in one's earn. *phr., informal* A hint; secret information given to someone to make him act; idea. *I saw Mary at the jeweler's admiring the diamond pin; I'll put a bug in Henry's ear.*

build a fire under *v. phr.* To urge or force (a slow or unwilling person) to action; get (someone) moving; arouse. *The health department built a fire under the restaurant owner and got him to clean the place up by threatening to cancel his license.*

build castles in the air *or* **build castles in Spain** *v. phr.* To make impossible or imaginary plans, dream about future successes that are unlikely. *He liked to build castles in the air, but never succeeded in anything. To build castles in Spain is natural for young people and they may work hard enough to get part of their wishes.*

build on sand *v. phr.* To lay a weak or insufficient foundation for a building, a business, or a relationship. *"I don't want to build my business on sand," John said, "so please, Dad, give me that loan I requested."*

build up *v.* **1.** To make out of separate pieces or layers; construct from parts. *Johnny built up a fort out of large balls of snow. Lois built up a cake of three layers.* **2.** To cover over or fill up with buildings. *The fields where Tom's father played as a boy are all built up now. A driver should slow down when he comes to an area that is built up.* **3a.** To increase slowly or by small amounts; grow. *John built up a bank account by saving regularly. The noise built up until Mary couldn't stand it any longer.* **3b.** To make stronger or better or more effective. *Fred exercised to build up his muscles. Joanne was studying to build up her algebra.* **3c.** *informal* To advertise quickly and publicize so as to make famous. *The press agent built up the young actress. The movie company spent much money building up its new picture.*

build up to *v. phr.* To be in the process of reaching a culmination point. *The clouds were building up to a violent storm. Their heated words were building up to a premature divorce.*

bull in a china shop *n. phr.* A rough or clumsy person who says or does something to anger others or upset plans; a tactless person. *We were talking politely and carefully with the teacher about a class party, but John came in like a bull in a china shop and his rough talk made the teacher say no.*

bull session *n., slang* A long informal talk about something by a group of persons. *After the* game the boys in the dormitory had a bull session until the lights went out.

bullshit n., vulgar, but gaining in acceptance by some Exaggerated or insincere talk meant to impress others. "Joe, this is a lot of bullshit!"

bullshit v., vulgar to informal, gaining in social acceptance by some To exaggerate or talk insincerely in an effort to make yourself seem impressive. "Stop bullshitting me, Joe, I can't believe a word of what you're saying."

bullshit artist n., slang, vulgar, but gaining in social acceptance A person who habitually makes exaggerated or insincerely flattering speeches designed to impress others. Joe is a regular bullshit artist, small wonder he keeps getting promoted ahead of everyone else.

bump off v., slang To kill in a violent way; murder in gangster fashion. Hoodlums in a speeding car bumped him off with Tommy guns.

bum steer n. Wrong or misleading directions given naively or on purpose. Man, you sure gave me a bum steer when you told me to go north on the highway; you should have sent me south!

bundle of laughs n. phr. A very amusing person, thing, or event. Uncle Lester tells so many jokes that he is a bundle of laughs.

burn a hole in one's pocket v. phr. To make you want to buy something; be likely to be quickly spent. Money burns a hole in Linda's pocket. The sil-

ver dollar that Don got for his birthday was burning a hole in his pocket, and Don hurried to a dime store.

burn one's bridges also **burn one's boats** v. phr. To make a decision that you cannot change; remove or destroy all the ways you can get back out of a place you have got into on purpose; leave yourself no way to escape a position. Bob was a good wrestler but a poor boxer. He burned his boats by letting Mickey choose how they would fight. When Dorothy became a nun, she burned her bridges behind her.

burn one's fingers v. phr., informal To get in trouble doing something and fear to do it again; learn caution through an unpleasant experience. He had burned his fingers in the stock market once, and didn't want to try again. Some people can't be told; they have to burn their fingers to learn.

burn out v. phr. **1.** To destroy by fire or by overheating. Mr. Jones burned out the clutch on his car. **2.** To destroy someone's house or business by fire so that they have to move out. Three racists burned out the Black family's home. **3a.** To go out of order; cease to function because of long use or overheating. The light bulb in the bathroom burned out, and Father put in a new one. The electric motor was too powerful, and it burned out a fuse. **3b.** To break, tire, or wear out by using up all the power, energy, or strength of. Bill burned himself out in the first part of the race *and could not finish. The farmer burned out his field by planting the same crop every year for many years.*

burn-out *n.* A point of physical or emotional exhaustion. *There are so many refugees all over the world that charitable organizations as well as individuals are suffering from donor burn-out.*

burn the candle at both ends *v. phr.* To work or play too hard without enough rest; get too tired. *He worked hard every day as a lawyer and went to parties and dances every night; he was burning the candle at both ends.*

burn the midnight oil *v. phr.* To study late at night. *Exam time was near, and more and more pupils were burning the midnight oil.*

burn up *v.* **1.** To burn completely; destroy or be destroyed by fire. *Mr. Scott was burning up old letters. The house burned up before the firemen got there.* **2.** *informal* To irritate, anger, annoy. *The boy's laziness and rudeness burned up his teacher. The breakdown of his new car burned Mr. Jones up.*

burn up the road *v. phr., informal* To drive a car very fast. *In his eagerness to see his girl again, he burned up the road on his way to see her. Speed demons burning up the road often cause accidents.*

burst at the seams *v. phr., informal* To be too full or too crowded. *John ate so much he was bursting at the seams. Mary's album was so full of*

pictures it was bursting at the seams.

burst into *v. phr.* **1.** To enter suddenly. *Stuart burst into the room, screaming angrily.* **2.** To break out. *The crowd burst out cheering when the astronauts paraded along Fifth Avenue.*

burst into flames *v. phr.* To begin to burn suddenly. *The children threw away some burning matches and the barn burst into flames.*

burst into tears *v. phr.* To suddenly start crying. *Mary burst into tears when she heard that her brother was killed in a car accident.*

bury the hatchet *v. phr., informal* To settle a quarrel or end a war; make peace. *The two men had been enemies a long time, but after the flood they buried the hatchet.*

busy work *n.* Work that is done not to do or finish anything important, but just to keep busy. *When the teacher finished all she had to say it was still a half hour before school was over. So she gave the class a test for busy work.*

butterflies in one's stomach *n. phr.* A queer feeling in the stomach caused by nervous fear or uncertainty; a feeling of fear or anxiety in the stomach. *When Bob walked into the factory office to ask for a job, he had butterflies in his stomach.*

butter up *v., informal* To try to get the favor or friendship of (a person) by flattery or pleasantness. *He began to butter up the boss in hope of being given a better job.*

butt in v., slang To join in with what other people are doing without asking or being asked; interfere in other people's business; meddle. *Mary was explaining to Jane how to knit a sweater when Barbara butted in.* Often used with *on. John butted in on Bill and Tom's fight, and got hurt.*

button one's lip also **zip one's lip** v. phr., slang To stop talking; keep a secret; shut your mouth; be quiet. *The man was getting loud and insulting and the cop told him to button his lip. John wanted to talk, but Dan told him to keep his lip buttoned.*

buy for a song v. phr. To buy something very cheaply. *Since the building on the corner was old and neglected, I was able to buy it for a song.*

buy off v. To turn from duty or purpose by a gift. *When the police threatened to stop the gambling business, the owner bought them off. The Indians were going to burn the cabins, but the men bought them off with gifts.*

buy out v. **1.** To buy the ownership or a share of; purchase the stock of. *He bought out several small stockholders.* **2.** To buy all the goods of; purchase the merchandise of. *Mr. Harper bought out a nearby hardware store.*

buy up v. phr. To purchase the entire stock of something. *The company is trying to buy up all the available shares.*

buzz word n. A word that sounds big and important in a sentence but, on closer inspection, means little except the speaker's indication to belong to a certain group. *The politician's speech was nothing but a lot of misleading statements and phony promises hidden in a bunch of buzz words.*

by a long shot adv. phr., informal By a big difference; by far.—Used to add emphasis. *Bert was the best swimmer in the race, by a long shot.* Often used with a negative. *Tom isn't the kind who would be fresh to a teacher, by a long shot. Our team didn't win—not by a long shot.*

by and large adv. phr. As it most often happens; more often than not; usually; mostly. *There were bad days, but it was a pleasant summer, by and large. By and large, women can bear pain better than men.*

by chance adv. phr. Without any cause or reason; by accident; accidentally. *Tom met Bill by chance. The apple fell by chance on Bobby's head.*

by choice adv. phr. As a result of choosing because of wanting to; freely. *John helped his father by choice. Mary ate a plum, but not by choice. Her mother told her she must eat it.*

by dint of prep. By the exertion of; by the use of; through. *By dint of sheer toughness and real courage, he lived through the jungle difficulties and dangers. His success in college was largely by dint of hard study.*

by ear adv. phr. **1.** By sound, without ever reading the printed music of the piece being played. *The church choir sang the hymns by ear.* **2.** Waiting to see what will happen. *I don't want to plan now; let's just play it by ear.*

by far *adv. phr.* By a large difference; much. *His work was better by far than that of any other printer in the city. The old road is prettier, but it is by far the longer way.*

by fits and starts or **jerks** *adv. phr.* With many stops and starts, a little now and a little more later; not all the time; irregularly. *He had worked on the invention by fits and starts for several years. You will never get anywhere if you study just by fits and starts.*

by heart *adv. phr.* By exact memorizing; so well that you remember it; by memory. *The pupils learned many poems by heart. He knew the records of the major league teams by heart.*

by hook or by crook *adv. phr.* By honest ways or dishonest in any way necessary. *The wolf tried to get the little pigs by hook or by crook. The team was determined to win that last game by hook or by crook, and three players were put out of the game for fouling.*

by leaps and bounds *adv. phr.* With long steps; very rapidly. *Production in the factory was increasing by leaps and bounds. The school enrollment was going up by leaps and bounds.*

by means of *prep.* By the use of; with the help of. *The fisherman saved himself by means of a floating log. By means of monthly payments, people can buy more than in the past.*

by mistake *adv. phr.* As the result of a mistake; through error. *He picked up the wrong hat by mistake.*

B.Y.O. *(Abbreviation) informal* Bring Your Own. Said of a kind of party where the host or hostess does not provide the drinks or food but people bring their own.

B.Y.O.B. *(Abbreviation) informal* Bring Your Own Bottle. Frequently written on invitations for the kind of party where people bring their own liquor.

by oneself *adv. phr.* **1.** Without any others around; separate from others; alone. *The house stood by itself on a hill. Tom liked to go walking by himself. Betty felt very sad and lonely by herself.* **2.** Without the help of anyone else; by your own work only. *John built a flying model airplane by himself. Lois cleaned the house all by herself.*

by the dozen or **by the hundred** or **by the thousand** *adv. phr.* Very many at one time; in great numbers. *Tommy ate cookies by the dozen.* Often used in the plural, meaning even larger numbers. *The ants arrived at the picnic by the hundreds. The enemy attacked the fort by the thousands.*

by the skin of one's teeth *adv. phr.* By a narrow margin; with no room to spare; barely. *The drowning man struggled, and I got him to land by the skin of my teeth. She passed English by the skin of her teeth.*

by the sweat of one's brow *adv. phr.* By hard work; by tiring effort; laboriously. *Even with modern labor-saving machinery, the farmer makes his living by the sweat of his brow.*

by the way *also* **by the bye** *adv. phr.* Just as some added fact or news; as something else that I think of.—Used to introduce something related to the general subject, or brought to mind by it. *We shall expect you; by the way, dinner will be at eight. I was reading when the earthquake occurred, and, by the way, it was* The Last Days of Pompeii *that I was reading.*

by turns *adv. phr.* First one and then another in a regular way; one substituting for or following another according to a repeated plan. *On the drive to Chicago, the three men took the wheel by turns. The teachers were on duty by turns. When John had a fever, he felt cold and hot by turns.*

by virtue of also **in virtue of** *prep.* On the strength of; because of; by reason of. *By virtue of his high rank and position, the President takes social leadership over almost everyone else. Plastic bags are useful for holding many kinds of food, by virtue of their clearness, toughness, and low cost.*

by way of *prep.* **1.** For the sake or purpose of; as. *By way of example, he described his own experience.* **2.** Through; by a route including; via. *He went from New York to San Francisco by way of Chicago.*

by word of mouth *adv. phr.* From person to person by the spoken word; orally. *The news got around by word of mouth. The message reached him quietly by word of mouth.*

calculated risk *n.* An action that may fail but is judged more likely to succeed. *The sending of troops to the rebellious island was a calculated risk.*

call a halt *v. phr.* To give a command to stop. *The scouts were tired during the hike, and the scoutmaster called a halt. When the children's play got too noisy, their mother called a halt.*

call a spade a spade *v. phr.* To call a person or thing a name that is true but not polite; speak bluntly; use the plainest language. *A boy took some money from Dick's desk and said he borrowed it, but I told him he stole it; I believe in calling a spade a spade.*

call down *also* **dress down** *v., informal* To scold. *Jim was called down by his teacher for being late to class. Mother called Bob down for walking into the kitchen with muddy boots.*

call for *v.* **1.** To come or go to get (someone or something). *John called for Mary to take her to the dance.* **2.** To need; require. *The cake recipe calls for two cups of flour. Success in school calls for much hard study.*

call girl *n., slang* A prostitute catering to wealthy clientele, especially one who is contacted by telephone for an appointment. *Rush Street is full of call girls.*

calling down *also* **dressing down** *n. phr., informal* A scolding; reprimand. *The judge gave the boy a calling down for speeding.*

call in question *or* **call into question** *or* **call in doubt** *v. phr.* To say (something) may be a mistake; express doubt about; question. *Bill called in question Ed's remark that basketball is safer than football.*

call it a day *v. phr.* To declare that a given day's work has been accomplished and go home; to quit for the day. *"Let's call it a day," the boss said, "and go out for a drink." It was nearly midnight, so Mrs. Byron decided to call it a day, and left the party, and went home. The four golfers played nine holes and then called it a day.*

call it a night *v. phr.* To declare that an evening party or other activity conducted late in the day is finished. *I am so tired that I am going to call it a night and go to bed.*

call it quits *v. phr., informal* **1.** To decide to stop what you are doing; quit. *When Tom had painted half the garage, he called it quits.* **2.** To agree that each side in a fight is satisfied; stop fighting because a wrong has been paid back; say things are even. *Pete called Tom a bad name, and they fought till*

Tom gave Pete a bloody nose; then they called it quits. **3.** To cultivate a habit no longer. *"Yes, I called it quits with cigarettes three years ago."*

all names *v. phr.* To use ugly or unkind words when speaking to someone or when talking about someone.—Usually used by or to children. *Bill got so mad he started calling Frank names.*

all off *v.* To stop (something planned); quit; cancel. *When the ice became soft and sloppy, we had to call off the ice-skating party. The baseball game was called off because of rain.*

all on or **call upon** *v.* **1.** To make a call upon; visit. *Mr. Brown called on an old friend while he was in the city.* **2.** To ask for help. *He called on a friend to give him money for the busfare to his home.*

all one's bluff *v. phr., informal* To ask someone to prove what he says he can or will do. (Originally from the card game of poker.) *Tom said he could jump twenty feet and so Dick called his bluff and said "Let's see you do it!"*

all one's shot *v. phr.* **1.** To tell before firing where a bullet will hit. *An expert rifleman can call his shot regularly. The wind was strong and John couldn't call his shots.* **2.** or **call the turn** To tell in advance the result of something before you do it. *Mary won three games in a row, just as she said she would. She called her turns well. Nothing ever happens as Tom says it will. He is very poor at calling his turns.*

call on the carpet *v. phr., informal* To call (a person) before an authority (as a boss or teacher) for a scolding or reprimand. *The worker was called on the carpet by the boss for sleeping on the job. The principal called Tom on the carpet and warned him to stop coming to school late.*

call the roll *v. phr.* To read out the names on a certain list, usually in alphabetical order. *The sergeant called the roll of the newly enlisted volunteers in the army.*

call the shots *v. phr., informal* To give orders; be in charge; direct; control. *Bob is a first-rate leader who knows how to call the shots. The quarterback called the shots well, and the team gained twenty yards in five plays.*

call the tune *v. phr., informal* To be in control; give orders or directions; command. *Bill was president of the club but Jim was secretary and called the tune. The people supported the mayor, so he could call the tune in city matters.*

call to account *v. phr.* **1.** To ask (someone) to explain why he did something wrong (as breaking a rule). *The principal called Jim to account after Jim left school early without permission.* **2.** To scold (as for wrong conduct); reprimand. *The father called his son to account for disobeying him.*

call to arms *v. phr.* To summon into the army. *During World War II millions of Americans were called to arms to fight for their country.*

call to mind *v. phr.* To remember; cause to remember. *Your story calls to mind a similar event that happened to us a few years back.*

call to order *v. phr.* **1.** To open (a meeting) formally. *The chairman called the committee to order. The president pounded with his gavel to call the convention to order.* **2.** To warn not to break the rules of a meeting. *The judge called the people in the court room to order when they talked too loud.*

call out *v. phr.* **1.** To shout; speak loudly. *My name was called out several times, but I was unable to hear it.* **2.** To summon someone. *If the rioting continues, the governor will have to call out the National Guard.*

call up *v.* **1.** To make someone think of; bring to mind; remind. *The picture of the Capitol called up memories of our class trip.* **2.** To tell to come (as before a court). *The district attorney called up three witnesses.* **3.** To bring together for a purpose; bring into action. *Jim called up all his strength, pushed past the players blocking him, and ran for a touchdown. The army called up its reserves when war seemed near.* **4.** To call on the telephone. *She called up a friend just for a chat.*

calm down *v. phr.* To become quiet; relax. *"Calm down, Mr. Smith," the doctor said with a reassuring smile. "You are going to live a long time."*

cancel out *v.* To destroy the effect of; balance or make use-

less. *The boy got an "A" in history to cancel out the "C" h got in arithmetic. Our trac team won the mile relay to can cel out the other team's advan tage in winning the half-mil relay. Tom's hot temper cancel out his skill as a player.*

cancer stick *n., slang* A ciga rette. *Throw away that cance stick! Smoking is bad for you!*

canned laughter *n., informa* The sounds of laughter hear on certain television program that were obviously not re corded in front of a live audi ence and are played for th benefit of the audience from stereo track to underscore th funny points. *"How can ther be an audience in this sho when it is taking place in th jungle?—Why, it's canne laughter you're hearing."*

canned music *n.* Recorde music, as opposed to musi played live. *"Let us go to a rea concert, honey," Mike said. " am tired of all this canned mu sic we've been listening to."*

can of worms *n., slang, infor mal* **1.** A complex problem, o complicated situation. *Let's no get into big city politics—that' a different can of worms.* **2.** A very restless, jittery person. *Jo can't sit still for a minute—he i a can of worms.*

can't see the wood for the tree *or* **can't see the woods for the trees** *or* **can't see the forest fo the trees** *v. phr.* To be un able to judge or understand th whole because of attention t the parts; criticize small thing and not see the value or th aim of the future achievement

Teachers sometimes notice language errors and do not see the good ideas in a composition; they cannot see the woods for the trees. The voters defeated a bond issue for the new school because they couldn't see the forest for the trees; they thought of their taxes rather than of their children's education. We should think of children's growth in character and understanding more than of their little faults and misdeeds; some of us can't see the wood for the trees.

card up one's sleeve *n. phr., informal* Another help, plan, or argument kept back and produced if needed; another way to do something. *John knew his mother would lend him money if necessary, but he kept that card up his sleeve. Bill always has a card up his sleeve, so when his first plan failed he tried another.*

car pool *n.* A group of people who own cars and take turns driving each other to work or on some other regular trip. *It was John's father's week to drive his own car in the car pool.*

carrot and stick *n. phr.* The promise of reward and threat of punishment, both at the same time. *John's father used the carrot and stick when he talked about his low grades.*

carry a torch *or* **carry the torch** *v. phr.* **1.** To show great and unchanging loyalty to a cause or a person. *Although the others gave up fighting for their rights, John continued to carry the torch.* **2.** *informal* To be in love, usually without success or return. *He is carrying a torch for Anna, even though she is in love with someone else.*

carry a tune *v. phr.* To sing the right notes without catching any false ones. *Al is a wonderful fellow, but he sure can't carry a tune and his singing is a pain to listen to.*

carry away *v.* To cause very strong feeling; excite or delight to the loss of cool judgment. *The music carried her away. He let his anger carry him away.*— Often used in the passive. *She was carried away by the man's charm. He was carried away by the sight of the flag.*

carry coals to Newcastle *v. phr.* To do something unnecessary; bring or furnish something of which there is plenty. *The man who waters his grass after a good rain is carrying coals to Newcastle. Joe was carrying coals to Newcastle when he told the doctor how to cure a cold.* [Newcastle is an English city near many coal mines, and coal is sent out from there to other places.]

carrying charge *n.* An extra cost added to the price of something bought on weekly or monthly payments. *The price of the bicycle was $50. Jim bought it for $5.00 a month for ten months plus a carrying charge of $1 a month.*

carry off *v.* **1.** To cause death of; kill. *Years ago smallpox carried off hundreds of Indians of the Sioux tribe.* **2.** To succeed in winning. *Bob carried off honors in science. Jim carried off two gold medals in the track* meet. **3.** To succeed somewhat unexpectedly in. *The spy planned to deceive the enemy soldiers and carried it off very well. In the class play, Lloyd carried off his part surprisingly well.*

carry on *v.* **1.** To work at; be busy with; manage. *Bill and his father carried on a hardware business. Mr. Jones and Mr. Smith carried on a long correspondence with each other.* **2.** To keep doing as before; continue. *After his father died, Bill carried on with the business. The colonel told the soldiers to carry on while he was gone. Though tired and hungry, the Scouts carried on until they reached camp.* **3a.** *informal* To behave in a noisy, foolish, and troublesome manner. *The boys carried on in the swimming pool until the lifeguard ordered them out.* **3b.** *informal* To make· too great a show of feeling, such as anger, grief, and pain. *John carried on for ten minutes after he hit his thumb with the hammer.* **4.** *informal* To act in an immoral or scandalous way; act disgracefully. *The townspeople said that he was carrying on with a neighbor girl.*

carry one's cross or (*literary*) **bear one's cross** *v. phr.* To live with pain or trouble; keep on even though you suffer or have trouble. *Weak ankles are a cross Joe carries while the other boys play basketball. We didn't know the cheerful woman was bearing her cross, a son in prison.*

carry out *v.* To put into action; follow; execute. *The gen-*

erals were determined to carry out their plans to defeat the enemy. John listened carefully and carried out the teacher's instructions.*

carry over *v.* **1.** To save for another time. *The store had some bathing suits it had carried over from last year. What you learn in school should carry over into adult life.* **2.** To transfer (as a figure) from one column, page, or book to another. *When he added up the figures, he carried over the total into the next year's account book.* **3.** To continue in another place. *The story was carried over to the next page.*

carry the ball *v. phr., informal* To take the most important or difficult part in an action or business. *None of the other boys would tell the principal about their breaking the window, and John had to carry the ball. When the going is rough, Fred can always be depended on to carry the ball.*

carry the day *v. phr., informal* To win completely; to succeed in getting one's aim accomplished. *The defense attorney's summary before the jury helped him carry the day.*

carry through *v.* **1a.** To put into action. *Mr. Green was not able to carry through his plans for a hike because he broke his leg.* **1b.** To do something you have planned; put a plan into action. *Jean makes good plans but she cannot carry through with any of them.* **2.** To keep (someone) from failing or stopping; bring through; help. *When the tire blew out, the rules Jim had learned in driving* *class carried him through safely.*

carry weight n. To be influential; have significance and/or clout; impress. *A letter of recommendation from a full professor carries more weight than a letter from an assistant professor.*

cart before the horse (to put) n. phr., informal Things in wrong order; something backwards or mixed up.—An overused expression. Usually used with *put* but sometimes with *get* or *have. When the salesman wanted money for goods he hadn't delivered, I told him he was putting the cart before the horse. To get married first and then get a job is getting the cart before the horse.*

case in point n. phr. An example that proves something or helps to make something clearer. *An American can rise from the humblest beginnings to become President. Abraham Lincoln is a case in point.*

case the joint v. phr., slang **1.** To study the layout of a place one wishes to burglarize. *The hooded criminals carefully cased the joint before robbing the neighborhood bank.* **2.** To familiarize oneself with a potential workplace or vacation spot as a matter of preliminary planning. "Hello Fred," he said. "Are you working here now?" "No, not yet," Fred answered. "I am merely casing the joint."*

cash-and-carry[1] adj. Selling things for cash money only and letting the customer carry them home, not having the store deliver them; also sold in this way. *This is a cash-and-carry store only. You can save money at a cash-and-carry sale.*

cash-and-carry[2] adv. With no credit, no time payments, and no deliveries. *Some stores sell cash-and-carry only. It is cheaper to buy cash-and-carry.*

cash crop n. A crop grown to be sold. *Cotton is a cash crop in the South. They raise potatoes to eat, but tobacco is their cash crop.*

cash in v. **1.** To exchange (as poker chips or bonds) for the value in money. *He paid the bill by cashing in some bonds. When the card game ended, the players cashed in their chips and went home.* **2.** or **cash in one's chips** slang To die. *When the outlaw cashed in his chips, he was buried with his boots on. He was shot through the body and knew he was going to cash in.*

cash in on v., informal To see (a chance) and profit by it; take advantage of (an opportunity or happening). *Mr. Brown cashed in on people's great interest in camping and sold three hundred tents.*

cash on the barrelhead n. phr., informal Money paid at once; money paid when something is bought. *Father paid cash on the barrelhead for a new car. Some lawyers want cash on the barrelhead.*

cast or **shed** or **throw light upon** v. phr. To explain; illuminate; clarify. *The letters that were found suddenly cast a new light on the circumstances of Tom's disappearance. Einstein's General Theory of Relativity threw* *light upon the enigma of our universe.*

cast off v. **1a.** or **cast loose** To unfasten; untie; let loose (as a rope holding a boat). *The captain of the boat cast off the line and we were soon out in open water.* **1b.** To untie a rope holding a boat or something suggesting a boat. *We cast off and set sail at 6 A.M.* **2.** To knit the last row of stitches. *When she had knitted the twentieth row of stitches she cast off.* **3.** To say that you do not know (someone) any more; not accept as a relative or friend. *Mr. Jones cast off his daughter when she married against his wishes.*

cast pearls before swine or **cast one's pearls before swine** n. phr., literary To waste good acts or valuable things on someone who won't understand or be thankful for them, just as pigs won't appreciate pearls.—Often used in negative sentences. *I won't waste good advice on John any more because he never listens to it. I won't cast pearls before swine.*

cast the first stone v. phr., literary To be the first to blame someone, lead accusers against a wrongdoer. *Jesus said that a person who was without sin could cast the first stone. Although Ben saw the girl cheating, he did not want to cast the first stone.*

catch-as-catch-can[1] adv. phr. In a free manner; in any way possible; in the best way you can. *On moving day everything is packed and we eat meals catch-as-catch-can.*

catch-as-catch-can[2] adj. phr. Using any means or method; unplanned; free. *Rip van Winkle seems to have led a catch-as-catch-can life. Politics is rather a catch-as-catch-can business.*

catch cold v. phr. **1.** or **take cold** To get a common cold-weather sickness that causes a running nose, sneezing, and sometimes sore throat and fever or other symptoms. *Don't get your feet wet or you'll catch cold.* **2.** informal To catch unprepared or not ready for a question or unexpected happening. *I had not studied my lesson carefully, and the teacher's question caught me cold. The opposing team was big and sure of winning, and they were caught cold by the fast, hard playing of our smaller players.*

catch (someone) dead v. phr., informal To see or hear (someone) in an embarrassing act or place at any time. Used in the negative usually in the passive. *You won't catch Bill dead taking his sister to the movies. John wouldn't be caught dead in the necktie he got for Christmas.*

catch fire v. phr. **1.** To begin to burn. *When he dropped a match in the leaves, they caught fire.* **2.** To become excited. *The audience caught fire at the speaker's words and began to cheer. His imagination caught fire as he read.*

catch hold of v. phr. To grasp a person or a thing. *"I've been trying to catch hold of you all week," John said, "but you* were out of town." The mountain climber successfully caught hold of his friend's hand and thereby saved his life.

catch it or **get it** v. phr., informal To be scolded or punished.—Usually used of children. John knew he would catch it when he came home late for supper. Wow, Johnny! When your mother sees those torn pants, you're going to get it.

catch off balance v. phr. To confront someone with physical force or with a statement or question he or she is not prepared to answer or deal with; to exploit the disadvantage of another. The smaller wrestler caught his opponent off balance and managed to throw him on the floor in spite of his greater weight and strength. Your question has caught me off balance; please give me some time to think about your problem.

catch off guard v. phr. To challenge or confront a person at a time of lack of preparedness or sufficient care. The suspect was caught off guard by the detective and confessed where he had hidden the stolen car.

catch on v., informal **1.** To understand; learn about.—Often used with to. You'll catch on to the job after you've been here awhile. Don't play any tricks on Joe. When he catches on, he will beat you. **2.** To become popular; be done or used by many people. The song caught on and was sung and played everywhere. **3.** To be hired; get a job. The ball player

caught on with a big league team last year.

catch one's breath v. phr. **1.** To breathe in suddenly with fear or surprise. The beauty of the scene made him catch his breath. **2a.** To rest and get back your normal breathing, as after running. After running to the bus stop, we sat down to catch our breath. **2b.** To relax for a moment after any work. After the day's work we sat down over coffee to catch our breath.

catch one's death of or **take one's death of** v. phr., informal To become very ill with (a cold, pneumonia, flu). Johnny fell in the icy water and almost took his death of cold. Sometimes used in the short form "catch your death." "Johnny! Come right in here and put your coat and hat on. You'll catch your death!"

catch one's eye v. phr. To attract your attention. I caught his eye as he moved through the crowd, and waved at him to come over. The dress in the window caught her eye when she passed the store.

catch red-handed v. phr. To apprehend a person during the act of committing an illicit or criminal act. Al was caught red-handed at the local store when he was trying to walk out with a new camera he had not paid for.

catch sight of v. phr. To see suddenly or unexpectedly. Allan caught sight of a kingbird in a maple tree.

catch some rays v. phr., slang, informal To get tanned while sunbathing. *Tomorrow I'll go to the beach and try to catch some rays.*

catch some Z's *v. phr., slang, informal* To take a nap, to go to sleep. (Because of the *z* sound resembling snoring.) *I want to hit the sack and catch some Z's.*

catch-22 *n., informal* From Joseph Heller's novel *Catch-22*, set in World War II. A regulation or situation that is self-contradictory or that conflicts with another regulation. In Heller's book it referred to the regulation that flight crews must report for duty unless excused for reasons of insanity, but that any one claiming such an excuse must, by definition, be sane. *Government rules require workers to expose any wrongdoing in their office, but the Catch-22 prevents them from their doing so, because they are not allowed to disclose any information about their work.* **2.** A paradoxical situation. *The Catch-22 of job-hunting was that the factory wanted to hire only workers who had experience making computers but the only way to get the experience was by working at the computer factory.*

catch up *v.* **1.** To take or pick up suddenly; grab (something). *She caught up the book from the table and ran out of the room.* **2.** To capture or trap (someone) in a situation; concern or interest very much.— Usually used in the passive with *in. The Smith family was caught up in the war in Europe and we did not see them again till it was over. We were so* caught up in the movie we forgot what time it was. **3.** To go fast enough or do enough so as not to be behind; overtake; come even.—Often used with *to* or *with. Johnny ran hard and tried to catch up to his friends. Mary missed two weeks of school; she must work hard to catch up with her class.* **4.** To find out about or get proof to punish or arrest.—Usually used with *with. A man told the police where the robbers were hiding, so the police finally caught up with them.* **5.** To result in something bad; bring punishment.—Usually used with *with. The boy's fighting caught up with him and he was expelled from school. Smoking will catch up with you.* **6.** To finish; not lose or be behind.—Used with *on* and often in the phrase *get caught up on. Frank stayed up late to get caught up on his homework. I have to catch up on my sleep. We caught up on all the latest news when we got back to school and saw our friends again.*

catch with one's pants down *v. phr., slang* To surprise someone in an embarrassing position or guilty act. *They thought they could succeed in the robbery, but they got caught with their pants down. When the weather turned hot in May, the drive-in restaurant was caught with its pants down, and ran out of ice cream before noon.*

cat got one's tongue You are not able or willing to talk because of shyness. Usually used about children or as a question to children. *Tommy's father asked Tommy if the cat had got* *his tongue. The little girl had a poem to recite, but the cat got her tongue.*

cathouse *n., slang* A house of ill repute, a house of prostitution. *Massage parlors are frequently cathouses in disguise.*

caught short *adj. phr., informal* Not having enough of something when you need it. *Mrs. Ford was caught short when the newspaper boy came for his money a day early. The man was caught short of clothes when he had to go on a trip.*

cave in *v.* **1.** To fall or collapse inward. *The mine caved in and crushed three miners. Don't climb on that old roof. It might cave in.* **2.** *informal* To weaken and be forced to give up. *The children begged their father to take them to the circus until he caved in. After the atomic bomb, Japan caved in and the war ceased.*

cease fire *v.* To give a military command ordering soldiers to stop shooting. *"Cease fire!" the captain cried, and the shooting stopped.*

cease-fire *n.* A period of negotiated nonaggression, when the warring parties involved promise not to attack. *Unfortunately, the cease-fire in Bosnia was broken many times by all parties concerned.*

chain letter *n.* A letter which each person receiving it is asked to copy and send to several others. *Most chain letters die out quickly.*

chain-smoke *v.* To smoke cigarettes or cigars one after another without stopping. *Mr. Jones is very nervous. He chain-smokes cigars.* **chain**

smoker *n. Mr. Jones is a chain smoker.* **chain-smoking** *adj. or n. Chain smoking is very dangerous to health.*

chain stores *n.* A series of stores in different locations, joined together under one ownership and general management. *The goods in chain stores tend to be more uniform than in independent ones.*

chalk up *v., informal* **1.** To write down as part of a score; record. *The scorekeeper chalked up one more point for the home team.* **2.** To make (a score or part of a score); score. *The team chalked up another victory. Bob chalked up a home run and two base hits in the game. Mary chalked up good grades this term.*

change hands *v. phr.* To change or transfer ownership. *Ever since our apartment building changed hands, things are working a lot better.*

change horses in the middle of a stream *or* **change horses in midstream** *v. phr.* To make new plans or choose a new leader in the middle of an important activity. *When a new President is to be elected during a war, the people may decide not to change horses in the middle of a stream.*

change off *v., informal* To take turns doing something; alternate. *John and Bill changed off at riding the bicycle. Bob painted one patch of wall and then he changed off with Tom.*

change of heart *n. phr.* A change in the way one feels or thinks about a given task, idea or problem to be solved. *Joan had a change of heart and sud-*

denly broke off her engagement to Tim. Fred got admitted to medical school, but he had a change of heart and decided to go into the Foreign Service instead.

change of life *n. phr.* The menopause (primarily in women). *Women usually undergo a change of life in their forties or fifties.*

change of pace *n. phr.* A quick change in what you are doing. *John studied for three hours and then read a comic book for a change of pace. The doctor told the man he needed a change of pace.*

change one's mind *v. phr.* To alter one's opinion or judgment on a given issue. *I used to hate Chicago, but as the years passed I gradually changed my mind and now I actually love living here.*

change one's tune *v. phr., informal* To make a change in your story, statement, or claim; change your way of acting. *The man said he was innocent, but when they found the stolen money in his pocket he changed his tune. Bob was rude to his teacher, but she threatened to tell the principal and he changed his tune.*

charge account *n.* An agreement with a store through which you can buy things and pay for them later. *Mother bought a new dress on her charge account. Mr. Jones has a charge account at the garage on the corner.*

charge something to something *v.* **1.** To place the blame on; make responsible for. *John failed to win a prize, but he*

charged it to his lack of experience. The coach charged the loss of the game to the team's disobeying his orders. **2.** To buy something on the credit of. *Mrs. Smith bought a new pocketbook and charged it to her husband. Mr. White ordered a box of cigars and had it charged to his account.*

charge up *v. phr.* **1.** To submit to a flow of electricity in order to make functional. *I mustn't forget to charge up my razor before we go on our trip.* **2.** To use up all the available credit one has on one's credit card(s). *"Let's charge dinner on the Master Card," Jane said. "Unfortunately I can't," Jim replied. "All of my credit cards are completely charged up."*

charge with *v. phr.* To accuse someone in a court of law. *The criminal was charged with aggravated kidnapping across a state line.*

charmed life *n.* A life often saved from danger; a life full of lucky escapes. *He was in two airplane accidents, but he had a charmed life. During the war a bullet knocked the gun out of his hand, but he had a charmed life.*

cheapskate *n., informal* A selfish or stingy person; a person who will not spend much.—*An insulting term.* *None of the girls like to go out on a date with him because he is a cheapskate.*

cheat on someone *v. phr., informal* To be unfaithful (to one's wife or husband, or to one's sweetheart or fiancee). *It is rumored that Joe cheats on his wife.*

check in *v.* **1a.** To sign your name (as at a hotel or convention). *The last guests to reach the hotel checked in at 12 o'clock.* **1b.** *informal* To arrive. *The friends we had invited did not check in until Saturday.* **2.** To receive (something) back and make a record of it. *The coach checked in the football uniforms at the end of the school year. The students put their books on the library desk, and the librarian checked them in.*

check off *v.* To put a mark beside (the name of a person or thing on a list) to show that it has been counted. *The teacher checked off each pupil as he got on the bus. Bill wrote down the names of all the states he could remember, and then he checked them off against the list in his book.*

check on someone/thing or **check up on someone/thing** *v.* To try to find out the truth or rightness of; make sure of; examine; inspect; investigate. *We checked on Dan's age by getting his birth record. Mrs. Brown said she heard someone downstairs and Mr. Brown went down to check up on it. You can check on your answers at the back of the book. The police are checking up on the man to see if he has a police record. Grandfather went to have the doctor check on his health.*

check out *v.* **1a.** To pay your hotel bill and leave. *The last guests checked out of their rooms in the morning.* **1b.** *informal* To go away; leave. *I hoped our guest would stay but he had to check out before*

Monday. **2a.** To make a list or record of. *They checked out all the goods in the store.* **2b.** To give or lend (something) and make a record of it. *The boss checked out the tools to the workmen as they came to work.* **2c.** To get (something) after a record has been made of it. *I checked out a book from the library.* **3.** *informal* To test (something, like a part of a motor). *The mechanic checked out the car battery.* "*He checked out from the motel at nine,*" *said the detective,* "*then he checked out the air in the car tires and his list of local clients.*" **4.** *slang* To die. *He seemed too young to check out.*

check up *v.* To find out or try to find out the truth or correctness of something; make sure of something; investigate. *Mrs. Brown thought she had heard a burglar in the house, so Mr. Brown checked up, but found nobody. Bill thought he had a date with Janie, but phoned her to check up.*

check-up *n.* A periodic examination by a physician or of some equipment by a mechanic. *I am overdue for my annual physical check-up. I need to take my car in for a check-up.*

check with *v. phr.* **1.** To consult. *I want to check with my lawyer before I sign the papers.* **2.** To agree with. *Does my reconciliation of our account check with the bank statement?*

cheer up *v.* **1.** To feel happy; stop being sad or discouraged; become hopeful, joyous, or glad. *Jones was sad at losing the business, but he cheered up* *at the sight of his daughter. Cheer up! The worst is over.* **2.** To make cheerful or happy. *The support of the students cheered up the losing team and they played harder and won. We went to the hospital to cheer up a sick friend. Flowers cheer up a room.*

cheesecake *n., slang, informal* A showing of the legs of an attractive woman or a display of her breasts as in certain magazines known as cheesecake magazines. *Photographer to model: "Give us some cheesecake in that pose!"*

chew out *v., slang* To scold roughly. *The boy's father chewed him out for staying up late. The coach chews out lazy players.*

chew the fat *or* **chew the rag** *v. phr., slang* To talk together in an idle, friendly fashion; chat. *We used to meet after work, and chew the fat over coffee and doughnuts. The old man would chew the rag for hours with anyone who would join him.*

chew the scenery *v. phr., slang* To act overemotionally in a situation where it is inappropriate; to engage in histrionics. *I don't know if Joe was sincere about our house, but he sure chewed up the scenery!*

chicken-brained *adj.* Stupid; narrowminded; unimaginative. *I can't understand how a bright woman like Helen can date such a chicken-brained guy as Oliver.*

chicken feed *n., slang* A very small sum of money. *John and Bill worked very hard, but they were only paid chicken feed.*

Mr. Jones is so rich he thinks a thousand dollars is chicken feed.

chicken-livered *adj., slang, colloquial* Easily scared; cowardly. *Joe sure is a chicken-livered guy.*

chicken out *v. phr., informal* To stop doing something because of fear; to decide not to do something after all even though previously having decided to try it. *I used to ride a motorcycle on the highway, but I've chickened out. I decided to take flying lessons but just before they started I chickened out.*

chickens come home to roost *informal* Words or acts come back to cause trouble for a person; something bad you said or did receives punishment; you get the punishment that you deserve. *Fred's chickens finally came home to roost today. He was late so often that the teacher made him go to the principal.*—Often used in a short form. *Mary's selfishness will come home to roost some day.*

chicken switch *n., slang, Space Engli..h* **1.** The emergency eject button used by test pilots in fast and high flying aircraft by means of which they can parachute to safety if the engine fails; later adopted by astronauts in space capsules. *Don't pull the chicken switch, unless absolutely necessary.* **2.** The panic button; a panicky reaction to an unforeseen situation, such as unreasonable or hysterical telephone calls to friends for help. *Joe pulled the chicken switch on his neighbor* when the grease started burning in the kitchen.

child's play *adj.* Easy; requiring no effort. *Mary's work as a volunteer social worker is so agreeable to her that she thinks of it as child's play.*

chime in *v.* **1.** *informal* To join in. *The whole group chimed in on the chorus. When the argument got hot, John chimed in.* **2.** To agree; go well together.—Usually used with *with. Dick was happy, and the holiday music chimed in with his feelings. When Father suggested going to the shore for the vacation, the whole family chimed in with the plan.*

chip in or **kick in** *v., informal* To give together with others, contribute. *The pupils chipped in a dime apiece for the teacher's Christmas present. All the neighbors kicked in to help after the fire. Lee chipped in ten points in the basketball game. Joe didn't say much but chipped in a few words.*

chip off the old block *n. phr.* A person whose character traits closely resemble those of his parents. *I hear that Tom plays the violin in the orchestra his father conducts; he sure is a chip off the old block.*

chip on one's shoulder *n. phr., informal* A quarrelsome nature; readiness to be angered. *He went through life with a chip on his shoulder. Jim often gets into fights because he goes around with a chip on his shoulder.*

choke off *v.* To put a sudden end to; stop abruptly or forcefully. *It was almost time for the meeting to end, and the presid-*

ing officer had to move to choke off debate. The war choked off diamond shipments from overseas.

choke up *v.* **1a.** To come near losing calmness or self-control from strong feeling; be upset by your feelings. *When one speaker after another praised John, he choked up and couldn't thank them. When Father tried to tell me how glad he was to see me safe after the accident, he choked up and was unable to speak.* **1b.** *informal* To be unable to do well because of excitement or nervousness. *Bill was a good batter, but in the championship game he choked up and did poorly.* **2.** To fill up; become clogged or blocked; become hard to pass through. *The channel had choked up with sand so that boats couldn't use it.*

claim check *n.* A ticket needed to get back something. *The man at the parking lot gave Mrs. Collins a claim check. The boy put the dry cleaning claim check in his billfold. The man told Mary the pictures would be ready Friday and gave her a claim check.*

clamp down *v., informal* To put on strict controls; enforce rules or laws. *After the explosion, police clamped down and let no more visitors inside the monument. The school clamped down on smoking. When the crowds became bigger and wilder, the police clamped down on them and made everyone go home.*

clam up *v., slang* To refuse to say anything more; stop talking. *The suspect clammed up,* *and the police could get no more information out of him.*

clean bill of health *n. phr.* **1.** A certificate that a person or animal has no infectious disease. *The government doctor gave Jones a clean bill of health when he entered the country.* **2.** *informal* A report that a person is free of guilt or fault. *The stranger was suspected in the bank robbery, but the police gave him a clean bill of health.*

clean break *n. phr.* A complete separation. *Tom made a clean break with his former girlfriends before marrying Pamela.*

clean out *v.* **1.** *slang* To take everything from; empty; strip. *George's friends cleaned him out when they were playing cards last night. The sudden demand for paper plates soon cleaned out the stores.* **2.** *informal* To get rid of; remove; dismiss. *The new mayor promised to clean the crooks out of the city government.*

clean slate *n. phr.* A record of nothing but good conduct, without any errors or bad deeds; past acts that are all good without any bad ones. *Johnny was sent to the principal for whispering. He had a clean slate so the principal did not punish him. Mary stayed after school for a week, and after that the teacher let her off with a clean slate.*

clean up *v. phr.* **1.** To wash and make oneself presentable. *After quitting for the day in the garage, Tim decided to clean up and put on a clean shirt.* **2.** To finish; terminate. *The secretary promised her boss to clean up*

all the unfinished work before leaving on her Florida vacation. **3.** *informal* To make a large profit. *The clever investors cleaned up on the stock market last week.*

clean-up *n.* **1.** An act of removing all the dirt from a given set of objects. *What this filthy room needs is an honest clean-up.* **2.** The elimination of pockets of resistance during warfare or a police raid. *The FBI conducted a clean-up against the drug pushers in our district.*

clear-cut *adj.* Definite; well defined. *The President's new policy of aggressive action is a clear-cut departure from his old methods of unilateral appeasement.*

clear one's name *v. phr.* To prove someone is innocent of a crime or misdeed of which he has been accused. *The falsely accused rapist has been trying in vain to clear his name.*

clear out *v.* **1.** To take everything out of; empty. *When Bill was moved to another class he cleared out his desk.* **2.** *informal* To leave suddenly; go away; depart. *The cop told the boys to clear out. Bob cleared out without paying his room rent. Clear out of here! You're bothering me.*

clear the air *v. phr.* To remove angry feelings, misunderstanding, or confusion. *The President's statement that he would run for office again cleared the air of rumors and guessing. When Bill was angry at Bob, Bob made a joke, and it cleared the air between them.*

clear up v. **1.** To make plain or clear; explain; solve. *The teacher cleared up the harder parts of the story. Maybe we can clear up your problem.* **2.** To become clear. *The weather cleared up after the storm.* **3.** To cure. *The pills cleared up his stomach trouble.* **4.** To put back into a normal, proper, or healthy state. *The doctor can give you something to clear up your skin. Susan cleared up the room.* **5.** To become cured. *This skin trouble will clear up in a day or two.*

cliffdweller n., slang, informal A city person who lives on a very high floor in an apartment building. *Joe and Nancy have become cliffdwellers—they moved up to the 30th floor.*

cliffhanger n., informal A sports event or a movie in which the outcome is uncertain to the very end, keeping the spectators in great suspense and excitement. *Did you see The Fugitive? It's a regular cliffhanger.*

climb the wall v. phr., slang. informal **1.** To react to a challenging situation with too great an emotional response, frustration, tension, and anxiety. *By the time I got the letter that I was hired, I was ready to climb the wall.* **2.** To be so disinterested or bored as to be most anxious to get away at any cost. *If the chairman doesn't stop talking, I'll climb the wall.*

clip joint n. slang A low-class night club or other business where people are cheated. *The man got drunk and lost all his money in a clip joint. The angry*

woman said the store was a clip joint.

clip one's wings v. phr. To limit or hold you back, bring you under control; prevent your success. *When the new president tried to become dictator, the generals soon clipped his wings. Jim was spending too much time on dates when he needed to study so his father stopped his allowance; that clipped his wings.*

cloak-and-dagger adj. Of or about spies and secret agents. *It was a cloak-and-dagger story about some spies who tried to steal atomic secrets. The book was written by a retired colonel who used to take part in cloak-and-dagger plots.* [From the wearing of cloaks and daggers by people in old adventure stories.]

close call or **shave** n. phr. A narrow escape. *That sure was a close call when that truck came near us from the right! When Tim fell off his bicycle in front of a bus, it was a very close shave.*

closed book n. A secret; something not known or understood. *The man's early life is a closed book. For Mary, science is a closed book. The history of the town is a closed book.*

close down or **shut down** v. To stop all working, as in a factory; stop work entirely; also: to stop operations in. *The factory closed down for Christmas. The company shut down the condom plant for Easter.*

closed shop n. phr. **1.** A plant or factory that employs only union workers. *Our firm has* *been fighting the closed shop policy for many years now.* **2.** A profession or line of work dominated by followers of a certain mode of thinking and behaving that does not tolerate differing views or ideas. *Certain groups of psychologists, historians, and linguists often behave with a closed-shop mentality.*

close in *v.* To come in nearer from all sides. *We wanted the boat to reach shore before the fog closed in.*—Often used with *on. The troops were closing in on the enemy.*

close-knit *adj.* Closely joined together by ties of love, friendship, or common interest; close. *The Joneses are a close-knit family. The three boys are always together. They form a very close-knit group.*

close out *v.* To sell the whole of; end (a business or a business operation) by selling all the goods; *also,* to sell your stock and stop doing business. *The store closed out its stock of garden supplies. Mr. Jones closed out his grocery. Mr. Randall was losing money in his shoe store, so he decided to close out.*

close ranks *v. phr.* **1.** To come close together in a line especially for fighting. *The soldiers closed ranks and kept the enemy away from the bridge.* **2.** To stop quarreling and work together; unite and fight together. *The Democrats and Republicans closed ranks to win the war. The leader asked the people to close ranks and plan a new school.*

close the books *v. phr.* To

stop taking orders; end a bookkeeping period. *The tickets were all sold, so the manager said to close the books. The department store closes its books on the 25th of each month.*

close the door *or* **bar the door** *or* **shut the door** *v. phr.* To prevent any more action or talk about a subject. *The President's veto closed the door to any new attempt to pass the bill. Joan was much hurt by what Mary said, and she closed the door on Mary's attempt to apologize. After John makes up his mind, he closes the door to any more arguments.*

close to home *adv. phr.* Too near to someone's personal feelings, wishes, or interests. *When John made fun of Bob's way of walking, he struck close to home. When the preacher spoke about prejudice, some people felt he had come too close to home.*

close-up *n.* A photograph, motion picture, or video camera shot taken at very close range. *Directors of movies frequently show close-ups of the main characters.*

close up shop *v. phr.* **1.** To shut a store at the end of a day's business, *also,* to end a business. *The grocer closes up shop at 5 o'clock. After 15 years in business at the same spot, the garage closed up shop.* **2.** *informal* To stop some activity; finish what you are doing. *After camping out for two weeks, the scouts took down their tents and closed up shop. The committee finished its business and closed up shop.*

coast is clear No enemy or danger is in sight; there is no one to see you. *When the teacher had disappeared around the corner, John said, "Come on, the coast is clear." The men knew when the night watchman would pass. When he had gone, and the coast was clear, they robbed the safe. When Father stopped the car at the stop sign, Mother said, "The coast is clear on this side."*

cock-and-bull story *n. phr.* An exaggerated or unbelievable story. *"Stop feeding me such cock-and-bull stories," the detective said to the suspect.*

cockeyed *adj.* Drunk; intoxicated. *Frank has been drinking all day and, when we met, he was so cockeyed he forgot his own address.*

C.O.D. *n. phr.* Abbreviation of "cash on delivery." *If you want to receive a piece of merchandise by mail and pay when you receive it, you place a C.O.D. order.*

coffee break *n.* A short recess or time out from work in which to rest and drink coffee. *The girls in the office take a coffee break in the middle of the morning and of the afternoon.*

coffin nail *n., slang* A cigarette. *"I stopped smoking," Algernon said. "In fact, I haven't had a coffin nail in well over a year."*

cold cash *or* **hard cash** *n.* Money that is paid at the time of purchase; real money; silver and bills. *Mr. Jones bought a new car and paid cold cash for it. Some stores sell things only for cold cash.*

cold feet *n. phr., informal* A loss of courage or nerve; a failure or loss of confidence in yourself. *Ralph was going to ask Mary to dance with him but he got cold feet and didn't.*

cold fish *n., informal* A queer person; a person who is unfriendly or does not mix with others. *No one knows the new doctor, he is a cold fish. Nobody invites Eric to parties because he is a cold fish.*

cold-shoulder *v., informal* To act towards a person; with dislike or scorn; be unfriendly to. *Fred cold-shouldered his old friend when they passed on the street. It is impolite and unkind to cold-shoulder people.*

cold shoulder *n., informal* Unfriendly treatment of a person, a showing of dislike for a person or of looking down on a person.—Used in the clichés *give the cold shoulder* or *turn a cold shoulder to* or *get the cold shoulder. When Bob asked Mary for a date she gave him the cold shoulder. The membership committee turned a cold shoulder to Jim's request to join the club.*

cold snap *n.* A short time of quick change from warm weather to cold. *The cold snap killed everything in the garden.*

cold turkey *adv., slang, informal* **1.** Abruptly and without medical aid to withdraw from the use of an addictive drug or from a serious drinking problem. *Joe is a very brave guy; he kicked the habit cold turkey.* **2.** *n.* An instance of withdrawal from drugs, alcohol, or cigarette smoking. *Joe did a cold turkey.*

cold war *n.* A struggle that is carried on by other means and not by actual fighting; a war without shooting or bombing. *After World War II, a cold war began between Russia and the United States.*

come about *v.* To take place; happen; occur. *Sometimes it is hard to tell how a quarrel comes about. When John woke up he was in the hospital, but he didn't know how that had come about.*

come a cropper **1.** To fall off your horse. *John's horse stumbled, and John came a cropper.* **2.** To fail. *Mr. Brown did not have enough money to put into his business and it soon came a cropper.*

come across *v.* **1.** *or* **run across** To find or meet by chance. *He came across a dollar bill in the suit he was sending to the cleaner. The other day I ran across a book that you might like. I came across George at a party last week; it was the first time I had seen him in months.* **2.** To give or do what is asked. *The robber told the woman to come across with her purse. For hours the police questioned the man suspected of kidnapping the child, and finally he came across with the story.*

come again *v., informal* Please repeat; please say that again.—Usually used as a command. *"Harry has just come into a fortune," my wife said. "Come again?" I asked her, not believing it. "Come again," said the hard-of-hearing man.*

come alive *or* **come to life** *v.* **1.** *informal* To become alert or attentive; wake up and look alive; become active. *When Mr. Simmons mentioned money, the boys came alive. Bob pushed the starter button, and the engine came alive with a roar.* **2.** To look real; take on a bright, natural look. *Under skillful lighting, the scene came alive. The President came alive in the picture as the artist worked.*

come along *v.* To make progress; improve; succeed. *He was coming along well after the operation. Rose is coming right along on the piano.*

come a long way *v. phr.* To show much improvement; make great progress. *The school has come a long way since its beginnings. Little Jane has come a long way since she broke her leg.*

come apart at the seams *v. phr., slang, informal* To become upset to the point where one loses self-control and composure as if having suffered a sudden nervous breakdown. *After his divorce Joe seemed to be coming apart at the seams.*

come at *v.* **1.** To approach; come to or against; advance toward. *The young boxer came at the champion cautiously.* **2.** To understand (a word or idea) or master (a skill); succeed with. *The sense of an unfamiliar word is hard to come at.*

come back *v., informal* **1.** To reply; answer. *The lawyer came back sharply in defense of his client. No matter how the audience heckled him, the comedian always had an answer to come back with.* **2.** To get a former place or position back, reach again a place which you have lost. *After a year off to have her baby, the singer came back to even greater fame. It is hard for* *a retired prize fighter to come back and beat a younger man.*

comeback *n., v. phr., slang, citizen's band radio jargon* A return call. *Thanks for your comeback.*

come back to earth *or* **come down to earth** *v. phr.* To return to the real world; stop imagining or dreaming; think and behave as usual. *After Jane met the movie star it was hard for her to come back to earth. Bill was sitting and daydreaming so his mother told him to come down to earth and to do his homework.*

come between *v.* To part; divide; separate. *John's mother-in-law came to live in his home, and as time passed she came between him and his wife. Bill's hot rod came between him and his studies, and his grades went down.*

come by *v.* To get; obtain; acquire. *A good job like that is hard to come by. Money easily come by is often easily spent. How did she come by that money?*

come clean *v. phr., slang* To tell all; tell the whole story; confess. *The boy suspected of stealing the watch came clean after long questioning.*

comedown *n.* Disappointment; embarrassment; failure. *It was quite a comedown for Al when the girl he took for granted refused his marriage proposal.*

come down *v.* **1.** To reduce itself; amount to no more than.—Followed by *to. The quarrel finally came down to a question of which boy would do the dishes.* **2.** To be handed

down or passed along, descend from parent to child; pass from older generation to younger ones. *Mary's necklace had come down to her from her grandmother.*

come down hard on *v., informal* **1.** To scold or punish strongly. *The principal came down hard on the boys for breaking the window.* **2.** To oppose strongly. *The minister in his sermon came down hard on drinking.*

come down with *v., informal* To become sick with; catch. *We all came down with the mumps. After being out in the rain, George came down with a cold.*

come full circle *v. phr., informal* **1.** To become totally opposed to one's own earlier conviction on a given subject. *Today's conservative businessperson has come full circle from former radical student days.* **2.** To change and develop, only to end up where one started. *From modern permissiveness, ideas about child raising have come full circle to the views of our grandparents.*

come hell or high water *adv. phr., informal* No matter what happens; whatever may come. *Grandfather said he would go to the fair, come hell or high water.*

come in *v.* **1.** To finish in a sports contest or other competition. *He came in second in the hundred-yard dash.* **2.** To become the fashion; begin to be used. *Swimming trunks for men came in after World War I; before that men used full swim suits.*

come in for *v.* To receive. *He came in for a small fortune when his uncle died. His conduct came in for much criticism.*

come in handy *v. phr., informal* To prove useful. *Robinson Crusoe found tools in the ship which came in handy when he built a house. The French he learned in high school came in handy when he was in the army in France.*

come into *v.* To receive, especially after another's death; get possession of. *He came into a lot of money when his father died. He came into possession of the farm after his uncle died.*

come into one's own *v. phr.* To receive the wealth or respect that you should have. *John's grandfather died and left him a million dollars; when John is 21, he will come into his own. With the success of the Model T Ford, the automobile industry came into its own.*

come off *v.* **1.** To take place; happen. *The picnic came off at last, after being twice postponed.* **2.** *informal* To do well; succeed. *The attempt to bring the quarreling couple together again came off, to people's astonishment.*

come off it *also* **get off it** *v. phr., slang* Stop pretending; bragging, or kidding; stop being silly.—Used as a command. *"So I said to the duchess" Jimmy began. "Oh, come off it," the other boys sneered. Fritz said he had a car of his own. "Oh, come off it," said John. "You can't even drive."*

come off *or* **through with flying colors** *v. phr.* To succeed; triumph. *John came off with flying colors in his final exams at college.*

come off second best *v. phr.* To not win first but only second, third, etc. place. *Our home team came off second best against the visitors. Sue complains that she always comes off second best when she has a disagreement with her husband.*

come on *v.* **1.** To begin; appear. *Rain came on toward morning. He felt a cold coming on.* **2.** To grow or do well; thrive. *The wheat was coming on. His business came on splendidly.* **3.** *or* **come upon.** To meet accidentally; encounter; find. *He came on an old friend that day when he visited his club. He came upon an interesting idea in reading about the French Revolution.* **4.** *informal* Let's get started; let's get going; don't delay; don't wait.—Used as a command. *"Come on, or we'll be late," said Joe, but Lou still waited.* **5.** *informal* Please do it!—Used in begging someone to do something. *Sing us just one song, Jane, come on! Come on, Laura, you can tell me. I won't tell anybody.*

come-on *n., slang* An attractive offer made to a naive person under false pretenses in order to gain monetary or other advantage. *Joe uses a highly successful come-on when he sells vacant lots on Grand Bahama Island.*

come on strong *v. phr., slang* To overwhelm a weaker person with excessively strong language, personality, or mannerisms; to insist extremely strongly and claim something with unusual vigor. *Joe came on very strong last night about the war in Indochina; most of us felt embarrassed.*

come out *v.* **1.** *Of a girl:* To be formally introduced to polite society at about age eighteen, usually at a party; begin to go to big parties. *In society, girls come out when they reach the age of about eighteen, and usually it is at a big party in their honor; after that they are looked on as adults.* **2.** To be published. *The book came out two weeks ago.* **3.** To become publicly known. *The truth finally came out at his trial.* **4.** To end; result; finish. *How did the story come out? The game came out as we had hoped. The snapshots came out well.* **5.** To announce support or opposition; declare yourself (for or against a person or thing). *The party leaders came out for an acceptable candidate. Many Congressmen came out against the bill.* **6. coming-out** *adj.* Introducing a girl to polite society. *Mary's parents gave her a coming-out party when she was 17.*

come out for *v. phr.* To support; declare oneself in favor of another, especially during a political election. *Candidates for the presidency of the United States are anxious for the major newspapers to come out for them.*

come out in the open *v. phr.* **1.** To reveal one's true identity or intentions. *Fred finally came out in the open and admitted that he was gay.* **2.** To declare one's position openly. *The conservative Democratic candidate came out in the open and declared that he would join the Republican party.*

come out with *v. phr.* **1.** To make a public announcement of; make known. *He came out with a clear declaration of his principles.* **2.** To say. *He comes out with the funniest remarks you can imagine.*

come over *v.* To take control of; cause sudden strong feeling in; happen to. *A sudden fit of anger came over him. A great tenderness came over her. What has come over him?*

come round *or* **come around** *v.* **1.** To happen or appear again and again in regular order. *And so Saturday night came around again. I will tell him when he comes round again.* **2.** *informal* To get back health or knowledge of things; get well from sickness or a faint. *Someone brought out smelling salts and Mary soon came round. Jim has come around after having had stomach ulcers.* **3.** To change direction. *The wind has come round to the south.* **4.** *informal* To change your opinion or purpose to agree with another's. *Tom came round when Dick told him the whole story.*

come through *v., informal* To be equal to a demand; meet trouble or a sudden need with success; satisfy a need. *When the baseball team needed a hit, Willie came through with a double. John needed money for college and his father came through.*

come to *v.* (stress on *to*) **1.** To

wake up after losing consciousness; get the use of your senses
back again after fainting or being knocked out. *She fainted in
the store and found herself in
the first aid room when she
came to. The boxer who was
knocked out did not come to
for five minutes. The doctor
gave her a pill and after she
took it she didn't come to for
two days.* **2.** (stress on *come*)
To get enough familiarity or
understanding; learn to;
grow to.—Used with an infinitive. *John was selfish at first,
but he came to realize that other
people counted, too. During her
years at the school, Mary came
to know that road well.* **3.** To
result in or change to; reach
the point of; arrive at. *Mr.
Smith lived to see his invention
come to success. Grandfather
doesn't like the way young people act today; he says, "I don't
know what the world is coming
to."* **4.** To have something to do
with; be in the field of; be
about.—Usually used in the
phrase *when it comes to. Joe is
not good in sports, but when it
comes to arithmetic he's the
best in the class. The school has
very good teachers, but when it
comes to buildings, the school
is poor.*

come to a dead end *v. phr.* To
reach a point from which one
cannot proceed further, either
because of a physical obstacle
or because of some forbidding
circumstance. *Our car came to
a dead end; the only way to get
out was to drive back in re-
verse. The factory expansion
project came to a dead end because of a lack of funds.*

come to blows *v. phr.* To begin to fight. *The two quarreling
boys came to blows after
school. The two countries came
to blows because one wanted to
be independent from the other.*

come to grief *v. phr.* To have
a bad accident or disappointment; meet trouble or ruin;
end badly; wreck; fail. *Bill
came to grief learning to drive a
car. Nick's hopes for a new
house came to grief when the
house he was building burned
down. The fishing boat came to
grief off Cape Cod.*

come to grips with *v. phr.* **1.**
To get hold of (another wrestler) in close fighting. *After cir-
cling around for a minute, the
two wrestlers came to grips with
each other.* **2.** To struggle seriously with (an idea or problem). *Mr. Blake's teaching
helps students come to grips
with the important ideas in the
history lesson. Harry cannot be
a leader, because he never quite
comes to grips with a problem.*

come to light *v. phr.* To be
discovered; become known; appear. *John's thefts from the
bank where he worked came to
light when the bank examiners
made an inspection. When the
old woman died it came to light
that she was actually rich. New
facts about ancient Egypt have
recently come to light.*

come to mind *v. phr.* To occur
to someone. *A new idea for the
advertising campaign came to
mind as I was reading your
book.*

come to nothing *also formal*
come to naught *v. phr.* To
end in failure; fail; be in vain.
The dog's attempts to climb the

tree after the cat came to nothing.

come to one's senses *v. phr.* **1.** Become conscious again; wake up. *The boxer was knocked out and did not come to his senses for several minutes. The doctors gave Tom an anesthetic before his operation; then the doctor took out Tom's appendix before he came to his senses.* **2.** To think clearly; behave as usual or as you should; act sensibly. *A boy threw a snowball at me and before I could come to my senses he ran away. Don't act so foolishly. Come to your senses!*

come to pass *v. phr., literary* To happen; occur. *Strange things come to pass in troubled times. It came to pass that the jailer visited him by night. His hopes of success did not come to pass.*

come to terms *v. phr.* To reach an agreement. *Management and the labor union came to terms about a new arrangement and a strike was prevented.*

come to the point *or* **get to the point** *v. phr.* To talk about the important thing; reach the important facts of the matter; reach the central question or fact. *Henry was giving a lot of history and explanation, but his father asked him to come to the point. A good newspaper story must come right to the point and save the details for later.*

come to think of it *v. phr., informal* As I think again; indeed; really. *Come to think of it, he has already been given what he needs. Come to think*
of it, I should write my daughter today.

come true *v.* To really happen; change from a dream or a plan into a fact. *It took years of planning and saving, but their seagoing vacation came true at last. It was a dream come true when he met the President. His hope of living to 100 did not come true.*

come up *v.* **1.** To become a subject for discussion or decision to talk about or decide about. *"He was a good salesman, and price never came up until the very last," Mary said. The question of wage increases came up at the board meeting. Mayor Jones comes up for re-election this fall.* **2.** To be equal; match in value.—Used with *to*. *The new model car comes up to last year's.* **3.** To approach; come close. *We saw a big black bear coming up on us from the woods. Christmas is coming up soon. The team was out practicing for the big game coming up.* **4.** To provide; supply; furnish.—Used with *with*. *For years Jones kept coming up with new and good ideas. The teacher asked a difficult question, but finally Ted came up with a good answer.*

come up smelling like a rose *v. phr.* To escape from a difficult situation or misdeed unscathed or without punishment. *It is predicted that Congressman Brown, in spite of the current investigation into his financial affairs, will come up smelling like a rose at the end.*

come up with *v. phr.* **1.** To offer. *We can always depend on John Smith to come up with a* *good solution for any problem we might have.* **2.** To produce on demand. *I won't be able to buy this car, because I cannot come up with the down payment you require.* **3.** To find. *How on earth did you come up with such a brilliant idea?*

coming and going *or* **going and coming** adv. phr. **1.** Both ways; in both directions. *The truck driver stops at the same cafe coming and going. John was late. He got punished both going and coming; his teacher punished him and his parents punished him.* **2.** Caught or helpless; in your power; left with no way out of a difficulty.—Used after *have. If Beth stayed in the house, Mother would make her help with the cleaning; if she went outside, Father would make her help wash the car—they had her coming and going. Uncle Mike is a good checker player, and he soon had me beat coming and going.*

comings and goings *n. pl., informal* **1.** Times of arriving and going away; movements. *I can't keep up with the children's comings and goings.* **2.** Activities; doings; business. *Mary knows all the comings and goings in the neighborhood.*

common ground *n.* Shared beliefs, interests, or ways of understanding; ways in which people are alike. *Bob and Frank don't like each other because they have no common ground. The only common ground between us is that we went to the same school.*

common touch *n.* The ability to be a friend of the people; friendly manner with everyone. *Voters like a candidate who has the common touch.*

compare notes *v. phr., informal* To exchange thoughts or ideas about something; discuss together. *Mother and Mrs. Barker like to compare notes about cooking.*

conk out *v. phr., slang, informal* To fall asleep suddenly with great fatigue or after having drunk too much. *We conked out right after the guests had left.*

conversation piece *n.* Something that interests people and makes them talk about it; something that looks unusual, comical, or strange. *Uncle Fred has a glass monkey on top of his piano that he keeps for a conversation piece.*

cook one's goose *v. phr., slang* To ruin someone hopelessly; destroy one's future expectations or good name. *The bank treasurer cooked his own goose when he stole the bank's funds. She cooked John's goose by reporting what she knew to the police. The dishonest official knew his goose was cooked when the newspapers printed the story about him.*

cook up *v., informal* To plan and put together; make up; invent. *The boys cooked up an excuse to explain their absence from school.*

cool as a cucumber *adj. phr., informal* Very calm and brave; not nervous, worried, or anxious; not excited; composed. *Bill is a good football* *quarterback, always cool as a cucumber.*

cool customer *n.* Someone who is calm and in total control of himself; someone showing little emotion. *Jim never gets too excited about anything; he is a cool customer.*

cool down *or* **cool off** *v.* To lose or cause to lose the heat of any deep feeling (as love, enthusiasm, or anger); make or become calm, cooled or indifferent; lose interest. *A heated argument can be settled better if both sides cool down first. John was deeply in love with Sally before he left for college, but he cooled off before he got back. Their friendship cooled off when Jack gave up football. The neighbor's complaint about the noise cooled the argument down.*

cool one's heels *v. phr., slang* To be kept waiting by another's pride or rudeness; be forced to wait by someone in power or authority; wait. *He cooled his heels for an hour in another room before the great man would see him. I was left to cool my heels outside while the others went into the office.*

coop up *v. phr.* To hedge in; confine; enclose in a small place. *How can poor Jane work in that small office, cooped up all day long?*

cop a plea *v. phr., slang, colloquial* To plead guilty during a trial in the hope of getting a lighter sentence as a result. *The murderer of Dr. Martin Luther King, Jr., copped a plea of guilty, and got away with a*

life sentence instead of the death penalty.

cop out *v. phr., slang, informal* To avoid committing oneself in a situation where doing so would result in difficulties. *Nixon copped out on the American people with Watergate.*

cop-out *n. phr., slang, informal* An irresponsible excuse made to avoid something one has to do, a flimsy pretext. *Come on, Jim, that's a cheap cop-out, and I don't believe a word of it!*

copy cat *n.* Someone who copies another person's work or manner.—Usually used by children or when speaking to children. *He called me a copy cat just because my new shoes look like his.*

corn ball *n., slang, informal* **1.** A superficially sentimental movie or musical in which the word love is mentioned too often; a theatrical performance that is trivially sentimental. *That movie last night was a corn ball.* **2.** A person who behaves in a superficially sentimental manner or likes performances portraying such behavior. *Suzie can't stand Joe; she thinks he's a corn ball.*

couch case *n., slang, informal* A person judged emotionally so disturbed that people think he ought to see a psychiatrist (who, habitually, make their patients lie down on a couch). *Joe's divorce messed him up so badly that he became a couch case.*

couch doctor *n., slang, colloquial* A psychoanalyst who puts his patients on a couch following the practice established by Sigmund Freud. *I didn't know your husband was a couch doctor, I thought he was a gynecologist!*

couch potato *n.* A person who is addicted to watching television all day. *Poor Ted has become such a couch potato that we can't persuade him to do anything.*

cough up *v., slang* **1.** To give (money) unwillingly; pay with an effort. *Her husband coughed up the money for the party with a good deal of grumbling.* **2.** To tell what is secret; make known. *He coughed up the whole story for the police.*

couldn't care less *v. phr., informal* To be indifferent; not care at all. *The students couldn't care less about the band; they talk all through the concert.* Also heard increasingly as *could care less* (nonstandard in this form.)

countdown *n., Space English, informal* **1.** A step-by-step process which leads to the launching of a rocket. *Countdown starts at 23:00 hours tomorrow night and continues for 24 hours.* **2.** Process of counting inversely during the acts leading to a launch; liftoff occurs at zero. **3.** The time immediately preceding an important undertaking, borrowed from Space English. *We're leaving for Hawaii tomorrow afternoon; this is countdown time for us.*

count off *v.* **1.** To count aloud from one end of a line of men to the other, each man counting in turn. *The soldiers counted off from right to left.* **2.** To place into a separate group or groups by counting. *The coach counted off three boys to carry in the equipment. Tom counted off enough newspapers for his route.*

count on *v.* To depend on; rely on; trust. *The team was counting on Joe to win the race. I'll do it; you know you can count on me. The company was counting on Brown's making the right decision.*

count one's chickens before they're hatched *v. phr., informal* To depend on getting a profit or gain before you have it; make plans that suppose something will happen; be too sure that something will happen. Usually used in negative sentences. *When Jim said that he would be made captain of the team, John told him not to count his chickens before they were hatched. Maybe some of your customers won't pay, and then where will you be? Don't count your chickens before they're hatched.*

count out *v.* **1.** To leave (someone) out of a plan; not expect (someone) to share in an activity; exclude. *"Will this party cost anything? If it does, count me out, because I'm broke."* When the coach was planning who would play in the big game he counted Paul out, because Paul had a hurt leg.* **2.** To count out loud to ten to show that (a boxer who has been knocked down in a fight) is beaten or knocked out if he does not get up before ten is counted. *The champion was*

counted out in the third round.
3a. To add up; count again to be sure of the amount. *Mary counted out the number of pennies she had.* **3b.** To count out loud, (especially the beats in a measure of music). *The music teacher counted out the beats "one-two-three-four," so the class would sing in time.*

count to ten *v. phr., informal* To count from one to ten so you will have time to calm down or get control of yourself; put off action when angry or excited so as not to do anything wrong. *Father always told us to count to ten before doing anything when we got angry.*

cover girl *n.* A pretty girl or woman whose picture is put on the cover of a magazine. *Ann is not a cover girl, but she is pretty enough to be.*

cover ground or **cover the ground** *v. phr.* **1.** To go a distance; travel. *Mr. Rogers likes to travel in planes, because they cover ground so quickly.* **2.** *informal* To move over an area at a speed that is pleasing; move quickly over a lot of ground. *The new infielder really covers the ground at second base. Herby's new car really covers ground!* **3.** To give or receive the important facts and details about a subject. *If you're thinking about a trip to Europe, the airline has a booklet that covers the ground pretty well. The class spent two days studying the Revolutionary War, because they couldn't cover that much ground in one day.*

cover one's tracks or **cover up one's tracks** *v. phr.* **1.** To hide and not leave anything, especially foot marks, to show where you have been, so that no one can follow you. *The deer covered his tracks by running in a stream.* **2.** *informal* To hide or not say where you have been or what you have done; not tell why you do something or what you plan to do. *The boys covered their tracks when they went swimming by saying that they were going for a walk.*

cover the waterfront *v. phr.* To talk or write all about something; talk about something all possible ways. *The principal pretty well covered the waterfront on student behavior.*

cover up *v., informal* **1.** To hide something wrong or bad from attention. *The spy covered up his picture-taking by pretending to be just a tourist. A crooked banker tried to cover up his stealing some of the bank's money by starting a fire to destroy the records.* **2.** In boxing: To guard your head and body with your gloves, arms, and shoulders. *Jimmy's father told him to cover up and protect his chin when he boxed.* **3.** To protect someone else from blame or punishment; protect someone with a lie or alibi.—Often used with *for*. *The teacher wanted to know who broke the window and told the boys not to try to cover up for anyone. The burglar's friend covered up for him by saying that he was at his home when the robbery occurred.*

cover-up *n., slang* A plan or excuse to escape blame or punishment; lie, alibi. *When the* men robbed the bank, their cover-up was to dress like policemen. Joe's cover-up to his mother after he had been fighting was that he fell down.

cowboy n., slang, informal A person who drives his car carelessly and at too great a speed in order to show off his courage. Joe's going to be arrested some day—he is a cowboy on the highway.

cow college n., slang 1. An agricultural college; a school where farming is studied. A new, bigger kind of apple is being grown at the cow college. 2. A new or rural college not thought to be as good as older or city colleges. John wanted to go to a big college in New York City, not to a cow college.

cozy up v., slang To try to be close or friendly; try to be liked.—Usually used with to. John is cozying up to Henry so he can join the club.

crack a book v. phr., slang To open a book in order to study.—Usually used with a negative. John did not crack a book until the night before the exam. Many students think they can pass without cracking a book.

crack a joke v. phr., informal To make a joke; tell a joke. The men sat around the stove, smoking and cracking jokes.

crack a smile v. phr., informal To let a smile show on one's face; permit a smile to appear. Bob told the whole silly story without even cracking a smile. Scrooge was a gloomy man, who never cracked a smile. When we gave the shy little boy an ice cream cone, he finally cracked a smile.

crack down v. phr., informal To enforce laws or rules strictly; require full obedience to a rule. After a speeding driver hit a child, the police cracked down.—Often used with on. Police suddenly cracked down on the selling of liquor to minors. The coach cracked down on the players when he found they had not been obeying the training rules.

crack of dawn n. phr. The time in the morning when the sun's rays first appear. The rooster crows at the crack of dawn and wakes up everybody on the farm.

cracked up adj. phr., informal Favorably described or presented; praised.—Usually used in the expression not what it's cracked up to be. The independent writer's life isn't always everything it's cracked up to be. In bad weather, a sailing cruise isn't what it's cracked up to be.

crackpot n., attrib. adj., informal 1. n. An eccentric person with ideas that don't make sense to most other people. Don't believe what Uncle Noam tells you—he is a crackpot. 2. attrib. adj. That's a crackpot idea.

crack the whip v. phr., informal To get obedience or cooperation by threats of punishment. If the children won't behave when I reason with them, I have to crack the whip.

crack up v. 1. To wreck or be wrecked; smash up. The airplane cracked up in landing. He cracked up his car. 2. informal

To become mentally ill under physical or mental overwork or worry. *He had kept too busy for years, and when failures came, he cracked up. It seemed to be family problems that made him crack up.* 3. Burst into laughter or cause to burst into laughter. *That comedian cracks me up.*

cramp one's style *v. phr., informal* To limit your natural freedom; prevent your usual behavior; limit your actions or talk. *It cramped his style a good deal when he lost his money. Army rules cramped George's style.*

crash dive *n.* A sudden dive made by a submarine to escape an enemy; a dive made to get deep under water as quickly as possible. *The captain of the submarine told his crew to prepare for a crash dive when he saw the enemy battleship approaching.*

crash-dive *v.* 1. To dive deep underwater in a submarine as quickly as possible. *We shall crash-dive if we see enemy planes coming.* 2. To dive into (something) in an airplane. *When the plane's motor was hit by the guns of the enemy battleship, the pilot aimed the plane at the ship and crash-dived into it.*

crash the gate *v. phr., slang* To enter without a ticket or without paying; attend without an invitation or permission. *Bob got into the circus without paying. He crashed the gate. Three boys tried to crash the gate at our party but we didn't let them in.*

cream of the crop *n. phr.* The best of a group; the top choice. *May Queen candidates were lovely, but Betsy and Nancy were the cream of the crop. The students had drawn many good pictures and the teacher chose the cream of the crop to hang up when the parents came to visit.*

credibility gap *n.,* hackneyed phrase, politics An apparent discrepancy between what the government says and what one can observe for oneself. *There was a tremendous credibility gap in the USA during the Watergate years.*

creep up on *v.* 1. To crawl towards; move along near the ground; steal cautiously towards so as not to be seen or noticed. *The mouse did not see the snake creeping up on it over the rocks. Indians were creeping up on the house through the bushes.* 2. *or* **sneak up on** To come little by little; arrive slowly and unnoticed. *The woman's hair was turning gray as age crept up on her. Winter is creeping up on us little by little. The boys didn't notice the darkness creeping up on them while they were playing.*

crew cut *or* **crew haircut** *n.* A boy's or man's hair style, cut so that the hair stands up in short, stiff bristle. *Many boys like to get crew cuts during the summer to keep cooler.*

crocodile tears *n.* Pretended grief; a show of sorrow that is not really felt. *When his rich uncle died, leaving him his money, John shed crocodile tears.* [From the old legend that crocodiles make weeping sounds to attract victims and then shed tears while eating them.]

crop out *v.* To appear at the surface; come through or show through from hiding or concealment. *Rocks often crop out in New England pasture land. A hidden hate cropped out in his words.*

crop up *v.* To come without warning; appear or happen unexpectedly. *Problems cropped up almost every day when Mr. Reed was building his TV station. Serious trouble cropped up just when Martin thought the problem of his college education was solved.*

cross a bridge before one comes to it *v. phr.* To worry about future events or trouble before they happen—Usually used in negative sentences, often as a proverb. *"Can I be a soldier when I grow up, Mother?" asked Johnny. "Don't cross that bridge until you come to it," said his mother.*

cross fire *n.* **1.** Firing in a fight or battle from two or more places at once so that the lines of fire cross. *The soldiers on the bridge were caught in the cross fire coming from both sides of the bridge.* **2.** Fast or angry talking back and forth between two or more people; also, a dispute; a quarrel. *There was a cross fire of excited questions and answers between the parents and the children who had been lost in the woods. The principal and the graduates quarreled about the football team, and the coach was caught in the cross fire and lost his job.*

cross one's fingers *v. phr.* **1a.**

To cross two fingers of one hand for good luck. *Mary crossed her fingers during the race so that Tom would win.* **1b.** *or* keep one's fingers crossed *informal* To wish for good luck. *Keep your fingers crossed while I take the test.* **2.** To cross two fingers of one hand to excuse an untruth that you are telling. *Johnny crossed his fingers when he told his mother the lie.*

cross one's heart *or* **cross one's heart and hope to die** *v. phr., informal* To say that what you have said is surely true; promise seriously that it is true.— Often used by children in the longer form. Children often make a sign of a cross over the heart as they say it, for emphasis. *"Cross my heart, I didn't hide your bicycle," Harry told Tom. "I didn't tell the teacher what you said. Cross my heart and hope to die," Mary said to Lucy.*

cross one's mind *or* **pass through one's mind** *v. phr.* To be a sudden or passing thought; be thought of by someone; come to your mind; occur to you. *At first Bob was puzzled by Virginia's waving, but then it crossed his mind that she was trying to tell him something. When Jane did not come home by midnight, many terrible fears passed through Mother's mind.*

cross one's path *v. phr.* To meet or encounter someone; to come upon someone more by accident than by plan. *Surprisingly, I crossed John's path in Central Park one afternoon.*

cross street *n.* A street that

crosses a main street and runs on both sides of it. *Elm Street is a cross street on Main Street and there is a traffic light there.*

cross swords *v. phr., literary* To have an argument with; fight.—Often used with *with*. *Don't argue with the teacher; you're not old enough to cross swords with her.*

cross the wire *v. phr.* To finish a race. *The Russian crossed the wire just behind the American.*

crux of the matter *n. phr.* The basic issue at hand; the core essence that one must face. *The crux of the matter is that he is incompetent and we will have to fire him.*

cry or **scream bloody murder** *v. phr.* To bitterly and loudly complain against an indignity. *Pete cried bloody murder when he found out that he didn't get the promotion he was hoping for.*

cry for or **cry out for** *v., informal* To need badly; to be lacking in. *It has not rained for two weeks and the garden is crying for it. The school is crying out for good teachers.*

cry out *v.* **1.** To call out loudly; shout; scream. *The woman in the water cried out "Help!"* **2.** To complain loudly; protest strongly.—Used with *against*. *Many people are crying out against the new rule.*

cry over spilled milk or **cry over spilt milk** *v. phr., informal* To cry or complain about something that has already happened; be unhappy about something that cannot be helped. *After the baby tore up Sue's picture book, Sue's mother told her there was no*

use crying over spilled milk. *You have lost the game but don't cry over spilt milk.*

crystal ball *n.* A ball, usually made of quartz crystal (glass) that is used by fortune-tellers. *The fortune-teller at the fair looked into her crystal ball and told me that I would take a long trip next year.* **2.** Any means of predicting the future. *My crystal ball tells me you'll be making the honor roll.*

cry wolf *v. phr.* To give a false alarm; warn of a danger that you know is not there. *The general said that the candidate was just crying wolf when he said that the army was too weak to fight for the country.* [From an old story about a shepherd boy who falsely claimed a wolf was killing his sheep, just to start some excitement.]

cue in *v. phr., informal* To add new information to that which is already known. *Let's not forget to cue in Joe on what has been happening.*

culture vulture *n., slang, informal* A person who is an avid cultural sightseer, one who seeks out cultural opportunities ostentatiously, such as going to the opera or seeing every museum in a town visited, and brags about it. *My Aunt Mathilda is a regular culture vulture; she spends every summer in a different European capital going to museums and operas.*

cup of tea also **dish of tea** *n. phr., informal* **1.** Something you enjoy or do well at; a special interest, or favorite occupation. Used with a possessive. *You could always get him to go* *for a walk: hiking was just his cup of tea.* **2.** Something to think about; thing; matter. *That's another cup of tea.*

curiosity killed the cat *informal* Getting too nosy may lead a person into trouble.—A proverb. *"Curiosity killed the cat," Fred's father said, when he found Fred hunting around in closets just before Christmas.*

curl one's hair *v. phr., slang* To shock; frighten; horrify; amaze. *Wait till you read what it says about you—this'll curl your hair. The movie about monsters from another planet curled his hair.*

curry favor *v.* To flatter or serve someone to get his help or friendship. *Joe tried to curry favor with the new teacher by doing little services that she didn't really want. Jim tried to curry favor with the new girl by telling her she was the prettiest girl in the class.*

cut a class *v. phr.* To be truant; to deliberately miss a class and do something else instead. *"If you keep cutting classes the way you do, you will almost surely flunk this course," John's professor said to him.*

cut a figure *v. phr.* To make a favorable impression; carry off an activity with dignity and grace. *With his handsome face and sporty figure, Harry cuts quite a figure with all the ladies.*

cut across *v.* **1.** To cross or go through instead of going around; go a short way. *John didn't want to walk to the corner and turn, so he cut across the yard to the next street.* **2.** To go beyond to include; stretch over to act on; affect. *The love*

for reading cuts across all classes of people, rich and poor.

cut-and-dried *adj. phr.* Decided or expected beforehand; following the same old line; doing the usual thing. *The decision of the judge was cut-and-dried. The ways of the king's court were cut-and-dried. People at the convention heard many cut-and-dried speeches.*

cut back *v.* **1.** To change direction suddenly while going at full speed. *The halfback started to his left, cut back to his right, and ran for a touchdown.* **2.** To use fewer or use less. *After the big job was finished, the builder cut back the number of men working for him. The school employed forty teachers until a lower budget forced it to cut back.*

cut back *v. phr.* To diminish; lessen; decrease (said of budgets). *The state had to cut back on the university budget.*

cutback *n.* An act of decreasing monetary sources. *The cutback in military spending has caused many bases to be closed.*

cut both ways or **cut two ways** *v. phr.* To have two effects; cause injury to both sides. *People who gossip find it cuts both ways.*

cut corners *v. phr.* **1.** To take a short way; not go to each corner. *He cut corners going home in a hurry.* **2.** To save cost or effort; manage in a thrifty way; be saving. *John's father asked him to cut corners all he could in college.* **3.** To do less than a very good job; do only what you must do on a job. *He had cut corners in building his* *house, and it didn't stand up well.*

cut down *v.* To lessen; reduce; limit. *Tom had to cut down expenses. The doctor told Mr. Jones to cut down on smoking.*

cut down to size *v. phr., informal* To prove that someone is not as good as he thinks. *The big boy told John he could beat him, but John was a good boxer and soon cut him down to size.*

cut ice *v. phr., informal* To make a difference; make an impression; be accepted as important.—Usually used in negative, interrogative, or conditional sentences. *When Frank had found a movie he liked, what others said cut no ice with him. Jones is democratic; a man's money or importance never cuts any ice with him. Does comfort cut any ice with you? I don't know if beauty in a woman cuts any ice with him.*

cut in *v.* **1.** To force your way into a place between others in a line of cars, people, etc.; push in. *After passing several cars, Fred cut in too soon and nearly caused an accident.*—Often used with *on*. *A car passed Jean and cut in on her too close; she had to brake quickly or she would have hit it. The teacher beside the lunch line saw Pete cut in, and she sent him back to wait his turn.* **2.** To stop a talk or program for a time; interrupt. *While Mary and Jim were talking on the porch, Mary's little brother cut in on them and began to tell about his fishing trip. While we were watching the late show, an announcer cut in to tell who won the election.* **3.** *informal* To tap a dancer on the shoulder and claim the partner. *Mary was a good dancer and a boy could seldom finish a dance with her; someone always cut in.*—Often used with *on*. *At the leap year dance, Jane cut in on Sally because she wanted to dance with Sally's handsome date.* **4.** To connect to an electrical circuit or to a machine. *Harry threw the switch and cut in the motor. The airplane pilot cut in a spare gas tank.* **5.** *informal* To take in; include. *When John's friends got a big contract, they cut John in.*

cut into *v.* **1.** To make less; reduce. *The union made the company pay higher wages, which cut into the profits. The other houses got old and shabby, and that cut into the value of his house. At first Smith led in votes, but more votes came in and cut into his lead.* **2.** To get into by cutting in. *She heard the other women gossiping and cut into the talk. While Bill was passing another car, a truck came around a curve heading for him, and Bill cut back into line quickly.*

cut no ice *v. phr.* To have no effect; achieve no result; be insignificant. *The fact that the accused is a millionaire will cut no ice with this particular judge.*

cut off *v.* **1.** To separate or block. *The flood cut the townspeople off from the rest of the world. The woods cut off the view. His rudeness cuts him off from friends he might have.* **2.** To interrupt or stop. *The television show was cut off by a special news report. We were told* to pay the bill or the water would be cut off. **3.** To end the life of; cause the death of. *Disease cut Smith off in the best part of life.* **4.** To give nothing to at death; leave out of a will. *Jane married a man her father hated, and her father cut her off. Frank's uncle cut him off without a penny.* **5.** To stop from operating; turn a switch to stop. *The ship cut off its engines as it neared the dock.*

cut off one's nose to spite one's face *v. phr.* To suffer from an action intended originally to harm another person. *In walking out and leaving his employer in the lurch, John really cut off his nose to spite his face, since no business wanted to hire him afterwards.*

cut one's throat *v. phr., informal* To spoil one's chances; ruin a person. *He cut his own throat by his carelessness. The younger men in the company were cutting each other's throats in their eagerness to win success. John cut Freddie's throat with Mary by telling her lies.*

cut out¹ *v., slang* **1.** To stop; quit. *All right, now—let's cut out the talking. He was teasing the dog and Joe told him to cut it out.* **2.** To displace in favor. *Tony cut Ed out with Mary. John cut out two or three other men in trying for a better job.*

cut out² *adj.* **1.** Made ready; given for action; facing. *Mary agreed to stay with her teacher's children all day; she did not know what was cut out for her.—*Often used in the phrase have one's work cut out for

one. *If Mr. Perkins wants to become a senator, he has his work cut out for him.* **2.** Suited to; fitted for. *Warren seemed to be cut out for the law. It was clear very early that Fred was cut out to be a doctor.*

cut rate¹ *n.* A lower price; a price less than usual. *Toys are on sale at the store for cut rates.*

cut-rate² *adj.* Sold for a price lower than usual; selling cheap things. *If you buy cut-rate things, be sure they are good quality first. John's brother bought a cut-rate bicycle at the second-hand store. There is a cut-rate drugstore on the corner.*

cut short *v.* To stop or interrupt suddenly; end suddenly or too soon. *Rain cut short the ball game. An auto accident cut short the man's life. When Dick began to tell about his summer vacation the teacher cut him short, saying "Tell us about that another time."*

cut the mustard *v. phr., slang* To do well enough in what needs to be done; to succeed. *His older brothers and sisters helped Max through high school, but he couldn't cut the mustard in college.*

cut-throat *adj.* Severe; intense; unrelenting. *There is cutthroat competition among the various software companies today.*

cut to pieces *v. phr.* **1.** To divide into small parts with something sharp; cut badly or completely. *Baby has cut the newspaper to pieces with scissors.* **2.** To destroy or defeat completely. *The soldiers were cut to pieces by the Indians. When Dick showed his book report to his big sister for correction, she cut it to pieces.*

cut to the bone *v. phr.* To make (something) the least or smallest possible amount; reduce severely; leave out everything extra or unnecessary from. *Father cut Jane's allowance to the bone for disobeying him. When Father lost his job, our living expenses had to be cut to the bone.*

cut to the quick *v. phr.* To hurt someone's feelings deeply. *The children's teasing cut Mary to the quick.*

cut up *v.* **1.** *informal* To hurt the feelings of; wound.—Usually used in the passive. *John was badly cut up when Susie gave him back his ring.* **2.** *slang* To act funny or rough; clown. *Joe would always cut up if there were any girls watching. At the party Jim and Ron were cutting up and broke a chair.*

D

damned if one does, damned if one doesn't *adj. phr.* No matter what one does, someone is likely to criticize one. *No matter what decisions I make, there are always some people who will approve them and those who won't. It is a classical case of "damned if I do, damned if I don't."*

dance to another tune *v. phr.* To talk or act differently, usually better because things have changed; be more polite or obedient because you are forced to do it. *Johnny refused to do his homework but punishment made him dance to another tune.*

dare say *v. phr.* To think probable; suppose; believe.— Used in first person. *Mary is unhappy now but I dare say she will be laughing about this tomorrow. There is no more ice cream on the table, but I dare say we can find some in the kitchen.*

dare one to do something *v. phr.* To challenge someone to do something. *"I dare you to jump off that rock into the sea," Fred said to Jack.*

dark horse *n., informal* A political candidate little known to the general voting public; a candidate who was not expected to run. *Every once in a while a dark horse candidate gets elected President.*

dark of the moon *n. phr., literary* A time when the moon is not shining or cannot be seen. *It was the dark of the moon when the scouts reached camp and they had to use flashlights to find their tents.*

dash light *n.* A light on the front inside of a car or vehicle. *Henry stopped the car and turned on the dash lights to read the road map.*

dash off *v.* To make, do, or finish quickly; especially, to draw, paint, or write hurriedly. *Ann took out her drawing pad and pencil and dashed off a sketch of the Indians. John can dash off several letters while Mary writes only one. Charles had forgotten to write his English report and dashed it off just before class.*

date back *v. phr.* To go back to a given period in the past. *My ancestors date back to the sixteenth century.*

dawn on *v.* To become clear to. *It dawned on Fred that he would fail the course if he did not study harder.*

day and night *or* **night and day** *adv.* **1.** For days without stopping; continually. *Some filling stations on great highways are open day and night 365 days a year. The three men took turns driving the truck, and they drove night and day for three days.* **2.** Every day and every evening. *The girl knitted day and night to finish the sweater before her mother's birthday.*

day by day adv. Gradually. *The patient got better day by day.*

day in and day out or **day in, day out** adv. phr. Regularly; consistently; all the time; always. *He plays good tennis day in and day out.*—Also used with several other time words in place of *day: week, month, year. Every summer, year in, year out, the ice cream man comes back to the park.*

day in court n. phr. A chance to be heard; an impartial hearing; a chance to explain what one has done. *The letters from the faculty members to the dean gave Professor Smith his day in court.*

daydream v. To spend time in reverie; be absentminded during the day. *John spends so much time daydreaming that he never gets anything done.*

day of reckoning n. phr. **1.** A time when one will be made to account for misdeeds. *When the criminal was caught and brought to trial his victims said, "finally, the day of reckoning has come."* **2.** A time when one's will and judgment are severely tested. *"You always wanted to run the department," the dean said to Professor Smith. "Now here is your chance; this is your day of reckoning."*

day off n. A day on which one doesn't have to work, not necessarily the weekend. *Monday is his day off in the restaurant, because he prefers to work on Saturdays and Sundays.*

day-to-day adj. Daily; common; everyday. *For best results,* students' homework should be checked on a day-to-day basis.

days are numbered (Someone or something) does not have long to live or stay. *The days of the old school building are numbered. When a man becomes ninety years old, his days are numbered.*

dead ahead adv., informal Exactly in front; before. *The school is dead ahead about two miles from here. Father was driving in a fog, and suddenly he saw another car dead ahead of him.*

deadbeat n., slang A person who never pays his debts and who has a way of getting things free that others have to pay for. *You'll never collect from Joe—he's a deadbeat.*

dead as a doornail adj. phr. Completely dead without the slightest hope of resuscitation. *This battery is dead as a doornail; no wonder your car won't start.*

dead center n. The exact middle. *The treasure was buried in the dead center of the island.* Often used like an adverb. *The arrow hit the circle dead center.*

dead duck n., slang A person or thing in a hopeless situation or condition; one to whom something bad is sure to happen. *When the pianist broke her arm, she was a dead duck.*

deadhead n., slang An excessively dull or boring person. *You'll never get John to tell a joke—he's a deadhead.*

dead letter n. phr. An undeliverable letter that ends up in a special office holding such letters. *There is a dead letter office in most major cities.*

deadline n. A final date by which a project, such as a term paper, is due. *The deadline for the papers on Shakespeare is November 10.*

dead loss n. phr. A total waste; a complete loss. *Our investment in Jack's company turned out to be a dead loss.*

dead on one's feet adv. phr., informal Very tired but still standing or walking; too tired to do more; exhausted. *Jimmy never leaves a job unfinished. He continues to work even when he's dead on his feet. After the soldiers march all night, they are dead on their feet.*

deadpan adj., adv., slang With an expressionless or emotionless face; without betraying any hint of emotion. *She received the news of her husband's death deadpan.*

dead ringer n. phr. A person who strongly resembles someone else. *Charlie is a dead ringer for his uncle.*

dead tired adj. phr., informal Very tired; exhausted; worn out. *She was dead tired at the end of the day's work.*

dead to the world adj. phr., informal **1.** Fast asleep. *Tim went to bed very late and was still dead to the world at 10 o'clock this morning.* **2.** As if dead; unconscious. *Tom was hit on the head by a baseball and was dead to the world for two hours.*

dead-end n. A street closed at one end; a situation that leads nowhere. *Jim drove into a dead-end street and had to back out. Mary was in a dead-end job.*

dead-end v. To not continue normally but end in a closure (said of streets). *Our street dead-ends on the lake.*

deal with v. phr. **1.** To conduct negotiations or business dealings with. *John refuses to deal with the firm of Brown and Miller.* **2.** To handle a problem. *Ted is a very strong person and dealt with the fact that his wife had left him much better than anyone else I know.*

dear me interj. Used to show surprise, fear, or some other strong feeling. *Dear me! My purse is lost, what shall I do now?*

death knell n. formal **1.** The ringing of a bell at a death or funeral. *The people mourned at the death knell of their friend.* **2.** literary Something which shows a future failure. *Bill's poor grade on his final examination sounded the death knell of his hope to be a doctor. His sudden deafness was the death knell of his hope to become President.*

decked out adj. phr., informal Dressed in fancy clothes; specially decorated for some festive occasion. *The school band was decked out in bright red uniforms with brass buttons. Main Street was decked with flags for the Fourth of July.*

deep-six v., slang To throw away; dispose of. *As the police boat came near, the drug smugglers deep-sixed their cargo.* (An expression originally used by sailors, suggesting throwing something into water six fathoms deep.)

deep water n. Serious trouble or difficulty. *When Dad tried to* *take Mom's place for a day, he found himself in deep water.*

deliver the goods v. phr. **1.** To carry things and give them to the person who wants them. *Lee delivered the goods to the right house.* **2.** slang To succeed in doing well what is expected. *The new pitcher delivered the goods by striking out 20 men in his first game. This personal computer surely delivers the goods.*

Dennis the Menace n. phr. After the notorious television character played by a young boy who always creates trouble for the grownups. Any hyperactive little boy who needs calming down. *"Your son, Joey, is becoming a regular 'Dennis the Menace',"* Jane said to Elvira.

devil-may-care adj. Not caring what happens; unworried. *Johnny has a devil-may-care feeling about his school work. Alfred was a devil-may-care youth but became more serious as he grew older.*

devil of it or **heck of it** n. phr. **1.** The worst or most unlucky thing about a trouble or accident; the part that is most regrettable. *Andy lost his notebook, and the devil of it was that the notebook contained all his homework for the coming week. When I had a flat tire, the devil of it was that my spare tire was flat too.* **2.** Fun from doing mischief.—Used after for. *The boys carried away Miss White's front gate just for the devil of it.*

diamond in the rough n. phr. A very smart person without a formal education who may

have untutored manners. *Jack never went to school but he is extremely talented; he is a veritable diamond in the rough.*

die away or **die down** v. To come slowly to an end; grow slowly less or weaker. *The wind died down. The music died away. He waited until the excitement had died down. His mother's anger died away.*

die is cast v. phr., literary To make an irrevocable decision. (From Julius Caesar's famous words in Latin, *alea iacta est,* when he crossed the river Rubicon, which meant war.) *Everything was ready for the invasion of Europe, the die had been cast, and there was no turning back now.*

die off v. To die one at a time. *The flowers are dying off because there has been no rain.*

die on the vine or **wither on the vine** v. phr. To fail or collapse in the planning stages. *The program for rebuilding the city died on the vine.*

die out v. To die or disappear slowly until all gone. *This kind of bird is dying out. If you pour salt water on grass, it dies out. The American colonists started colleges so that learning would not die out.*

dig in v., informal **1.** To dig ditches for protection against an enemy attack. *The soldiers dug in and waited for the enemy to come.* **2a.** To go seriously to work; work hard. *John dug in and finished his homework very quickly.* **2b.** To begin eating. *Mother set the food on the table and told the children to dig in.*

dig out v. **1.** To find by searching; bring out (something) that was put away. *Jack dug his sled out of the cellar. The newspaper printed an old story dug out of their records.* **2.** *informal* To escape.—Usually used with *of.* Often used in the phrase *dig oneself out of a hole. The pitcher dug himself out of a hole by striking the batter out.*

dig up *v., informal* To find or get (something) with some effort. *Sue dug up some useful material for her English composition. Jim asked each boy to dig up twenty-five cents to pay for the hot dogs and soda.*

dime a dozen *adj. phr., informal* Easy to get and so of little value; being an everyday thing because there are many of them; common. *Mr. Jones gives A's to only one or two students, but in Mr. Smith's class, A's are a dime a dozen.*

dine out *v. phr.* To not eat at home but to go to a restaurant. *"Let's dine out tonight, honey,"* she said to her husband. *"I am tired of cooking dinner every night."*

dip into *v. phr.* **1.** To scan or sample lightly and briefly (said of printed materials). *I didn't get a chance to read all of* War and Peace, *but I dipped into it here and there.* **2.** To take money out of a savings account or a piggy bank. *I am sorry to have to say that I had to dip into the piggy bank; I took out $6.75.*

dirt cheap *adj.* Extremely inexpensive. *The apartment we are renting is dirt cheap compared to other apartments of* similar size in this neighborhood.

dirty look *n., informal* A look that shows dislike. *Miss Parker sent Joe to the principal's office for giving her a dirty look.*

dirty old man *n. phr.* An older man who shows an unhealthy interest in young girls. *"Stay away from Uncle Algernon, Sally," her mother warned. "He is a dirty old man."*

dirty one's hands or **soil one's hands** *v. phr.* To lower or hurt one's character or good name; do a bad or shameful thing. *The teacher warned the children not to dirty their hands by cheating in the examination. I would not soil my hands by going with bad people and doing bad things.*

dirty story *n. phr.* An improper or obscene story. *Uncle Bill is much too fond of telling dirty stories in order to embarrass his friends.*

dirty trick *n. phr.* A treacherous action; an unfair act. *That was a dirty trick John played on Mary when he ran away with her younger sister.*

discretion is the better part of valor *literary* When you are in danger or trouble, good sense helps more than foolish risks; it is better to be careful than to be foolishly brave.—A proverb. *When you are facing a man with a knife, discretion is the better part of valor.*

dish out *v.* **1.** To serve (food) from a large bowl or plate. *Ann's mother asked her to dish out the beans.* **2.** *informal* To give in large quantities. *That teacher dished out so much homework that her pupils complained to their parents.* **3.** *slang* To scold; treat or criticize roughly. *Jim likes to dish it out, but he hates to take it.*

dish the dirt *v. phr., slang* To gossip, to spread rumors about others. *Stop dishing the dirt, Sally, it's really quite unbecoming!*

disk jockey *n.* An employee at a radio station or in a dance club who puts on the records that will be broadcast. *Jack is working as a disk jockey at the local FM station.*

dispose of *v.* **1.** To throw away; give away, or sell; get rid of. *John's father wants to dispose of their old house and buy a new one. The burglars had difficulty in disposing of the stolen jewelry.* **2.** To finish with; settle; complete. *The boys were hungry, and quickly disposed of their dinner. The committee soon disposed of all its business.* **3.** To destroy or defeat. *The champion disposed of the other fighter by knocking him out in the second round. Our planes disposed of two enemy planes.*

do a double take *v. phr., informal* To look again in surprise; suddenly understand what is seen or said. *John did a double take when he saw Bill in girls' clothes. When Evvie said she was quitting school, I did a double take.*

do a job on *v. phr., slang* To damage badly; do harm to; make ugly or useless. *The baby did a job on Mary's book. Jane cut her hair and really did a job on herself.*

do away with *v.* **1.** To put an end to; stop. *The teachers want to do away with cheating in their school. The city has decided to do away with overhead wires.* **2.** To kill; murder. *The robbers did away with their victims.*

doctor up *v. phr.* To meddle with; adulterate. *You don't have to doctor up this basic salad with a lot of extras as I am trying to lose weight.*

doesn't add up to a can of beans *v. phr.* To be of little or no value. (Said of plans, ideas, etc.) *"That's a fairly interesting concept you got there, Mike, but the competition is bound to say that it doesn't add up to a can of beans."*

do for *v., informal* To cause the death or ruin of; cause to fail.—Used usually in the passive form *done for. The poor fellow is done for and will die before morning. Andy's employer always does very well by him. If Jim fails that test, he is done for.*

dog days *n. phr.* The hottest days of the year in the Northern Hemisphere (July and August). (The ancient Romans associated this time with the "Dog Star"—Sirius—which becomes visible in the heavens at this time of year.) *"The dog days are upon us," John said. "It's time to go swimming in the lake."*

dog-eat-dog[1] *n.* A way of living in which every person tries to get what he wants for himself no matter how badly or cruelly he must treat others to get it; readiness to do anything to get what you want. *In some early frontier towns it was dog-eat-dog.*

dog-eat-dog[2] *adj.* Ready or willing to fight and hurt others to get what you want. *During the California gold rush, men had a dog-eat-dog life.*

dog in the manger *n. phr.* A person who is unwilling to let another use what he himself has no use for. *Although Valerie lives alone in that big house, she is like a dog in the manger when it comes to letting someone sharing it with her.*

dog one's steps *v. phr.* To follow someone closely. *All the time he was in Havana, Castro's police were dogging his steps.*

do in *v., slang* **1.** To ruin; destroy. *Mr. Smith's business was done in by a fire that burned down his store.* **2a.** To kill; murder. *The poor man was done in by two gangsters who ran away after the crime.* **2b.** To make tired; exhaust. *The boys were done in after their long hike.* **3.** To cheat; swindle. *Mr. Jones was done in by two men who claimed to be collecting money for orphans and widows.*

do justice to *v. phr.* **1.** To do (something) as well as you should; do properly. *Barbara had so many things to do that she could not do justice to her lessons. The newspaper man did not do justice to the story.* **2.** To eat or drink with enthusi-asm or enjoyment. *The boy did justice to the meal.*

dole out *v. phr.* To measure out sparingly. *Since the water ration was running low in the desert, the camp commandant doled out small cups of water to each soldier.*

doll up *v., slang* **1.** To dress in fine or fancy clothes. *The girls dolled up for the big school dance of the year. The girls were all dolled up for the Christmas party.* **2.** To make more pretty or attractive. *The classrooms were all dolled up with Christmas decorations.*

done for *adj. phr.* Finished; dead. *When the police burst in on the crooks, they knew they were done for.*

done with *adj. phr.* Finished; completed. *As soon as you're done with your work, give us a call.*

do one a good turn *v. phr.* To perform an act of kindness, friendship, or help to another person, unselfishly, without expectation of reward. *"I'll be happy to help you any time you need it," John said. "After all you have done me so many good turns."*

do one good *v. phr.* To benefit. *The fresh air will do you good after having been inside the house all day.*

do one good *or* **do one's heart good** *v. phr.* To give satisfaction; please; gratify. *It does my heart good to see those children play.*

do one's best *v. phr.* To perform at one's optimum capacity; spare no effort in fulfilling one's duties. *"I've really done my best teaching you people,"* the tired professor said on the last day of classes. "I hope you got something out of this course."

do one's bit *or* **part** *v. phr.* To shoulder one's share of responsibility in a communal undertaking; shirk one's obligation. *"Let me go home and rest, fellows," John said. "I think I've done my bit for this project."*

do one's thing *or* **do one's own thing** *v. phr., informal* **1.** To do what one does well and actually enjoys doing. *Two thousand fans paid $15 each to hear the rock group do their thing.* **2.** To follow one's bent; for example, to be engaged in left-wing politics, some sort of meditation, or use of drugs (particularly in the sixties). *The hippies were doing their own thing when the cops came and busted them.* **3.** To be engaged in an unusual activity that strikes others as odd. *Leave Jim alone, he's just doing his own thing when he's standing on his head.*

do one's worst *v. phr.* To do one's utmost by resorting to every foul means possible. *Hitler did his worst to drive out the Allied invasion from Europe, but he failed.*

do-or-die *adj.* Strongly decided, very eager and determined. *With a real do-or-die spirit the team scored two touchdowns in the last five minutes of the game. The other army was larger but our men showed a do-or-die determination and won the battle.*

dope out *v., slang* To think of something that explains. *The*

detectives tried to dope out why the man was murdered.

do someone out of something *v., informal* To cause to lose by trickery or cheating. *The clerk in the store did me out of $2.00 by overcharging me.*

dose of one's own medicine *or* **taste of one's own medicine** *n. phr.* Being treated in the same way you treat others; something bad done to you as you have done bad to other people. *Jim was always playing tricks on other boys. Finally they decided to give him a dose of his own medicine.*

do the honors *v. phr.* To act as host or hostess (as in introducing guests, carving, or paying other attentions to guests.) *The president of the club will do the honors at the banquet.*

do the trick *v. phr., informal* To bring success in doing something; have a desired result. *Jim was not passing in English, but he studied harder and that did the trick. The car wheels slipped on the ice, so Tom put sand under them, which did the trick.*

double back *v.* **1.** To turn back on one's way or course. *The escaped prisoner doubled back on his tracks.* **2.** To fold over; usually in the middle. *The teacher told Johnny to double back the sheet of paper and tear it in half.*

double check *n.* A careful second check to be sure that something is right; a careful look for errors. *The policeman made a double check on the doors in the shopping area.*

double-check *v.* **1.** To do a double check on; look at again very carefully. *When the last typing of his book was finished, the author double-checked it.* **2.** To make a double check; look carefully at something. *The proofreader double-checks against errors.*

double-cross *v.* To promise one thing and deliver another; to deceive. *The lawyer double-crossed the inventor by manufacturing the gadget instead of fulfilling his promise to arrange a patent for his client.*

double date *n., informal* A date on which two couples go together. *John and Nancy went with Mary and Bill on a double date.*

double-date *v., informal* To go on a double date; date with another couple. *John and Nancy and Mary and Bill double-date.*

double duty *n.* Two uses or jobs; two purposes or duties. *Matthew does double duty. He's the janitor in the morning and gardener in the afternoon. Our new washer does double duty; it washes the clothes and also dries them.*

double-header *n.* Two games or contests played one right after the other, between the same two teams or two different pairs of teams. *The Yankees and the Dodgers played a double-header Sunday afternoon. We went to a basketball double-header at Madison Square Garden and saw Seton Hall play St. John's and N.Y.U. play Notre Dame.*

double-park *v.* To park a car beside another car which is at the curb. *Jimmy's father dou-*ble-parked his car and the police gave him a ticket. If you double-park, you block other cars from passing.*

double-talk *n.* **1.** Something said that is worded, either on purpose or by accident, so that it may be understood in two or more different ways. *The politician avoided the question with double-talk.* **2.** Something said that does not make sense; mixed up talk or writing; nonsense. *The man's explanation of the new tax bill was just a lot of double-talk.*

double up *v.* **1.** To bend far over forward. *Jim was hit by the baseball and doubled up with pain.* **2.** To share a room, bed, or home with another. *When relatives came for a visit, Ann had to double up with her sister.*

do up *v.* **1a.** To clean and prepare for use or wear; launder. *Ann asked her mother to do up her dress.* **1b.** To put in order; straighten up; clean. *At camp the girls have to do up their own cabins.* **2.** To tie up or wrap. *Joan asked the clerk to do up her purchases.* **3a.** To set and fasten (hair) in place. *Grace helped her sister to do up her hair.* **3b.** *informal* To dress or clothe. *Suzie was done up in her fine new skirt and blouse.*

do with *v.* **1.** To find enough for one's needs; manage.— Usually follows *can. Some children can do with very little spending money.* **2.** To make use of; find useful or helpful.— Follows *can* or *could. After a hard day's work, a man can do with a good, hot meal.*

After cleaning out the basement, the boy could do with a bath.

do without *or* **go without** *v.* **1.** To live or work without (something you want); manage without. *Ann said that she likes candy, but can do without it. We had to go without hot food because the stove was broken.* **2.** To live or work without something you want; manage. *If George cannot earn money for a bicycle, he will have to do without.*

down and out *adj. phr.* Without money; without a job or home; broke. *Poor Sam lost his job after his wife had left him; he is really down and out.*

down in the dumps *or* **down in the mouth** *adj. phr., informal* Sad or discouraged; gloomy; dejected. *The boys were certainly down in the dumps when they heard that their team had lost.*

down on *adj. phr., informal* Having a grudge against; angry at. *John is down on his teacher because she gave him a low grade.*

down one's alley *or* **up one's alley** *adj. phr., slang* Suited to your tastes and abilities; what you like or like to do. *Baseball is right down Jim's alley.*

down on one's luck *adj., informal* Having bad luck; having much trouble; not successful in life. *Harry asked me to lend him ten dollars, because he was down on his luck. The teacher is easy on Jane because Jane has been down on her luck lately.*

down payment *n.* A retainer

paid to a prospective seller. *How much of a down payment do you require for this new car?*

down the drain *adj.* or adv. *phr., informal* Wasted; lost. *It is money down the drain if you spend it all on candy. Our plans to go swimming went down the drain when it rained.*

down the hatch! *v. phr., informal* Let us drink! *When we celebrated Mom's birthday, we all raised our glasses and cried in unison, "Down the hatch!"*

down the line *adv. phr., informal* **1.** Down the road or street; straight ahead. *The church is down the line a few blocks.* **2.** All the way; completely; thoroughly. *Bob always follows the teacher's directions right down the line.*

down-to-earth *adj.* Showing good sense; practical. *The committee's first plan for the party was too fancy, but the second was more down-to-earth. Mr. Jenkins never seems to know what is happening around him, but his wife is friendly and down-to-earth.*

down to the wire *adj., slang* **1.** Running out of time, nearing a deadline. *Bob is down to the wire on his project* **2.** Being financially almost broke, being very low on cash or other funds. *We can't afford going to a restaurant tonight—we're really down to the wire!]*

drag in *v.* To insist on bringing (another subject) into a discussion; begin talking about (something different.) *No matter what we talk about, Jim* *drags in politics. Whenever anyone mentions travel, Grace has to drag in the trip to Mexico she took ten years ago.*

drag on *or* **drag out** *v.* **1.** To pass very slowly. *The cold winter months dragged on until we thought spring would never come.* **2.** To prolong; make longer. *The meeting would have been over quickly if the members had not dragged out the argument about dues.*

drag one's feet *or* **drag one's heels** *v. phr.* To act slowly or reluctantly. *The children wanted to watch television, and dragged their feet when their mother told them to go to bed. The city employees said the mayor had promised to raise their pay, but was now dragging his feet.*

drag race *n., slang* An automobile race in which the drivers try to cover a certain distance (usually one quarter mile) in the shortest possible time. *Drag races are often held on airport landing strips. Holding drag races is a good way to stop teenage hot rod racing on public highways.*

draw a blank *v. phr., informal* **1.** To obtain nothing in return for an effort made or to get a negative result. *I looked up all the Joneses in the telephone book but I drew a blank every time I asked for Archibald Jones.* **2.** To fail to remember something. *I am trying to think of the name but I keep drawing a blank.* **3.** To be consistently unsuccessful at doing something. *I keep trying to pass that math exam but each time I try it I draw a blank.*

draw a conclusion *v. phr.* To make an inference. *After he failed to keep an appointment with me for the third time, I drew the conclusion that he was an unreliable person.*

draw a line *or* **draw the line** *v. phr.* **1.** To think of as different. *The law in this country draws a line between murder and manslaughter. Can you draw the line between a lie and a fib?* **2.** To set a limit to what will be done; say something cannot be done. *We would like to invite everybody to our party, but we have to draw a line somewhere.*—Often used with *at*. *Mrs. Jones draws the line at permitting the children to play in their father's den. People fighting for their freedom often do not draw the line at murder.*

draw back *v.* To move back; back away; step backward; withdraw; move away from. *When the man spotted the rattlesnake, he drew back and aimed his shotgun. The children drew back from the dog when it barked at them. When the pitcher drew back his arm to pitch the ball, Tom ran as fast as he could to steal second base. Some juice from the grapefruit that Father was eating squirted in his eye and he drew back in surprise.*

drawback *n.* Disadvantage; obstacle; hindrance. *The biggest drawback of Bill's plan is the cost involved.*

draw blood *v. phr., informal* To make someone feel hurt or angry. *If you want to draw blood, ask Jim about his last money-making scheme. Her* *sarcastic comments drew blood.*

draw fire *v. phr.* **1.** To attract or provoke shooting; be a target. *The general's white horse drew the enemy's fire.* **2.** To bring criticism or argument; make people say bad things about you. *Having the newest car in your group is sure to draw fire.*

drawing card *n.* The most important figure in a multi-person event; the top entertainer during a show; the best professor or researcher at a university, etc. *During the concert series Barbra Streisand was the biggest drawing card. The biggest drawing card at many a university is the resident Nobel Laureate.*

draw out *v. phr.* **1.** To take out; remove. *Johnny drew a dollar out of the bank to buy his mother a present. The hunter drew out his gun and shot the snake.* **2.** To make (a person) talk or tell something. *Jimmy was bashful but Mrs. Wilson drew him out by asking him about baseball.* **3.** To make come out; bring out. *The bell of the ice-cream truck drew the children out of the houses. Mary was drawn out of her silence by Billy's jokes.* **4.** To make longer or too long; stretch. *The Smiths drew out their vacation at the beach an extra week. It was a long drawn out meeting because everybody tried to talk at once. Mary and her mother drew out their goodbyes so long at the bus station that Mary almost missed the bus.*

draw to a close *v. phr.* To fin-

ish; terminate; come to an end. *The meeting drew to a close around midnight.*

draw up *v.* **1.** To write (something) in its correct form; put in writing. *The rich man had his lawyers draw up his will so that each of his children would receive part of his money when he died.* **2.** To plan or prepare; begin to write out. *The two countries drew up a peace treaty after the war ended. Plans are being drawn up for a new school next year.* **3.** To hold yourself straight or stiffly, especially because you are proud or angry. *When we said that Mary was getting fat, she drew herself up angrily and walked out of the room.* **4.** To stop or come to a stop. *The cowboy drew up his horse at the top of the hill. A big black car drew up in front of the house.*

dress up *v.* **1a.** To put on best or special clothes. *Billy hated being dressed up and took off his best suit as soon as he got home from church.* **1b.** To put on a costume for fun or clothes for a part in a play. *Mary was dressed up to play Cinderella in her school play.* **2.** To make (something) look different; make (something) seem better or more important. *A fresh coat of paint will dress up the old bicycle very much. Tommy dressed up the story of what he did on vacation and made it seem twice as interesting as it was.*

drift off *v. phr.* **1.** To fall asleep. *He kept nodding and drifting off to sleep while the lecturer was speaking.* **2.** To depart; leave gradually. *One by one, the sailboats drifted off over the horizon.*

drink down *v. phr.* To drink in one gulp; swallow entirely. *Steve was so thirsty that he drank down six glasses of orange juice in rapid succession.*

drink in *v. phr.* To absorb with great interest. *The tourists stood on the beach drinking in the wonderful Hawaiian sunset.*

drink like a fish *v. phr.* To drink (alcoholic beverages) in great quantities; to be addicted to alcohol. *John is a nice guy but, unfortunately, he drinks like a fish.*

drink up *v. phr.* To finish drinking; empty one's glass. *"Drink up that cough syrup," the nurse said, "and never mind the taste."*

drive a bargain *v. phr.* **1.** To buy or sell at a good price; succeed in a trade or deal. *Tom's collie is a champion; it should be easy for Tom to drive a bargain when he sells her puppies. Father drove a hard bargain with the real estate agent when we bought our new house.* **2.** To make an agreement that is better for you than for the other person; make an agreement to your advantage. *The French drove a hard bargain in demanding that Germany pay fully for World War I damages.*

drive at *v.* To try or want to say; mean. Used in the present participle. *John did not understand what the coach was driving at. He had been talking for half an hour before anyone realized what he was driving at.*

drive home *v. phr.* To argue

convincingly; make a strong point. *The doctor's convincing arguments and explanation of his X-ray pictures drove home the point to Max that he needed surgery.*

drive-in *adj. n.* A kind of movie theater, fast food restaurant, or church, where the customers, spectators, or worshippers do not leave their automobiles but are served the food inside their cars, can watch a motion picture from inside their cars, or can participate in a religious service in their cars. *Let's not waste time on the road; let's just eat at the next drive-in restaurant. There is a drive-in theater not far from where we live. Max and Hilde go to a drive-in church every Sunday.*

drive one ape, bananas, crazy, mad *or* **nuts** *v. phr., informal* To irritate, frustrate, or tickle someone's fancy so badly that they think they are going insane. *"Stop teasing me, Mary," John said. "You are driving me nuts." "You are driving me bananas with all your crazy riddles," Steve said.*

drop a line *v. phr.* To write someone a short letter or note. *Please drop me a line when you get to Paris; I'd like to know that you've arrived safely.*

drop back *v.* To move or step backwards; retreat. *The soldiers dropped back before the enemy's attack. The quarterback dropped back to pass the football.*

drop by or stop by *v.* **1.** *or* **drop around** To make a short or unplanned visit; go on a call or errand; stop at someone's home. *Drop by any time you're in town. My sister dropped around last night. Don't forget to stop by at the gas station.* **2.** or **drop into** To stop (somewhere) for a short visit or a short time. *We dropped by the club to see if Bill was there, but he wasn't. I dropped into the drugstore for some toothpaste and a magazine.*

drop dead *v., slang* To go away or be quiet; stop bothering someone.—Usually used as a command. *"Drop dead!" Bill told his little sister when she kept begging to help him build his model airplane. When Sally bumped into Kate's desk and spilled ink for the fifth time, Kate told her to drop dead.*

drop in *v.* To make a short or unplanned visit; pay a call.— Often used with *on. We were just sitting down to dinner when Uncle Willie dropped in. The Smiths dropped in on some old friends on their vacation trip to New York.*

drop in the bucket *n. phr.* A relatively small amount; a small part of the whole. *Our university needs several million dollars for its building renovation project; $50,000 is a mere drop in the bucket.*

drop name *v. phr.* To impress people by mentioning famous names. *He likes to pretend he's important by dropping a lot of names.*

drop off *v.* **1.** To take (someone or something) part of the way you are going. *Joe asked Mrs. Jones to drop him off at the library on her way downtown.* **2.** To go to sleep. *Jimmy was thinking of his birthday party as he dropped off to sleep.* **3.** To die. *The patient dropped off in his sleep.* **4.** or **fall off** To become less. *Business picked up in the stores during December, but dropped off again after Christmas.*

dropout *n.* Someone who did not finish school, high school and college primarily. *Tim is having a hard time getting a better job as he was a high-school dropout. Jack never got his B.A. as he became a college dropout.*

drop out *v.* To stop attending; quit; stop; leave. *In the middle of the race, Joe got a blister on his foot and had to drop out. Teenagers who drop out of high school have trouble finding jobs.*

drown out *v.* To make so much noise that it is impossible to hear (some other sound). *The children's shouts drowned out the music. The actor's words were drowned out by applause.*

drum up *v.* **1.** To get by trying or asking again and again; attract or encourage by continued effort. *The car dealer tried to drum up business by advertising low prices.* **2.** To invent. *I will drum up an excuse for coming to see you next week.*

duck out *v. phr.* To avoid; escape from something by skillful maneuvering. *Somehow or other Jack always manages to duck out of any hard work.*

duck soup *n., slang* **1.** A task easily accomplished or one that does not require much effort. *That history test was duck soup.* **2.** A person who offers no resistance; a pushover. *How's the* *new history teacher? He's duck soup.*

dumb bunny *n., slang, informal* Any person who is gullible and stupid. *Jack is a regular dumb bunny.*

dumbwaiter *n.* A small elevator for carrying food, dishes, etc., from one floor to another in hotels, restaurants, or large homes. *The banquet was delayed because the dumbwaiter broke down and the food had to be carried upstairs by hand.*

dust off *v., informal* **1.** To get ready to use again. *Four years after he graduated from school, Tom decided to dust off his algebra book.* **2.** To throw a baseball pitch close to. *The pitcher dusted off the other team's best hitter.*

dutch treat *n., informal* A meal in a restaurant or an outing at the movies, concert, or theater where each party pay his or her own way. *"I am willing to accept your invitation,"* Mary said, *"but it will have t be Dutch treat."*

dwell on *or* **dwell upon** *v.* T stay on a subject; not leav something or want to leave not stop talking or writin about. *Joe dwelt on his mistak long after the test was over. Ou eyes dwelled on the beautifu sunset. The principal dwelle on traffic safety in his talk.*

dyed-in-the-wool *adj. phr* Thoroughly committed; invet erate; unchanging. *He is dyed-in-the-wool Conservativ Republican.*

dying to *adj. phr.* Having great desire to; being ex tremely eager to. *Seymour i dying to date Mathilda, but sh keeps refusing him.*

E

each and every adj. phr. Every.—Used for emphasis. *The captain wants each and every man to be here at eight o'clock. The teacher must learn the name of each and every pupil.*

each other or **one another** pron. Each one the other; one the other. *That man and his wife love each other. Bill and Mary gave one another Christmas presents last year. All the children at the party were looking at one another trying to recognize one another in their masks and costumes. The birds fought each other over the bread.*

eager beaver n. phr., slang A person who is always eager to work or do anything extra, perhaps to win the favor of his leader or boss. *Jack likes his teacher and works hard for her, but his classmates call him an eager beaver. The man who was promoted to be manager was an eager beaver who got to work early and left late and was always offering to do extra work.*

eagle eye n. Sharp vision like that of an eagle; the ability to notice even the tiniest details. *The new boss keeps an eagle eye on all aspects of our operation.*

early bird n. An early riser from bed. *Jane and Tom are real birds; they get up at 6 A.M. every morning.*

early bird catches the worm or

early bird gets the worm A person who gets up early in the morning has the best chance of succeeding; if you arrive early or are quicker, you get ahead of others.—A proverb. *When Billy's father woke him up for school he said, "The early bird catches the worm." Charles began looking for a summer job in January; he knows that the early bird gets the worm.*

earn one's keep v. phr. To merit one's salary or keep by performing the labor or chores that are expected of one. *John earned his keep at the music conservatory by dusting off all the musical instruments every day.*

ear to the ground n. phr., informal Attention directed to the way things are going, or seem likely to go, or to the way people feel and think. *The city manager kept an ear to the ground for a while before deciding to raise the city employees' pay. Reporters keep an ear to the ground so as to know as soon as possible what will happen.*

ease off or **ease up** v. To make or become less nervous; relax; work easier. *When the boss realized that John had been overworking, he eased off his load. With success and prosperity, Mr. Smith was able to ease off.*

easy come, easy go truncated sent. informal Something you get quickly and easily may be lost or spent just as easily. *Grandfather thought Billy should have to work for the money Father gave him, saying "Easy come, easy go."*

easy does it *informal* Let's do it carefully, without sudden movements and without forcing too hard or too fast; let's try to just hard enough but not too hard. *"Easy does it," said the boss as they moved the piano through the narrow doorway.*

easy mark *n.* A foolishly generous person; one from whom it is easy to get money. *Bill is known to all the neighborhood beggars as an easy mark.*

easy money *n. informal* Money gained without hard work; money that requires little or no effort. *The movie rights to a successful play mean easy money to the writer of the play. Young people who look for easy money are usually disappointed.*

eat away *v.* **1.** To rot, rust, or destroy. *Rust was eating away the pipe. Cancer ate away the healthy flesh.* **2.** To gradually consume. *The ocean waves were gradually eating the volcanic rocks until they turned into black sand.*

eat crow *v. phr.* To admit you are mistaken or defeated; take back a mistaken statement. *John had boasted that he would play on the first team; but when the coach did not choose him, he had to eat crow. Fred said he could beat the new man in boxing, but he lost and had to eat crow.*

eat dirt *v. phr., informal* To act humble; accept another's insult or bad treatment. *Mr. Johnson was so much afraid of losing his job that he would eat dirt whenever the boss got mean.*

eat humble pie *v. phr.* To be humbled; to accept insult or shame; admit your error and apologize. *Tom told a lie about George, and when he was found out, he had to eat humble pie. In some old stories a boy with a stepfather has to eat humble pie.*

eat like a bird *v. phr.* To eat very little; have little appetite. *Mrs. Benson is on a diet and she eats like a bird. Alice's mother is worried about her; she eats like a bird and is very thin.*

eat like a horse *v. phr.* To eat a lot; eat hungrily. *The harvesters worked into the evening, and then came in and ate like horses.*

eat one out of house and home *v. phr.* **1.** To eat so much as to cause economic hardship. *Our teenaged sons are so hungry all the time that they may soon eat us out of house and home.* **2.** To overstay one's welcome. *We love Bob and Jane very much, but after two weeks we started to feel that they were eating us out of house and home.*

eat one's cake and have it too *v. phr.* To use or spend something and still keep it; have both when you must choose one of two things. Often used in negative sentences. *Roger can't make up his mind whether to go to college or get a job. You can't eat your cake and have it too. Mary wants to buy* *a beautiful dress she saw at the store, but she also wants to save her birthday money for camp. She wants to eat her cake and have it too.*

eat one's heart out *v. phr.* To grieve long and hopelessly; to become thin and weak from sorrow. *For months after her husband's death, Joanne simply ate her heart out. We sometimes hear of a dog eating its heart out for a dead owner.*

eat one's words also **swallow one's words** *v. phr.* To take back something you have said; admit something is not true. *John had called Harry a coward, but the boys made him eat his words after Harry bravely fought a big bully.*

eat out *v.* **1.** To eat in a restaurant; eat away from home. *Fred ate out often even when he wasn't out of town.* **2.** To rust, rot, or be destroyed in time. *Rust had eaten out the gun barrel.*

eat up *v.* **1.** To eat all of. *After hiking all afternoon, they quickly ate up all of the dinner.* **2.** To use all of. *Idle talk had eaten up the hour before they knew it.* **3.** *slang* To accept eagerly; welcome. *The girls told John he was a hero because he made the winning touchdown, and he ate up their praise. Jim told Martha that she was as smart as she was beautiful and Martha ate it up.*

edge in (on) *v. phr.* **1.** To gradually approach an individual or a group with the intent of taking over or wielding power. *Jack was edging in on the firm of Smith and Brown and after half a year actually*

became its vice president. **2.** To approach for capture (said of a group). *The hunters were edging in on the wounded leopard.*

edge on *adv. phr.* Edgewise; with the narrow side forward. *The board struck him edge on.*

edge out *v.* To defeat in competition or rivalry; take the place of; force out. *Harry edged out Tom for a place in Mary's affections. Signal lights on cars have gradually edged out hand signals.*

egg on *v.* To urge on; excite; lead to action. *Joe's wife egged him on to spend money to show off. The big boys egged on the two little boys to fight.*

eke out *v.* **1.** To fill out or add a little to; increase a little. *Mr. Jones eked out a country teacher's small salary by hunting and trapping in the winter. The modest meal was eked out with bread and milk.* **2.** To get (little) by hard work; to earn with difficulty. *Fred eked out a bare living by farming on a rocky hillside.*

elbow grease *n.* Exertion; effort; energy. *"You'll have to use a little more elbow grease to get these windows clean,"* Mother said to Ed.

elbow one's way into or out of *v. phr.* To force entry into a place by using one's elbows. *The bus was so crowded that, in order to get off in time, we had to elbow our way to the exit door.*

elbow room *n.* Adequate space to move around or to work in. *He doesn't require a huge office, but we must at least give him elbow room.*

end in itself *n. phr.* Something wanted for its own sake; a purpose, aim, or goal we want for itself alone and not as a way to something else. *The miser never spent his gold because for him it was an end in itself.*

end of one's rope *or* **end of one's tether** *n. phr., informal* The end of your trying or imagining; the last of your ability, or ideas of how to do more. *Frank was out of work and broke, and he was at the end of his rope. The doctor saw that Mother had reached the end of her tether, and told us to send her away for a holiday.*

end of the road *or* **end of the line** *n. phr.* The final result or end (as of a way of action or behavior); the condition that comes when you can do no more. *He had left a trail of forgery and dishonesty across seven states; he had got out of each trouble with a new trick. Now the police had caught up with him, and it was the end of the road. "When I get to the end of the line," Jones thought, "I'd like my children to like and respect me still."*

end run *n.* A football play in which a back tries to run around one end of the opponent's line. *Smith's end run scored the winning touchdown.*

end up *v.* **1.** To come to an end; be ended or finished; stop. *How does the story end up?* **2.** To finally reach or arrive; land. *I hope you don't end up in jail.* **3.** *informal* To die; be killed. *The gangster ended up in the electric chair.* **4.** *or* **finish up.** To put an end to; finish; stop. *The*

politician finally ended up his speech.

end zone *n.* Either of the marked areas behind the goal line. *He caught a pass in the end zone for a touchdown.*

enjoy oneself *v. phr.* To have a good time; be happy; feel pleasure. *Mary enjoyed herself at the party. "Enjoy yourselves, children," Mother urged the guests at our party.*

enough is enough That's enough, let's not have any more; that will do, let's cut it short; that's the limit, let's stop there. *"I don't mind good clean fun, but enough is enough," the principal said.*

every cloud has a silver lining Every trouble has something hopeful that you can see in it, like the bright edge around a dark cloud.—A proverb. *The doctor told Tommy to cheer up when he had measles. "Every cloud has a silver lining," he said.*

every dog has his day Everyone will have his chance or turn; everyone is lucky or popular at some time.—A proverb. *Mary will be able to go to dances like her sister when she grows up. Every dog has his day.*

every inch *adv. phr.* To the last part, in every way; completely. *He was every inch a man. Henry looked every inch a soldier.*

every now and then *or* **every now and again** *or* **every so often** *or* **every once in a while** *adv. phr.* At fairly regular intervals; fairly often; repeatedly. *John comes to visit me every now and then. It was hot work,* *but every so often Susan would bring us something cold to drink.*

every other *adj. phr.* Every second; every alternate. *The milkman comes every other day. On St. Patrick's Day, it seems as if every other man you meet is wearing a shamrock.*

every single *or* **every last** *adj. phr.* Every.—Used for emphasis. *She dropped the box, and when she opened it, every single glass was broken. When she got home she found every last tomato in the box was rotten.*

exception proves the rule Something unusual that does not follow a rule tests that rule to see if it is true; if there are too many exceptions, the rule is no good.—A proverb. *Frank is very short but is a good basketball player. He is the exception that proves the rule.*

excuse oneself *v. phr.* **1.** To think of reasons for not being to blame; think yourself not at fault. *John excused himself for his low grades on the ground that the teacher didn't like him.* **2.** To ask to be excused after doing something impolite. *John excused himself for his tardiness, saying his watch was wrong.* **3.** To ask permission to leave a group or place. *The committee meeting lasted so long that Mr. Wilkins excused himself to keep an appointment. John had to go to the dentist's, so he excused himself and left the classroom.*

exert oneself *v. phr.* To make an effort; try hard; work hard. *Susan exerted herself all year to earn good marks. Jerry exerted himself to please the new girl.*

eye-catcher *n.* Something that strongly attracts the eye. See catch one's eye. *That new girl in our class is a real eye-catcher.*

eye for an eye and a tooth for a tooth A blow or injury should be given back as hard as each one that is received; every crime or injury should be punished or paid back. *In ancient times if a man's eye was put out by his enemy, he might get revenge by putting his enemy's eye out. This was the rule of "an eye for an eye and a tooth for a tooth."* Sometimes used in a short form. *Churches today teach that we should forgive people who hurt us, not follow the rule of "an eye for an eye."* [From the old command in the Bible meaning when you pay back a person, you should not hurt him more than he hurt you.]

eye out Careful watch or attention; guard. Used after *keep, have* or *with*. *Keep an eye out. We're close to Joe's house.* Usually used with *for. Mary has her eye out for bargains. They went through the woods very quietly, with an eye out for Indians.*

eyes are bigger than one's stomach *informal* You want more food than you can eat. *Annie took a second big helping of pudding, but her eyes were bigger than her stomach. "Your eyes are bigger than your stomach," Mother told little Tommy when he piled up food on his plate.*

eyes in the back of one's head *n. phr., informal* Ability to know what happens when your back is turned. *Mother must* have eyes in the back of her head, because she always knows when I do something wrong.

eyes open 1. Careful watch or attention; readiness to see— Usually used with *for. Keep your eyes open for a boy in a red cap and sweater. The hunter had his eyes open for rabbits. They drove on with their eyes open for a gas station.* **2.** Full knowledge; especially of consequences; understanding of what will or might result.— Used with *have* or *with. Automobile racing is dangerous. Bob went into it with his eyes open. Betty had her eyes open when she got married.*

eyes pop out *informal* (You) are very much surprised.— Used with a possessive noun or pronoun. *Mary's eyes popped out when her mother entered her classroom. When Joan found a clock radio under the Christmas tree, her eyes popped out.*

face down v. phr. To get the upper hand over someone by behaving forcefully; disconcert someone by the displaying of great self-assurance. *The night guard faced down the burglar by staring him squarely in the face.*

face lift n. phr. **1.** A surgical procedure designed to make one's face look younger. *Aunt Jane, who is in her seventies, had an expensive face lift and now she looks as if she were 40.* **2.** A renovation, a refurbishing. *Our house needs a major face lift to make it fit in with the rest of the neighborhood.*

face the music v. phr., informal To go through trouble or danger, especially because of something you did; accept your punishment. *The boy was caught cheating in an examination and had to face the music. The official who had been taking bribes was exposed by a newspaper, and had to face the music. George knew his mother would cry when he told her, but he decided to go home and face the music.*

face-to-face adv. phr. **1.** With your face looking toward the face of another person; each facing the other. *Turning a corner, he found himself face-to-face with a policeman. The two teams for the spelling bee stood face-to-face on opposite sides of the classroom. The church and the school stand face-to-face across the street.* **2.** In the presence of another or others. *She was thrilled to meet the President face-to-face. I have heard about him, but I never met him face-to-face.* **3.** To the point where you must do something. Used with *with. The solution of the first problem brought him face-to-face with a second problem.*

face-to-face adj. Being in the presence of a person; being right with someone. *The British prime minister came to Washington for a face-to-face meeting with the President.*

face up to v. phr. **1.** To bravely confront a person or a challenge; admit. *Jack doesn't want to face up to the fact that Helen doesn't love him anymore. Jane cannot face up to her mother-in-law who always wins every argument they have.* **2.** To confess something to someone; confess to having done something. *Jim had to face up to having stolen a sweater from the department store.*

face value n. **1.** The worth or price printed on a stamp, bond, note, piece of paper money, etc. *The savings bond had a face value of $25.* **2.** The seeming worth or truth of something. *She took his stories at face value and did not know he was joking.*

faced with adj. phr. Confronted with. *We were all faced with the many wars that broke out in the wake of the collapse of communism.*

101

facts of life *n. phr.* **1.** The truth which we should know about sex, marriage, and births. *His father told him the facts of life when he was old enough.* **2.** The truths one learns about people and their good and bad habits of life, work or play. *As a cub reporter he would learn the facts of life in the newspaper world.*

fair and square *adv. phr., informal* Without cheating; honestly. *He won the game fair and square.*

fair-haired boy *n., informal* A person that gets special favors; favorite; pet. *If he wins the election by a large majority, he will become his party's fair-haired boy. The local boy playing first base could do no wrong; he was the fair-haired boy of the fans. Charles was a good student and behaved very well; he became the teacher's fair-haired boy.*

fair play *n.* Equal and right action (to another person); justice. *The visiting team did not get fair play in the game. The judges decided against Bob, but he said that he had gotten fair play. Sally's sense of fair play made her a favorite with her classmates.*

fair sex *n., informal* Women in general; the female sex. *"Better not use four-letter words in front of a member of the fair sex," Joe said.*

fair shake *n., informal* Honest treatment. *Joe has always given me a fair shake.*

fair-weather friend *n.* A person who is a friend only when you are successful. *Everyone knows that John's only a fair-weather friend.*

fairy godmother *n.* **1.** A fairy believed to help and take care of a baby as it grows up. **2.** A person who helps and does much for another. *The rich man played fairy godmother to the boys and had a baseball field made for them. Jane was a fairy godmother to her poorer friends.*

fall asleep at the switch *v. phr.* To fail to perform an expected task; be remiss in one's duty. *The two airplanes wouldn't have collided, if the control tower operator hadn't fallen asleep at the switch. The dean promised our department $250,000 but the foundation never sent the money because someone in the dean's office fell asleep at the switch.*

fall back *v.* To move back; go back.—Usually used with a group as subject. *The army fell back before their stubborn enemies. The crowd around the hurt boy fell back when someone shouted "Give him air!"*

fall back on or **fall back upon** *v.* **1.** To retreat to. *The enemy made a strong attack, and the soldiers fell back on the fort.* **2.** To go for help to; turn to in time of need. *When the big bills for Mother's hospital care came, Joe was glad he had money in the bank to fall back on. If Mr. Jones can't find a job as a teacher, he can fall back on his skill as a printer.*

fall behind *v.* To go slower than others and be far behind them. *When the campers took a hike in the woods, two boys fell behind and got lost. Frank's les-*

sons were too hard for him, and he soon fell behind the rest of the class. Mary was not promoted because she dreamed too much and fell behind in her lessons.

fall by the wayside also **drop by the wayside** v. phr. To give up or fail before the finish. The boys tried to make a 50-mile hike, but most of them fell by the wayside. George, Harry, and John entered college to become teachers, but Harry and John fell by the wayside, and only George graduated.

fall flat v., informal To be a failure; fail. The party fell flat because of the rain. His joke fell flat because no one understood it.

fall for v., slang 1. To begin to like very much. Dick fell for baseball when he was a little boy. 2. To begin to love (a boy or a girl.) Helen was a very pretty girl and people were not surprised that Bill fell for her. 3. To believe (something told to fool you.) Nell did not fall for Joe's story about being a jet pilot.

fall from grace v. phr. To go back to a bad way of behaving; do something bad again. The boys behaved well during dinner until they fell from grace by eating their dessert with their fingers instead of their forks. The boy fell from grace when he lied.

fall guy n. slang The "patsy" in an illegal transaction; a sucker; a dupe; the person who takes the punishment others deserve. When the Savings and Loan Bank failed, due to embezzlement, the vice president

had to be the fall guy, saving the necks of the owners.

fall in v. 1. To go and stand properly in a row like soldiers. The captain told his men to fall in. 2. to collapse. The explosion caused the walls of the house to fall in.

falling-out n. Argument; disagreement; quarrel. Mary and Jane had a falling-out about who owned the book. The boys had a falling-out when each said that the other had broken the rules.

fall in or **into place** v. phr. To suddenly make sense; find the natural or proper place for the missing pieces of a puzzle. When the detectives realized that a second man was seen at the place of the murder, the pieces of the puzzle began to fall into place.

fall in with v., informal 1. To meet by accident. Mary fell in with some of her friends downtown. 2. To agree to help with; support. I fell in with Jack's plan to play a trick on his father. 3. To become associated with a group detrimental to the newcomer. John fell in with a wild bunch; small wonder he flunked all of his courses.

fall off the wagon v. phr., slang alcoholism and drug culture To return to the consumption of an addictive, such as alcohol or drugs, after a period of abstinence. Poor Joe has fallen off the wagon again—he is completely incoherent today.

fall on or **fall upon** v. 1. To go and fight with; attack. The robbers fell on him from behind trees. 2. formal To meet (troubles). *The famous poet fell upon unhappy days.*

fallout *n.* **1.** Result of nuclear explosion; harmful radioactive particles. *Some experts consider fallout as dangerous as the bomb itself.* **2.** Undesirable aftereffects in general. *As a fallout of Watergate, many people lost their faith in the government.*

fall out *v.* **1.** To happen. *As it fell out, the Harpers were able to sell their old car.* **2.** To quarrel; fight; fuss; disagree. *The thieves fell out over the division of the loot.* **3.** To leave a military formation. *You men are dismissed. Fall out!* **4.** To leave a building to go and line up. *The soldiers fell out of the barracks for inspection.*

fall over backwards *or* **fall over oneself** *v. phr.* To do everything you can to please someone; try very hard to satisfy someone. *The hotel manager fell over backwards to give the movie star everything she wanted. The boys fell over themselves trying to get the new girl's attention.*

fall short *v.* To fail to reach (some aim); not succeed. *His jump fell three inches short of the world record. The movie fell short of expectations.*

fall through *v., informal* To fail; be ruined; not happen or be done. *Jim's plans to go to college fell through at the last moment. Mr. Jones' deal to sell his house fell through.*

fall to *v.* **1.** To begin to work. *The boys fell to and quickly cut the grass.* **2.** To begin to fight. *They took out their swords and fell to.* **3.** To begin to eat. *The hungry boys fell to before everyone sat down.* **4.** Begin; start. *The old friends met and fell to talking about their school days.*

far and wide *adv. phr.* Everywhere, in all directions. *The wind blew the papers far and wide. My old school friends are scattered far and wide now. The movie company looked far and wide for a boy to act the hero in the new movie.*

farfetched *adj.* Exaggerated; fantastic. *Sally told us some farfetched story about having been kidnapped by little green men in a flying saucer.*

far cry *n.* Something very different. *His last statement was a far cry from his first story. The first automobile could run, but it was a far cry from a modern car.*

farm out *v.* **1.** To have another person do (something) for you; send away to be done. *Our teacher had too many test papers to read, so she farmed out half of them to a friend.* **2.** To send away to be taken care of. *While Mother was sick, the children were farmed out to relatives.* **3.** To send a player to a league where the quality of play is lower. *The player was farmed out to Rochester to gain experience.*

far-out *adj.* **1.** Very far away; distant. *Scientists are planning rocket trips to the moon and far-out planets.* **2.** *informal* Very different from others; queer; odd, unusual. *He enjoyed being with beatniks and other far-out people. Susan did not like some of the paintings at* *the art show because they were too far-out for her.*

fast buck or **quick buck** *slang* Money earned quickly and easily, and sometimes dishonestly. *You can make a fast buck at the golf course by fishing balls out of the water trap. He isn't interested in a career; he's just looking for a quick buck.*

fast talker *n., slang, informal* A con artist or a swindler, one who is particularly apt to get away with illegitimate transactions because of the clever way he talks. *I wouldn't trust Uncle Joe if I were you,—he is a fast talker.*

fat chance *n. phr., slang* Little or no possibility; almost no chance. *A high school team would have a fat chance of beating a strong college team. Jane is pretty and popular; you will have a fat chance of getting a date with her.*

fat of the land *n. phr.* The best and richest food, clothes, everything. *When I'm rich I'll retire and live off the fat of the land.*

favorite son *n.* A man supported by his home state for President. *At a national convention, states often vote for their favorite sons first; then they change and vote for another man.*

feather in one's cap *n. phr.* Something to be proud of; an honor. *It was a feather in his cap to win first prize.* [From the medieval practice of placing a feather in the helmet of one who won honors in battle.]

feather one's nest *v. phr., informal* **1.** To use for yourself money and power, especially from a public office or job in which you are trusted to help other people. *The rich man told his lawyer to use his money after he died to build a hospital for poor people, but the lawyer feathered his own nest with the money instead. The man feathered his nest in politics by getting money from contractors who built roads.* **2.** To make your home pleasant and comfortable; furnish and decorate your house. *Furniture stores welcome young couples who want to feather their nests.*

fed up *(informal)* ALSO *(slang)* **fed to the gills** or **fed to the teeth** *adj. phr.* Having had too much of something; at the end of your patience; disgusted; bored; tired. *People get fed up with anyone who brags all the time. I've had enough of his complaints. I'm fed up. He was fed to the teeth with television and sold his set to a cousin. John quit football because he was fed to the gills with practice.*

feel for someone *v. phr., informal* To be able to sympathize with someone's problems. *I can really feel for you, John, for losing your job.*

feel like a new man *v. phr.* To feel healthy, vigorous, and well again after a major physical illness or emotional upheaval. *Ted felt like a new man after his successful heart bypass operation.*

feel one's way *v. phr.* To proceed cautiously by trial and error; probe. *I won't ask her to marry me directly; I will feel my way first.*

feel out *v.* To talk or act carefully with someone and find what he thinks or can do. *The pupils felt out the principal about a party after the game. John felt out his father about letting him have the car that evening. At first the boxers felt each other out.*

feel out of place *v. phr.* To experience the sensation of not belonging in a certain place or company. *Dave felt out of place among all those chess players as he knows nothing about chess.*

feel the pinch *v. phr.* To be short of money; experience monetary difficulties. *If we are going to have a recession, everybody will feel the pinch.*

feel up *v. phr., vulgar, avoidable* To arouse sexually by manual contact. *You mean to tell me that you've been going out for six months and he hasn't ever tried to feel you up?*

feel up to something *v. phr., informal* To feel adequately knowledgeable, strong, or equipped to handle a given task. *Do you feel up to jogging a mile a day with me?*

feet of clay *n. phr.* A hidden fault or weakness in a person which is discovered or shown. *The famous general showed he had feet of clay when he began to drink liquor. The banker seemed to be honest, but he had feet of clay and was arrested for stealing.*

feet on the ground *n. phr.* An understanding of what can be done; sensible ideas. Used with a possessive. *John has his feet on the ground; he knows he cannot learn everything at once. Ted dreams of sudden riches,*

but Henry keeps his feet on the ground and expects to work for his money. Mrs. Smith was a dreamer, but her husband was a man with his feet on the ground.*

fence-sitter *n.* A person unable to pick between two sides; a person who does not want to choose. *Daddy says he is a fence-sitter because he doesn't know which man he wants for President.*

fence-sitting *n. or adj.* Choosing neither side. *You have been fence-sitting for too long. It is time you made up your mind.*

ferret out *literary or* **smell out** *or* **sniff out** *v.* To hunt or drive from hiding; to bring out into the open; search for and find. *John ferreted out the answer to the question in the library. Jane smelled out the boys' secret hiding place in the woods.*

few and far between *adj. phr.* Not many; few and scattered; not often met or found; rare.— Used in the predicate. *People who will work as hard as Thomas A. Edison are few and far between. Places where you can get water are few and far between in the desert. Really exciting games are few and far between.*

fifty-fifty[1] *adv., informal* Equally; evenly. *The two boys divided the marbles they won fifty-fifty. When Dick and Sam bought an old car, they divided the cost fifty-fifty.*

fifty-fifty[2] *adj., informal* **1.** Divided or shared equally. *It will be a fifty-fifty arrangement; half the money for me and half for you.* **2.** Half for and half

against; half good and half bad.
*There is only a fifty-fifty chance
that we will win the game.*

fight fire with fire *v. phr.*
slightly formal, of Biblical origin To fight back in the same
way one was attacked; make a
defense similar to the attack.
*The candidate was determined
to fight fire with fire in the debate.*

fight off *v. phr.* **1.** To struggle
against someone so as to free
oneself; push an attacker back.
Suzy fought off her two attackers in Central Park with a couple of karate chops. **2.** To
strive to overcome something
negative. *After twelve hours at
the computer terminal, Jane
had to fight off her overwhelming desire to go to sleep.*

figure in *v.* **1.** *informal* To add
to a total; remember to put
down in figures. *We figured in
the travel expenses but forgot
the cost of meals.* **2.** To have a
part in; be partly responsible
for. *Joe figured in all our
touchdowns. Mary's good
grades figured in her choice as
class president.*

figure on *v.* **1.** To expect and
think about while making
plans. *We did not figure on
having so many people at the
picnic. He figured on going to
town the next day.* **2.** To depend on; be sure about. *You
can figure on him to be on
time.*

figure out *v.* **1.** To find an answer by thinking about (some
problem or difficulty); solve.
*Tom couldn't figure out the last
problem on the arithmetic test.
Sam couldn't figure out how to
print a program until the*

*teacher showed him how. Mary
couldn't figure out why her
cake tasted so funny until she
found salt mixed in the sugar
bag.* **2.** To learn how to explain; understand. *Laurence is
an odd boy; I can't figure him
out.*

figure up *v. phr.* To calculate;
add up. *If you can figure up
how many phone calls I've
made from your home, I will
pay you right away.*

fill in *v.* **1.** To write words
needed in blanks; put in; fill.
*You should fill in all the blanks
on an application for a job.* **2.**
informal To tell what you
should know. *The new boy
didn't know the rules so Bob
filled him in. The teacher filled
in Mary about class work done
while she was sick.* **3.** To take
another's place; substitute. *The
teacher was sick and Miss Jones
filled in for her.*

fill one's shoes *v. phr.* To take
the place of another and do as
well; to substitute satisfactorily
for. *When Jack got hurt, the
coach had nobody to fill his
shoes. Joe hopes to fill his father's shoes.* See in one's shoes.

fill out *v.* **1.** To put in what is
missing; complete; finish; especially, to complete (a printed
application blank or other
form) by writing the missing
facts in the blank spaces; to
write down facts which are
asked for in (a report or application.) *After Tom passed his
driving test he filled out an application for his driver's license.
The policeman filled out a report of the accident.* **2.** To become heavier and fatter; gain
weight. *When Bill was nineteen*

he began to fill out. The girl was pale and thin after her sickness, but in a few months she filled out.

fill the bill *v. phr., informal* To be just what is needed; be good enough for something; be just right. *The boss was worried about hiring a deaf boy, but after he tried Tom out for a few weeks, he said that Tom filled the bill. I thought I would need a special tool, but this wrench fills the bill.*

filthy rich *adj. phr.* Extremely rich but without cultural refinement; nouveau riche. *"The Murgatroyds are filthy rich," Ted complained. "They are rolling in money but they never learned how to behave properly at a dinner table."*

finders keepers *or* **finders keepers, losers weepers** *informal* Those who find lost things can keep them.—Used usually by children to claim the right to keep something they have found. *I don't have to give it back; it's finders keepers. Finders keepers, losers weepers! It's my knife now!*

find out *v.* **1.** To learn or discover (something you did not know before.) *One morning the baby found out for the first time that she could walk. I don't know how this car works, but I'll soon find out. He watched the birds to find out where they go. Mary was angry when Jane found out her secret.* **2.** To get facts; to get facts about. *He wrote to find out about a job in Alaska. She found out how much the house would cost.* **3.** To discover (someone) doing

wrong; catch. *Some children are bad when no one is watching them, but they are usually found out. The boy knew that i[f] he cheated on the test th[e] teacher would find him out.*

fine-tooth comb *n. phr.* Grea[t] care; careful attention so as no[t] to miss anything. *The polic[e] searched the scene of the crim[e] with a fine-tooth comb fo[r] clues. My room is so clean yo[u] couldn't find dirt if you wen[t] over it with a fine-tooth comb.*

finger in the pie *n. phr., infor-mal* Something to do wit[h] what happens; part interest o[r] responsibility. *When the girl[s] got up a Christmas party, I fe[lt] sure Alice had a finger in th[e] pie. The Jones Company wa[s] chosen to build the new hospita[l] and we knew Mr. Smith had [a] finger in the pie. Jack is a bo[y] with a finger in every pie a[t] school, from dramatics to foot[-] ball.*

firebug *n.* An arsonist; on[e] who willfully sets fire to prop[-] erty. *The police caught the fire[-] bug just as he was about to se[t] another barn ablaze in th[e] country.*

firing squad *n.* A group of sol[-] diers chosen to shoot a pris[-] oner to death or to fire shot[s] over a grave as a tribute. *A dic[-] tator often sends his enemie[s] before a firing squad. The dea[d] general was honored by a firin[g] squad.*

first come, first served *trun-cated sent. informal* If you ar[-] rive first, you will be serve[d] first; people will be waited o[n] in the order they come; th[e] person who comes first wi[ll] have his turn first. *Get in line for your ice cream, boys. First come, first served. The rule in the restaurant is first come, first served. The team's owners announced that tickets for the World Series would be sold on a first come, first served basis only. There are only a few seats left so it's first come, first served.*

first of all *adv. phr.* Chiefly; primarily; as the first thing. *After we get to Chicago, we will, first of all, try to find a reliable used car.*

first-run *adj. phr.* Shown for the first time; new. *The local theater showed only first-run movies.*

fish-and-chips *n. phr.* Fried fish and french fried potatoes. *The family went to a drive-in restaurant and had fish-and-chips.*

fish for *v., informal* To try to get or to find out (something), by hinting or by a roundabout way to try to lead someone else to give or tell you what you want by hinting. *Jerry was always fishing for an invitation to Bob's house. Near examination time, some of the students fish for information.*

fish for a compliment *v. phr.* To try to make someone pay a compliment. *When Jim showed me his new car, I could tell that he was fishing for a compliment.*

fish in muddy *or* **troubled waters** *v. phr.* To take advantage of a troubled or confusing situation; seek personal advantage. *With the police disorganized after the collapse of communism in*

Europe, many criminals started to fish in troubled waters.

fish out of water *n. phr.* A person who is out of his proper place in life; someone who does not fit in. *Because Ed could not swim, he felt like a fish out of water at the beach. She was the only girl at the party not in a formal dress and she felt like a fish out of water.*

fit as a fiddle *adj. phr.* In very good health. *The man was almost 90 years old but fit as a fiddle. Mary rested at home for a few weeks after her operation; then she felt fit as a fiddle.*

fit for *v. phr.* To be suited for; be prepared for. *"What kind of job is Ted fit for?" the social worker asked.*

fit in with *v. phr.* To fall into agreement or accord with. *His plans to take a vacation in early July fit in perfectly with the university schedule.*

fit like a glove *v. phr.* To fit perfectly. *Her new dress fits her like a glove.*

fit out *or* **fit up** *v.* To give things needed; furnish. *The soldiers were fitted out with guns and clothing. The government fitted out warships and got sailors for them. The house was fitted out very nicely. He fitted his room up as a photographic laboratory.*

fit to be tied[1] *adj. phr., informal* Very angry or upset. *She was fit to be tied when she saw the broken glass.*

fit to be tied[2] *adv. phr., substandard* Very hard.—Used for emphasis. *Uncle Willie was laughing fit to be tied at the surprised look on Mother's face.*

fix someone's wagon or **fix someone's little red wagon** *v. phr.*, *informal* **1.** (Said to a child as a threat) to administer a spanking. *Stop that right away or I'll fix your (little red) wagon!* **2.** (Said of an adult) to thwart or frustrate another, to engineer his failure. *If he sues me for slander, I will countersue him for malicious prosecution. That will fix his wagon!*

fix someone up with *v. phr.*, *informal* To help another get a date with a woman or man by arranging a meeting for the two. *Say Joe, can you possibly fix me up with someone this weekend? I am so terribly lonesome!*

fix up *v. phr.* **1.** To repair. *The school is having the old gym fixed up.* **2.** To arrange. *I think I can fix it up with the company so that John gets the transfer he desires.* **3.** To arrange a date that might lead to a romance or even to marriage. *Mary is a great matchmaker; she fixed up Ron and Betty at her recent party.*

fizzle out *v.*, *informal* **1.** To stop burning; die out. *The fuse fizzled out before exploding the firecracker.* **2.** To fail after a good start; end in failure. *The power mower worked fine for a while but then it fizzled out. The party fizzled out when everyone went home early.*

flag down *v.*, *informal* To stop by waving a signal flag or as if waving a signal flag. *The signalman flagged down the freight train. A policeman flagged down the car with his flashlight.*

flare up *v.* **1.** To burn brightly

for a short time especially aft having died down. *The fi flared up again and then die* **2.** To become suddenly angr *The mayor flared up at t reporter's remark. The moth flared up at her children.* **3.** begin again suddenly, esp cially for a short time after quiet time. *Mr. Gray's arthri flared up sometimes. Even aft they had conquered t country, revolts sometim flared up.*

flare-up *n.* The reoccurren of an infection or an arm conflict. *He had a flare-up his arthritis. There was a b flare-up of hostilities in son countries.*

flatfoot *n., slang, derogatory* policeman. *"What does Joe for a living?—He's a flatfoot.*

flat-out *adv. phr.*, *informal* Without hiding anythin plainly; openly. *The stude told his teacher flat-out that was not listening to her.* **2.** top speed; as fast as possibl *He saw two men running fle out from the wild rhinoceros.*

flea in one's ear *n. phr.*, *info mal* An idea or answer that not welcome; an annoying surprisingly sharp reply or hir *I'll put a flea in his ear if bothers me once more.*

flea market *n. phr.* A pla where antiques, second-ha things, and cheap articles a sold, and especially one in t open air. *The local antiq dealers held a flea market a fair on the high-school athle field. There are many outdo flea markets in Europe.*

flesh and blood *n.* **1.** A clo relative (as a father, daughte brother); close relatives. Used in the phrase one's own flesh and blood. *Such an answer from her—and she's my own flesh and blood, too!* **2.** The appearance of being real or alive. *The author doesn't give his characters any flesh and blood.* **3.** The human body. *Before child labor laws, small children often worked 50 or 60 hours a week in factories. It was more than flesh and blood could bear.*

flip one's lid *also* **flip one's wig** *slang* **1.** To lose one's temper. *When that pushy salesman came back Mom really flipped her lid.* **2.** To lose your mind; become insane. *When he offered me three times the pay I was getting, I thought he had flipped his lid.* **3.** To become unreasonably enthusiastic. *She flipped her lid over a hat she saw in the store window. He's flipped his lid over that new actress.*

flip out *v. phr., slang, informal* To go insane, to go out of one's mind. *It is impossible to talk to Joe today—he must have flipped out.*

flunk out *v. phr.* To have to withdraw from school or college because of too many failing grades. *Fred flunked out of college during his junior year.*

flush it *v. phr., slang* **1.** To fail (something). *I really flushed it in my math course.* **2.** *interj., used imperatively* Expression registering refusal to believe something considered stupid or false. *"You expect me to buy that story? Flush it!"*

fly blind *v. phr.* **1.** To fly an airplane by instruments alone. *In the heavy fog he had to fly blind.* **2.** *informal* To do something without understanding what you are doing. *I'm glad the car runs now; I was flying blind when I fixed it. He's flying blind when he talks about philosophy.*

fly-by-night[1] *adj.* Set up to make a lot of money in a hurry, then disappear so people can't find you to complain about poor work, etc.; not trustworthy; not reliable. *Mrs. Blank bought her vacuum cleaner from a new company; when she tried to have it fixed, she found it was a fly-by-night business.*

fly-by-night[2] *n., informal* **1.** A company that sells many cheap things for a big profit and then disappears. *A dependable company honors its guarantees, but a fly-by-night only wants your money.* **2.** A person who does not pay his bills, but sneaks away (as at night.) *Hotels are bothered by fly-by-nights.*

fly by the seat of one's pants *v. phr., slang* To fly an airplane by feel and instinct rather than with the help of the instruments. *Many pilots in World War I had to fly by the seat of their pants.*

flying high *adj., slang* Very happy; joyful. *Jack was flying high after his team won the game.*

fly in the face of *or* **fly in the teeth of** *v. phr.* To ignore; go against; show disrespect or disregard for. *You can't fly in the face of good business rules and expect to be successful. Floyd's friends tried to help him, but he flew in the teeth of their advice and soon became a drunkard.*

fly in the ointment *n. phr.*, *informal* An unpleasant part of a pleasant thing; something small that spoils your fun. *We had a lot of fun at the beach; the only fly in the ointment was George's cutting his foot on a piece of glass. Your new job sounds too good to be true—interesting work, high pay, short hours. Isn't there any fly in the ointment?*

fly off the handle *v. phr.*, *informal* To become very angry. *John flew off the handle whenever Mary made a mistake. The children's noise made the man next door fly off the handle.*

fly the coop *v. phr.*, *slang* To leave suddenly and secretly; run away. *The robbers flew the coop before the police arrived. His partner flew the coop with all the money.*

flying visit *n. phr.* A visit of very short duration. *Tom came to New York for only a flying visit. We had hardly eaten lunch when he had to leave.*

foam at the mouth *v. phr.*, *slang* To be very angry, like a mad dog. *By the time Uncle Henry had the third flat tire he was really foaming at the mouth.*

fob off *v.*, *informal* 1. To get something false accepted as good or real. *The peddler fobbed off pieces of glass as diamonds.* 2. To put aside; not really answer but get rid of. *Her little brother asked where she was going, but she fobbed him off with an excuse.*

follow in one's footsteps also **follow in one's tracks** *v. phr.* To follow someone's example; follow someone exactly. *He followed in his father's footsteps and became a doctor.*

follow one's nose *v. phr.*, *informal* 1. To go straight ahead; continue in the same direction. *Just follow your nose and you'll get there.* 2. To go any way you happen to think of. *Oh, I don't know just where I want to go. I'll just follow my nose and see what happens.*

follow suit *v. phr.* 1. To play a card of the same color and kind that another player has put down. *When diamonds were led, I had to follow suit.* 2. To do as someone else has done; follow someone's example. *When the others went swimming, I followed suit.*

follow through *v. phr.* 1. To finish a movement that you have started; continue an action to its natural ending. *A football passer should follow through after he throws the ball.* 2. To finish an action that you have started. *Bob drew plans for a table for his mother, but he did not follow through by making it.*

follow up *v. phr.*, *informal* 1. To chase or follow closely and without giving up. *The Indians followed up the wounded buffalo until it fell dead.* 2. Make (one action) more successful by doing something more. *After Mary sent a letter to apply for a job; she followed it up by going to talk to the personnel manager. The doctor followed up Billy's operation with x-rays and special exercises to make his foot stronger.* 3a. To hunt for (more news about something that has already been in the newspapers, radio or TV news); find more about. *The day after news of the fire at Brown's store, the newspaper sent a reporter to follow up Mr. Brown's future plans.* **3b.** To print or broadcast (more news about some happening that has been in the news before). *The fire story was printed Monday, and Tuesday's paper followed it up by saying that Mr. Brown planned to build a bigger and better store at the same place.*

follow-up *n.* Additional work or research by means of which an earlier undertaking's chances of success are increased. *I hope you'll be willing to do a bit of follow-up.*

fond of Having a liking for; attracted to by strong liking. *Alan is fond of candy. Uncle Bill was the children's favorite, and he was fond of them too.*

food for thought *n. phr.* Something to think about or worth thinking about; something that makes you think. *The teacher told John that she wanted to talk to his father, and that gave John food for thought. There is much food for thought in this book.*

fool around *or* **mess around** *or* **play around** *or* **monkey around** *v., informal* **1.** To spend time playing, fooling, or joking instead of being serious or working; waste time. *If you go to college, you must work, not fool around. The boys fooled around all afternoon in the park.* **2.** To treat or handle carelessly. *Bob cut himself by fooling around with a sharp knife. Suzie says she wishes John would quit playing around with the girls and get* married. **3.** *or* **fiddle around** To work or do something in an irregular or unplanned way; tinker. *Jimmy likes to monkey around with automobile engines. Alice is fooling around with the piano in her spare time.*

foot in the door *n. phr., informal* The first step toward getting or doing something; a start toward success; opening. *Don't let Jane get her foot in the door by joining the club or soon she'll want to be president.*

foot the bill *v. phr.* To cover the expenses of; pay for something. *The bride's father footed two-thirds of the bill for his daughter's wedding.*

footloose and fancy-free *adj. phr.* Free and free to do what one wants (said of unmarried men). *Ron is a merry bachelor and seems to enjoy greatly being footloose and fancy-free.*

for all 1. In spite of; even with; despite.—Used for contrast. *For all his city ways, he is a country boy at heart. There may be mistakes occasionally, but for all that, it is the best book on the subject. For all his money, he was very unhappy.* **2.** *also* **for aught** To the extent that.—Used like a negative with *care* and *know. For all I care, you can throw it away. For all he knows, we might be in Boston.*

for all one is worth With all of your strength; as hard as you can. *Roger ran for all he was worth to catch the bus.*

for all one knows *adv. phr.* According to the information one has; probably. *For all we know, Ron and Beth might* have eloped and been married in a French chateau.

for all that *adv. phr.* In spite of what has been said, alleged, or rumored. *Well, for all that, we think that she is still the most deserving candidate for Congress.*

for all the world *adv. phr.* **1.** Under no circumstances. *Betty said she wouldn't marry Jake for all the world.* **2.** Precisely; exactly. *It began for all the world like a successful baseball season for the UIC Flames, when suddenly they lost to the Blue Demons.*

for a song *adv. phr., informal* At a low price; for a bargain price; cheaply. *He sold the invention for a song and its buyers were the ones who got rich. They bought the house for a song and sold it a few years later at a good profit.*

for better or worse *or* **for better or for worse** *adv. phr.* **1.** With good or bad effect, depending on how one looks at the matter. *The historian did justice, for better or worse, to the careers of several famous men.* **2.** Under any eventuality; forever; always. *Alex and Masha decided to leave Moscow and come to Chicago, for better or for worse.* **3.** (Marriage vows) Forever, for as long as one may live. *With this ring I thee wed, for richer or poorer, in sickness and in health, for better or worse, til death do us part.*

force one's hand *v. phr.* To make you do something or tell what you will do sooner than planned. *Ben did not want to tell where he was going, but his friend forced his hand. Mr.*

Smith planned to keep his land until prices went up, but he had so many doctor bills that it forced his hand.

for crying out loud *informal* Used as an exclamation to show that you feel surprised or cross. *For crying out loud, look who's here! For crying out loud! that's the third time you've done it wrong.*

for days on end *adv. phr.* For a long time; for many days. *The American tourists tried to get used to Scottish pronunciation for days on end, but still couldn't understand what the Scots were saying.*

for dear life *adv. phr.* As though afraid of losing your life. *He was running for dear life toward town. When the horse began to run, she held on for dear life.*

forever and a day *adv. phr., informal* For a seemingly endless time; forever; always. Used for emphasis. *We waited forever and a day to find out who won the contest. They promised to remain friends forever and a day.*

forever and ever *adv. phr.* Forever; always.—Used for emphasis, usually about spiritual things. *God will live forever and ever.*

for good *also* **for good and all** Permanently, forever, for always. *The lost money was gone for good. He hoped that the repairs would stop the leak for good. When John graduated from school, he decided that he was done with study for good and all.*

for good measure *adv. phr.* As something more added to what is expected or needed; as an extra. *He sold me the car at a cheap price and included the radio for good measure. She puts in the spices the recipe calls for and then adds an extra pinch for good measure.* .

for Heaven's sake! *adv. phr.* Please. *"Help me, for Heaven's sake!" the injured man cried.*

for hours on end *adv. phr.* For many hours; for a very long time. *We have been trying to get this computer going for hours on end, but we need serious professional help.*

for keeps *adv. phr.* **1.** For the winner to keep. *They played marbles for keeps.* **2.** *informal* For always; forever. *He left town for keeps.* **3.** Seriously, not just for fun. *This is not a joke, it's for keeps.*—Often used in the phrase *play for keeps. The policeman knew that the robber was trying to shoot him. He was playing for keeps.*

fork over a lot of money *v. phr.* To pay an excessive amount of money often unwillingly. *"According to my divorce decree," Alan complained, "I have to fork over a lot of money to my ex-wife every month."*

fork over *or* **fork out** *also* **fork up** *v.* To pay; pay out. *He had to fork over fifty dollars to have the car repaired.*

for love or money *adv. phr.* For anything; for any price. Used in negative sentences. *I wouldn't give him my dog for love or money.*

for shame *interj.* Shame on you; you should be ashamed of yourself.—An exclamation no longer in common use, having been largely replaced by *shame* on you. *"For shame, John, taking the toy from your baby brother!"*

for short *adv. phr.* So as to make shorter; as an abbreviation or nickname. *The boy's name was Humperdink, or "Dink" for short. The National Broadcasting Company is called NBC for short.*

for sure *or* **for certain** *adv. phr.* **1.** Without doubt; certainly; surely. *He couldn't tell for sure from a distance whether it was George or Tom. He didn't know for certain which bus to take. I know for certain that he has a car.* **2.** *slang* Certain. *"That car is smashed so badly it's no good any more." "That's for sure!"*

for that matter *adv. phr.* With regard to that; about that. *I don't know, and for that matter, I don't care. Alice didn't come, and for that matter, she didn't even telephone.*

for the asking *adv. phr.* By asking; by asking for it; on request. *John said I could borrow his bike any time. It was mine for the asking. Teacher said her advice was free for the asking.*

for the better *adj. or adv. phr.* With a better result; for something that is better. *The doctor felt that moving Father to a dry climate would be for the better. The new large print in the book is a change for the better.*

for the birds *adj. phr., slang* Not interesting; dull; silly; foolish; stupid. *I think history is for the birds. I saw that movie. It's for the birds.*

for the life of one *adv., informal* No matter how hard you try.—Used for emphasis with negative statements. *I can't for the life of me remember his name.*

foul ball *n.* A batted baseball that lands outside the foul line. *Mickey hit a long foul ball that landed on the roof.*

foul line *n.* **1.** Either of two lines separating fair from foul ground in baseball. *Willie hit the ball just inside the foul line for a double.* **2.** A line across the upper end of a bowling alley across which a bowler must not step. *John bowled a strike but it didn't count because he stepped over the foul line.* **3.** A line on the floor in front of the basket in basketball, from which foul shots are made. *Tony scored eight points from the foul line.*

foul play *n.* Treachery; a criminal act (such as murder). *After they discovered the dead body, the police suspected foul play. "She must have met with foul play," the chief inspector said when they couldn't find the 12-year-old girl who had disappeared.*

foul up *v., informal* **1.** To make dirty. *The birds fouled up his newly washed car.* **2.** To tangle up. *He tried to throw a lasso but he got the rope all fouled up.* **3.** To ruin or spoil by stupid mistakes; botch. *He fouled the whole play up by forgetting his part.* **4.** To make a mistake; to blunder. *Blue suit and brown socks! He had fouled up again.* **5.** To go wrong. *Why do some people foul up and become criminals?*

foul-up *n.* (stress on *foul*) **1.** *informal* A confused situation; confusion; mistake. *The lunch-eon was handled with only one or two foul-ups.* **2.** *informal* A breakdown. *There was a foul-up in his car's steering mechanism.* **3.** *slang* A person who fouls up or mixes things. *He had gotten a reputation as a foul-up.*

fraidy-cat *or* **fraid-cat** *or* **scaredy-cat** *or* **scared cat** *n., informal* A shy person; someone who is easily frightened.—Usually used by or to children. *Tom was a fraidy-cat and wouldn't go in the water.*

frame of mind *n. phr.* One's mental outlook; the state of one's psychological condition. *There is no use trying to talk to him while he is in such a negative frame of mind.*

freak *n., slang* **1.** A good, or well-liked person, the opposite of a square, someone with long hair and who is likely (or known) to be a marijuana smoker or a drug user. Also said of homosexuals. *Is Joe a square, establishment type?—Oh no, he's a regular freak.* **2.** _____ **freak** An enthusiast, a person who does or cultivates something in excess. *Ellen is a film-freak.*

freak-out[1] *n., slang* An act of losing control; a situation that is bizarre or unusual. *The party last night was a regular freak-out.*

freak out[2] *v. phr., slang* To lose control over one's conscious self due to the influence of hallucinogenic drugs. *Joe freaked out last night.*

free and easy *adj.* Not strict; relaxed or careless. *The teacher was free and easy with his students. He had a free and easy* *way of acting that attracted many friends. They were free and easy with their money and it was soon gone.*

free enterprise *n. phr.* A system in which private business is controlled by as few government rules as possible. *The United States is proud of its free enterprise.*

free hand *n.* Great freedom. *The teacher had a free hand in her classroom. Bob put paint on the fence with a free hand.*

freeload *v.* To have oneself supported in terms of food and housing at someone else's expense. *When are you guys going to stop freeloading and do some work?*

free rein *n.* Freedom to do what you want. *The king had free rein in his country. Father is strict with the children, but Mother gives them free rein.*

free-for-all *n.* **1.** Unlimited, free access to something everybody wants. *The Smith's party was a lavish free-for-all; everybody could eat and drink as much as they wanted.* **2.** A barroom, tavern, or street fight in which everybody participates. *The celebration after the soccer game victory turned into an uncontrollable free-for-all.*

freeze out *v., informal* To force out or keep from a share or part in something by unfriendly or dishonest treatment. *The other boys froze John out of the club.*

freeze over *v.* To become covered with ice. *The children wanted the lake to freeze over so they could ice-skate.*

from hand to hand *adv. phr.* From one person to another and another. *The box of candy was passed from hand to hand. Jane brought her engagement ring, and it passed from hand to hand until all the girls had admired it.*

from rags to riches *adv. phr.* Suddenly making a fortune; becoming rich overnight. *The Smiths went from rags to riches when they unexpectedly won the lottery.*

from scratch *adv. phr., informal* With no help from anything done before; from the beginning; from nothing. *Dick built a radio from scratch. In sewing class, Mary already knew how to sew a little, but Jane had to start from scratch.*

from the bottom of one's heart or **with all one's heart** *adv. phr.* With great feeling; sincerely. *A mother loves a baby from the bottom of her heart. John thanked his rescuer from the bottom of his heart. The people welcomed the returning soldiers from the bottom of their hearts.*

from the heart *adv.* Sincerely; honestly. *John always speaks from the heart.*

from time to time *adv. phr.* Not often; not regularly; sometimes; occasionally; at one time and then again at another time. *Even though the Smiths have moved, we still see them from time to time. Mother tries new recipes from time to time, but the children never like them.*

from way back *adv. phr.* From a previous time; from a long time ago. *They have known one another from way back when they went to the same elementary school.*

fuck around v. phr., vulgar, avoidable **1.** To be promiscuous. *John fucks around with the secretaries.* **2.** To play at something without purpose, to mess around. *He doesn't accomplish anything, because he fucks around so much.*

fuck off v. phr., vulgar, avoidable **1.** Go away! *Can't you see you're bothering me? Fuck off!* **2.** To be lazy. *John said "I don't feel like working, so I'll fuck off today."*

fuck up v. phr., vulgar, avoidable To make a mess of something or oneself. *Because he was totally unprepared, he fucked up his exam. He is so fucked up he doesn't know whether he is coming or going.*

fuck-up n. vulgar, avoidable A mess; a badly botched situation. *What a fuck-up the dissolution of the USSR created!*

fuddy-duddy n. A person whose ideas and habits are old-fashioned. *His students think Professor Jones is an old fuddy-duddy.*

full blast adv. At full capacity. *With all the research money at their disposal, the new computer firm was going ahead full blast.*

full-bodied adj. Mature; of maximum quality. *The wines from that region in California have a rich, full-bodied flavor.*

full-fledged adj. Having everything that is needed to be something; complete. *A girl needs three years of training to be a full-fledged nurse. The book was a full-fledged study of American history.*

full of beans adj. phr., slang **1.** Full of pep; feeling good; in high spirits. *The football team was full of beans after winning the tournament. The children were full of beans as they got ready for a picnic.* **2.** also **full of prunes**. Being foolish and talking nonsense. *You are full of prunes; that man's not 120 years old.*

full tilt adv. At full speed; at high speed. *He ran full tilt into the door and broke his arm.*

fun and games n., slang, informal **1.** A party or other entertaining event. **2.** Something trivially easy. **3.** Petting, or sexual intercourse. **4.** (Ironically) An extraordinary difficult task. *How was your math exam? (With a dismayed expression):—Yeah, it was all fun and games, man.*

fun house n. A place where people see many funny things and have tricks played on them to make them laugh or have a good time. *The boys and girls had a good time looking at themselves in mirrors in the fun house.*

funny bone n. **1.** The place at the back of the elbow that hurts like electricity when accidentally hit. *He hit his funny bone on the arm of the chair.* **2.** or informal **crazy bone** Sense of humor; understanding jokes. *Her way of telling the story tickled his funny bone.*

G

gain ground v. phr. **1.** To go forward; move ahead. *The soldiers fought hard and began to gain ground.* **2.** To become stronger; make progress; improve. *The sick man gained ground after being near death. Under Lincoln, the Republican Party gained ground.*

gallows' humor n. phr. Bitter joke(s) that make fun of a very serious matter, e.g. death, imprisonment, etc. *When the criminal was led to the electric chair on Monday morning, he said, "Nice way to start the week, eh?"*

gang up on or **gang up against** v. phr., informal To jointly attack someone, either physically or verbally; take sides in a group against an individual. *The class bully was stronger than all the other boys, so they had to gang up on him to put him in his place.*

garbage down v. phr., slang To eat eagerly and at great speed without much regard for manners or social convention. *The children garbaged down their food.*

gas up v., informal **1.** To fill the gasoline tank of. *The mechanics gassed up the planes for their long trip.* **2.** To fill the tank with gasoline. *The big truck stopped at the filling station and gassed up.*

gee whiz interj., informal Used as an exclamation to show surprise or other strong feeling. Rare in written English. *Gee whiz! I am late again.*

generation gap n., informal, hackneyed phrase The difference in social values, philosophies, and manners between children and their parents, teachers and relatives which causes a lack of understanding between them and frequently leads to violent confrontations. *My daughter is twenty and I am forty, but we have no generation gap in our family.*

generous to a fault adj. phr. Excessively generous. *Generous to a fault, my Aunt Elizabeth gave away all her rare books to her old college.*

get across v. **1.** To explain clearly, make (something) clear; to make clear the meaning of. *Mr. Brown is a good coach because he can get across the plays.* **2.** To become clear. *The teacher tried to explain the problem, but the explanation did not get across to the class.*

get a fix or **give a fix** v. phr., slang, drug culture To provide (someone) with an injection of narcotics. *The neighborhood pusher gave Joe a fix.*

get a fix on v. phr., informal Receive a reading of a distant object by electronic means, as by radar or sonar. *Can you get a fix on the submarine?*

get after v., informal **1.** To try or try again to make someone do what he is supposed to do. *Ann's mother gets after her to*

119

hang up her clothes. **2.** To scold or make an attack on. *Bob's mother got after him for tracking mud into the house. The police are getting after the crooks in the city.*

get a grip on *v. phr.* To take firm control of something. *If Tim wants to keep his job, he had better get a grip on himself and start working harder.*

get ahead *v.* **1.** *informal* To become successful. *Mr. Brown was a good lawyer and soon began to get ahead. The person with a good education finds it easier to get ahead.* **2.** To be able to save money; get out of debt. *In a few more years he will be able to get ahead. After Father pays all the doctor bills, maybe we can get a little money ahead and buy a car.*

get a head start on *v. phr.* To receive preliminary help or instruction in a particular subject so that the recipient is in a favorable position compared to his or her peers. *At our school, children get a head start on their reading ability thanks to a special program.*

get a kick out of *v. phr.* To be greatly thrilled; derive pleasure from. *Tom and Marty get a kick out of playing four hands on the piano.*

get a line on *v. phr.* To receive special, sometimes even confidential, information about something. *Before Bill accepted his new position, he got a line on how the business was being run.*

get a load of *v. phr., slang* **1.** To take a good look at; see (something unusual or interesting.)—Often used to show surprise or admiration. *Get a load of that pretty girl! Get a load of Dick's new car!* **2.** To listen to carefully or with interest, especially exciting news.—Often used as a command: *Get a load of this: Alice got married yesterday!*

get along *also* **get on** *v.* **1.** To go or move away; move on. *The policeman told the boys to get along.* **2.** To go forward; make progress; advance. *John is getting along well in school. He is learning more every day.* **3.** To advance; become old or late. *It is getting along towards sundown. Grandmother is 68 and getting along.* **4.** To get or make what you need; manage. *It isn't easy to get along in the jungle. We can get along on $100 a week.* **5.** To live or work together in a friendly way; agree, cooperate; not fight or argue. *We don't get along with the Jones family. Jim and Jane get along fine together. Don't be hard to get along with.*

get a move on *informal or slang*
get a wiggle on *v. phr.* To hurry up; get going.—Often used as a command. *Get a move on, or you will be late.*

get a raise *v. phr.* To receive an increment in salary. *Because of his good work, Ted got a raise after May 1.*

get a rise out of *v. phr., slang* **1.** To have some fun with (a person) by making (him) angry; tease. *The boys get a rise out of Joe by teasing him about his girl friend.* **2.** *vulgar, avoidable* To be sexually aroused (said of males) *Jim always gets a rise out of watching adult movies.*

get around v. **1a.** To go to different places; move about. *Mary's father really gets around; Monday he was in Washington; Wednesday he was in Chicago; and today he is in New York. Fred broke his leg, but he is able to get about on crutches.* **1b.** *or* **get about** To become widely known especially by being talked about. *Bad news gets around quickly.* **2a.** *informal* To get by a trick or flattery what you want from (someone). *Mary knows how to get around her father.* **2b.** *informal* To find a way of not obeying or doing; escape from. *Some people try to get around the tax laws. John did not weigh enough to join the Navy, but he got around that; he drank a lot of water before his physical examination.*

get around to v. To do (something) after putting it off; find time for. *Mr. Lee hopes to get around to washing his car next Saturday.*

get at v. **1.** To reach an understanding of; find out the meaning. *This book is very hard to get at.* **2.** To do harm to. *The cat is on the chair trying to get at the canary.* **3.** To have a chance to do; attend to. *I hope I have time to get at my homework tonight.* **4.** To mean; aim at; hint at. *What was Betty getting at when she said she knew our secret? What the teacher was getting at in this lesson was that it is important to speak correctly.*

get away v. **1.** To get loose or get free; become free from being held or controlled; succeed in leaving; escape. *As Jim was trying the bat, it got away from him and hit Tom. Someone left the door open, and the puppy got away. Mary tried to catch a butterfly, but it got away from her. The bank robbers used a stolen car to get away. If Mr. Graham can get away from his store this afternoon, he will take Johnny fishing.* **2.** To begin; start. *We got away early in the morning on the first day of our vacation. The race got away to a fast start.*

getaway car n. phr. A vehicle parked near the scene of a crime in which the criminals escape. *The police intercepted the getaway car at a major crossroads.*

get away with v., *informal* To do (something bad or wrong) without being caught or punished. *Some students get away without doing their homework.*

get away with murder v. phr., *informal* To do something very bad without being caught or punished. *John is scolded if he is late with his homework, but Robert gets away with murder. Mrs. Smith lets her children get away with murder.*

get a word in or **get a word in edgewise** also **get a word in edgeways** v. phr. To find a chance to say something when others are talking. *The little boy listened to the older students and finally got in a word. Mary talked so much that Jack couldn't get a word in edgewise.*

get back at v., *informal* To do something bad to (someone who has done something bad to you) hurt in return. *John* *played a joke on Henry, and next day Henry got back at him. The elephant waited many years to get back at the man who fed him red pepper.*

get back on one's feet *v. phr.* To once again become financially solvent; regain one's former health or income, or health. *Max got back on his feet soon after his open heart surgery. Tom's business was ruined due to the inflation, but he got back on his feet again.*

get behind *v.* **1.** To go too slowly; be late; do something too slowly. *The post office got behind in delivering Christmas mail.* **2.** *informal* To support; help. *A club is much better if members get behind their leaders. We got behind Mary to be class president.* **3.** *informal* To explain; find out the reason for. *The police are questioning many people to try and get behind the bank robbery.*

get by *v., informal* **1.** To be able to get past; pass. *The cars moved to the curb so that the fire engine could get by.* **2.** To satisfy the need or demand. *Mary can get by with her old coat this winter. The janitor does just enough work to get by.* **3.** Not to be caught and scolded or punished. *The soldier thought he could get by with his dirty rifle. The boy got by without answering the teacher's question because a visitor came in.*

get cracking *v. phr., slang, informal* To hurry up, to start moving fast. (Used mostly as an imperative). *Come on, you guys, let's get cracking! (Let's hurry up!)*

get down to *v., informal* To get started on, being on. *Joe wasted a lot of time before he got down to work. Let's get down to work.*

get down to brass tacks *also* **get down to cases** *v. phr., informal* To begin the most important work or business; get started on the most important things to talk about or know. *The men talked about little things and then got down to brass tacks. A busy doctor wants his patients to get down to brass tacks.*

get down to business *or* **work** *v. phr.* To start being serious; begin to face a problem to be solved, or a task to be accomplished. *Gentlemen, I'm afraid the party is over and we must get down to business.*

get even *v., informal* **1.** To owe nothing. *Mr. Johnson has a lot of debts, but in a few years he will get even.* **2.** To do something bad to pay someone back for something bad; get revenge; hurt back. *Jack is waiting to get even with Bill for tearing up his notebook. Last April First Mr. Harris got fooled by Joe, and this year he will get even.*

get going *v., informal* **1.** To excite; stir up and make angry. *The boys' teasing gets John going. Talking about her freckles gets Mary going.* **2.** *or chiefly British* **get cracking** To begin to move; get started. *The teacher told Walter to get going on his history lesson. The foreman told the workmen to get cracking. Let's get going. It's almost supper time.*

get hitched *v. phr.* To get

married. *After a long period of dating, Fred and Mary finally got hitched.*

get hold of v. **1.** To get possession of. *Little children sometimes get hold of sharp knives and cut themselves.* **2.** To find a person so you can speak with him. *Mr. Thompson spent several hours trying to get hold of his lawyer.*

get in v. phr. **1.** To be admitted. *Andy wants to go to medical school but his grades aren't good enough for him to get in.* **2.** To arrive. *What time does the plane from New York get in?* **3.** To enter. *"Get in the car, and let's go," Tom said in a hurry.* **4.** To put in stock; receive. *The store just got in a new shipment of shoes from China.*

get in on v. phr. To be permitted to participate; become privy to; be included. *This is your chance to get in on a wonderful deal with the new company if you're willing to make an investment.*

get in on the ground floor v. phr. To be one of the first members or employees to participate in the growth of a firm, educational institution, etc. *Elliott got in on the ground floor and made a fortune at the company. Mr. Smith, who joined the new college as an instructor, got in on the ground floor, and wound up as its president after twenty years.*

get it all together v. phr. **1.** To be in full possession and control of one's mental faculties; have a clear purpose well pursued. *You've sure got it all together, haven't you?* **2.**

Retaining one's self-composure under pressure. *A few minutes after the burglars left he got it all together and called the police.* **3.** To be well built, stacked (said of girls and women.) *Sue's sure got it all together, hasn't she?*

get lost v. phr., slang Go away!—Used as a command. *Get lost! I want to study. John told Bert to get lost.*

get off v. **1.** To come down from or out of. *The ladder fell, and Tom couldn't get off the roof. The bus stopped, the door opened, and Father got off.* **2.** To take off. *Joe's mother told him to get his wet clothes off.* **3.** To get away; leave. *Mr. Johnson goes fishing whenever he can get off from work. William got off early in the morning.* **4.** To go free. *Mr. Andrews got off with a $5 fine when he was caught passing a stop sign.* **5.** To make (something) go. *The halfback got off a long pass. John got a letter off to his grandmother.* **6.** To tell. *The governor got off several jokes at the beginning of his speech.*

get off easy v. phr., informal To have only a little trouble; escape something worse. *The children who missed school to go to the fair got off easy. John got off easy because it was the first time he had taken his father's car without permission.*

get off one's back v. phr., slang, colloquial To stop criticizing or nagging someone. *"Get off my back! Can't you see how busy I am?"*

get off one's case or **back** or **tail** v. phr. To stop bothering and constantly checking up on someone; quit hounding one. *"Get off my case!" he cried angrily. "You're worse than the cops."* Contrast on one's case.

get off on the wrong foot *v. phr.* To make a bad start; begin with a mistake. *Peggy got off on the wrong foot with her new teacher; she chewed gum in class and the teacher didn't like it.*

get off the ground *v. phr., informal* To make a successful beginning; get a good start; go ahead; make progress. *Our plans for a party didn't get off the ground because no one could come.*

get off to a flying or running start *v. phr.* To have a promising or successful beginning. *Ron got off to a flying start in business school when he got nothing but A's.*

get on *or* **get onto** *v., informal* **1.** To speak to (someone) roughly about something he did wrong; blame; scold. *Mrs. Thompson got on the girls for not keeping their rooms clean. The fans got on the new shortstop after he made several errors.* **2.** To grow older. *Work seems harder these days; I'm getting on, you know.*

get one down *v. phr., informal* **1.** To make (someone) unhappy; cause low spirits; cause discouragement. *Low grades are getting Helen down. Three straight losses got the team down.* **2.** To swallow; digest. *The medicine was so bitter I couldn't get it down.* **3.** To depress a person's spirit. *Working at such an awful job got Mike down.*

get one's back up *v. phr., informal* To become or make angry or stubborn. *Fred got his back up when I said he was wrong. Our criticisms of his actions just got his back up.*

get one's brains fried *v. phr., slang also used colloquially* **1.** To sit in the sun and sunbathe for an excessive length of time. *Newcomers to Hawaii should be warned not to sit in the sun too long—they'll get their brains fried.* **2.** To get high on drugs. *He can't make a coherent sentence anymore—he's got his brains fried.*

get one's dander up *or* **get one's Irish up** *v. phr.* To become or make angry. *The boy got his dander up because he couldn't go to the store. The children get the teacher's dander up when they make a lot of noise.*

get one's feet wet *v. phr., informal* To begin; do something for the first time. *The party was at Bill's house and when Ruth and I got there the party had already started. "Jump right in and don't be afraid to get your feet wet," said Bill. "It's not hard to dance once you get your feet wet," said the teacher.*

get one's goat *v. phr., informal* To make a person disgusted or angry. *The boy's laziness all summer got his father's goat. The slow service at the cafe got Mr. Robinson's goat.*

get one's rear in gear *v. phr., slang* To hurry up, to get going. *I'm gonna have to get my rear in gear.*

get one's teeth into *or* **sink one's teeth into** *v. phr., informal* To have something real or solid to think about; go to work on seriously; struggle with. *After dinner, John got his teeth into the algebra lesson. Frank chose a subject for his report that he could sink his teeth into.*

get on one's nerves *v. phr.* To make you nervous. *John's noisy eating habits get on your nerves. Children get on their parents' nerves by asking so many questions.*

get on the stick *v. phr., slang, informal* To stop being idle and to start working vigorously. *All right, man, let's get on the stick!*

get over *v.* **1.** To finish. *Tom worked fast to get his lesson over.* **2.** To pass over. *It was hard to get over the muddy road.* **3.** To get well from; recover from. *The man returned to work after he got over his illness.* **4.** To accept or forget (a sorrow or surprise.) *It is hard to get over the death of a member of your family. We could not get over the speed of Mary's recovery from pneumonia.*

get rattled *v. phr.* To become confused, overexcited, or nervous. *The thief got so rattled when he saw the police following him that he drove his car into a ditch.*

get set *v. phr.* To get ready to start. *The runners got set. The seniors are getting set for the commencement.*

get something out of one's system *v. phr.* **1.** To eliminate some food item or drug from one's body. *John will feel much better once he gets the addictive sleeping pills out of his system.* **2.** To free oneself of yearning for something in order to liber-

ate oneself from an unwanted preoccupation. *Ted bought a new cabin cruiser that he'd been wanting for a long time, and he says he is glad that he's finally got it out of his system.*

get stuck *v. phr.* **1.** To be victimized; be cheated. *The Smiths sure got stuck when they bought that secondhand car; it broke down just two days after they got it.* **2.** To become entrapped or embroiled in a physical, emotional, or social obstacle so as to be unable to free oneself. *Last winter our car got stuck in the snow and we had to walk home. Poor Jeff is stuck in a terrible job. Tom and Jane are stuck in a bad marriage.*

get the ax *v. phr., slang* **1.** To be fired from a job. *Poor Joe got the ax at the office yesterday.* **2.** To be dismissed from school for improper conduct, such as cheating. *Joe got caught cheating on his final exam and he got the ax.* **3.** To have a quarrel with one's sweetheart or steady ending in a termination of the relationship. *Joe got the ax from Betsie—they won't see each other again.*

get the ball rolling *or* **set the ball rolling** *or* **start the ball rolling** *informal* To start an activity or action; make a beginning; begin. *George started the ball rolling at the party by telling a new joke.*

get the better of *or* **get the best of** *v. phr.* **1.** To win over, beat; defeat. *Our team got the best of the visitors in the last quarter. George got the better of Robert in a game of checkers. When the opposing player fouled*

John, John let his anger get the better of his good sense and hit the boy back. Dave wanted to study till midnight, but sleepiness got the best of him. **2.** or **have the best of** or **have the better of** To win or be ahead in (something); gain most from (something). *Bill traded an old bicycle tire for a horn; he got the best of that deal. Our team had the best of it today, but they may lose the game tomorrow. The champion had all the better of it in the last part of the fight.*

get the eye *v. phr., informal* **1.** To be looked at with interest and liking. *The pretty girl got the eye as she walked past the boys on the street corner.* **2.** To be looked at or stared at, especially in a cold, unfriendly way. *When Mary asked if she could take home the fur coat and pay later, she got the eye from the clerk.*

get the feel of *v. phr.* To become used to or learn about, especially by feeling or handling; get used to the experience or feeling of; get skill in. *John had never driven a big car, and it took a while for him to get the feel of it. You'll get the feel of the job after you've been there a few weeks.*

get the go-ahead or **get the green light** *v. phr.* To receive the permission or signal to start or to proceed. *We had to wait until we got the go-ahead on our research project.*

get the goods on or **have the goods on** *v. phr. slang* To find out true and, often, bad information about; discover what is wrong with; be able to prove the guilt of. *Tell the truth, Johnny. We know who your girl is because we've got the goods on you. The police had the goods on the burglar before he came to trial.*

get the lowdown on *v. phr.* To receive the full inside information on a person or thing. *We need to get the lowdown on Peter before we can decide whether or not to hire him.*

get the message or **get the word** *v. phr., slang* To understand clearly what is meant. *The principal talked to the students about being on time, and most of them got the message. Mary hinted to her boyfriend that she wanted to break up, but he didn't get the message.*

get the sack *v. phr., slang* **1.** To be fired or dismissed from work. *John got the sack at the factory last week.* **2.** To be told by one's lover that the relationship is over. *Joanna gave Sam the sack.*

get the show on the road *v. phr., informal* To start a program; get work started. *It was several years before the rocket scientists got the show on the road.*

get the worst of also **have the worst of** *v. phr.* To lose; be defeated or beaten in; suffer most. *Joe got the worst of the argument with Molly.* Often used in the phrase *the worst of it.* *If you start a fight with Jim, you may get the worst of it. Bill had the worst of it in his race with Al. Jack traded his knife for a few marbles; he got the* *worst of it in that trade. The driver of the car got the worst of it in the accident.*

get through *v. phr.* **1.** To finish. *Barry got through his homework by late evening.* **2.** To pass a course or an examination. *I got through every one of my courses except mathematics.*

get through one's head *v. phr.* **1.** To understand or believe. *Jack couldn't get it through his head that his father wouldn't let him go to camp if his grades didn't improve. At last Mary got it through her head that she had failed to pass the test.* **2.** To make someone understand or believe. *I'll get it through his head if it takes all night.*

get through to *v.* To be understood by; make (someone) understand. *The little boy could not get through to his housemother. Deaf people sometimes find it hard to get through to strangers. When the rich boy's father lost his money, it took a long time for the idea to get through to him that he'd have to work and support himself.*

get to *v. phr., informal* **1.** To begin by chance; begin to.— Used with a verbal noun or an infinitive. *George meant to save his dollar, but he got to thinking how good an ice cream cone would taste, and he spent it. On a rainy day, Sally got to looking around in the attic and found some old pictures of Father. I got to know Mary at the party. I was just getting to know John when he moved away.* **2.** To have a chance to; be able to. *The Taylors wanted to go to the beach Saturday, but it*

rained and they didn't get to. Did you get to see the king?

get to first base *or* **reach first base** *v. phr.* To make a good start; really begin; succeed. *Joe had a long paper to write for history class, but when the teacher asked for it, Joe hadn't got to first base. Suppose Sam falls in love with Betty. Can he even get to first base with her? George wants to go to college and become a teacher, but I'll be surprised if he even reaches first base. If you don't dress neatly, you won't get to first base when you look for a job.*

get together *v.* To come to an agreement; agree. *Mother says I should finish my arithmetic lesson, and Father says I should mow the lawn. Why don't you two get together?*

get-together *n.* A party; a gathering. *I hate to break up this nice get-together but we must leave. We manage to have a get-together with our old friends once or twice a year.*

get to the bottom of *v. phr.* To find out the real cause of. *The superintendent talked with several students to get to the bottom of the trouble. The doctor made several tests to get to the bottom of the man's headaches.*

get to the heart of *v. phr.* To find the most important facts about or the central meaning of; understand the most important thing about. *You can often get to the heart of people's unhappiness by letting them talk. "If you can find a topic sentence, often it will help you get* *to the heart of the paragraph,"* said the teacher.

get under one's skin *v. phr.* To bother; upset. *The students get under Mary's skin by talking about her freckles. Children who talk too much in class get under the teacher's skin.*

get up *v.* **1.** To get out of bed. *John's mother told him that it was time to get up.* **2.** To stand up; get to your feet. *A man should get up when a woman comes into the room.* **3.** To prepare; get ready. *Mary got up a picnic for her visitor. The students got up a special number of the newspaper to celebrate the school's 50th birthday.* **4.** To dress up. *One of the girls got herself up as a witch for the Halloween party.* **5.** To go ahead. *The wagon driver shouted, "Get up!" to his horses.*

get up *or* **rise with the chickens** *v. phr.* To rise very early in the morning. *All the farmers in this village get up with the chickens.*

get-up *n.* (stress on *get*) Fancy dress or costume. *Some get-up you're wearing!*

get-up-and-go *also* **get-up-and-get** *n. phr., informal* Energetic enthusiasm; ambitious determination; pep; drive; push. *Joe has a lot of get-up-and-go and is working his way through school.*

get up on the wrong side of the bed *v. phr., informal* To awake with a bad temper. *Henry got up on the wrong side of the bed and wouldn't eat breakfast. The man went to bed very late and got up on the wrong side of the bed.*

get up the nerve *v. phr.* To build up your courage until you are brave enough; become brave enough. *Jack got up the nerve to ask Ruth to dance with him. The hungry little boy got up nerve to ask for another piece of cake.*

get what's coming to one *or* slang **get one's** *v. phr.* To receive the good or bad that you deserve; get what is due to you; get your share. *At the end of the movie the villain got what was coming to him and was put in jail. John didn't think he was getting what was coming to him, so he quit the job. Mother told Mary that she'd get hers if she kept on being naughty.*

get wind of *v. phr.* To get news of; hear rumors about; find out about. *The police got wind of the plans to rob the bank. The captain didn't want the sailors to get wind of where the ship was going.*

get wise *v. phr., slang* To learn about something kept secret from you; become alert. *One girl pretended to be sick on gym days when she had athletics, until the teacher got wise and made her go anyway. Often used with to. The boys got wise to Jack's fondness for bubble gum. If you don't get wise to yourself and start studying, you will fail the course.*

get with it *v. phr., slang* To pay attention; be alive or alert; get busy. *The students get with it just before examinations. The coach told the team to get with it.*

ghost of a Least trace of; slightest resemblance to; smallest bit even of; a very little. Usually used with *chance* or *idea* in negative sentences, or with *smile*. *There wasn't a ghost of a chance that Jack would win. We didn't have the ghost of an idea where to look for John. The teacher scolded Harold for drawing a funny picture on the chalkboard, but she had a ghost of a smile.*

ghost-writer *n.* A writer whose identity remains a secret and who writes for another who receives all the credit. *It is rumored that John Smith's best-selling novel was written by a ghost-writer.*

girl friend *n., informal* 1. A female friend or companion. *Jane is spending the night at her girl friend's house.* 2. A boy's steady girl; the girl or woman partner in a love affair; girl; sweetheart. *John is taking his girl friend to the dance.*

give a hard time *v. phr., informal* 1. To give trouble by what you do or say; complain. *Jane gave her mother a hard time on the bus by fighting with her sister and screaming. Don't give me a hard time, George. I'm doing my best on this job.* 2. To get in the way by teasing or playing; kid. *Don't give me a hard time, boys. I'm trying to study.*

give-and-take *n. phr.* 1. A sharing; giving and receiving back and forth between people; a giving up by people on different sides of part of what each one wants so that they can agree. *Jimmy is too selfish. He has no notion of give-and-take with the other children but wants everything for himself.*

There has to be give-and-take between two countries before they can be friends. 2. Friendly talking or argument back and forth. Friendly sharing of ideas which may not agree; also: an exchange of teasing remarks. *After the meeting there was a lot of give-and-take about plans for the dance.*

give an ear to or **lend an ear to** *v. phr., literary* To listen to. *Children should give an ear to their parents' advice. The king lent an ear to the complaints of his people.*

give away *v.* 1. To give as a present. *Mrs. Jones has several kittens to give away.* 2. To hand over (a bride) to her husband at the wedding. *Mr. Jackson gave away his daughter.* 3. To let (a secret) become known; tell the secret of. *The little boy gave away his hiding place when he coughed. Mary said she didn't care anything about John, but her blushing face gave her away.*

giveaway or **dead giveaway** *n.* (stress on *give*) 1. An open secret. *By mid-afternoon, it was a dead giveaway who the new boss would be.* 2. A forced or sacrifice sale at which items are sold for much less than their market value. *The Simpson's garage sale was actually a big giveaway.* 3. A gift; something one doesn't have to pay for. *The tickets to the concert were a give-away.*

give a wide berth *v. phr.* To keep away from; keep a safe distance from. *Mary gave the barking dog a wide berth. Jack gave a wide berth to the fallen electric wires. After Tom got*

Bob into trouble, Bob gave him a wide berth.

give birth to *v. phr.* **1.** To bear live offspring. *The mother gave birth to twin baby girls.* **2.** To bring about; create; occasion. *Beethoven gave birth to a new kind of symphony.*

give chase *v. phr.* To chase or run after someone or something. *The dog saw a rabbit and gave chase. The policeman gave chase to the man who robbed the bank.*

give ground *v. phr.* To go backward under attack; move back; retreat. *After fighting for a while the troops slowly began to give ground. Although they were outnumbered by the enemy, the men refused to give ground.*

give in *v.* To stop fighting or arguing and do as the other person wants; give someone his own way; stop opposing someone. *Mother kept inviting Mrs. Smith to stay for lunch, and finally she gave in. After Billy proved that he could ride a bicycle safely, his father gave in to him and bought him one.*

give it to *v. phr., informal* **1.** To give punishment to; beat. *The crowd yelled for the wrestler to give it to his opponent.* **2.** To scold. *Jerry's mother gave it to him for coming home late.*

give it to one straight *v. phr.* To be direct; be frank. *I asked the doctor to give it to me straight how long I have to live.*

give no quarter *v. phr.* To be ruthless and show no mercy. *The enemy soldiers gave no quarter and shot all the prisoners.*

give notice *v. phr.* To inform an employer, an employee, a landlord, or a tenant of the termination of a contractual agreement of service or tenancy. *Max gave notice at the bank where he was working. Sally was given notice by her landlord.*

given to *adj. phr.* Having a tendency to; addicted to. *Phil is given to telling fantastic tales about his chateau in France.*

give off *v.* To send out; let out; put forth. *Rotten eggs give off a bad smell. Burning leaves give off thick smoke.*

give one a lift *v. phr.* **1.** To give someone a ride. *Jack gave me a lift in his new car.* **2.** To comfort someone. *Talking to my doctor yesterday gave me a lift.*

give one an inch, and he will take a mile If you give some people a little or yield anything, they will want more and more; some people are never satisfied. *I gave Billy a bite of candy and he wanted more and more. If you give him an inch, he'll take a mile. The counselor said to Jack, "No, I can't let you get a haircut until Saturday. I.'s against the rules, and if I give an inch, someone will take a mile."*

give one a piece of one's mind *v. phr., informal* To scold angrily; say what you really think to (someone). *Mr. Allen gave the other driver a piece of his mind. The sergeant gave the soldier a piece of his mind for not cleaning his boots.*

give one a ring *also informal* **give a buzz** To call on the telephone. *Mrs. Jacobs promised to give her husband a ring* *in the afternoon. Alice will give her friend a buzz tonight.*

give one enough rope and he will hang himself *informal* Give a bad person enough time and freedom to do as he pleases, and he may make a bad mistake or get into trouble and be caught.—A proverb. *Johnny is always stealing and hasn't been caught. But give him enough rope and he'll hang himself.* Often used in a short form, *give one enough rope. Mother didn't know who robbed the cookie jar, but she thought she could catch him if she gave him enough rope.*

give oneself up to *v. phr.* Not to hold yourself back from; let yourself enjoy. *Uncle Willie gave himself up to a life of wandering. John came inside from the cold and gave himself up to the pleasure of being in a warm room.*

give one some of his or her own medicine *v. phr.* To treat someone the way he or she treats others (used in the negative). *The gangster beat up an innocent old man, so when he resisted arrest, a policeman gave him a little of his own medicine.*

give one's due *v. phr.* To be fair to (a person), give credit that (a person) deserves. *The boxer who lost gave the new champion his due. We should give a good worker his due.*

give one's right arm for *v. phr.* To give something of great value; sacrifice. *During our long hike in the desert, I would have given my right arm for an ice cold drink.*

give one's word *v. phr.* To seriously promise. *"You gave me your word you would marry me,"* Mary bitterly complained, *"but you broke your word."*

give one the eye *v. phr., slang* **1.** To look at, especially with interest and liking. *A pretty girl went by and all the boys gave her the eye.* **2.** To look or stare at, especially in a cold or unfriendly way. *Mrs. Jones didn't like Mary and didn't speak. She just gave her the eye when they met on the street.*

give or take *v. phr.* To add or subtract. Used with a round number or date to show how approximate it is. *The house was built in 1900, give or take five years.*

give out *v.* **1.** To make known; let it be known; publish. *Mary gave out that she and Bob were going to be married.* **2.** To let escape; give. *The cowboy gave out a yell.* **3.** to give to people; distribute. *The barber gives out free lollipops to all the children.* **4.** To fail; collapse. *Tom's legs gave out and he couldn't run any farther. The chair gave out under the fat man.* **5.** To be finished or gone. *When the food at the party gave out, they bought more. The teacher's patience gave out.* **6.** *slang* Not to hold back; act freely; let yourself go.—Often used in the imperative. *You're not working hard, Charley. Give out!* **7.** *informal* To show how you feel. *When Jane saw the mouse, she gave out with a scream. Give out with a little smile.*

give pause *v. phr.* To cause you to stop and think; make you doubt or worry. *The heavy* monthly payments gave Mr. Smith pause in his plans to buy a new car. The bad weather gave Miss Carter pause about driving to New York City.

give rise to v. phr. To be the reason for; cause. A branch floating in the water gave rise to Columbus' hopes that land was near. John's black eye gave rise to rumors that he had been in a fight.

give someone his rights or **read someone his rights** v. phr., informal 1. The act of advising arrested criminals that they have the right to remain silent and that everything they say can be held against them in a court of law; that they have the right to the presence of an attorney during questioning and that if they can't afford one and request it, an attorney will be appointed for them by the state. The cops gave Smith his rights immediately after the arrest. 2. To sever a relationship by telling someone that he or she can go and see a divorce lawyer or the like. Sue gave Mike his rights before she slammed the door in his face.

give the ax v. phr., colloquial 1. Abruptly to finish a relationship. She gave me the ax last night. 2. To fire an employee in a curt manner. His boss gave John the ax last Friday.

give the benefit of the doubt v. phr. To believe (a person) is innocent rather than guilty when you are not sure. The money was stolen and John was the only boy who had known where it was, but the teacher gave him the benefit of the doubt. George's grade was higher than usual and he might have cheated, but his teacher gave him the benefit of the doubt.

give the devil his due v. phr. To be fair, even to someone who is bad; tell the truth about a person even though you don't like him. I don't like Mr. Jones, but to give the devil his due, I must admit that he is a good teacher.

give the glad eye v. phr., slang To give (someone) a welcoming look as if saying "come over here, I want to talk to you." I was surprised when Joe gave me the glad eye.

give the slip v. To escape from (someone); run away from unexpectedly; sneak away from. An Indian was following, but Boone gave him the slip by running down a hill. Some boys were waiting outside the school to beat up Jack, but he gave them the slip.

give to understand v. phr., informal 1. To make a person think that something is true but not tell him; suggest; hint. Mr. Johnson gave Billy to understand that he would pay him if he helped him clean the yard. 2. To make a person understand by telling him very plainly or boldly. Frank was given to understand in a short note from the boss that he was fired.

give up v. 1a. To stop trying to keep; surrender; yield. The dog had the ball in his mouth and wouldn't give it up. Jimmy is giving up his job as a newsboy when he goes back to school. 1b. To allow; permit. Ford gave up two walks in the first inning. 2. To stop doing or having; abandon; quit. *The doctor told Mr. Harris to give up smoking. Jane hated to give up her friends when she moved away.* **3.** To stop hoping for, waiting for, or trying to do. *Johnny was given up by the doctors after the accident, but he lived just the same. When Mary didn't come by nine o'clock, we gave her up. I couldn't do the puzzle so I gave it up.* **4.** To stop trying; quit; surrender. *The war will be over when one of the countries gives up. The other team gave up after we scored three touchdowns.*

give up the ghost *v. phr.* To die; stop going. *After a long illness, the old woman gave up the ghost. The motor turned over a few times and gave up the ghost.*

give up the ship *v. phr.* To stop fighting and surrender; stop trying or hoping to do something. "Don't give up the ship, John," said his father when John failed a test.*

give voice *v. phr., formal* To tell what you feel or think; especially when you are angry or want to object.—Used with *to. The students gave voice to their pleasure over the new building. Little Willie gave voice to his pain when the dog bit him by crying loudly.*

give way *v.* **1.** To go back; retreat. *The enemy army is giving way before the cannon fire.* **2.** To make room, get out of the way. *The children gave way and let their mother through the door.* **3.** To lose control of yourself; lose your courage or hope; yield. *Mrs. Jones didn't give way during the flood, but she was very frightened.* **4.** To collapse; fail. *The river was so high that the dam gave way. Mary's legs gave way and she fainted.* **5.** To let yourself be persuaded; give permission. *Billy kept asking his mother if he could go to the movies and she finally gave way.*

glad hand *n., informal* A friendly handshake; a warm greeting. *Father went to the front door to give Uncle Fred the glad hand when he arrived. The politician went down the street on election day giving everyone the glad hand.*

gloss over *v.* To try to make what is wrong or bad seem right or not important; try to make a thing look easy; pretend about; hide. *Billy broke a window and Mother tried to gloss it over by saying it wouldn't cost much to have it fixed, but Father spanked Billy anyway. John glossed over his mistake by saying that everybody did the same thing.*

glutton for punishment *n. phr.* A greedy person; someone who wants too much of something, such as food or drink, which will make him sick. *Fred eats so much red meat that he is a regular glutton for punishment.*

go about one's business *v. phr.* To mind one's own affairs. *Fred kept bothering me with his questions all day, so I finally told him to go about his business and leave me alone.*

go after *v.* To try to get. "First find out what job you want and then go after it," said Jim's father.*

go ahead v. To begin to do something; not wait. *The teacher told the students not to write on the paper yet, but John went ahead and wrote his name. "May I ask you a question?" "Go ahead."*

go astray v. phr. To become lost. *The letter has obviously gone astray; otherwise it would have been delivered a long time ago.*

go along v. **1.** To move along; continue. *Uncle Bill made up the story as he went along.* **2.** To go together or as company; go for fun. Often used with *with. Mary went along with us to Jane's house. John just went along for the ride to the ball game. He didn't want to play. When one filling station cuts gasoline prices, the others usually go along.* **3.** To agree; cooperate. Often used with *with. "Jane is a nice girl." "I'll go along with that," said Bill. Just because the other boys do something bad, you don't have to go along with it.*

go ape v. phr., slang To become highly excited or behave in a crazy way. *Amy went ape over the hotel and beautiful beaches. The electric door opener malfunctioned and caused the garage door to go ape.*

go around v. **1a.** To go from one place or person to another. *Mr. Smith is going around looking for work. Don't go around telling lies like that. Chicken pox is going around the neighborhood. A rumor is going around school that we will get the afternoon off.* **1b.** To go together; keep company. —Usually used with *with. Bill goes around with boys older than he is because he is big for his age.* **2.** To be enough to give to everyone; be enough for all. *There are not enough desks to go around in the classroom.*

go around in circles See in a circle.

goat See get one's goat.

go at v. **1.** To start to fight with; attack. *The dog and the cat are going at each other again.* **2.** To make a beginning on; approach; tackle. *How are you going to go at the job of fixing the roof?*

go at it hammer and tongs v. phr., informal **1.** To attack or fight with great strength or energy; have a bad argument. *Bill slapped George's face and now they're going at it hammer and tongs in back of the house. Helen and Mary have been arguing all day, and now they are going at it hammer and tongs again.* **2.** To start or do something with much strength, energy, or enthusiasm. *The farmer had to chop down a tree and he went at it hammer and tongs. Charles had a lot of homework to do and he went at it hammer and tongs till bedtime.*

go back on v. phr. **1.** To turn against; not be faithful or loyal to. *Many of the man's friends went back on him when he was sent to prison. The boy's father told him not to go back on his promise.* **2.** To fail to do necessary work; not work. *Grandfather's eyes are going back on him.*

go back on one's word *v. phr.* To renege; break a promise. *Patrick went back on his word when he refused to marry Karen in spite of his earlier promise.*

go broke *v. phr., slang* To lose all one's money; especially by taking a chance; owe more than you can pay. *The inventor went broke because nobody would buy his machine. Dan had a quarter but he went broke matching pennies with Fred.*

go-between *n.* An intermediary. *They expect Mr. Smith to act as a go-between in the dispute between management and labor.*

God forbid *interj.* May God prevent (something from happening); I hope that will not happen or is not true. *Someone told the worried mother that her son might have drowned. She said, "God forbid!" God forbid that the dam break and flood the valley!*

God knows or **goodness knows** or **heaven knows** *informal* **1.** Maybe God knows but I don't know and no one else knows. —Often used with *only. Do you know where Susan is? God only knows!* **2.** Surely; certainly. *Goodness knows, the poor man needs the money. Heaven only knows, I have tried hard enough.*

go down *v. phr.* **1.** To deteriorate in quality. *This hotel, which used to be one of the best, has gone down during the past few years.* **2.** To become lower in price. *It is said that the price of milk is expected to go down soon.* **3.** To sink. *The*

Titanic went down with a lot of people aboard.

go down in history or **go down in the records** *v. phr.* To be remembered or recorded for always. *The lives of great men go down in history. Babe Ruth went down in history as a home run hitter. The boy's straight A's for four years of college went down in the records. The President said that the day the war ended would go down in history.*

go down the drain *v. phr.* To be lost or wasted forever. *If he doesn't pass the bar examination tomorrow, his best efforts to become a lawyer will go down the drain.*

go Dutch *v. phr., informal* To go out for fun together but have each person pay for himself. *High school students often go Dutch to basketball games. Sometimes boys and girls go Dutch on dates. The girl knew her boyfriend had little money, so she offered to go Dutch.*

go fly a kite *v. phr., slang* To go away; leave. Usually used as a command, to show that you do not accept someone's ideas. *Harry was tired of John's advice and told him to go fly a kite. After Mary stood around telling Sue what was wrong with her dress, Sue told her to go fly a kite.*

go for *v. phr., informal* **1.** To try to get; aim for; try for. *Our team is going for the championship in the game tonight. The dog went for Bob's leg.* **2.** To favor; support; like. *Little Susie really goes for ice cream. Bob goes for Jane in a big way.*

3. To attack; begin to fight or argue with. *The Indian jumped out of the bush and went for Daniel. Molly went for James about being late as soon as he got home.*

go for broke *v. phr., slang* To risk everything on one big effort; use all your energy and skill; try as hard as possible. *The racing car driver decided to go for broke in the biggest race of the year.*

go from bad to worse *adv. phr.* To change from a bad position or condition to a worse one; become worse. *Dick's typing went from bad to worse when he was tired. Jack's conduct in school has gone from bad to worse.*

go from strength to strength *v. phr.* To move forward, increasing one's fame, power, or fortune in a series of successful achievements. *Our basketball team has gone from strength to strength.*

go-getter *n.* A person who works hard to become successful; an active, ambitious person who usually gets what he wants. *The governor of the state has always been a go-getter. The best salesmen are the go-getters.*

go-go *adj., slang, informal* **1.** Vigorous youthful, unusually active. *Joe is a go-go kind of guy.* **2.** Of a discotheque or the music or dances performed there. **3a.** Unrestrained **3b.** Very up-to-date, hip. *Mary wore handsome go-go boots to the discotheque last night.*

go haywire *v. phr., informal* Mixed-up, out of order, not in regular working condition. *My electric typewriter has gone all haywire; I have to call the repair man.*

go hog wild *v. phr., slang* To become extremely agitated and go out of control. *After the soccer game was won, the fans went hog wild.*

go in for *v. phr., informal* To try to do; take part in; take pleasure in. *Most girls do not go in for rough games. Mrs. Henry goes in for simple meals.*

going through changes *v. phr., slang, informal* To be in trouble, to have difficulties, to be trapped in unfavorable circumstances. *"What's the matter with Joe?"—"He's going through changes."*

go in one ear and out the other *v. phr., informal* To be not really listened to or understood; be paid no attention. *The teacher's directions to the boy went in one ear and out the other. Mother scolded Martha, but it went in one ear and out the other.*

go into *v.* **1a.** To go or fit inside of; able to be put in. *The table is too big to go into the closet.* **1b.** To be able to be divided into; be divisible into. *Two goes into four two times.* **2.** To enter a state or condition of; pass into. *John went into a fit of temper when he didn't get his own way. The sick man went into a coma. The country went into mourning when the king died.* **3.** To be busy in or take part in; enter as a job or profession. *The mayor went into politics as a very young man. Mr. Johnson is going into* *business for himself. Bill wants to go into law when he gets out of school.* **4.** To start to talk about; bring up the subject of; examine. *We'll talk about the dead mouse after dinner, Billy. Let's not go into it now. The teacher went into the subject of newspapers today.*

go into a tailspin *or* **go into a nose dive** *v. phr., informal* **1.** To fall or go down badly; collapse; give up trying. *The team went into a tailspin after their captain was hurt, and they were badly beaten.* **2.** *informal* To become very anxious, confused, or mentally sick; give up hope. *The man went into a tailspin after his wife died and he never got over it.*

go into orbit *v. phr., slang* **1.** To become very happy or successful. *Our team has gone into orbit.* **2.** To lose one's temper or control completely; become very angry. *John was afraid his father would go into orbit when he found out about the car accident.*

go jump in the lake *v. phr., informal* To go away and quit being a bother. *George was tired of Tom's advice and told him to go jump in the lake.*

goldfish bowl *n., slang, informal* **1.** A situation in which it is not possible to keep things secret for any length of time. *Washington Society is a goldfish bowl.* **2.** An apartment or place that provides no privacy for its occupant, e.g., an office that has too many windows. *Joe's office is a goldfish bowl, that's why I didn't let him kiss me there.*

go legit *v. phr.* To start practicing a legitimate business after having been operating outside of the law. *"The old days are over," the crime boss said to his friends. "We are going legit as of right now."*

go native *v. phr.* To behave like a native (said of European Americans in tropical countries). *Mainlanders often go native in Hawaii.*

gone with the wind *adj. phr.* Gone forever; past; vanished. *All the Indians who used to live here are gone with the wind. Joe knew that his chance to get an "A" was gone with the wind when he saw how hard the test was.*

good buddy *n., slang, citizen's band radio jargon* Salutation used by truckers and automobile drivers who have CB radios. *What's the Smokey situation, good buddy?*

good deal *or* **great deal** *n., informal* A large amount; much. —Used with *a*. *Mrs. Walker's long illness cost her a good deal. George spends a great deal of his time watching television.*—Often used like an adverb. *Cleaning up after the party took a great deal more work than the girls expected. Usually it takes Father half an hour to drive to work, but in bad weather it takes a good deal longer. Mother likes the gloves Mary gave her, and she uses them a good deal. George is a good deal like his father; they both love to eat.*

good egg *slang or informal* **good scout** *n. phr.* A friendly, kind or good-natured person, a nice fellow. *Tommy is such a good egg that everybody wants to be his friend.*

good-for-nothing *adj. phr.* Worthless. *While Janice works hard each day, her good-for-nothing husband hangs around in the bars.*

good grief! *interj., informal* Wow! Indication of surprise, good or bad. *"Good grief," Joe cried out loud. "Is this all you will pay me for my hard work?" What a figure Melanie has, good grief! I wonder if she would be willing to go out with me.*

good nature *n.* Readiness to please others and to be pleased. Cheerfulness, pleasantness. *Everybody likes Mr. Crowe because of his good nature. Miss Reynolds was remembered by her students for her good nature.*

goodness gracious *interj., slightly archaic* Exclamation of surprise and a certain degree of disapproval. *"Can my boyfriend stay overnight, Dad?" Melanie asked. "Goodness gracious, most certainly not!" her father replied. "What would the neighbors think?"*

good riddance *n.* A loss that you are glad about. Often used as an exclamation, and in the sentence *good riddance to bad rubbish.* To show that you are glad that something or somebody has been taken or sent away. *The boys thought it was good riddance when the troublemaker was sent home. When Mr. Roberts' old car was stolen he thought it was good riddance. Betty thought it was* good riddance when her little brother broke his toy drum. *"I'm going and won't come back," said John. "Good riddance to bad rubbish!" said Mary.*

good show! *adj. phr.* Excellent; terrific; wonderful. *"Good show, boys!" the coach cried, when our team won the game.*

go off *v.* **1.** To leave; to depart. *Helen's mother told her not to go off without telling her.* **2a.** To be fired; explode. *The firecracker went off and scared Jack's dog.* **2b.** To begin to ring or buzz. *The alarm clock went off at six o'clock and woke Father.* **3.** To happen. *The party went off without any trouble. The parade went off without rain.*

go off half-cocked *also* **go off at half cock** *v. phr., informal* To act or speak before getting ready; to do something too soon. *Bill often goes off half cocked. Mr. Jones was thinking about quitting his job, but his wife told him not to go at half cock.*

go off the deep end *or* **go overboard** *v. phr., informal* To act excitedly and without careful thinking. *John has gone off the deep end about owning a motorcycle. Mike warned his roommate not to go off the deep end and get married. Some girls go overboard for handsome movie and television actors.*

goof off *v., slang* To loaf or be lazy; not want to work or be serious; fool around. *Tom didn't get promoted because he goofed off all the time and never did* she was the prettiest girl in the world, Mother just said, "Oh, go on, Charles." "Aunt May, your picture is in the paper." "Go on with you, boy!"

go on record *v. phr.* To make an official statement as opposed to an informal one; say something officially that may be quoted with the person's name added for reference. *I want to go on record that I oppose the merger with the firm of Catwallender and Swartvik.*

go one's way *v. phr.* **1.** To start again or continue to where you are going. *The milkman left the milk and went his way. The man stopped and asked me for a match, then went his way.* **2.** To go or act the way you want to or usually do. *Joe just wants to go his way and mind his own business. Don't tell me how to do my job. You go your way and I'll go mine. George was not a good sport; when the game did not go his way, he became angry and quit.*

goose bumps *or* **goose pimples** *n. plural, informal* Small bumps that come on a person's skin when he gets cold or afraid. *Nancy gets goose bumps when she sees a snake. Ann, put on your sweater; you're so cold you have goose pimples on your arms.*

go out of one's way *v. phr.* To make an extra effort; do more than usual. *Jane went out of her way to be nice to the new girl. Don did not like Charles, and he went out of his way to say bad things about Charles.*

go out the window *v. phr., informal* To go out of effect; be

his homework. If you goof off on the job too much, you'll be fired.

go on *v.* **1a.** To continue; not stop. *After he was hit by the ball, Billy quit pitching and went home, but the game went on. The TV picture began to jump, and it went on like that until Father turned a knob. I asked Jane a question but she went on reading and didn't answer. Mother told Jim to stop, but he went on hitting Susan.* **1b.** To continue after a pause; begin with the next thing. *"Go on! I'm listening," said Mother. The teacher pointed to the map, and went on, "But the land that Columbus came to was not India."*—Often used before an infinitive. *Father said Mother had gone to the hospital, and went on to say that Grandmother was coming to take care of us.* **1c.** Of time: To pass. *As time went on, Mary began to wonder if John had forgotten their date. The years went on, and Betty's classmates became gray-haired men and women.* **2.** To happen. *Mr. Scott heard the noise and went to see what was going on in the hall. The teacher knows what goes on when she leaves the room.* **3.** To talk for too long, often angrily. *We thought Jane would never finish going on about the amount of homework she had.* **4.** To fit on; be able to be worn. *My little brother's coat wouldn't go on me. It was too small.* **5.** Stop trying to fool me; I don't believe you.—Used as a command, sometimes with with. *When Father told Mother* abandoned. *During the war, the school dress code went out the window.*

go over *v.* **1.** To examine; think about or look at carefully. *The teacher went over the list and picked John's name. The police went over the gun for fingerprints.* **2.** To repeat; do again. *Don't make me go all over it again. We painted the house once, then we went over it again.* **3.** To read again; study. *After you finish the test, go over it again to look for mistakes. They went over their lessons together at night.* **4.** To cross; go to stop or visit; travel. *We went over to the other side of the street. I'm going over to Mary's house. We went over to the next town to the game.* **5.** To change what you believe. *Father is a Democrat, but he says that he is going over to the Republicans in the next election. Many of the natives on the island went over to Christianity after the white men came.* **6.** To be liked; succeed.—Often used in the informal phrase *go over big. Bill's joke went over big with the other boys and girls. Your idea went over well with the boss.*

go over like a lead balloon *v. phr., informal* To fail to generate a positive response or enthusiasm; to meet with boredom or disapproval. *The president's suggested budget cuts went over like a lead balloon. Jack's off-color jokes went over like a lead balloon.*

go over one's head *v. phr.* **1.** To be too difficult to understand. *Penny complains that what her math teacher says simply goes over her head.* **2.** To do something without the permission of one's superior. *Fred went over his boss's head when he signed the contract on his own.*

go somebody one better *v. phr., informal* To do something better than (someone else); do more or better than; beat. *Bill's mother gave the boys in Bill's club hot dogs for refreshments, so Tom's mother said that she would go her one better next time by giving them hot dogs and ice cream. John made a good dive into the water, but Bob went him one better by diving in backwards.*

go stag *v. phr.* **1.** To go to a dance or party without a companion of the opposite sex. *When Sally turned him down, Tom decided to go stag to the college prom.* **2.** To participate in a party for men only. *Mrs. Smith's husband frequently goes stag, leaving her at home.*

go steady *v. phr.* To go on dates with the same person all the time; date just one person. *At first Tom and Martha were not serious about each other, but now they are going steady. Jean went steady with Bob for a year; then they had a quarrel and stopped dating each other.*

go straight *v. phr., slang* To become an honest person; lead an honest life. *After the man got out of prison, he went straight. Mr. Wright promised to go straight if the judge would let him go free.*

got a thing going *v. phr., slang, informal* To be engaged in pleasurable or profitable activi-

y with someone else as a part-
er either in romance or in mu-
ually profitable business.
*You two seem to have got a
ning going, haven't you?"
You've got a good thing going
ith your travel bureau, why
uit now?"*

the whole hog *or* **go whole
og** *v. phr., informal* To do
omething completely or thor-
ughly; to give all your
trength or attention to some-
ing. *When Bob became
iterested in model airplanes,
e went the whole hog. The
imily went whole hog at the
air, and spent a lot of
oney.*

through *v.* **1.** To examine or
ink about carefully; search. *I
ent through the papers look-
1g for Jane's letter. Mother
ent through the drawer look-
1g for the sweater.* **2.** To expe-
ence; suffer; live through.
rank went through many dan-
ers during the war.* **3.** To do
hat you are supposed to do;
o what you promised. *I went
rough my part of the bargain,
ut you didn't go through your
art.* **4.** To go or continue to
ie end of; do or use all of.
ick went through the maga-
ine quickly. We went through
ll our money at the circus.* **5.**
o be allowed; pass; be agreed
n. *I hope the new law we want
oes through Congress. The
ale of the store went through
uickly.*

through with *v. phr.* To fin-
h; do as planned or agreed;
ot stop or fail to do. *The boys
on't think Bob will go through
ith his plans to spend the sum-
er at a camp. Mr. Trent hopes*

*the city won't go through with
its plans to widen the street.*

go to bat for *v. phr., informal*
To help out in trouble or need;
give aid to. *Everybody else
thought Billy had broken the
window, but Tom went to bat
for him. Mary went to bat for
the new club program.*

go to bed with the chickens *v.
phr., informal* To go to bed
early at night. *On the farm
John worked hard and went to
bed with the chickens. Mr.
Barnes goes to bed with the
chickens because he has to get
up at 5 A.M.*

go together *v.* **1.** To go with the
same boy or girl all the time;
date just one person. *Herbert
and Thelma go together.* **2.** To
be suitable or agreeable with
each other; match. *Roast turkey and cranberries go together. Ice cream and cake go
together. Green and yellow go
together.*

go to one's head *v. phr.* **1.** To
make one dizzy. *Beer and wine
go to a person's head. Looking
out the high window went to the
woman's head.* **2.** To make
someone too proud; make a
person think he is too important. *Being the star player went
to John's head. The girl's fame
as a movie actress went to her
head.*

go to pieces *v. phr.* To become very nervous or sick from
nervousness; become wild.
*Mrs. Vance went to pieces when
she heard her daughter was in
the hospital. The man went to
pieces when the judge said he
would have to go to prison for
life. Mary goes to pieces when
she can't have her own way.*

go to pot v. phr., informal To be ruined; become bad; be destroyed. Mr. Jones' health has gone to pot. The motel business went to pot when the new highway was built.

go to seed or **run to seed** v. phr. **1.** To grow seeds. Onions go to seed in hot weather. **2.** To lose skill or strength; stop being good or useful. Sometimes a good athlete runs to seed when he gets too old for sports. Mr. Allen was a good carpenter until he became rich and went to seed.

go to show or **go to prove** v. phr., informal To seem to prove; act or serve to show (a fact); demonstrate.—Often used after it. Our team beat a bigger team, and it just goes to show you can win if you play hard enough. The hard winter at Valley Forge goes to show that our soldiers suffered a great deal to win the Revolution.

go to the devil v. phr., informal **1.** To go away, mind your own business. Used as a command; considered rude. George told Bob to go to the devil. "Go to the devil!" said Jack, when his sister tried to tell him what to do. **2.** To become bad or ruined; become useless. The boy got mixed up with bad company and began to steal and rob his friends. He went to the devil. Mr. Jones went to the devil after he lost his business.

go to the dogs v. phr., informal To go to ruin; to be ruined or destroyed. The man went to the dogs after he started drinking. After the death of the owner, the business went to the dogs.

The team went to the dogs wh its best players got hurt.

go to town v. phr., slang **1.** [To] do something quickly or wi[th] great force or energy; work fa[st] or hard. The boys went to tow[n] on the old garage, and had [it] torn down before Father ca[me] home from work. While Sa[lly] was slowly washing the dishe[s] she remembered she had a da[te] with Pete that evening; then s[he] really went to town. **2.** or [go] **places.** To do a good job; su[c]ceed. Our team is going to tow[n] this year. We have won all fi[ve] games that we played. Dan w[as] a good student and a good at[h]lete; we expect him to go plac[es] in business.

go to waste v. phr. To [be] wasted or lost; not used. T[he] strawberries went to waste b[e]cause there was nobody to pi[ck] them. Joe's work on the mo[del] automobile went to waste wh[en] he dropped it.

go up in smoke or **go up [in] flames** v. phr. To burn; [be] destroyed by fire. **1.** The ho[use] went up in flames. The barn f[ull] of hay went up in smoke. [2.] Disappear; fail; not come tru[e.] Jane's hopes of going to colle[ge] went up in smoke when her [fa]ther lost his job. The tea[m's] chances to win went up [in] smoke when their captain w[as] hurt.

go up in the air v. phr. To b[e]come angry; lose one's tempe[r.] Herb is so irritable these da[ys] that he goes up in the air for [no] reason at all.

go without saying v. phr. [To] be too plain to need talkin[g] about; not be necessary to s[ay] or mention. *It goes without saying that children should not be given knives to play with. A person with weak eyes should wear glasses. That goes without saying.*

go wrong *v. phr.* **1.** To fail; go out of order. *Something went wrong with our car and we stalled on the road.* **2.** To sink into an immoral or criminal existence. *In a large city many young people go wrong every year.*

grand slam *n.* A home run hit when there are three men on the bases. *Tony's grand slam won the game for the Yankees, 4–0.*

grandstand *v., slang, informal* To show off, to perform histrionics needlessly. *Stop grandstanding and get down to honest work!*

grandstander *n., slang, informal* A showoff, a person who likes to engage in histrionics. *Many people think that Evel Knievel is a grandstander.*

grasp at straws *or* **clutch at straws** *v. phr.* To depend on something that is useless or unable to help in a time of trouble or danger; try something with little hope of succeeding. *To depend on your memory without studying for a test is to grasp at straws. The robber clutched at straws to make excuses. He said he wasn't in the country when the robbery happened.*

grass is always greener on the other side of the fence *or* **grass is always greener on the other side of the hill** *We are often*

not satisfied and want to be somewhere else; a place that is far away or different seems better than where we are. *John is always changing his job because the grass always looks greener to him on the other side of the fence.*

graveyard shift *n. phr.* The work period lasting from sundown to sunup, when one has to work in the dark or by artificial light. *"Why are you always so sleepy in class?" Professor Brown asked Sam. "Because I have to work the graveyard shift beside going to school," Sam answered.*

gravy train *n., slang, informal* The kind of job that brings in a much higher income than the services rendered would warrant. *Jack's job at the Athletic Club as Social Director is a regular gravy train.*

grease one's palm *or* **grease the palm** *slang* **1.** To pay a person for something done or given, especially dishonestly; bribe. *Some politicians will help you if you grease their palms.* **2.** To give a tip; pay for a special favor or extra help. *We had to grease the palm of the waiter to get a table in the crowded restaurant.*

greasy spoon *n., informal* Any small, inexpensive restaurant patronized by workers or people in a hurry; a place not noted for its excellence of cuisine or its decor. *I won't have time to eat lunch at the club today; I'll just grab a sandwich at the local greasy spoon.*

great guns *adv. phr., informal*

1. Very fast or very hard.— Usually used in the phrases *blow great guns, go great guns. The wind was blowing great guns, and big waves beat the shore. The men were going great guns to finish the job.* **2.** Very well; successfully. *Smith's new store opened last week and it's going great guns.*

green around the gills *or* **pale around the gills** *adj. phr., slang* Pale-faced from fear or sickness; sickly; nauseated. *Bill's father took him for a ride in his boat while the waves were rough, and when he came back he was green around the gills. The car almost hit Mary crossing the street, and she was pale around the gills because it came so close.*—Also used with other prepositions besides *around,* as *about, at, under,* and with other colors, as *blue, pink, yellow, white.*

green thumb *n., informal* A talent for gardening; ability to make things grow.—Considered trite by many. *Mr. Wilson's neighbors say his flowers grow because he has a green thumb.*

green with envy *adj. phr.* Very jealous; full of envy. *Alice's girlfriends were green with envy when they saw her new dress. The other boys were green with envy when Joe bought a second-hand car.*

grind to a halt *v. phr., informal* To slow down and stop like a machine does when turned off. *The old car ground to a halt in front of the house. The Cardinals' offense ground to a halt before the stubborn Steeler defense.*

ground floor *n.* **1.** First floor of a house or building. *Mrs. Turner has an apartment on the ground floor.* **2.** *informal* The first or best chance, especially in a business. *That man got rich because he got in on the ground floor of the television business.*

ground rule *n.* **1.** A rule in sports that is made especially for the grounds or place where a game is played.—Usually used in the plural. *There was such a big crowd at the baseball game, that the ground rules of the field were changed in case a ball went into the crowd.* **2.** A rule, usually not written, of what to do or how to act in case certain things happen. — Usually used in the plural. *When you go to a new school, you don't know the ground rules of how you are supposed to behave.*

growing pains *n.* **1.** Pains in children's legs supposed to be caused by changes in their bodies and feelings as they grow. *The little girl's legs hurt, and her mother told her she had growing pains.* **2.** *informal* Troubles when something new is beginning or growing. *The factory has growing pains.*

grow on *or* **grow upon** *v.* **1.** To become stronger in; increase as a habit of. *The habit of eating before going to bed grew upon John.* **2.** To become more interesting to or liked by. *The more Jack saw Mary, the more she grew on him. Football grew on Billy as he grew older.*

grow out of *v. phr.* **1.** To outgrow; become too mature for. *As a child he had a habit of* scratching his chin all the time, but he grew out of it. **2.** To result from; arise. *Tom's illness grew out of his tendency to overwork and neglect his health.*

grow up *v.* To increase in size or height; become taller or older; reach full height. **1.** *Johnny is growing up; his shoes are too small for him. I grew up on a farm. The city has grown up since I was young.* **2.** To become adult in mind or judgment; become old enough to think or decide in important matters. *Tom wants to be a coach when he grows up. Grow up, you're not a baby any more!*

gum up *v., slang* To cause not to work or ruin; spoil; make something go wrong.—Often used in the phrase *gum up the works. Jimmy has gummed up the typewriter.*

gun for *v., informal* **1.** To hunt for with a gun; look hard for a chance to harm or defeat. *The cowboy is gunning for the man who stole his horse. Bob is gunning for me because I got a higher mark than he did.* **2.** To try very hard to get. *The man is gunning for first prize in the golf tournament.*

gung-ho *adj., colloquial* Enthusiastic, full of eagerness in an uncritical or unsophisticated manner. *Suzie is all gung-ho on equal rights for women, but fails to see the consequences.*

gut feeling *n. phr.* An instinctive reaction. *I have a gut feeling that they will never get married in spite of all they say.*

gut reaction *n. phr.* A mental or physical response that springs from one's depths. *My gut reaction was to get out of here as fast as possible.*

gut talk *n. phr.* Sincere, honest talk. *We admire people who speak gut talk and tell exactly what they think and feel.*

had better *or* **had best** *informal*
Should; must. *I had better leave now, or I'll be late. If you want to stay out of trouble, you had best not make any mistakes. Jim decided he had better do his homework instead of playing ball.*

hair stand on end *informal*
The hair of your head rises stiffly upwards as a sign or result of great fright or horror. *When he heard the strange cry, his hair stood on end. The sight of the dead man made his hair stand on end.*

hale and hearty *adj. phr.* In very good health; well and strong. *Grandfather will be 80 years old tomorrow, but he is hale and hearty. That little boy looks hale and hearty, as if he is never sick.*

half-baked *adj., informal* Not thought out or studied thoroughly; not worth considering or accepting. *We wish Tom would not take our time at meetings to offer his half-baked ideas. We cannot afford to put the government in the hands of people with half-baked plans.*

half-hearted *adj.* Lacking enthusiasm or interest. *Phil made several half-hearted attempts to learn word processing, but we could see that he didn't really like it.*

half the battle *n. phr.* A large part of the work. *When you write an essay for class, making the outline is half the battle. To*
see your faults and decide to change is half the battle of self-improvement.*

hammer and tongs *adv. phr.* Violently. *Mr. and Mrs. Smith have been at it all day, hammer and tongs.*

hammer out *v.* **1.** To write or produce by hard work. *The President sat at his desk till midnight hammering out his speech for the next day.* **2.** To remove, change, or work out by discussion and debate; debate and agree on (something). *Mrs. Brown and Mrs. Green have hammered out their difference of opinion. The club members have hammered out an agreement between the two groups.*

hand down *v.* To arrange to give or leave after death. *Joe will have his father's gold watch because it is handed down in the family. In old times, property was usually handed down to the oldest son at his father's death.*

hand it to *v. phr., informal* To admit the excellence of; give credit or praise to. *You have to hand it to Jim; he is very careful and hard-working in all he does. The teacher said, "I hand it to Jane for the way she managed the Music Club."*

handle with gloves *or* **handle with kid gloves** *v. phr., informal* **1.** To treat very gently and carefully. *An atomic bomb is handled with kid gloves.* **2.** To treat with great tact and diplomacy. *Aunt Jane is so irritable that we have to treat her with kid gloves.*

hand-me-down *n., informal* Something given away after another person has no more use for it; especially, used clothing. *Alice had four older sisters, so all her clothes were hand-me-downs.*

handout *n.* 1. A free gift of food, clothes, etc. *The homeless people were standing in a long line for various handouts.* 2. A typed and photocopied sheet or sheets of paper outlining the main points made by a speaker. *Please look at page three of the handout.*

hand out *v., informal* To give (things of the same kind) to several people. *The teacher handed out the examination papers. At the Christmas party Santa Claus handed out the presents under the tree. Handing out free advice to all your friends will not make them like you.*

hand over *v.* To give control or possession of; give (something) to another person. *When the teacher saw Johnny reading a comic book in study period, she made him hand over the book. When Mr. Jones gets old, he will hand over his business to his son.*

hand over fist *adv. phr., informal* Fast and in large amounts. *Fred may get a pony for Christmas because his father is making money hand over fist. Business is so bad that the store on the corner is losing money hand over fist.*

hands-down *adj., informal* 1.

Easy. *The Rangers won a hands-down victory in the tournament.* 2. Unopposed; first; clear. *Johnny was the hands-down favorite for president of the class.*

hands down *adv., informal* 1. Without working hard; easily. *The Rangers won the game hands down.* 2. Without question or doubt; without any opposition; plainly. *Johnny was hands down the best player on the team.*

hands off *informal* Keep your hands off or do not interfere; leave that alone.—Used as a command. *I was going to touch the machine, but the man cried, "Hands off!" and I let it alone.*

hands-off *adj., informal* Leaving alone, not interfering; inactive. *The United States told the European governments to follow a hands-off policy toward Latin America. I did not approve of his actions, but I have a hands-off rule in personal matters, so I said nothing.*

hands up *informal* Hold up your hands! Put your hands up high and keep them there!— Used as a command. *The sheriff pointed his gun at the outlaws and called out, "Hands up!"*

hand something to someone on a silver platter *v. phr.* To give a person a reward that has not been earned. *The lazy student expected his diploma to be handed to him on a silver platter.*

hand-to-mouth *adj.* Not providing for the future; living from day to day; not saving for later. *Many native tribes lead a hand-to-mouth existence, con-*

tent to have food for one day at a time. John is not a saving boy; he spends his money without thought for the future, and lives a hand-to-mouth life.

handwriting on the wall *n. phr.* A sign that something bad will happen. *When Bill's team lost four games in a row, he saw the handwriting on the wall. John's employer had less and less work for him; John could read the handwriting on the wall and looked for another job.*

hang around *v., informal* **1.** To pass time or stay near without any real purpose or aim; loaf near or in. *The principal warned the students not to hang around the corner drugstore after school.* **2.** To spend time or associate. *Jim hangs around with some boys who live in his neighborhood.*

hang back or **hang off** or **hang behind** **1.** To stay some distance behind or away, be unwilling to move forward. *Mary offered the little girl candy, but she was shy and hung back.* **2.** To hesitate or be unwilling to do something. *Lou wanted Fred to join the club, but Fred hung off.*

hang by a thread or **hang by a hair** *v. phr.* To depend on a very small thing; be in doubt. *For three days Tom was so sick that his life hung by a thread. As Joe got ready to kick a field goal, the result of the game hung by a hair.*

hang in (there) *v. phr., slang, informal* To persevere; not to give up; to stick to a project and not lose faith or courage. *Hang in there old buddy; the worst is yet to come.*

hang it *interj. informal* An exclamation used to express annoyance or disappointment. *Oh, hang it! I forgot to bring the book I wanted to show you. Hang it all, why don't you watch where you're going?*

hang on *v.* **1.** To hold on to something, usually tightly. *Jack almost fell off the cliff, but managed to hang on until help came.* **2a.** To continue doing something; persist. *The grocer was losing money every day, but he hung on, hoping that business would improve.* **2b.** To hold a lead in a race or other contest while one's opponents try to rally. *The favorite horse opened an early lead and hung on to win as two other horses almost passed him in the final stretch. Bunning, staked to a 6–0 lead in the first inning, hung on to beat the Dodgers 6–4.* **3.** To continue to give trouble or cause suffering. *Lou's cold hung on from January to April.* **4.** To continue listening on the telephone. *Jerry, asked John, who had called him on the phone, to hang on while he ran for a pencil and a sheet of paper.*

hang on to *v.* To hold tightly; keep firmly. *The child hung on to its mother's apron, and would not let go. John did not like his job, but decided to hang on to it until he found a better one.*

hang out *v.* **1.** *slang* To spend your time idly or lounging about. *The teacher complained that Joe was hanging out in poolrooms instead of doing his homework.* **2.** *slang* To live; reside. *Two policemen stopped*

the stranger and asked him
where he hung out. **3.** To reach
out farther than the part below. *The branches of the trees
hung out over the road. The upper floor of that house hangs
out above the first.*

hang out one's shingle *v. phr.,
informal* To give public notice
of the opening of an office, especially a doctor's or lawyer's
office, by putting up a small
signboard. *The young doctor
hung out his shingle and soon
had a large practice.*

hang up *v.* **1.** To place on a
hook, peg, or hanger. *When the
children come to school, they
hang up their coats in the cloak-
room.* **2a.** To place a telephone
receiver back on its hook and
break the connection. *Carol's
mother told her she had talked
long enough on the phone and
made her hang up.* **2b.** To put
a phone receiver back on its
hook while the other person is
still talking.—Used with *on. I
said something that made Joe
angry, and he hung up on me.*
3a. *informal* To cause to be
stuck or held so as to be immovable.—Usually used in the passive. *Ann's car was hung up in
a snowdrift and she had to call
a garageman to get it out.* **3b.**
informal To stick or get held so
as to be immovable. *A big
passenger ship hung up on a
sandbar for several hours.* **4.** *informal* To cause a wait; delay.
*Rehearsals for the school play
were hung up by the illness of
some of the actors.* **5.** *informal*
To set (a record.) *Bob hung up a
school record for long distance
swimming.*

hang-up *n., informal* (stress on

hang) **1.** A delay in some process. *The mail has been late for
several days; there must be
some hang-up with the trucks
somewhere.* **2.** A neurotic reaction to some life situation
probably stemming from a
traumatic shock which has
slipped into the unconscious.
*Doctor Simpson believes that
Suzie's frigidity is due to some
hang-up about men.*

happy hour *n., informal* A
time in bars or restaurants
when cocktails are served at a
reduced rate, usually one hour
before they start serving
dinner. *Happy hour is between
6 and 7 P.M. at Celestial
Gardens.*

hard-and-fast *adj.* Not to be
broken or changed; fixed;
strict. *The teacher said that
there was a hard-and-fast rule
against smoking in the school.*

hard as nails *adj. phr., informal*
1. Not flabby or soft; physically
very fit; tough and strong. *After a summer of work in the
country, Jack was as hard as
nails, without a pound of extra
weight.* **2.** Not gentle or mild;
rough; stern. *Johnny works for
a boss who is as hard as nails
and scolds Johnny roughly
whenever he does something
wrong.*

hard feeling *n.* Angry or bitter
feeling; enmity.—Usually used
in the plural. *Jim asked Andy
to shake hands with him, just to
show that there were no hard
feelings. Bob and George once
quarreled over a girl, and there
are still hard feelings between
them.*

hard-nosed *adj., slang* Tough
or rugged; very strict; not weak

or soft; stubborn, especially in a fight or contest. *Joe's father was a hard-nosed army officer who had seen service in two wars. Pete is a good boy; he plays hard-nosed football.*

hard nut to crack *also* **tough nut to crack** *n. phr., informal* Something difficult to understand or to do. *Tom's algebra lesson was a hard nut to crack. Mary found knitting a hard nut to crack.*

hard of hearing *adj.* Partially deaf. *Some people who are hard of hearing wear hearing aids.*

hard-on *n. vulgar, avoidable.* An erection of the male sexual organ.

hard sell *n., informal* A kind of salesmanship characterized by great vigor, aggressive persuasion, and great eagerness on the part of the person selling something; opposed to "soft sell." *Your hard sell turns off a lot of people; try the soft sell for a change, won't you?*

hard up *adj., informal* Without enough money or some other needed thing. *Dick was hard up and asked Lou to lend him a dollar. The campers were hard up for water because their well had run dry.*

hatchet job *n. phr., slang* **1.** The act of saying or writing terrible things about someone or something, usually on behalf of one's boss or organization. *When Phil makes speeches against the competition exaggerating their weaknesses, he is doing the hatchet job on behalf of our president.* **2.** A ruthless, wholesale job of editing a script whereby entire paragraphs or pages are omitted. *Don, my editor, did a hatchet job on my new novel.*

hatchet man *n., colloquial* **1.** A politician or newspaper columnist whose job is to write and say unfavorable things about the opposition. *Bill Lerner is the hatchet man for the Mayor's Party; he smears all the other candidates regularly.* **2.** An executive officer in a firm whose job it is to fire superfluous personnel, cut back on the budget, etc., in short, to do the necessary but unpleasant things. *The firm hired Cranhart to be hatchet man; his title is that of Executive Vice President.*

hate one's guts *v. phr., slang* To feel a very strong dislike for someone. *Dick said that he hated Fred's guts because Fred had been very mean to him.*

have a ball *v. phr., slang* Enjoy yourself very much; have a wonderful time. *Johnny had a ball at camp. Mary and Tim have a ball exploring the town. After their parents left, the children had a ball.*

have a fit *or* **have fits** *or* **throw a fit** *v. phr.* **1.** To have a sudden illness with stiffness or jerking of the body. *Our dog had a fit yesterday.* **2.** *informal* To become angry or upset. *Father will throw a fit when he sees the dent in the car. Howard will have a fit when he learns that he lost the election. When John decided to drop out of college, his parents had fits.*

have a go at *v. phr., informal* To try, especially after others have tried. *Bob asked Dick to let him have a go at shooting at the target with Dick's rifle. She* *had a go at archery, but did not do very well.*

have a hand in *v. phr.* To have a part in or influence over; to be partly responsible for. *Sue's schoolmates respect her and she has a hand in every important decision made by the Student Council. Ben had a hand in getting ready the senior play.*

have all one's buttons *or* **have all one's marbles** *v. phr., slang* To have all your understanding; be reasonable.—Usually used in the negative or conditionally. *Mike acts sometimes as if he didn't have all his buttons. He would not go to town barefooted if he had all his marbles.*

have an edge on *v. phr., informal* 1. To have an advantage over someone or something else in the course of an evaluative comparison. *I can't beat you at tennis, but I have an edge on you in ping-pong.* 2. To be mildly intoxicated; to have had a few drinks. *Joe sure had an edge on when I saw him last night.*

have an eye for *v. phr.* To be able to judge correctly of; have good taste in. *She has an eye for color and style in clothes. He has an eye for good English usage.*

have an eye on *or* **have one's eye on** *v. phr., informal* 1. To look at or think about (something wanted); have a wish for; have as an aim. *I bought ice cream, but Jimmy had his eye on some candy. John has his eye on a scholarship so he can go to college.*

have a screw loose *v. phr., slang* To act in a strange way;

to be foolish. *Now I know he has a screw loose—he stole a police car this time. He was a smart man but had a screw loose and people thought him odd.*

have a time *v. phr., informal* 1. To have trouble; have a hard time. *Poor Susan had a time trying to get the children to go to bed. John had a time passing his math course.* 2. To have a good time; to have fun.—Used with a reflexive pronoun. *Bob had himself a time going to every night club in town. Mary had herself a time dancing at the party.*

have a way with *v. phr.* To be able to lead, persuade, or influence. *Dave has such a way with the campers that they do everything he tells them to do. Ted will be a good veterinarian, because he has a way with animals.*

have dibs on *or* **put dibs on** *v. phr., slang* To demand a share of something or to be in line for the use of an object usable by more than one person. *Don't throw your magazine away! I put (my) dibs on it, remember?*

have eyes only for *v. phr.* To see or want nothing else but; give all your attention to; be interested only in. *Of all the horses in the show, John had eyes only for the big white one. All the girls liked Fred, but he had eyes only for Helen.*

have had it *v. phr., slang* To have experienced or suffered all you can; to have come to the end of your patience or life. *"I've had it," said Lou, "I'm resigning from the job of* *chairman right now." When the doctor examined the man who had been shot, he said, "He's had it."*

have it *v. phr.* **1.** To hear or get news; understand. *I have it on the best authority that we will be paid for our work next week.* **2.** To do something in a certain way. *Make up your mind, because you can't have it both ways. You must either stay home or come with us. Bobby must have it his way and play the game by his rules.* **3.** To claim; say. *Rumor has it that the school burned down. Gossip has it that Mary is getting married. The man is very smart the way his family has it, but I think he's silly.* **4.** To allow it—Usually used with *will* or *would* in negative sentences. *Mary wanted to give the party at her house, but her mother wouldn't have it.* **5.** To win. *When the senators vote, the ayes will have it.* **6.** To get or find the answer; think of how to do something. "I have it!" said John to Mary. "We can buy Mother a nice comb for her birthday."* **7.** *informal* To have an (easy, good, rough, soft) time; have (certain kinds of) things happen to you; be treated in a (certain) way by luck or in life. *Everyone liked Joe and he had it good until he got sick. Mary has it easy; she doesn't have to work.*

have it coming *v. phr.* To deserve the good or bad things that happen to you. *I feel sorry about Jack's failing that course, but he had it coming to him. Everybody said that Eve had it*

coming when she won the scholarship.

have it in for *v. phr., informal* To wish or mean to harm; have a bitter feeling against. *George has it in for Bob because Bob told the teacher that George cheated in the examination. After John beat Ted in a fight, Ted always had it in for John.*

have it made *v. phr., slang* To be sure of success; have everything you need. *With her fine grades Alice has it made and can enter any college in the country. The other seniors think Joe has it made because his father owns a big factory.*

have it out *v. phr.* To settle a difference by a free discussion or by a fight. *Joe called Bob a bad name, so they went back of the school and had it out. Joe got a bloody nose and Bob got a black eye. The former friends finally decided to have it out in a free argument and they became friends again.*

have on *v.* **1.** To be dressed in; wear. *Mary had on her new dress.* **2.** To have (something) planned; have an appointment; plan to do. *Harry has a big weekend on. I'm sorry I can't attend your party, but I have a meeting on for that night.*

have one's ass in a sling *v. phr., slang, vulgar, avoidable* To be in an uncomfortable predicament; to be in the doghouse; to be at a disadvantage. *Al sure had his ass in a sling when the boss found out about his juggling the account.*

have one's cake and eat it too *v. phr.* To enjoy two opposite advantages. *You can either spend your money going to*

Europe or save it for a down payment on a house, but you can't do both. That would be having your cake and eating it, too.

have one's hands full *v. phr.* To have as much work as you can do; be very busy. *The plumber said that he had his hands full and could not take another job for two weeks. With three small children to take care of, Susie's mother has her hands full.*

have rocks in one's head *v. phr., informal* To be stupid; not have good judgment. *When Mr. James quit his good job with the coal company to begin teaching school, some people thought he had rocks in his head.*

have something going for one *v. phr., slang, informal* To have ability, talent; good looks, and/or influence in important places helping one to be successful. *Well now, Pat Jones, that's another story—she's got something going for her.*

have something on *v. phr., informal* To have information or proof that someone did something wrong. *Mr. Jones didn't want to run for office because he knew the opponents had something on him. Mr. Smith keeps paying blackmail to a man who has something on him. Although Miss Brown is not a good worker, her boss does not fire her because she has something on him.*

have something on the ball *v. phr., slang, colloquial* To be smart, clever; to be skilled and*

have the necessary know-how. *You can trust Syd; he's got a lot on the ball OR he's got something on the ball.*

have the last laugh *or* **get the last laugh** *v. phr.* To make someone seem foolish for having laughed at you. *Other schools laughed at us when our little team entered the state championship, but we had the last laugh when we won it.*

have to *or* **have got to** *v., informal* To be obliged or forced to; need to; must. *Do you have to go now? He had to come. His parents made him. I have got to go to the doctor. I have to go to church.*

have to do with *v. phr.* **1.** To be about; be on the subject of or connected with. *The book has to do with airplanes.* **2.** To know or be a friend of; work or have business with.—Usually used in negative sentence. *Tom said he didn't want to have anything to do with the new boy. I had nothing to do with the party; I was home that night.*

have two strikes against one *or* **have two strikes on one** *v. phr., informal* To have things working against you; be hindered in several ways; be in a difficult situation; be unlikely to succeed. *Children from the poorest parts of a city often have two strikes against them before they enter school. George has two strikes against him already. Everybody is against what he wants to do.* [In baseball, three strikes are out. If the umpire calls two strikes against the batter, he has only one strike left and will be out if he gets one more strike.]

head above water *n. phr.* out of difficulty; clear of trouble. *How are your marks at school? Are you keeping your head above water? Business at the store is bad. They can't keep their heads above water.*

head-hunting *n.*, *slang*, *informal* **1.** The custom of seeking out, decapitating, and preserving the heads of enemies as trophies **2.** A search for qualified individuals to fill certain positions. *The president sent a committee to the colleges and universities to do some head-hunting; we hope he finds some young talent.* **3.** A systematic destruction of opponents, especially in politics. *Billings was hired by the party to do some head-hunting among members of the opposition.*

head off *v.* **1.** To get in front of and stop, turn back, or turn aside. *The sheriff said to head the cattle thieves off at the pass.* **2.** To block; stop; prevent. *He will get into trouble if someone doesn't head him off.*

head-on *adj.* or *adv. phr.* **1.** With the head or front pointing at; with the front facing; front end to front end. *Our car skidded into a head-on crash with the truck. In the fog the boat ran head-on into a log. There is a head-on view of the parade from our house.* **2.** In a way that is exactly opposite; against or opposed to in argument. *If you think a rule should be changed, a head-on attack against it is best. Tom did not want to argue head-on what*

the teacher said, so he sai[d] nothing.

head out *v.* **1.** To go or poin[t] away. *The ship left port an[d] headed out to sea. The car wa[s] parked beside the house. It wa[s] headed out towards the street.* **2.** *informal* Leave; start out. *have a long way to go befor[e] dark. I'm going to head out.*

head over heels *also* **heels over head 1a.** In a somersault; up[side] side down; head first. *It was s[o] dark Bob fell head over hee[ls] into a big hole in the ground.* **1b.** In great confusion or disor[der] der; hastily. *The children a[ll] tried to come in the door a[t] once, head over heels.* **2.** *infor[mal]* mal Completely; deeply. *H[e] was head over heels in deb[t]. She was head over heels in love*

head shrinker *n.*, *slang*, *infor[mal]* mal A psychoanalyst, als[o] called a shrink. *Forrester is fall[ing] ing apart; his family physicia[n] sent him to a head shrinker (t[o] a shrink).*

head start *n.* **1.** A beginning be[fore] fore someone; lead or advan[tage] tage at the beginning. *Th[e] other racers knew they couldn['t] catch Don if he got too big [a] head start. Joe has a head start[.] He began to study earlier tha[n] we did.* **2.** A good beginning[.] *Let's get a head start in paintin[g] the house by getting up early[.] The teacher gave the class [a] head start on the exercise b[y] telling them the answers to th[e] first two problems.*

head up *v.*, *informal* **1.** To be a[t] the head or front of. *The ele[-] phants headed up the whole pa[-] rade.* **2.** To be the leader o[r] boss of. *Mr. Jones will head u[p]* *the new business. The class planned a candy sale, and they elected Mary to head it up.*

heap coals of fire on one's head *v. phr., literary* To be kind or helpful to someone who has done wrong to you, so that he is ashamed. *Alice heaped coals of fire on Mary's head by inviting her to a party after Mary had gossiped about her. Jean Valjean stole the Bishop's silver, but the Bishop heaped coals of fire on his head by giving the silver to him.*

heart goes out to *formal* You feel very sorry for; you feel pity or sympathy for. Used with a possessive. *Frank's heart went out to the poor children playing in the slum street. Our hearts went out to the young mother whose child had died.*

heart is in the right place or **have one's heart in the right place.** To be kind-hearted, sympathetic or well-meaning; have good intentions. *All the tramps and stray dogs in the neighborhood knew that Mrs. Brown's heart was in the right place. Tom looks very rough but his heart is in the right place.*

heart of gold *n. phr.* A kind, generous, or forgiving nature. *John has a heart of gold. I never saw him angry at anyone. Mrs. Brown is a rich woman with a heart of gold.*

heart of stone *n. phr.* A nature without pity. *Mr. Smith has a heart of stone. He whipped his horse until it fell down.*

heart skip a beat or **heart miss a beat 1.** The heart leaves out or

seems to leave out a beat; the heart beats hard or leaps from excitement or strong feeling. —Often considered trite. *When Paul saw the bear standing in front of him, his heart skipped a beat.* **2.** To be startled or excited from surprise, joy, or fright. *When Linda was told that she had won, her heart missed a beat.*

heart stand still *v. phr.* To be very frightened or worried. *Johnny's heart stood still when he saw his dog run into the street in front of a car. Everybody's heart stood still when the President announced that war was declared.*

heart-to-heart *adj.* Speaking freely and seriously about something private. *The father decided to have a heart-to-heart talk with his son about smoking. She waited until they were alone so she could have a heart-to-heart talk with him.*

heavy heart *n. phr.* A feeling of being weighed down with sorrow; unhappiness. *They had very heavy hearts as they went to the funeral.*

hedge about or **hedge in 1.** To surround with a hedge or barrier; protect or separate by closing in. *The house is hedged about with bushes and trees. The little garden is hedged in to keep the chickens out.* **2.** To keep from getting out or moving freely; keep from acting freely; block in. *The boys are hedged in today. They can only play in the backyard. The king said he could not make new laws if he was so hedged in by old ones.*

he laughs best who laughs last A person should go ahead with what he is doing and not worry when others laugh at him. When he succeeds he will enjoy laughing at them for being wrong more than they enjoyed laughing at him.—A proverb. *Everyone laughed at Mary when she was learning to ski. She kept falling down. Now she is the state champion. He laughs best who laughs last.*

hell and high water *n. phr.* Troubles or difficulties of any kind. *After John's father died he went through hell and high water, but he managed to keep the family together.*

hell-on-wheels *n., slang* A short-tempered, nagging, or crabby person especially one who makes another unhappy by constantly criticizing him even when he has done nothing wrong. *Finnegan complains that his wife is hell on wheels; he is considering getting a divorce.*

helter-skelter *adv.* **1.** At a fast speed, but in confusion. *The batted ball broke Mr. Jones's window, and the boys ran away helter-skelter. When the bell rang, the pupils ran helter-skelter out of the door.* **2.** In a confusing group; in disorder. *The movers piled the furniture helter-skelter in the living room of the new house. Mary fell down and her books, papers, and lunch landed helter-skelter over the sidewalk.*

he-man *n., informal* A man who is very strong, brave, and healthy. *Larry was a real he-*
man when he returned from service with the Marines.

hem and haw *v. phr.* **1.** To pause or hesitate while speaking, often with little throat noises. *The man was a poor lecturer because he hemmed and hawed too much.* **2.** To avoid giving a clear answer; be evasive in speech. *The principal asked Bob why he was late to school, and Bob only hemmed and hawed.*

here goes *interj., informal* I am ready to begin; I am now ready and willing to take the chance; I am hoping for the best.—Said especially before beginning something that takes skill, luck, or courage. *"Here goes!" said Charley, as he jumped off the high diving board. "Here goes!" said Mary as she started the test.*

here goes nothing *interj., informal* I am ready to begin, but this will be a waste of time; this will not be anything great. Used especially before beginning something that takes skill, luck or courage. *"Here goes nothing," said Bill at the beginning of the race.*

hide one's head in the sand *or* **bury one's head in the sand** *or* **have one's head in the sand** To keep from seeing, knowing, or understanding something dangerous or unpleasant; to refuse to see or face something. *If there is a war, you cannot just bury your head in the sand.*

hide one's light under a bushel *v. phr.* To be very shy and modest and not show your abilities or talents; be too modest in letting others see what you can do. *When Joan is with her close friends she has a wonderful sense of humor, but usually she hides her light under a bushel. Mr. Smith is an expert in many fields, but most people think he is not very smart because he hides his light under a bushel. All year long Tommy hid his light under a bushel and the teacher was surprised to see how much he knew when she read his exam paper.*

high and dry *adv. or adj. phr.* **1.** Up above the water; beyond the reach of splashing or waves. *Mary was afraid she had left her towel where the tide would reach it, but she found it high and dry. When the tide went out the boat was high and dry.* **2.** Without anyone to help; alone and with no help. *When the time came to put up the decorations, Mary was left high and dry. At first the other boys helped, but when the work got hard, Bob found himself high and dry.*

high-and-mighty *adj., informal* Feeling more important or superior to someone else; too proud of yourself. *John wasn't invited to the party, because he acted too high-and-mighty. Mary became high-and-mighty when she won the prize, and Joan would not go around with her any more.*

high gear *n. phr., informal* Top speed; full activity. *Production got into high gear after the vacation. An advertising campaign for the new tooth-*paste promptly moved into high gear.

high-handed *adj.* Depending on force rather than right; bossy; dictatorial. *With high-handed daring, John helped himself to the best food on the table. Mr. Smith was a high-handed tyrant in his office.*

high seas *n. phr.* The open ocean, not the waters near the coast. *It was a big powerful liner built to sail on the high seas. The ships of every country have the right to sail on the high seas.*

high time *adj. phr., used predicatively* (stress on *time*) Dire, necessary, and sufficient circumstances prompting action. *It is high time we sold the old house; it will fall apart within a year.*

highway robbery *n. phr.* **1.** A hold-up of or theft from a person committed on an open road or street usually by an armed man. *Highway robbery was common in England in Shakespeare's day.* **2.** An extremely high price or charge; a profiteer's excessive charge. *To someone from a small town, the prices of meals and theater tickets in New York often seem to be highway robbery.*

hire out *v., informal* **1.** To accept a job; take employment. *Frank hired out as a saxophonist with a dance band.* **2.** To rent (as owner). *John used to hire out his tractor sometimes when he didn't need it himself.*

hit-and-run *adj.* **1.** Of or about an accident after which a motorist drives away without giving his name and offering help.

Judges are stern with hit-and-run drivers. **2.** Striking suddenly and leaving quickly. *The bandits often made hit-and-run attacks on wagon trains.*

hit between the eyes *v. phr., informal* To make a strong impression on; surprise greatly. *Helen hit Joe right between the eyes the moment he saw her. It was a wonderfully lifelike picture, and it hit Sol right between the eyes. To learn that his parents had endured poverty for his sake hit John between the eyes.*

hit bottom or **touch bottom** *v. phr., informal* **1.** To be at the very lowest. *In August there was a big supply of corn and the price hit bottom. When Johnny failed the exam his spirits hit bottom.* **2.** To live through the worst; not to be able to go any lower. *After all their troubles, they thought they had hit bottom and then something else happened. When they lost all their money they thought they had touched bottom and things would have to get better.*

hitch one's wagon to a star *v. phr.* To aim high; follow a great ambition or purpose. *In trying to be a famous pianist, Mary had hitched her wagon to a star. John hitched his wagon to a star and decided to try to become President.*

hither and thither or **hither and yon** *adv. phr., literary* In one direction and then in another. *Bob wandered hither and thither looking for a playmate.*

hit it off *v. phr., informal* To enjoy one another's company; be happy and comfortable in each other's presence. *Tom and Fred hit it off well with each other. Mary and Jane hit it off from the first.*

hit on or **hit upon** *v.* To happen to meet, find, or reach; to choose or think by chance. *John hit on a business that was just starting to grow rapidly. There seemed to be several explanations of the crime, but the detectives hit on the right one the first time.*

hit-or-miss also **hit-and-miss** *adj.* Unplanned; uncontrolled; aimless; careless. *John did a lot of hit-or-miss reading, some of it about taxes. Mary packed her bag in hurried, hit-or-miss fashion.*

hit or miss also **hit and miss** *adv.* In an unplanned or uncontrolled way; aimlessly; carelessly. *George didn't know which house on the street was Jane's, so he began ringing doorbells hit or miss.*

hit parade *n.* **1.** A list of songs or tunes arranged in order of popularity. *Tom was overjoyed when his new song was named on the hit parade on the local radio station.* **2.** *slang* A list of favorites in order of popularity. *Jack is no longer number one on Elsie's hit parade.*

hit the books *v. phr., informal* To study your school assignments, prepare for classes. *Jack broke away from his friends, saying, "I've got to hit the books."*

hit the bull's-eye *v. phr., informal* To go to the important part of the matter; reach the main question. *John hit the bull's-eye when he said the big* *question was one of simple honesty.*

hit the ceiling *or* **hit the roof** *v. phr., slang* To become violently angry; go into a rage. *When Elaine came home at three in the morning, her father hit the ceiling. Bob hit the roof when Joe teased him.*

hit the deck *v. phr.* To get up from bed, to start working. (From sailor's language as in "All hands on the deck!") *OK boys, it's time to hit the deck!*

hit the dirt *v. phr., slang military* To take cover under gunfire by falling on the ground. *We hit the dirt the moment we heard the machine gun fire.*

hit the fan *v. phr., informal* To become a big public problem or controversy. *The whole mess hit the fan when the judge was arrested for drunken driving for the second time.*

hit the hay *or* **hit the sack** *v. phr., slang* To go to bed. *The men hit the hay early, in order to be out hunting at dawn. Louis was so tired that he hit the sack soon after supper.*

hit the high spots *v. phr.* To consider, mention, or see only the more important parts of something such as a book, war, or school course. *In his lecture, the speaker hit the high spots of his subject. The first course in general science hits only the high spots of the physical sciences. The Bakers went to the fair for one day, and only hit the high spots.*

hit the jackpot *v. phr., slang* To be very lucky or successful. *Mr. Brown invented a new gadget which hit the jackpot.*

Mrs. Smith hit the jackpot when she got Lula for a maid.

hit the nail on the head *v. phr.* To get something exactly right; speak or act in the most fitting or effective way. *The mayor's talk on race relations hit the nail on the head.*

hit the road *v. phr., slang* **1.** To become a wanderer; to live an idle life; become a tramp or hobo. *When Jack's wife left him, he felt a desire to travel, so he hit the road.* **2.** To leave, especially in a car. *It is getting late, so I guess we will hit the road for home. He packed his car and hit the road for California.*

hit the sauce *v. phr., slang* To drink alcoholic beverages—especially heavily and habitually. *When Sue left him, Joe began to hit the sauce.*

hit the spot *v. phr., informal* To refresh fully or satisfy you; bring back your spirits or strength—used especially of food or drink. *A cup of tea always hits the spot when you are tired. Mother's apple pie always hits the spot with the boys.*

hit town *v. phr.* To arrive in town. *Give me a phone call as soon as you hit town.*

hoist with one's own petard *adj. phr.* Caught in your own trap or trick. *Jack carried office gossip to the boss until he was hoisted by his own petard.* [From Shakespeare; literally, blown up with one's own bomb.]

hold a candle to *also* **hold a stick to** *v. phr.* To be fit to be compared with; be in the same class with.—A trite phrase used in negative, interrogative, and conditional sentences. *Henry thought that no modern ball club could hold a candle to those of 50 years ago.*

hold all the trumps *v. phr.* To have the best chance of winning; have all the advantages; have full control. *Most of the team wants John for captain and he is the best player. He will be elected captain because he holds all the trumps. Freddy has a quarter and I have no money, so he holds all the trumps and can buy whatever he wants with it.*

hold back *v.* **1.** To stay back or away; show unwillingness. *The visitor tried to get the child to come to her, but he held back. John held back from social activity because he felt embarrassed with people.* **2.** To keep someone in place; prevent from acting. *The police held back the crowd.*

hold court *v. phr.* **1.** To hold a formal meeting of a royal court or a court of law. *Judge Stephens allowed no foolishness when he held court.* **2.** *informal* To act like a king or queen among subjects. *Even at sixteen, Judy was holding court for numbers of charmed boys.*

hold down *v.* **1.** To keep in obedience; keep control of; continue authority or rule over. *Kings used to know very well how to hold down the people.* **2.** *informal* To work satisfactorily at. *John had held down a tough job for a long time.*

hold forth *v.* **1.** To offer; propose. *As a candidate, Jones held forth the promise of a bright future.* **2.** To speak in public; preach.—Usually used

with little respect. *Senator Smith was holding forth on free trade.*

hold good *v.* **1.** To continue to be good; last. *The coupon on the cereal box offered a free toy, but the offer held good only till the end of the year. Attendance at the basketball games held good all winter.* **2.** To continue; endure; last. *The demand for new houses held good all that year. The agreement between the schools held good for three years.*

hold off *v.* **1a.** To refuse to let (someone) become friendly. *The president's high rank and chilly manner held people off.* **1b.** To be rather shy or unfriendly. *Perkins was a scholarly man who held off from people.* **2.** To keep away by fighting; oppose by force. *The man locked himself in the house and held off the police for an hour.* **3.** To wait before (doing something); postpone; delay. *Jack held off paying for the television set until the dealer fixed it. Mr. Smith held off from building while interest rates were high.*

hold on *v.* **1.** To keep holding tightly; continue to hold strongly. *As Ted was pulling on the rope, it began to slip and Earl cried, "Hold on, Ted!"* **2.** To wait and not hang up a telephone; keep a phone for later use. *Mr. Jones asked me to hold on while he spoke to his secretary.* **3.** To continue a business or job in spite of difficulties. *It was hard to keep the store going during the depression, but Max held on and at last met with success.* **4.** *infor-*

mal To wait a minute; stop. Usually used as a command. "Hold on!" John's father said, "I want the car tonight."

hold one's breath *v. phr.* **1.** To stop breathing for a moment when you are excited or nervous. *The race was so close that everyone was holding his breath at the finish.* **2.** To endure great nervousness, anxiety, or excitement. *John held his breath for days before he got word that the college he chose had accepted him.*

hold one's fire or hold fire *v. phr.* To keep back arguments or facts; keep from telling something. *Tom could have hurt Fred by telling what he knew, but he held his fire. Mary held fire until she had enough information to convince the other club members.*

hold one's horses *v. phr., informal* To stop; wait; be patient. —Usually used as a command. May be considered rude. "Hold your horses!" Mr. Jones said to David when David wanted to call the police.

hold one's own *v. phr.* To keep your position; avoid losing ground; keep your advantage, wealth, or condition without loss. *Mr. Smith could not build up his business, but he held his own. The team held its own after the first quarter. Mary had a hard time after the operation, but soon she was holding her own.*

hold one's peace *v. phr., formal* To be silent and not speak against something; be still; keep quiet. *I did not agree with the teacher, but held my peace as he was rather angry.*

hold one's tongue *v. phr.* To be silent; keep still; not talk.— May be considered rude. *The teacher told Fred to hold his tongue. If people would hold their tongues from unkind speech, fewer people would be hurt.*

hold on to *v. phr.* **1a.** *or* **hold to** To continue to hold or keep; hold tightly. *When Jane played horse with her father, she held on to him tightly. The teacher said that if we believed something was true and good we should hold on to it. The old man held on to his job stubbornly and would not retire.* **1b.** To stay in control of. *Ann was so frightened that she had to hold on to herself not to scream.* **2.** To continue to sing or sound. *The singer held on to the last note of the song for a long time.*

holdout *n.* A rebel who refuses to go with the majority. *Sam was a lone holdout in town; he refused to sell his old lakefront cottage to make place for a skyscraper.*

hold out *v. phr.* **1.** To put forward; reach out; extend; offer. *Mr. Ryan held out his hand in welcome. The clerk held out a dress for Martha to try on. The company held out many fine promises to Jack in order to get him to work for them.* **2.** To keep resisting; not yield; refuse to give up. *The city held out for six months under siege.* **3.** To refuse to agree or settle until one's wishes have been agreed to. *The strikers held out for a raise of five cents an hour.* **4.** *slang* To keep something from;

refuse information or belongings to which someone has a right. *Mr. Porter's partner held out on him when the big payment came in. Mother gave Bobby cookies for all the children in the yard, but he held out on them and ate the cookies himself. John knew that the family would go to the beach Saturday, but he held out on his brother.*

holdover *n.* **1.** A successful movie or theater production that plays longer than originally planned. *Because of its great popularity,* Star Wars *was a holdover in most movie theaters.* **2.** A reservation not used at the time intended, but used later. *They kept my seat at the opera as a holdover because I am a patron.*

hold over *v.* **1.** To remain or keep in office past the end of the term. *The city treasurer held over for six months when the new treasurer died suddenly. The new President held the members of the Cabinet over for some time before appointing new members.* **2.** To extend the engagement of; keep longer. *The theater held over the feature film for another two weeks.* **3.** To delay action on; to postpone; to defer. *The directors held over their decision until they could get more information.*

hold the fort *v. phr.* **1.** To defend a fort successfully; fight off attackers. *The little group held the fort for days until help came.* **2.** *informal* To keep a position against opposing forces. *Friends of civil liberties held the fort during a long de-*bate. **3.** *informal* To keep service or operations going. *It was Christmas Eve, and a few workers held the fort in the office. Mother and Father went out and told the children to hold the fort.*

holdup *n.* **1.** Robbery. *John fell victim to a highway holdup.* **2.** A delay, as on a crowded highway. *Boy we're late! What's causing this holdup?.*

hold up *v.* **1.** To raise; lift. *John held up his hand.* **2.** To support; bear; carry. *The chair was too weak to hold up Mrs. Smith.* **3.** To show; call attention to; exhibit. *The teacher held up excellent models of composition for her class to imitate.* **4.** To check; stop; delay. *The wreck held up traffic on the railroad's main line tracks.* **5.** *informal* To rob at gunpoint. *Masked men held up the bank.* **6.** To keep one's courage or spirits up; remain calm; keep control of oneself. *The grieving mother held up for her children's sake.* **7.** To remain good; not get worse. *Sales held up well. Our team's luck held up and they won the game. The weather held up and the game was played.* **8.** To prove true. *The police were doubtful at first, but Tony's story held up.* **9.** To delay action; defer; postpone. Often used with *on. The college held up on plans for the building until more money came in. The President held up on the news until he was sure of it.*

holier-than-thou *adj.* Acting as if you are better than others in goodness, character, or reverence for God; acting as if morally better than other people. *Most people find holier-than-thou actions in others hard to accept. After Mr. Howard stopped smoking, he had a holier-than-thou manner toward his friends who still smoked.*

holy cats *or* **holy cow** *or* **holy mackerel** *or* **holy Moses** *interj.*, *informal* Used to express strong feeling (as astonishment, pleasure, or anger); used in speech or when writing conversation. *"Holy cats! That's good pie!" said Dick. "Holy cow! They can't do that!" Mary said when she saw the boys hurting a much smaller boy.*

holy terror *n.*, *informal* A very disobedient or unruly child; brat. *All the children are afraid of Johnny because he's a holy terror.*

honeymoon is over The first happy period of friendship and cooperation between two persons or groups is over. *A few months after a new President is elected, the honeymoon is over and Congress and the President begin to criticize each other. The honeymoon was soon over for the new foreman and the men under him.*

honky-tonk *n.* A cheap nightclub or dance hall. *There were a number of honky-tonks near the army camp.*

hook, line and sinker *adv. phr.*, *informal* Without question or doubt; completely. *Johnny was so easily fooled that he fell for Joe's story, hook, line and sinker. Mary was such a romantic girl that she swallowed the story Alice told her about her date, hook, line and sinker. Bobby trusted Jim so he was*

taken in by his hard-luck story hook, line and sinker.

hookup *n.* A connection, electrical or otherwise, between two instruments or two individuals. *Edwin and Hermione are a perfect couple; they have got the right hookup.*

hook up *v. phr.* To connect or fit together. *The company sent a man to hook up the telephone. They could not use the gas stove because it had not been hooked up.*

hope against hope *v. phr.* To try to hope when things look black; hold to hope in bad trouble. *The mother continued to hope against hope although the plane was hours late. Jane hoped against hope that Joe would call her.*

hop to it *v. phr.*, *slang* To get started; start a job; get going. *"There's a lot to do today, so let's hop to it," the boss said.*

hopped up *adj.*, *slang* **1.** Doped with a narcotic drug. *Police found Jones hiding in an opium den, among other men all hopped up with the drug.* **2.** Full of eagerness; excited. *Fred was all hopped up about going over the ocean.*

horn in *v.*, *slang* To come in without invitation or welcome; interfere. Often used with *on*. *Jack would often horn in on conversations discussing things he knew nothing about. Lee horned in on Ray and Annie and wanted to dance with Annie.*

horse around *v.*, *slang* To join in rough teasing; play around. *They were a bunch of sailors on shore leave, horsing around where there were girls and* drinks. *John horsed around with the dog for a while when he came in from school.*

horse of a different color or **horse of another color** *n. phr., informal* Something altogether separate and different. *Anyone can be broke, but to steal is a horse of a different color. Do you mean that the boy with that pretty girl is her brother? I thought he was her boyfriend. Well, that's a horse of another color.*

horse sense *n., informal* A good understanding about what to do in life; good judgment; wisdom in making decisions. *Bill had never been to college, but he had plenty of horse sense. Some people are well educated and read many books, but still do not have much horse sense.*

horse trade *n.* **1.** The sale of a horse or the exchange of two horses. *It was a horse trade in which the owner of the worse animal gave a rifle to make the trade equal.* **2.** *informal* A business agreement or bargain arrived at after hard and skillful discussion. *Party leaders went around for months making horse trades to get support for their candidate. The horse trade finally called for a new car for the radio station in exchange for several weeks of advertising for the car dealer.*

hot air *n., informal* Nonsense, exaggerated talk, wasted words characterized by emotion rather than intellectual content. *That was just a lot of hot air what Joe said.*

hot and bothered *adj., informal* Excited and worried, dis-

pleased, or puzzled.—A hackneyed phrase. *Fritz got all hot and bothered when he failed in the test. Leona was all hot and bothered when her escort was late in coming for her. Jerry was hot and bothered about his invention when he couldn't get it to work. It is a small matter; don't get so hot and bothered.*

hot dog *n. phr., informal* A frankfurter or wiener in a roll. *The boys stopped on the way home for hot dogs and coffee.*

hot dog *interj., informal* Hurrah!—A cry used to show pleasure or enthusiasm. *"Hot dog!" Frank exclaimed when he unwrapped a birthday gift of a small record player.*

hot potato *n., informal* A question that causes strong argument and is difficult to settle. *Many school boards found segregation a hot potato in the 1960s.*

hot rod *n., informal* An older automobile changed so that it can gain speed quickly and go very fast. *Hot rods are used by young people especially in drag racing.*

hot water *n. informal* Trouble.—Used with *in, into, out of. John's thoughtless remark about religion got John into a lot of hot water. It was the kind of trouble where it takes a friend to get you out of hot water.*

house of cards *n. phr.* Something badly put together and easily knocked down; a poorly founded plan, hope, or action. *John's business fell apart like a house of cards..*

how about or **what about** *interrog.*—Used to ask for a decision, action, opinion, or explanation. **1.** Will you have or agree on? *How about another piece of pie? What about a game of tennis? How about going to the dance with me Saturday?* **2.** Will you lend or give me? *How about five dollars until Friday? What about a little help with these dishes?* **3.** What is to be done about? *What about the windows? Shall we close them before we go?* **4.** How do you feel about? What do you think about? What is to be thought or said? *What about women in politics? How about this button on the front of the typewriter?*

how come *informal also nonstandard* **how's come** *interrog.* How does it happen that? Why? *How come you are late? You're wearing your best clothes today. How come?*

how do you do *formal* How are you?—Usually as a reply to an introduction; it is in the form of a question but no answer is expected. *"Mary, I want you to meet my friend Fred. Fred, this is my wife, Mary." "How do you do, Mary?" "How do you do, Fred?"*

how's that *informal* What did you say? Will you please re-

peat that? *"I've just been up in a balloon for a day and a half." "How's that?" "The courthouse is on fire." "How's that again?"*

hue and cry *n.* **1.** An alarm and chase after a supposed wrongdoer; a pursuit usually by shouting men. *"Stop, thief," cried John as he ran. Others joined him, and soon there was a hue and cry.* **2.** An excited mass protest, alarm, or outcry of any kind. *The explosion was so terrible that people at a distance raised a great hue and cry about an earthquake.*

hush-hush *adj., informal* Kept secret or hidden; kept from public knowledge; hushed up; concealed. *The company had a new automobile engine that it was developing, but kept it a hush-hush project until they knew it was successful.*

hush up *v.* **1.** To keep news of (something) from getting out; prevent people from knowing about. *It isn't always easy to hush up a scandal.* **2.** *informal* To be or make quiet; stop talking, crying, or making some other noise.—Often used as a command. *"Hush up," Mother said, when we began to repeat ugly gossip.*

I

idiot box n. A television set. *Phil has been staring at the idiot box all afternoon.*

if the hill will not come to Muhammad, Muhammad will go to the hill If one person will not go to the other, then the other must go to him.—A proverb. *Grandfather won't come to visit us, so we must go and visit him. If the hill won't come to Muhammad, then Muhammad will go to the hill.*

if the shoe fits, wear it If what is said describes you, you are meant.—A proverb. *I won't say who, but some children are always late. If the shoe fits, wear it.*

if worst comes to worst If the worst thing that be imagined happens; if the worst possible thing happens; if troubles grow worse. *If worst comes to worst and Mr. Jones loses the house, he will send his family to his mother's farm. If worst comes to worst, we shall close the school for a few days.*

ill at ease adj. phr. Not feeling at ease or comfortable; anxious; worried; unhappy. *Donald had never been to a big party before and he was ill at ease. When Joe first went to dancing school, he was ill at ease, not knowing how to act.*

in a bind or **in a box** adv. phr., informal Likely to have trouble whether you do one thing or another. *Sam is in a bind because if he carries home his aunt's groceries, his teacher will be angry because he is late, and if he doesn't, his aunt will complain.*

in a circle or **in circles** adv. phr. Without any progress; without getting anywhere; uselessly. *The committee debated for two hours, just talking in circles. If you don't have a clear aim, you can work a long time and still be going in circles. He seemed to be working hard, but was just running around in circles.*

in a family way or **in the family way** adj. phr., informal Going to have a baby. *Sue and Liz are happy because their mother is in the family way. The Ferguson children are promising kittens to everyone because their cat is in a family way.*

in a hole or **in a spot** adj. phr., informal In an embarrassing or difficult position; in some trouble. *When the restaurant cook left at the beginning of the busy season, it put the restaurant owner in a hole.*

in and out adv. phr. Coming in and going out often. *He was very busy Saturday and was in and out all day.*

in a nutshell adv. phr., informal In a few words; briefly, without telling all about it. *We are in a hurry, so I'll give you the story in a nutshell. In a nutshell, the car is no bargain.*

in any case also **in any event** or **at all events** adv. phr. **1.** No matter what happens; surely; without fail; certainly; anyhow; anyway. *It may rain tomorrow, but we are going home in any case. I may not go to Europe, but in any event, I will visit you during the summer.* **2.** Regardless of anything else; whatever else may be true; anyhow; anyway. *Tom was not handsome and he was not brilliant, but at all events he worked hard and was loyal to his boss. I don't know if it is a white house or a brown house. At all events, it is a big house on Main Street.*

in a pig's eye *adv., slang, informal* Hardly; unlikely; not so. *Would I marry him? In a pig's eye.*

in a pinch *adv. phr., informal* In an emergency. *Dave is a good friend who will always help out in a pinch.*

in arms *adv. phr.* Having guns and being ready to fight; armed. *When our country is at war, we have many men in arms.*

in a way *adv. phr.* **1.** *also informal* **in a kind of way** *or informal* **in a sort of way** To a certain extent; a little; somewhat. *I like Jane in a way, but she is very proud.* **2.** In one thing. *In a way, this book is easier; it is much shorter.*

in a world of one's own *or* **in a world by oneself** **1.** In the place where you belong; in your own personal surroundings; apart from other people. *They are in a little world of their own in their house on the mountain.* **2a.** In deep thought or concentration. *Mary is in a world of her own when she is*

playing the piano. **2b.** *slang* Not caring about or connected with other people in thoughts or actions.—Usually used sarcastically. *That boy is in a world all by himself. He never knows what is happening around him.*

in case *adv. phr., informal* **1.** In order to be prepared; as a precaution; if there is need. — Usually used in the phrase *just in case. The bus is usually on time, but start early, just in case. The big dog was tied up, but John carried a stick, just in case.* **2. in case** *or* **in the event** *conj.* If it happens that; if it should happen that; if; lest. *Tom took his skates in case they found a place to skate. Let me know in case you're not coming. The night watchman is in the store in case there is ever a fire. Keep the window closed in case it rains. I stayed home in case you called. In the event that our team wins, there will be a big celebration. What shall we do in case it snows?*

in character *adv. or adj. phr.* **1.** In agreement with a person's character or personality; in the way that a person usually behaves or is supposed to behave; as usual; characteristic; typical; suitable. *John was very rude at the party, and that was not in character because he is usually very polite. The way Judy comforted the little girl was in character. She did it gently and kindly.* **2.** Suitable for the part or the kind of part being acted; natural to the way a character in a book or play is supposed to act. *The fat actor in the movie was in character because* the character he played was supposed to be fat and jolly. It would not have been in character for Robin Hood to steal from a poor man.

in charge *adv. or adj. phr.* **1.** In authority or control; in a position to care for or supervise; responsible. *If you have any questions, ask the boss. He's in charge.* **2.** Under care or supervision. *The sick man was taken in charge by the doctor. During your visit to the library, you will be in the librarian's charge.*

in charge of *prep.* **1.** Responsible for; having supervision or care of. *Marian is in charge of selling tickets. The girl in charge of refreshments forgot to order the ice cream for the party. When our class had a play, the teacher put Harold in charge of the stage curtain.* **2.** or **in the charge of** Under the care or supervision of. *Mother puts the baby in the charge of the baby-sitter while she is out. The money was given in charge of Mr. Jackson for safe-keeping.*

in check *adv. phr.* In a position where movement or action is not allowed or stopped; under control; kept quiet or back. *The boy was too small to keep the big dog in check, and the dog broke away from his leash. The soldiers tried to keep the attacking Indians in check until help came. Mary couldn't hold her feelings in check any longer and began to cry.*

in clover or **in the clover** *adv. or adj. phr., informal* In rich comfort; rich or successful; having a pleasant or easy life. *They live in clover because*

their father is rich. When we finish the hard part we'll be in the clover.

in cold blood *adv. phr.* Without feeling or pity; in a purposely cruel way; coolly and deliberately. *The bank robbers planned to shoot in cold blood anyone who got in their way. The bandits planned to murder in cold blood all farmers in the village by the river.*

in common *adv. phr.* Shared together or equally; in use or ownership by all. *Mr. and Mrs. Smith own the store in common. The four boys grew up together and have a lot in common. The swimming pool is used in common by all the children in the neighborhood.*

in deep *adj. phr.* Seriously mixed up in something, especially in trouble. *George began borrowing small sums of money to bet on horses, and before he knew it he was in deep.*

in fact also **in point of fact** *adv. phr.* Really truthfully. Often used for emphasis. *No one believed it but, in fact, Mary did get an A on her book report. It was a very hot day; in fact, it was 100 degrees.*

in for *prep., informal* Unable to avoid; sure to get. *The naughty puppy was in for a spanking. On Christmas morning we are in for some surprises. We saw Father looking angrily out of the broken window, and we knew we were in for it.*

in good time or **in good season** *adv. phr.* **1.** A little early; sooner than necessary. *The school bus arrived in good* *time. The students finished their school work in good time. We reached the station in good season to catch the 9:15 bus for New York.* **2.** *or* **in due course** *or* **in due season** *or* **in due time** In the usual amount of time; at the right time; in the end. *Spring and summer will arrive in due course. Sally finished her spelling in due course.*

in hand *adv. or adj. phr.* **1.** Under control. *The principal was happy to find that the new teacher had her class in hand. The baby-sitter kept the children well in hand. Mabel was frightened when the barking dog ran at her, but she soon got herself in hand and walked on.* **2.** In your possession; with you. —Often used in the phrase *cash in hand. Tom figured that his cash in hand with his weekly pay would be enough to buy a car.* **3.** Being worked on; with you to do. *We should finish the work we have in hand before we begin something new.*

in kind *adv. phr.* In a similar way; with the same kind of thing. *My neighbor pays me in kind for walking her dog. Lois returned Mary's insult in kind.*

in league with *or informal* **in cahoots with** *prep.* In secret agreement or partnership with (someone); working together secretly with, especially for harm. *People once believed that some women were witches in league with the devil. The mayor's enemies spread a rumor that he was in cahoots with gangsters.*

in light of *also* **in the light of** *adj. phr.* **1.** As a result of new information; by means of new ideas. *The teacher changed John's grade in the light of the extra work in the workbook.* **2.** Because of. *In light of the muddy field, the football team wore their old uniforms.*

in line[1] *adv. phr.* In or into a straight line. *The boys stood in line to buy their tickets. Tom set the chairs in line along the wall. The carpenter put the edges of the boards in line.*

in line[2] *adj. phr.* **1.** In a position in a series or after someone else. *John is in line for the presidency of the club next year. Mary is fourth in line to be admitted to the sorority.* **2.** Obeying or agreeing with what is right or usual; doing or being what people expect or accept; within ordinary or proper limits. *The coach kept the excited team in line. When the teacher came back into the room, she quickly brought the class back in line. The government passed a new law to keep prices in line.*

in love *adj. phr.* Liking very much; loving. *John is in love with Helen. Tom and Ellen are in love. Mary is in love with her new wristwatch.*

in luck *adj. phr.* Being lucky; having good luck; finding something good by chance. *Bill was in luck when he found the money on the street. Mary dropped her glasses and they did not break. She was in luck.*

in memory of *prep.* As something that makes people remember (a person or thing); as a reminder of; as a memorial to. *The building was named Ford Hall in memory of a man* named James Ford. Many special ceremonies are in memory of famous men.

in no time or **in nothing flat** adv. phr., informal In a very little time; soon; quickly. When the entire class worked together they finished the project in no time. The bus filled with students in nothing flat.

in on prep. **1.** Joining together for. The children collected money from their classmates and went in on a present for their teacher. **2.** Told about; having knowledge of. Bob was in on the secret. The other girls wouldn't let Mary in on what they knew.

in one's element adv. phr. **1.** In one's natural surroundings. The deep-sea fish is in his element in deep ocean water. **2.** Where you can do your best. John is in his element working on the farm.

in one's face adv. phr. **1.** Against your face. The trick cigar blew up in the clown's face. A cold wind was in our faces as we walked to school. **2.** In front of you. The maid slammed the door in the salesman's face. I told the boys that they were wrong, but they laughed in my face.

in one's good graces or **in one's good books** adv. phr. Approved of by you; liked by someone. Ruth is in her mother's good graces because she ate all her supper. Bill is back in the good graces of his girlfriend because he gave her a box of candy.

in one's hair adj. phr., informal Bothering you again and again; always annoying. Johnny got in Father's hair when he was trying to read the paper by running and shouting. The grown-ups sent the children out to play so that the children wouldn't be in their hair while they were talking.

in one's mind's eye adv. phr. In the memory; in the imagination. In his mind's eye he saw again the house he had lived in when he was a child. In his mind's eye, he could see just what the vacation was going to be like.

in one's shell or **into one's shell** adv. or adj. phr., informal In or into bashfulness; into silence; not sociable; unfriendly. After Mary's mother scolded her, she went into her shell. The teacher tried to get Rose to talk to her, but she stayed in her shell.

in one's shoes also **in one's boots** adv. phr. In or into one's place or position. How would you like to be in a lion tamer's boots?

in one's tracks adv. phr., informal Just where one is at the moment; abruptly; immediately. The hunter's rifle cracked and the rabbit dropped in his tracks. Mary stopped dead in her tracks, turned around, and ran back home.

in order to or **so as to** conj For the purpose of; to.—Used with an infinitive. In order to follow the buffalo, the Indians often had to move their camps. We picked apples so as to make a pie.

in part adv. phr. To some extent; partly; not wholly.—

IN THE AIR 171

Often used with *large* or *small*. *We planted the garden in part with flowers. But in large part we planted vegetables. Tom was only in small part responsible.*

in particular *adv. phr.* In a way apart from others; more than others; particularly; especially. *The speaker talked about sports in general and about football in particular. All the boys played well and Bill in particular. Margaret liked all her classes, but she liked sewing class in particular.*

ins and outs *n. phr.* The special ways of going somewhere or doing something; the different parts. *The janitor knows all the ins and outs of the big school building. Jerry's father is a good life insurance salesman; he knows all the ins and outs of the business.*

in short supply *adj. phr.* Not enough; in too small a quantity or amount; in less than the amount or number needed. *The cookies are in short supply, so don't eat them all up. We have five people and only four beds, so the beds are in short supply.*

inside out *adv.* **1.** So that the inside is turned outside. *Mother turns the stockings inside out when she washes them.* **2.** *or* **inside and out** *also in* **and out** In every part; throughout; completely. *David knows the parts of his bicycle inside out. We searched the house inside and out for the kitten.*

inside track *n. phr.* **1.** The inside, shortest distance around a curved racetrack; the place that is closest to the inside

fence. *A big white horse had the inside track at the start of the race.* **2.** *informal* An advantage due to special connections or information. *I would probably get that job if I could get the inside track.*

in spite of *prep. phr.* Against the influence or effect of; in opposition to; defying the effect of; despite. *In spite of the bad storm John delivered his papers on time. In spite of all their differences, Joan and Ann remain friends.*

in stitches *adj. phr., informal* Laughing so hard that the sides ache; in a fit of laughing hard. *The comedian was so funny that he had everyone who was watching him in stitches.*

in stock *adj. phr.* Having something ready to sell or use; in present possession or supply; to be sold. *The store had no more red shoes in stock, so Mary chose brown ones instead.*

in store *adj. or adv. phr.* **1.** Saved up in case of need; ready for use or for some purpose. *If the electricity goes off, we have candles in store in the closet. The squirrel has plenty of nuts in store for the winter.* **2.** Ready to happen; waiting.—Often used in the phrase *hold* or *have in store. What does the future hold in store for the boy who ran away? There is a surprise in store for Helen when she gets home.*

in the air *adv. phr.* **1.** In everyone's thoughts. *Christmas was in the air for weeks before. The war filled people's thoughts every day; it was in the air.* **2.**

Meeting the bodily senses; surrounding you so as to be smelled or felt. *Spring is in the air. Rain is in the air.*

in the bag *adj. phr., informal* Sure to be won or gotten; certain. *Jones had the election in the bag after the shameful news about his opponent came out. We thought we had the game in the bag.*

in the black *adv. or adj. phr., informal* In a successful or profitable way; so as to make money. *The big store was running in the black. A business must stay in the black to keep on.* Contrast in the red.

in the cards *also* **on the cards** *adj. phr., informal* To be expected; likely to happen; foreseeable; predictable. *It was in the cards for the son to succeed his father as head of the business. John finally decided that it wasn't in the cards for him to succeed with that company.*

in the clear *adj. phr.* **1.** Free of anything that makes moving or seeing difficult; with nothing to limit action. *The plane climbed above the clouds and was flying in the clear. Jack passed the ball to Tim, who was in the clear and ran for a touchdown.* **2.** *informal* Free of blame or suspicion; not thought to be guilty. *After John told the principal that he broke the window, Martin was in the clear. Steve was the last to leave the locker room, and the boys suspected him of stealing Tom's watch, but the coach found the watch and put Steve in the clear.* **3.** Free of debt; not owing money to anyone. *Bob borrowed a*

thousand dollars from his father to start his business, but at the end of the first year he was in the clear.

in the clouds *adj. phr.* Far from real life; in dreams; in fancy; in thought. *When Alice agreed to marry Jim, Jim went home in the clouds.*—Often used with *head, mind, thoughts. Mary is looking out the window, not at the chalkboard; her head is in the clouds again. A good teacher should have his head in the clouds sometimes, but his feet always on the ground.*

in the dark *adj. phr.* In ignorance; without information. *John was in the dark about the job he was being sent to. If the government controls the news, it can keep people in the dark on any topic it chooses. Mary had a letter from Sue yesterday, but she was left in the dark about Sue's plans to visit her.*

in the doghouse *adj. phr., slang* In disgrace or disfavor. *Our neighbor got in the doghouse with his wife by coming home drunk. Jerry is in the doghouse because he dropped the ball, and the other team won because of that.*

in the groove *adj. phr., slang* Doing something very well; near perfection; at your best. *The band was right in the groove that night. It was an exciting football game; every player was really in the groove.*

in the hole *adv. or adj. phr., informal* **1a.** Having a score lower than zero in a game, especially a card game; to a score below zero. *John went three points in the hole on the first* *hand of the card game.* **1b.** Behind an opponent; in difficulty in a sport or game. *We had their pitcher in the hole with the bases full and no one out.* **2.** In debt; behind financially. *John went in the hole with his hot dog stand. It's a lot easier to get in the hole than to get out again.*

in the line of duty *adj. phr.* Done or happening as part of a job. *The policeman was shot in the line of duty. The soldier had to clean his rifle in the line of duty.*

in the long run *adv. phr.* In the end; in the final result. *John knew that he could make a success of the little weekly paper in the long run. You may make good grades by studying only before examinations, but you will succeed in the long run only by studying hard every day.*

in the market for *adj. phr.* Wishing to buy; ready to buy. *Mr. Jones is in the market for a new car. People are always in the market for entertainment.*

in the red *adv. or adj. phr., informal* In an unprofitable way; so as to lose money. *A large number of American radio stations operate in the red. A rich man who has a farm or ranch often runs it in the red, but makes his money with his factory or business.* [From the fact that people who keep business records usually write in red ink how much money they lose and in black ink how much money they gain.]

in the saddle *adv. or adj. phr.* In command; in control; in a position to order or boss

others. *Mr. Park was in the saddle when he had over half the company's stock. Getting appointed chief of police put Stevens in the saddle.*

in the same boat *adv. or adj. phr.* In the same trouble; in the same fix; in the same bad situation. *When the town's one factory closed and hundreds of people lost their jobs, all the storekeepers were in the same boat. Dick was disappointed when Fern refused to marry him, but he knew others were in the same boat.*

in the soup *adj. phr., slang* In serious trouble; in confusion; in disorder. *When his wife overdrew their bank account without telling him, Mr. Phillips suddenly found himself really in the soup. The police misunderstood Harry's night errand, and arrested him, which put him in the soup with the boss.*

in the swim *adj. phr.* Doing the same things that other people are doing; following the fashion (as in business or social affairs); busy with what most people are doing. *Jim found some college friends at the lake that summer, and soon was in the swim of things. Mary went to New York with introductions to writers and artists, and that winter she was quite in the swim.*

in the wake of *prep., literary* As a result of; right after; following. *Many troubles follow in the wake of war. There were heavy losses of property in the wake of the flood.*

in the wind *adj. phr.* Seeming probable; being planned; soon to happen. *Changes in top* *management of the company had been in the wind for weeks. Tom's close friends knew that marriage was in the wind.*

in the works *adv. or adj. phr.* In preparation; being planned or worked on; in progress. *John was told that the paving of his street was in the works. It was reported that the playwright had a new play in the works. The manager told the employees that a raise in wages was in the works.*

in the wrong *adj. phr.* With moral or legal right or truth against you; against justice, truth, or fact; wrong. *In attacking a smaller boy, Jack was plainly in the wrong. Mary was in the wrong to drink from a finger bowl. Since he had put pennies behind the fuses, Bill was in the wrong when fire broke out.*

in time *adv. or adj. phr.* **1.** Soon enough. *We got to Washington in time for the cherry blossoms. We got to the station just in time to catch the bus. John liked to get to work in good time and talk to the man who worked on his machine before him.* **2.** In the end; after a while; finally. *Fred and Jim did not like each other at first, but in time they became friends.* **3.** In the right rhythm; in step. *The marchers kept in time with the band. Johnny didn't play his piano piece in time.*

into thin air *adv. phr.* Without anything left; completely. *When Bob returned to the room, he was surprised to find that his books had vanished into thin air.*

in touch *adj. phr.* Talking or writing to each other; giving and getting news. *John kept in touch with his school friends during the summer. Police anywhere in the U.S. can get in touch instantly with any other police department by teletype. The man claimed to be in touch with people on another planet.*

in tow *adj. phr.* **1.** Being pulled. *The tugboat had the large ocean liner in tow as they came into the harbor. An engine came with a long string of cars in tow.* **2.** Being taken from place to place; along with someone. *Janet took the new girl in tow and showed her where to go. Mrs. Hayes went to the supermarket with her four little children in tow.*

in tune *adv. or adj. phr.* **1.** At the proper musical pitch; high or low enough in sound. *The piano is in tune.* **2.** Going well together; in agreement; matching; agreeable.—Often used with *with. In his new job, John felt in tune with his surroundings and his associates.*

in turn *adv. phr.* According to a settled order; each following another. *Each man in turn got up and spoke. Two teachers supervised the lunch hour in turn. Two of the three boys tease their younger brother—John, the biggest, teases Bob, the middle boy; and Bob in turn teases Tim, the youngest.*

in two shakes of a lamb's tail *adv., informal* Quickly; in no time at all. *I'll be back in two shakes of a lamb's tail.*

in vain *adv. phr.* Without effect; without getting the desired result; without success. *The drowning man called in vain for help. To cry over spilled milk is to cry in vain.*

in view *adv. or adj. phr.* **1.** In sight; visible. *We came around a bend and there was the ocean in view.* **2.** As a purpose, hope, or expectation. *John had his son's education in view when he began to save money. The end that we must keep always in view is peace with justice.*

in view of *prep.* After thinking about; because of. *Schools were closed for the day in view of the heavy snowstorm. In view of rising labor costs, many companies have turned to automation.*

in with *prep.* In friendship, favor, or closeness with; in the trust or liking of. *We trusted on Byrd's being in with the mayor, not knowing that the mayor no longer liked him. It took the new family some time to get in with their neighbors.*

I.O.U. *adj. phr.* I owe you, abbreviated; a promissory note. *I had to borrow some money from John and, in order to repay him both of us, I wrote him an I.O.U. note for $250.*

iron in the fire *n. phr.* Something you are doing; one of the projects with which a person is busy; job. *John had a number of irons in the fire, and he managed to keep all of them hot.*—Usually used in the phrase *too many irons in the fire.* "*Ed has a dozen things going all the time, but none of them seem to work out." "No*

wonder. *He has too many irons in the fire.*"

iron out *v., informal* To discuss and reach an agreement about (a difference); find a solution for (a problem); remove (a difficulty). *The company and its workers ironed out their differences over hours and pay. The House and Senate ironed out the differences between their two different tax bills.*

itching palm *n., slang* A wish for money; greed. *He was born with an itching palm. The bellboys in that hotel seem always to have itching palms.*

it's a cinch *informal sentence* It is very easy. "*What about the final exam?" Fred asked. "It was a cinch," Sam answered.*

it's a deal *informal sentence* Consider it done; OK; it is agreed. "*How much for this used car?" Bill asked. "Two thousand," the man answered. "I'll give $1,500," Bill said. "It's a deal!" the owner answered as they sealed the transaction.*

it's high time *informal sentence* It is overdue. *It is high time for John Browning to be promoted to full professor; he has written a great deal but his books went unnoticed.*

Ivy League *n.* A small group of the older and more famous eastern U.S. colleges and universities. *Several Ivy League teams play each other regularly each year. Harvard, Yale, and Princeton were the original Ivy League.*

jack of all trades n., informal (Often followed by the words "master of none.") A person who is knowledgeable in many areas. Can be used as praise, or as a derogatory remark depending on the context and the intonation. *Peter is a jack of all trades; he can survive anywhere!* "How come Joe did such a sloppy job?" Mary asked. "He's a jack of all trades," Sally answered.

jack up v. **1.** To lift with a jack. *The man jacked up his car to fit a flat tire.* **2.** informal To make (a price) higher; raise. *Just before Christmas, some stores jack up their prices.*

jailbait n., slang A girl below the legal age of consent for sex; one who tempts you to intimacy which is punishable by imprisonment. *Stay away from Arabella, she is a jailbait.*

jawbreaker n. **1.** A large piece of hard candy or bubblegum. *Billy asked his mother for a quarter to buy some jawbreakers and a chocolate bar.* **2.** informal A word or name that is hard to pronounce. *His name, Nissequogue, is a real jawbreaker.*

jazz up v., slang To brighten up; add more noise, movement, or color; make more lively or exciting. *The party was very dull until Pete jazzed it up with his drums.*

John Doe n. A name used for an unknown person, especially in police and law business. *The alarm went out for a John Doe who stole the diamonds from the store.*

John Hancock or **John Henry** n., informal Your signature; your name in writing. *The man said, "Put your John Hancock on this paper." Joe felt proud when he put his John Henry on his very first driver's license.*

Johnny-come-lately n. Someone new in a place or group; newcomer; also: a new person who takes an active part in group affairs before the group has accepted him; upstart. *Everybody was amazed when a Johnny-come-lately beat the old favorite in the race. When it looked as though Mr. Brown had a good chance of winning, many Johnny-come-latelies began to support him.*

Johnny-on-the-spot adj. phr. At the right place when needed; present and ready to help; very prompt; on time. *A good waterboy is always Johnny-on-the-spot. The firemen were Johnny-on-the-spot and put out the fire in the house soon after it started.*

jump at v. To take or accept quickly and gladly. *Johnny jumped at the invitation to go swimming with his brother.*

jump bail or **skip bail** v. phr., informal To run away and fail to come to trial, and so to give up a certain amount of money already given to a court of law to hold with the promise that you would come. *The robber paid $2000 bail so he wouldn't be put in jail before his trial, but he jumped bail and escaped to Mexico. The man skipped bail because he was afraid the court might put him in jail for a long time.*

jump ball *n.* The starting of play in basketball by tossing the ball into the air between two opposing players, each of whom jumps and tries to hit the ball to a member of his own team. *Two players held onto the ball at the same time and the referee called a jump ball.*

jump down one's throat *v. phr.* To suddenly become very angry at someone; scold severely or angrily. *The teacher jumped down Billy's throat when Billy said he did not do his homework.*

jumping-off place *n. phr.* **1.** A place so far away that it seems to be the end of the world. *Columbus' sailors were afraid they would arrive at the jumping-off place if they sailed farther west. So you visited Little America? That sounds like the jumping-off place!* **2.** The starting place of a long, hard trip or of something difficult or dangerous. *The jumping-off place for the explorer's trip through the jungle was a little village.*

jump on *or* **jump all over** *or* **land on** *or* **land all over** *v. phr., informal* To scold; criticize; blame. *Tom's boss jumped all over Tom because he made a careless mistake. Janice landed on Robert for dressing carelessly for their date. "I don't*

know why Bill is always jumping on me; I just don't understand him," said Bob.*

jump on the bandwagon *or* **get on the bandwagon** *v. phr., informal* To join a popular cause or movement. *At the last possible moment, the senator jumped on the winning candidate's bandwagon.*

jump out of one's skin *v. phr., informal* To be badly frightened; be very much surprised. *The lightning struck so close to Bill that he almost jumped out of his skin.*

jump the gun *also* **beat the gun** *v. phr.* **1.** To start before the starter's gun in a race. *The runners were called back because one of them jumped the gun.* **2.** *informal* To start before you should; start before anyone else. *The new students were not supposed to come before noon, but one boy jumped the gun and came to school at eight in the morning. The students planned to say happy birthday to the principal when the teacher raised her hand, but Sarah jumped the gun and said it when he came into the room.*

jump the track *v. phr.* **1.** To go off rails; go or run the wrong way. *The train jumped the track and there was a terrible accident. The pulley of the clothesline jumped the track and Mother's washing fell down.* **2.** *informal* To change from one thought or idea to another without plan or reason; change the thought or idea you are talking about to something different. *Bob didn't finish his algebra homework because his mind kept jumping the track to* think about the new girl in class.

jump through a hoop v. phr., informal To do whatever you are told to do; obey any order. Bob would jump through a hoop for Mary.

jump to a conclusion v. phr. To decide too quickly or without thinking or finding the facts. Jerry saw his dog limping on a bloody leg and jumped to the conclusion that it had been shot.

junked up adj. or v. phr., slang, drug culture To be under the influence of drugs, especially heroin. You can't talk to Billy, he's all junked up.

just about adv., informal Nearly; almost; practically. Just about everyone in town came to hear the mayor speak. The dress came down to just about the middle of her knee. Has

Mary finished peeling the potatoes? Just about.

just so[1] adj. Exact; exactly right. Mrs. Robinson likes to keep her house just so, and she makes the children take off their shoes when they come in the house.

just so[2] conj. Provided; if. Take as much food as you want, just so you don't waste any food.

just the other way or **the other way around** adv. phr. Just the opposite. One would have thought that Goliath would defeat David, but it was the other way around.

just what the doctor ordered n. phr., informal Exactly what is needed or wanted. "Ah! Just what the doctor ordered!" exclaimed Joe when Mary brought him a cold soda.

kangaroo court *n.* A self-appointed group that decides what to do to someone who is supposed to have done wrong. *The Chicago mob held a kangaroo court and shot the gangster who competed with Al Capone.*

keel over *v.* **1.** To turn upside down; tip over; overturn.—Usually refers to a boat. *The strong wind made the sailboat keel over and the passengers fell into the water.* **2.** *informal* To fall over in a faint; faint. *It was so hot during the assembly program that two girls who were standing on the stage keeled over. When the principal told the girl her father died, she keeled right over.*

keep after *v.*, *informal* To speak to (someone) about something again and again; remind over and over again. *Some pupils will do sloppy work unless the teacher keeps after them to write neatly. Sue's mother had to keep after her to clean her bedroom.*

keep an eye on *or* **keep one's eye on** *or* **have one's eye on** *v. phr.* **1.** To watch carefully; not stop paying attention to. *Keep an eye on the stove in case the coffee boils. You must keep your eye on the ball when you play tennis. A good driver keeps his eye on the road. The teacher had her eye on me because she thought I was cheating. Billy keeps a jealous eye on* his toys. *The lion tamer keeps a sharp eye on the lions when he is in the cage.* **2.** To watch and do what is needed for; mind. *Mother told Jane to keep an eye on the baby while she was in the store. Mr. Brown told John to keep an eye on the store while he was out.*

keep a stiff upper lip *v. phr.* To be brave; face trouble bravely. *He was very much worried about his sick daughter, but he kept a stiff upper lip. Although he was having some trouble with the engine, the pilot kept a stiff upper lip and landed the plane safely.*

keep at *v.* To continue to do; go on with. *Mary kept at her homework until she finished it.*

keep body and soul together *v. phr.* To keep alive; survive. *John was unemployed most of the year and hardly made enough money to keep body and soul together.*

keep books *v. phr.* To keep records of money gained and spent; do the work of a bookkeeper. *Miss Jones keeps the company's books.*

keep down *v.* Keep from progressing or growing; keep within limits; control. *The children could not keep their voices down. We hoe the garden to keep down the weeds. You can't keep a good man down.*

keep house *also* **play house** *v. phr.*, *informal* To live together without being married.

Bob and Nancy keep house these days.

keep on *v.* **1.** To go ahead; not stop; continue. *The neighbors asked them to stop making noise, but they kept right on. Columbus kept on until he saw land.*—Often used before a present participle. *Columbus kept on sailing until he saw land. The boy kept on talking even though the teacher had asked him to stop.* **2.** To allow to continue working for you. *The new owner kept Fred on as gardener.*

keep one's chin up *v. phr.* To be brave; be determined; face trouble with courage. *He didn't think that he would ever get out of the jungle alive, but he kept his chin up.*

keep one's eye on the ball *v. phr.* **1.** To watch the ball at all times in a sport, usually in order to hit it or get it; not stop watching the ball. *Keep your eye on the ball or you won't be able to hit it.* **2.** *informal* To be watchful and ready; be wide-awake and ready to win or succeed; be smart. *Tom is just starting on the job but if he keeps his eye on the ball, he will be promoted.*

keep one's head *also* **keep one's wits about one** *v. phr.* To stay calm when there is trouble or danger. *When Tim heard the fire alarm he kept his head and looked for the nearest exit.*

keep one's mouth shut *v. phr., informal* To be or stay silent.—A rude expression when used as a command. *When the crooks were captured by the police, their leader warned them to*

keep their mouths shut. *Charles began to tell Barry how to kick the ball, and Barry said angrily,* "Keep your mouth shut!"

keep one's nose clean *v. phr., slang* To stay out of trouble; do only what you should do. *The boss said Jim could have the job as long as he kept his nose clean and worked hard. The policeman warned the boys to keep their noses clean unless they wanted to go to jail.*

keep one's nose to the grindstone *or* **have one's nose to the grindstone** *or* **hold one's nose to the grindstone** *v. phr., informal* To work hard all the time; keep busy with boring or tiresome work. *Sarah keeps her nose to the grindstone and saves as much as possible to start her own business.*

keep one's own counsel *v. phr., formal* To keep your ideas and plans to yourself. *John listened to what everyone had to say in the discussion, but he kept his own counsel. Although everybody gave Mrs. O'Connor advice about what to do with her house, she kept her own counsel.*

keep one's shirt on *v. phr., slang* To calm down; keep from losing your temper or getting impatient or excited. *Bob got very angry when John accidentally bumped into him, but John told him to keep his shirt on.*—Usually used as a command; may be considered impolite. *John said to Bob,* "Keep your shirt on."

keep pace *v. phr.* To go as fast; go at the same rate; not get behind. *When they go for a* walk, Johnny has to take long steps to keep pace with his father. When Billy was moved to a more advanced class, he had to work hard to keep pace.

keep tab on or **keep tabs on** v. phr., informal **1.** To keep a record of. The government tries to keep tabs on all the animals in the park. **2.** To keep a watch on; check. The house mother kept tabs on the girls to be sure they were clean and neat.

keep the ball rolling v. phr., informal To keep up an activity or action; not allow something that is happening to slow or stop. Clyde kept the ball rolling at the party by dancing with a lamp shade on his head.

keep the wolf (wolves) from the door v. phr. To avoid hunger, poverty, and/or creditors. "I don't like my job," Mike complained, "but I must do something to keep the wolves from the door."

keep track v. phr. To know about changes; stay informed or up-to-date; keep a count or record. What day of the week is it? I can't keep track.—Usually used with of. Mr. Stevens kept track of his business by telephone when he was in the hospital. The farmer has so many chickens, he can hardly keep track of them all.

keep under one's hat v. phr., informal To keep secret; not tell. Mr. Jones knew who had won the contest, but he kept it under his hat until it was announced publicly.—Often used as a command. Keep it under your hat.

keep up v. **1a.** To go on; not stop; continue. The rain kept up for two days and the roads were flooded. **1b.** To go on with (something); continue steadily; never stop. Mrs. Smith told John to keep up the good work. The teacher asked Dick to stop bothering Mary, but he kept it up. **2a.** To go at the same rate as others. John had to work hard to keep up. Billy was the youngest boy on the hike, but he kept up with the others. **2b.** To keep (something) at the same level or rate or in good condition. The shortage of tomatoes kept the prices up. Grandfather was too poor to keep up his house. **3.** To keep informed.—Usually used with on or with. Mary is interested in politics and always keeps up with the news.

keep up with the Joneses v. phr. To follow the latest fashion; try to be equal with your neighbors. Mrs. Smith kept buying every new thing that was advertised. Finally Mr. Smith told her to stop trying to keep up with the Joneses and to start thinking for herself.

keep watch v. phr. To be vigilant; be alert; guard. The police have asked the neighborhood to keep watch against an escaped convict.

kettle of fish v. phr., informal Something to be considered; how things are; a happening; business. I thought he needed money, but it was another kettle of fish—his car had disappeared.—Usually used with pretty, fine, nice, but meaning bad trouble. He had two flat tires and no spare on a country road at night, which was certainly a pretty *kettle of fish.* This is a fine *kettle of fish!* I forgot my book.

keyed up *adj., informal* Excited; nervous; anxious to do something. *Mary was all keyed up about the exam. Mother would not let Tom read a ghost story at bedtime; she said it would get him keyed up.*

kick around *v., informal* **1.** To act roughly or badly to; treat badly; bully. *John likes to kick around the little boys. Mr. Jones is always kicking his dog around.* **2.** To lie around or in a place; be treated carelessly; be neglected. *This old coat has been kicking around the closet for years. The letter kicked around on my desk for days.* **3.** *slang* To talk easily or carelessly back and forth about; examine in a careless or easygoing way. *Bob and I kicked around the idea of going swimming, but it was hot and we were too lazy.* **4.** To move about often; go from one job or place to another; become experienced. *Harry has kicked around all over the world as a merchant seaman.*

kick back *v., slang, informal* To pay money illegally for favorable contract arrangements. *I will do it if you kick back a few hundred for my firm.*

kickback *n., slang, informal* Money paid illegally for favorable treatment. *He was arrested for making kickback payments.*

kick down *v. phr., slang* To shift an automobile, jeep, or truck into lower gear by handshifting. *Joe kicked the jeep down from third to second, and we slowed down.*

kick it *v. phr., slang* To end a bad or unwanted habit such as drinking, smoking, or drug addiction. *Farnsworth finally kicked it; he's in good shape.*

kickoff *n.* The start of something, like a new venture, a business, a sports event, or a concert season. *Beethoven's Ninth will be the kickoff for this summer season at Ravinia.*

kick off *v. phr.* **1.** To make the kick that begins a football game. *John kicked off and the football game started.* **2.** *informal* To begin; launch; start. *The candidate kicked off his campaign with a speech on television. The fund raising drive was kicked off with a theater party.* **3.** *slang* To die. *Mr. Jones was almost ninety years old when he kicked off.*

kick oneself *v. phr., informal* To be sorry or ashamed; regret. *When John missed the train, he kicked himself for not having left earlier. Mary could have kicked herself for letting the secret out before it was announced officially.*

kick out *or* **boot out** *v., informal* To make (someone) go or leave; get rid of; dismiss. *The boys made so much noise at the movie that the manager kicked them out. The chief of police was booted out of office because he was a crook.*

kick over *v.* **1.** Of a motor: To begin to work. *He had not used his car for two months and when he tried to start it, the motor would not kick over.* **2.**

slang To pay; contribute. *The gang forced all the storekeepers on the block to kick over $5 a week.* **3.** *slang* To die. *Mrs. O'Leary's cow kicked over this morning.*

kick the bucket *v. phr., slang* To die. *Old Mr. Jones kicked the bucket just two days before his ninety-fourth birthday.*

kick up a fuss *or* **kick up a row** *or* **raise a row** *also* **kick up a dust** *v. phr., informal* To make trouble; make a disturbance. *When the teacher gave the class five more hours of homework, the class kicked up a fuss. When the teacher left the room, two boys kicked up a row.*

kick up one's heels *v. phr., informal* To have a merry time; celebrate. *When exams were over the students went to town to kick up their heels. Mary was usually very quiet but at the farewell party she kicked up her heels and had a wonderful time.*

kill off *v.* To kill or end completely; destroy. *The factory dumped poisonous wastes into the river and killed off the fish. The President suggested a new law to Congress but many members of Congress were against the idea and they killed it off. Mother made Nancy practice her dancing an hour every day; Nancy got tired of dancing and that killed off her interest.*

kill the goose that laid the golden egg To spoil something that is good or something that you have, by being greedy.—A proverb. *Mrs. Jones gives you an apple from her tree whenever you go by her house, but don't kill the goose that laid the golden egg by bothering her too much.*

kill time *v. phr.* To cause the time to pass more rapidly; waste time. *The plane trip to Hong Kong was long and tiring, but we managed to kill time by watching several movies.*

kill two birds with one stone *v. phr.* To succeed in doing two things by only one action; get two results from one effort. *Mother stopped at the supermarket to buy bread and then went to get Jane at dancing class; she killed two birds with one stone. The history teacher told us that making an outline kills two birds with one stone; it makes us study the lesson till we understand it, and it gives us notes to review before the test.*

knock about *or* **knock around** *v.* To travel without a plan; go where you please. *After he graduated from college, Joe knocked about for a year seeing the country before he went to work in his father's business.*

knocked out *adj., slang* Intoxicated; drugged; out of one's mind. *Jim sounds so incoherent, he must be knocked out.*

knock it off *v. phr., slang, informal* **1.** To stop talking about something considered not appropriate or nonsensical by the listener.—Used frequently as an imperative. *Come on, Joe, knock it off, you're not making any sense at all!* **2.** To cease doing something; to quit.—Heavily favored in the imperative. *Come* *on boys, knock it off, you're breaking the furniture in my room!*

knock off *v. phr., slang* **1.** To burglarize someone. *They knocked off the Manning residence.* **2.** To murder someone. *The gangsters knocked off Herman.*

knock off one's feet *v. phr.* To surprise (someone) so much that he does not know what to do. *Her husband's death knocked Mrs. Jones off her feet. When Charlie was given the prize, it knocked him off his feet for a few minutes.*

knock one's block off *v. phr., slang* To hit someone very hard; beat someone up. *Stay out of my yard or I'll knock your block off. Jim will knock your block off if he catches you riding his bike.*

knock oneself out *v. phr., informal* To work very hard; make a great effort. *Mrs. Ross knocked herself out planning her daughter's wedding. Tom knocked himself out to give his guests a good time.*

knock on wood *v. phr.* To knock on something made of wood to keep from having bad luck.—Many people believe that you will have bad luck if you talk about good luck or brag about something, unless you knock on wood; often used in a joking way. *Charles said, "I haven't been sick all winter." Grandfather said, "You'd better knock on wood when you say that."*

knockout *n., slang* **1.** Strikingly beautiful woman. *Sue is a regular knockout.* **2.** A straight punch in boxing that causes

one's opponent to fall and lose consciousness. *The champion won the fight with a straight knockout.*

knock out *v. phr.* To make helpless, unworkable, or unusable. *The champion knocked out the challenger in the third round. The soldier knocked out two enemy tanks with his bazooka.*

knock the living daylights out of *v. phr., slang, informal* To render (someone) unconscious (said in exaggeration). *The news almost knocked the living daylights out of me.*

know-it-all *n.* A person who acts as if he knows all about everything; someone who thinks no one can tell him anything new. *After George was elected as class president, he wouldn't take suggestions from anyone; he became a know-it-all.*—Also used like an adjective. *The other students didn't like George's know-it-all attitude.*

know one's stuff To have experience and skill in an activity. *Before trying to make any pottery, it is better to get advice from someone who knows his stuff in ceramics.*

know which side one's bread is buttered on *v. phr.* To know who can help you and try to please him; know what is for your own gain. *Dick was always polite to the boss; he knew which side his bread was buttered on.*

knuckle under *v. phr.* To do something because you are forced to do it. *Bobby refused to knuckle under to the bully.*

L

labor of love *n. phr.* Something done for personal pleasure and not pay or profit. *Building the model railroad was a labor of love for the retired engineer.*

lady friend *n.* **1.** A woman friend. *His aunt stays with a lady friend in Florida during the winter.* **2.** A woman who is the lover of a man.—Used by people trying to appear more polite, but not often used by careful speakers. *The lawyer took his lady friend to dinner.*

lady-killer *n., informal* **1.** Any man who has strong sex appeal toward women. *Joe is a regular lady-killer.* **2.** A man who relentlessly pursues amorous conquests, is successful at it, and then abandons his heart-broken victims. *The legendary Don Juan of Spain is the most famous lady-killer of recorded history.*

lady's man *n.* A man or boy who likes to be with women or girls very much and is popular with them. *Charlie is quite a lady's man now.*

laid up *adj.* Sick; confined to bed. *I was laid up for a couple of weeks with an ear infection.*

lame duck *n., informal* An elected public official who has been either defeated in a new election or whose term cannot be renewed, but who has a short period of time left in office during which he can still perform certain duties, though

with somewhat diminished powers. *In the last year of their second terms, American presidents are lame ducks.*

lap up *v.* **1.** To eat or drink with the tip of the tongue. *The kitten laps up its milk.* **2.** *informal* To take in eagerly. *She flatters him all the time and he just laps it up. William is interested in rockets and space, and he laps up all he can read about them.*

lash out *v.* **1.** To kick. *The horse lashed out at the man behind him.* **2.** To try suddenly to hit. *The woman lashed out at the crowd with her umbrella.* **3.** To attack with words. *The senator lashed out at the administration. The school newspaper lashed out at the unfriendly way some students treated the visiting team.*

last but not least *adv. phr.* In the last place but not the least important. *Billy will bring sandwiches, Alice will bring cake, Susan will bring cookies, John will bring potato chips, and last but not least, Sally will bring the lemonade.*

last ditch *n.* The last place that can be defended; the last resort. *They will fight reform to the last ditch.*

last-ditch *adj.* Made or done as a last chance to keep from losing or failing. *He threw away his cigarettes in a last-ditch effort to stop smoking.*

last straw *or* **straw that breaks the camel's back** *n. phr.* A small trouble which follows other troubles and makes one lose patience and be unable to bear them. *Bill had a bad day in school yesterday. He lost his knife on the way home, then he fell down, and when he broke a shoe lace, that was the last straw and he began to cry. Mary didn't like it when the other girls said she was proud and lazy, but when they said she told fibs it was the straw that broke the camel's back and she told the teacher.*

last word *n.* **1.** The last remark in an argument. *I never win an argument with her. She always has the last word.* **2.** The final say in deciding something. *The superintendent has the last word in ordering new desks.* **3.** *informal* The most modern thing. *Mrs. Green's stove is the last word in stoves.*

laugh off *v.* To dismiss with a laugh as not important or not serious; not take seriously. *He had a bad fall while ice skating but he laughed it off. You can't laugh off a ticket for speeding.*

lay a finger on *v. phr.* To touch or bother, even a little.—Used in negative, interrogative, and conditional sentences. *Don't you dare lay a finger on the vase! Suppose Billy takes his brother with him; will the mean, tough boy down the street dare lay a finger on him? If you so much as lay a finger on my boy, I'll call the police.*

lay an egg *v. phr., slang* To fail to win the interest or favor of an audience. *His joke laid an egg. Sometimes he is a successful speaker, but sometimes he lays an egg.*

lay away *v.* **1.** To save. *She laid a little of her pay away each week.* **2.** To bury (a person).—Used to avoid the word *bury,* which some people think is unpleasant. *He was laid away in his favorite spot on the hill.*

lay-away plan *n.* A plan for buying something that you can't pay cash for; a plan in which you pay some money down and pay a little more when you can, and the store holds the article until you have paid the full price. *She could not afford to pay for the coat all at once, so she used the lay away plan.*

lay down the law *v. phr.* **1.** To give strict orders. *The teacher lays down the law about homework every afternoon.* **2.** To speak severely or seriously about a wrongdoing; scold. *The principal called in the student and laid down the law to them about skipping classes.*

lay eyes on *or* **set eyes on** *v. phr.* To see. *She knew he was different as soon as she laid eyes on him. I didn't know the man; in fact, I had never set eyes on him.*

lay hands on *v. phr.* **1.** To get hold of; find; catch. *The treasure hunters can keep any treasure they can lay hands on. If the police can lay hands on him they will put him in jail.* **2.** To do violence to; harm; hurt. *They were afraid that if they left him alone in his disturbed condition he would lay hands on himself.*

lay hold of *v. phr.* **1.** To take hold of; grasp; grab. *He laid hold of the rope and pulled the boat ashore.* **2.** To get possession of. *He sold every washing machine he could lay hold of.* **3.** *Chiefly British* To understand. *Some ideas in this science book are hard to lay hold of.*

lay in *v.* To store up a supply of; to get and keep for future use. *Mrs. Mason heard that the price of sugar might go up, so she laid in a hundred pounds of it. Before school starts, the principal will lay in plenty of paper for the students' written work.*

lay into *or* **light into** *v., informal* **1.** To attack physically; go at vigorously. *The two fighters laid into each other as soon as the bell rang. John loves Italian food and he really laid into the spaghetti.* **2.** *slang* To attack with words. *The senator laid into the opponents of his bill.*

lay it on *or* **lay it on thick** *also* **put it on thick** *or* **spread it on thick** *or* **lay it on with a trowel** *v. phr., informal* To persuade someone by using very much flattery; flatter. *Bob wanted to go to the movies. He laid it on thick to his mother. Mary was caught fibbing. She sure spread it on thick.*

lay low *v.* **1.** To knock down; to force into a lying position; to put out of action. *Many trees were laid low by the storm. Jane was laid low by the flu.* **2.** To kill. *The hunters laid low seven pheasants.*

layoff *n.* A systematic or periodical dismissal of employees from a factory or a firm. *Due to the poor economy, the car manufacturer announced a major layoff starting next month.*

lay off *v. phr.* **1.** To mark out the boundaries or limits. *He laid off a baseball diamond on the vacant lot.* **2.** To put out of work. *The company lost the contract for making the shoes and laid off half its workers.* **3.** *slang* To stop bothering; leave alone.—Usually used in the imperative. *Lay off me, will you? I have to study for a test.* **4.** *slang* To stop using or taking. *His doctor told him to lay off cigarettes.*

lay one's cards on the table *or* **lay down one's cards** *or* **put one's cards on the table** *v. phr., informal* To let someone know your position and interest openly; deal honestly; act without trickery or secrets. *In talking about buying the property, Peterson laid his cards on the table about his plans for it. Some of the graduates of the school were unfriendly toward the new superintendent, but he put his cards on the table and won their support.*

lay oneself out *v. phr., informal* To make an extra hard effort; try very hard. *Larry wanted to win a medal for his school, so he really laid himself out in the race.*

lay one's hands on *or* **get one's hands on** *v. phr.* **1.** To seize in order to punish or treat roughly. *If I ever lay my hands on that boy he'll be sorry.* **2.** To get possession of. *He was unable to lay his hands on a Model T Ford for the school play.* **3.** *or* **lay one's hand on** *or* **put one's hand on** To find;

locate. *He keeps a file of letters so he can lay his hands on one whenever he needs it.*

lay on the line *or* **put on the line** *v. phr., informal* **1.** To pay or offer to pay. *The sponsors had to lay nearly a million dollars on the line to keep the show on TV. The bank is putting $5,000 on the line as a reward to anyone who catches the robber.* **2.** To say plainly so that there can be no doubt; tell truthfully. *I'm going to lay it on the line for you, Paul. You must work harder if you want to pass.* **3.** To take a chance of losing; risk. *The champion is laying his title on the line in the fight tonight. Frank decided to lay his job on the line and tell the boss that he thought he was wrong.*

lay out *v. phr.* **1.** To prepare (a dead body) for burial. *The corpse was laid out by the undertaker.* **2.** *slang* To knock down flat; to hit unconscious. *A stiff right to the jaw laid the boxer out in the second round.* **3.** To plan. *Come here, Fred, I have a job laid out for you.* **4.** To mark or show where work is to be done. *The foreman laid out the job for the new machinist.* **5.** To plan the building or arrangement of; design. *The architect laid out the interior of the building. The early colonists laid out towns in the wilderness.* **6.** *slang* To spend; pay. *How much did you have to lay out for your new car?* **7.** *or* **lay out in lavender** *slang* To scold; lecture. *He was laid out in lavender for arriving an hour late for the dance.*

layout *n.* General situation; arrangement; plan. *The layout*

of their apartment overlooking Lake Michigan was strikingly unusual.*

layover *n.* A stopover, usually at an airport or in a hotel due to interrupted air travel. *There were several layovers at O'Hare last month due to bad weather.*

lay over *v.* **1.** To put off until later; delay; postpone. *We voted to lay the question over to our next meeting for decision.* **2.** To arrive in one place and wait some time before continuing the journey. *We had to lay over in St. Louis for two hours waiting for a plane to Seattle.*

lay to rest *v. phr., informal* **1.** To put a dead person into a grave or tomb; bury. *President Kennedy was laid to rest in Arlington National Cemetery.* **2.** To get rid of; put away permanently; stop. *The Scoutmaster's fears that Tom had drowned were laid to rest when Tom came back and said he had gone for a boat ride. The rumor that the principal had accepted another job was laid to rest when he said it wasn't true.*

lay up *v.* **1.** To collect a supply of; save for future use; store. *Bees lay up honey for the winter.* **2.** To keep in the house or in bed because of sickness or injury; disable. *Jack was laid up with a twisted knee and couldn't play in the final game.* **3.** To take out of active service; put in a boat dock or a garage. *Bill had to lay up his boat when school started. If you lay up a car for the winter, you should take out the battery.*

lay waste *v. phr., literary* To cause wide and great damage to; destroy and leave in ruins; wreck. *Enemy soldiers laid waste the land.*

lead a dog's life *v. phr., informal* To live a hard life, work hard, and be treated unkindly. *A new college student of long ago led a dog's life.*

lead a merry chase *v. phr.* To delay or escape capture by (someone) skillfully; make (a pursuer) work hard. *The deer led the hunter a merry chase. Valerie is leading her boyfriend a merry chase.*

lead by the nose *v. phr., informal* To have full control of; make or persuade (someone) to do anything whatever. *Many people are easily influenced and a smart politician can lead them by the nose. Don't let anyone lead you by the nose; use your own judgment and do the right thing.*

lead off *v.* To begin; start; open. *Richardson led off the inning with a double. We always let Henry lead off. Mr. Jones led off with the jack of diamonds. When the teacher asked if the film helped them to understand, Phil led off by saying that he learned a lot from it.*

lead on *v. phr.* To encourage you to believe something untrue or mistaken. *Tom led us on to believe that he was a world traveler, but we found out that he had never been outside our state. We were led on to think that Jeanne and Jim were engaged to be married.*

lead the way *v. phr.* To go before and show how to go somewhere; guide. *The boys need someone to lead the way on their hike. The men hired an In-*

dian to lead the way to the Pueblo ruins. *That school led the way in finding methods to teach reading.*

lean on *v. phr., slang, informal* To pressure (someone) by blackmailing, threats, physical violence, or the withholding of some favor in order to make the person comply with a wish or request. *I would gladly do what you ask if you only stopped leaning on me so hard!*

leave a bad taste in one's mouth *v. phr.* To feel a bad impression; make you feel disgusted. *Seeing a man beat his horse leaves a bad taste in your mouth. His rudeness to the teacher left a bad taste in my mouth.*

leave hanging *or* **leave hanging in the air** *v. phr.* To leave undecided or unsettled. *Because the committee could not decide on a time and place, the matter of the spring dance was left hanging. Ted's mother didn't know what to do about the broken window, so his punishment was left hanging in the air until his father came home.*

leave holding the bag *or* **leave holding the sack** *v. phr., informal* **1.** To cause (someone) not to have something needed; leave without anything. *In the rush for seats, Joe was left holding the bag.* **2.** To force (someone) to take the whole responsibility or blame for something that others should share. *When the ball hit the glass, the team scattered and left George holding the bag. After the party, the other girls on the clean-up committee went away* *with their dates, and left Mary holding the bag.*

leave in the lurch *v. phr.* To desert or leave alone in trouble; refuse to help or support. *The town bully caught Eddie, and Tom left him in the lurch. Bill quit his job, leaving his boss in the lurch.*

leave no stone unturned *v. phr.* To try in every way; miss no chance; do everything possible.—Usually used in the negative. *The police will leave no stone unturned in their search for the bank robbers.*

leave off *v.* To come or put to an end; stop. *There is a high fence where the school yard leaves off and the woods begin. Don told the boys to leave off teasing his little brother. Marion put a marker in her book so that she would know where she left off.*

left-handed compliment An ambiguous compliment which is interpretable as an offense. *I didn't know you could look so pretty! Is that a wig you're wearing?*

leg man *n., informal* **1.** An errand boy; one who performs messenger services, or the like. *Joe hired a leg man for the office.* **2.** *Slang, semi-vulgar, avoidable* A man who is particularly attracted to good looking female legs and pays less attention to other parts of the female anatomy. *Herb is a leg man.*

leg to stand on *n. phr.* A firm foundation of facts; facts to support your claim.—Usually used in the negative. *Jerry's answering speech left his opponent without a leg to stand on.*

Amos sued for damages, but did not have a leg to stand on.

leg work *n., informal* The physical end of a project, such as the typing of research reports; the physical investigating of a criminal affair; the carrying of books to and from libraries; etc. *Joe, my research assistant, does a lot of leg work for me.*

let alone *conj. phr.* **1.** Even less; certainly not.—Used after a negative clause. *I can't add two and two, let alone do fractions. Jim can't drive a car, let alone a truck.* **2. let alone** *or* **leave alone** *v.* To stay away from; keep hands off; avoid. *When Joel gets mad, just let him alone. Little Patsy was warned to leave the birthday cake alone.*

let bygones be bygones *v. phr.* To let the past be forgotten. *After a long, angry quarrel the two boys agreed to let bygones be bygones and made friends again. We should let bygones be bygones and try to get along with each other.*

letdown *n.* A disappointment; a heartbreak. *It was a major letdown for John when Mary refused to marry him.*

let down *v. phr.* **1.** To allow to descend; lower. *Harry let the chain saw down on a rope and then climbed down himself.* **2.** To relax; stop trying so hard; take it easy. *The horse let down near the end of the race and lost. The team let down in the fourth quarter because they were far ahead.* **3.** To fail to do as well as (someone) expected; disappoint. *The team felt they had let the coach down.*

let down easy *v. phr.* To refuse or say no to (someone) in a pleasant manner; to tell bad news about a refusal or disappointment in a kindly way. *The teacher had to tell George that he had failed his college examinations, but she tried to let him down easy. The boss tried to let Jim down easy when he had to tell him he was too young for the job.*

let go *v.* **1a.** To stop holding something; loosen your hold; release. *The boy grabbed Jack's coat and would not let go.*—Often used with *of. When the child let go of her mother's hand, she fell down.* **1b.** To weaken and break under pressure. *The old water pipe suddenly let go and water poured out of it.* **2.** To pay no attention to; neglect. *Robert let his teeth go when he was young and now he has to go to the dentist often. After she was married, Jane let herself go and was not pretty anymore.* **3.** To allow something to pass; do nothing about. *When Charles was tardy, the teacher scolded him and let it go at that. The children teased Frank, but he smiled and let it go.* **4.** To discharge from a job; fire. *Mr. Wilson got into a quarrel with his boss and was let go.* **5.** To make (something) go out quickly; shoot; fire. *The soldiers let go a number of shots. Robin Hood let go an arrow at the deer. Paul was so angry that he let go a blow at the boy. The truck driver saw the flat tire and let go a loud curse. The pitcher let go a fast ball and the batter swung and missed.* **6.** *or* **let oneself go** *informal* To be free in one's actions or talk; relax. *Judge Brown let go at the reunion of his old class and had a good time. The cowboys worked hard all week, but on Saturday night they went to town and let themselves go.*

let grass grow under one's feet *v. phr.* To be idle; be lazy; waste time.—Used in negative, conditional, and interrogative sentences. *The new boy joined the football team, made the honor roll, and found a girlfriend during the first month of school. He certainly did not let any grass grow under his feet.*

let it all hang out *v. phr., slang, informal* Not to disguise anything; to let the truth be known. *Sue can't deceive anyone; she just lets it all hang out.*

let it lay *v. phr., used imperatively, slang* Forget it; leave it alone; do not be concerned or involved. *Don't get involved with Max again—just let it lay.*

let it rip *v. phr., used imperatively, slang* **1.** Don't be concerned; pay no attention to what happens. *Why get involved? Forget about it and let it rip.* **2.** (Imperatively) Do become involved and make the most of it; get in there and really try to win. *Come on man, give it all you've got and let it rip!*

let know *v. phr.* To inform. *Please let us know the time of your arrival.*

let loose *v.* **1a.** *or* **set loose** *or* **turn loose** To set free; loosen or give up your hold on. *The farmer opened the gate and let the bull loose in the pasture. They turned the balloon loose* *to let it rise in the air.* **1b.** *or* **turn loose** To give freedom (to someone) to do something; to allow (someone) to do what he wants. *Mother let Jim loose on the apple pie. The children were turned loose in the toy store to pick the toys they wanted.* **1c.** To stop holding something; loosen your hold. *Jim caught Ruth's arm and would not let loose.* **2a.** *informal* To let or make (something) move fast or hard; release. *The fielder let loose a long throw to home plate after catching the ball.* **2b.** *informal* To release something held. *Those dark clouds are going to let loose any minute.* **3.** *informal* To speak or act freely; disregard ordinary limits. *The teacher told Jim that some day she was going to let loose and tell him what she thought of him. Mother let loose on her shopping trip today and bought things for all of us.*

let off *v.* **1.** To discharge (a gun); explode; fire. *Willie accidentally let off his father's shotgun and made a hole in the wall.* **2.** To permit to go or escape; excuse from a penalty, a duty, or a promise. *Two boys were caught smoking in school but the principal let them off with a warning. Mary's mother said that she would let Mary off from drying the supper dishes. The factory closed for a month in the summer and let the workers off.* **3.** *or informal* **let off the hook** To miss a chance to defeat or score against, especially in sports or games. *We almost scored a touchdown in the first play*

against Tech but we let them off the hook by fumbling the ball. The boxer let his opponent off the hook many times.

let off steam *or* **blow off steam** *v. phr.* **1.** To let or make steam escape; send out steam. *The janitor let off some steam because the pressure was too high.* **2.** *informal* To get rid of physical energy or strong feeling through activity; talk or be very active physically after forced quiet. *After the long ride on the bus, the children let off steam with a race to the lake. When the rain stopped, the boys let off steam with a ball game. Bill's mother was very angry when he was late in coming home, and let off steam by walking around and around. Bill had to take his foreman's rough criticisms all day and he would blow off steam at home by scolding the children.*

let on *v. informal* **1.** To tell or admit what you know.—Usually used in the negative. *Frank lost a quarter but he didn't let on to his mother.* **2.** To try to make people believe; pretend. *The old man likes to let on that he is rich.*

let one in on *v. phr.* To reveal a secret to; permit someone to share in. *If I let you in on something big we're planning, will you promise not to mention it to anyone?*

let one's hair down *or* **let down one's hair** *v. phr., informal* Act freely and naturally; be informal; relax. *Kings and queens can seldom let their hair down. After the dance, the college girls let their hair down and compared dates.*

let out v. **1a.** To allow to go out or escape. *The guard let the prisoners out of jail to work in the garden. Mother won't let us out when it rains.* **1b.** *informal* To make (a sound) come out of the mouth; utter. *A bee stung Charles. He let out a yell and ran home. Father told Betty to sit still and not let out a peep during church.* **2.** To allow to be known; tell. *I'll never tell you another secret if you let this one out.* **3.** To make larger (as clothing) or looser; allow to slip out (as a rope). *Mary's mother had to let out her dress because Mary is growing so tall. Father hooked a big fish on his line. He had to let the line out so the fish wouldn't break it.* **4.** *informal* To allow to move at higher speed. *The rider let out his horse to try to beat the horse ahead of him.* **5.** *informal* To free from blame, responsibility, or duty.—Often used with *of*. *Last time I let you out of it when you were late. I'll have to punish you this time. Frank has shoveled the snow from the sidewalk. That lets me out.* **6.** *informal* To discharge from a job; fire. *The shop closed down and all the men were let out.* **7.** *informal* To dismiss or be dismissed. *The coach let us out from practice at 3 o'clock. I'll meet you after school lets out.*

let ride v. phr., *informal* To allow to go on without change; accept (a situation or action) for the present. *The committee could not decide what to do about Bob's idea, so they let the matter ride for a month or so. The class was rather noisy but the teacher let it ride because it was near Christmas. Ruth's paper was not very good, but the teacher let it ride because she knew Ruth had tried.*

let sleeping dogs lie Do not make (someone) angry and cause trouble or danger; do not make trouble if you do not have to.—A proverb. *Don't tell Father that you broke the window. Let sleeping dogs lie.*

let the cat out of the bag v. phr., *informal* To tell about something that is supposed to be a secret. *We wanted to surprise Mary with a birthday gift, but Allen let the cat out of the bag by asking her what she would like.*—Sometimes used in another form. *Well, the cat is out of the bag—everybody knows about their marriage.*

let the chips fall where they may v. phr. To pay no attention to the displeasure caused others by your actions. *The senator decided to vote against the bill and let the chips fall where they may. The police chief told his men to give tickets to all speeders and let the chips fall where they may.*

let up v., *informal* **1.** To become less, weaker, or quiet; become slower or stop. *It's raining as hard as ever. It's not letting up at all. It snowed for three days before it let up and we could go outdoors.* **2.** To do less or go slower or stop; relax; stop working or working hard. *Grandfather has been working all his life. When is he going to let up? Let up for a minute. You can't work hard all day. Jim ran all the way home without letting up once.* **3.** To become easier, kinder, or less strict.—Usually used with *on*. *Let up on Jane. She is sick.* **4.** or **change up** To pitch a ball at less than full speed in baseball.—Usually used with *on*. *John pitched a ball that was very fast and the batter missed it. Then he let up on the next pitch and the batter was badly fooled.*

let well enough alone or **leave well enough alone** *v. phr.* To be satisfied with what is good enough; not try to improve something because often that might cause more trouble. *John wanted to make his kite go higher, but his father told him to let well enough alone because it was too windy. Ed polished up his car until his friends warned him to leave well enough alone. Ethel made a lot of changes in her test paper after she finished. She should have let well enough alone, because she made several new mistakes.*

lie in state *v. phr.* Of a dead person: To lie in a place of honor, usually in an open coffin, and be seen by the public before burial. *When the President died, thousands of people saw his body lying in state.*

lie in wait *v. phr.* To watch from hiding in order to attack or surprise someone; to ambush. *The driver of the stagecoach knew that the thieves were lying in wait somewhere along the road.*

lie low or nonstandard **lay low** *v., informal* **1.** To stay quietly out of sight; try not to attract attention; hide. *After holding up the bank, the robbers lay*

low for a while. **2.** To keep secret one's thoughts or plans. *I think he wants to be elected president, but he is lying low and not saying anything.*

life of Riley *n. phr., informal* A soft easy life; pleasant or rich way of living. *He's living the life of Riley. He doesn't have to work anymore.* Compare bed of roses, in clover, live high off the hog.

lift a finger or **lift a hand** also **raise a hand** *v. phr.* To do something; do your share; to help.—Usually used in the negative. *We all worked hard except Joe. He wouldn't lift a finger. The king did not lift a hand when his people were hungry.*

light up *v.* Suddenly to look pleased and happy. *Martha's face lit up when she saw her old friend. Tom will really light up when he sees his new bike!*

like father, like son A son is usually like his father in the way he acts.—A proverb. *Frank's father has been on the city council; he is now the mayor, and is running for governor. Frank is on the student council and is likely to be class president. Like father, like son. Mr. Jones and Tommy are both quiet and shy. Like father, like son.*

like hell *adv., slang, vulgar, avoidable* **1.** With great vigor. *As soon as they saw the cops, they ran like hell.* **2.** *interj.* Not so; untrue; indicates the speaker's lack of belief in what he heard. *Like hell you're gonna bring me my dough!*

like mad or **like crazy** *adv., slang, informal* With great enthusiasm and vigor; very fast. *We had to drive like mad (like crazy) to get there on time.*

like two peas in a pod *adj. phr.* Closely similar; almost exactly alike. *The twin sisters Eve and Agnes are like two peas in a pod.*

like water off a duck's back *adv. phr., informal* Without changing your feelings or opinion; without effect. *Advice and correction roll off him like water off a duck's back. Many people showed him they didn't like what he was doing, but their disapproval passed off him like water off a duck's back.*

lineup *n.* **1.** An alignment of objects in a straight line. *A lineup of Venus and the moon can be a very beautiful sight in the night sky.* **2.** An arrangement of suspects through a one-way mirror so that the victim or the witness of a crime can identify the wanted person. *She picked out her attacker from a police lineup.*

line up *v. phr.* **1.** To take places in a line or formation; stand side by side or one behind another; form a line or pattern. *The boys lined up and took turns diving off the springboard. The football team lined up in a "T" formation.* **2.** To put in line. *John lined up the pool balls.* **3.** To adjust correctly. *The garage man lined up the car's wheels.* **4a.** *informal* To make ready for action; complete a plan or agreement for; arrange. *Henry's friends lined up so many votes for him that he won the election. Roger lined up a summer job before school*

was out. *The superintendent lined up all the new teachers he needed before he went on vacation.* **4b.** *informal* To become ready for action; come together in preparation or agreement. *The football schedule is lining up well; the coach has arranged all games except one. Larry wanted to go to the seashore for the family vacation, but the rest of the family lined up against him.*

lip service *n.* Support shown by words only and not by actions; a show of loyalty that is not proven in action.—Usually used with *pay. By holding elections, communism pays lip service to democracy, but it offers only one candidate per office. Some people pay lip service to education, but don't vote taxes for better schools.*

little frog in a big pond *or* **small frog in a big pond** *n. phr.* An unimportant person in a large group or organization. *In a large company, even a fairly successful man is likely to feel like a little frog in a big pond. When Bill transferred to a larger high school, he found himself a small frog in a big pond.*

little pitchers have big ears Little children often overhear things they are not supposed to hear, or things adults do not expect they would notice.—A proverb. *Be especially careful not to swear in front of little children. Little pitchers have big ears.*

live and let live To live in the way you prefer and let others live as they wish without being bothered by you. *Father scolds*

Mother because she wears her hair in curlers and Mother scolds Father because he smokes a smelly pipe. Grandfather says it's her hair and his pipe; live and let live.

live down *v.* To remove (blame, distrust or unfriendly laughter) by good conduct; cause (a mistake or fault) to be forgiven or forgotten by not repeating it. *John's business failure hurt him for a long time, but in the end he lived it down. Frank was rather a bad boy, but he lived it down as he grew up. Sandra called her principal the wrong name at the banquet, in front of everyone, and she thought she would never live it down.*

live from hand to mouth *v. phr.* To live on little money and spend it as fast as it comes in; live without saving for the future; have just enough. *Mr. Johnson got very little pay, and the family lived from hand to mouth when he had no job. These Indians live from hand to mouth on berries, nuts, and roots.*

live it up *v. phr., informal* To pursue pleasure; enjoy games or night life very much; have fun at places of entertainment. *Joe had had a hard winter in lonesome places; now he was in town living it up. The western cowboys usually went to town on Saturdays to live it up.*

live off someone *v. phr.* To be supported by someone. *Although Eric is already 40 years old, he has no job and continues to live off his elderly parents.*

live up to *v.* To act according to; come up to; agree with; follow. *So far as he could, John had always tried to live up to the example he saw in Lincoln. Bob was a man who lived up to his promises. The new house didn't live up to expectations.*

living end *adj., slang* Great; fantastic; the ultimate. *That show we saw last night was the living end.*

lock the barn door after the horse is stolen To be careful or try to make something safe when it is too late.—A proverb. *After Mary failed the examination, she said she would study hard after that. She wanted to lock the barn door after the horse was stolen.*

lock up *v. phr., slang* To be assured of success. *How did your math test go?—I locked it up, I think.*

long face *n.* A sad look; disappointed look. *He told the story with a long face.*—Often used in the phrase *pull a long face. Don't pull a long face when I tell you to go to bed.*

longhair[1] **1.** *n., slang* A male hippie. *Who's that longhair?—It's Joe.* **2.** An intellectual who prefers classical music to jazz or acid rock. *Catwallender is a regular longhair; he never listens to modern jazz.*

longhair[2] *adj., slang* Pertaining to classical art forms, primarily in dancing and music. *Cut out that longhair Mozart Symphony and put on a decent pop record!*

long haul or **long pull** *n., informal* **1.** A long distance or trip. *It is a long haul to drive across* the country. **2.** A long length of time during which work continues or something is done; a long time of trying. *A boy crippled by polio may learn to walk again, but it may be a long haul.*—Often used in the phrase *over the long haul. Over the long haul, an expensive pair of shoes may save you money.*

long shot *n.* A bet or other risk taken though not likely to succeed. *The horse was a long shot, but it came in and paid well. Jones was a long shot for mayor. The business long shot that succeeds often pays extremely well.*

look a gift horse in the mouth To complain if a gift is not perfect.—A proverb. Usually used with a negative. *John gave Joe a baseball but Joe complained that the ball was old. His father told him not to look a gift horse in the mouth.*

look at the world through rose-colored glasses *or* **see with rose-colored glasses** *v. phr.* To see everything as good and pleasant; not see anything hard or bad. *When Jean graduated from high school, she looked at the world through rose-colored glasses. If you see everything through rose-colored glasses, you will often be disappointed.*

look down on *also* **look down upon** *v.* To think of (a person or thing) as less good or important; feel that (someone) is not as good as you are, or that (something) is not worth having or doing; consider inferior. *Mary looked down on her classmates because she was bet-*

ter dressed than they were. Jack looked down on Al for his poor manners. Miss Tracy likes tennis but she looks down on football as too rough.

look down one's nose at *v. phr., informal* To think of as worthless; feel scorn for. *The banker's wife has beautiful china cups, and she looked down her nose at the plastic cups that Mrs. Brown used. Harry has never had to work, and he looks down his nose at people in business. Jerry was the athlete who looked down his nose at the weak student.*

look for *v.* **1.** To think likely; expect. *We look for John to arrive any day now. The frost killed many oranges, and housewives can look for an increase in their price. Bob wouldn't go for a ride with the boys because he was looking for a phone call from Julie.* **2.** To try to find; search for; hunt. *Fred spent all day looking for a job. Mary and Joe looked for the Smiths at the play.* **3.** To do things that cause (your own trouble); make (trouble) for yourself; provoke. *Joe often gets into fights because he is always looking for trouble. If you say the opposite of everything that others say, you are looking for a quarrel.*

look forward to *v.* **1.** To expect. *At breakfast, John looked forward to a difficult day.* **2.** To expect with hope or pleasure. *Frank was looking forward to that evening's date.*

look in on *v.* To go to see; make a short visit with; make a call on. *On his way downtown,*

Jim looked in on his aunt. The doctor looked in on Mary each day when he went by.

look into *v.* To find out the facts about; examine; study; inspect. *The mayor felt he should look into the decrease of income from parking meters. Mr. Jones said he was looking into the possibility of buying a house.*

look like a million dollars *v. phr., informal* To look well and prosperous; appear healthy and happy and lucky; look pretty and attractive. *John came back from Florida driving a fine new car, tanned and glowing with health. He looked like a million dollars. Dressed in the new formal and in a new hairdo, Betty looked like a million dollars.*

look like the cat that ate the canary *or* **look like the cat that swallowed the canary** *v. phr.* To seem very self-satisfied; look as if you had just had a great success. *Peter bet on the poorest horse in the race and when it won, he looked like the cat that ate the canary. When she won the prize, she went home looking like the cat that swallowed the canary.*

look out *or* **watch out** *v.* **1.** To take care; be careful; be on guard.—Usually used as a command or warning. *"Look out!" John called, as the car came toward me. "Look out for the train," the sign at the railroad crossing warns.* **2.** To be alert or watchful; keep watching. *A collector of antique cars asked Frank to look out for a 1906 gas head lamp.* **3.** *informal* To watch or keep (a person or

thing) and do what is needed provide protection and care.— Used with *for. Lillian looked out for her sister's children one afternoon a week. Uncle Fred looked out for his brother's orphan son until the boy was through college.*

look to *v.* **1.** To attend to; get ready for; take care of. *Plans had been prepared that looked to every possibility. The President assigned a man to look to our needs.* **2.** To go for help to; depend on. *The child looks to his mother to cure his hurts.*

look to one's laurels To make sure that your reputation is not spoiled; protect your good name; keep your record from being beaten by others. *Tom won the broad jump, but he had to look to his laurels. Look to your laurels, Joan. Betty says she is going to run against you for head cheerleader.*

look up *v.* **1.** *informal* To improve in future chances; promise more success. *The first year was tough, but business looked up after that.* **2.** To search for; hunt for information about; find. *It is a good habit to look up new words in a dictionary.* **3.** To seek and find. *While he was in Chicago, Henry looked up a friend of college days.*

look up to *v.* To think of (someone) as a good example to copy; honor; respect. *Mr. Smith had taught for many years, and all the students looked up to him. Young children look up to older ones, so older children should be good examples.*

lord it over *v. phr.* To act as

the superior and master of; dominate; be bossy over; control. *John learned early to lord it over other children. The office manager lorded it over the clerks and typists.*

ose face *v.* To be embarrassed or shamed by an error or failure; lose dignity, influence or reputation; lose self-respect or the confidence of others. *Many Japanese soldiers were killed in World War II because they believed that to give up or retreat would make them lose face. John's careless work made him lose face with his employer. The banker lost face when people found out he bet on horse races.*

ose ground 1. To go backward; retreat. *The soldiers began to lose ground when their leader was killed.* **2.** To become weaker; get worse; not improve. *The sick man began to lose ground when his cough grew worse. When the Democrats are in power, the Republicans lose ground.*

ose heart *v. phr.* To feel discouraged because of failure; to lose hope of success. *The team had won no games and it lost heart.*

ose one's heart *v. phr.* To fall in love; begin to love. *She lost her heart to the soldier with the broad shoulders and the deep voice. Bill lost his heart to the puppy the first time he saw it.*

ose one's shirt *v. phr., slang* To lose all or most of your money. *Uncle Joe spent his life savings to buy a store, but it failed, and he lost his shirt. Mr. Matthews lost his shirt betting on the horses.*

lose out *v.* To fail to win; miss first place in a contest; lose to a rival. *John lost out in the rivalry for Mary's hand in marriage. Fred didn't want to lose out to the other salesman.*

lose touch *v. phr., informal* To fail to keep in contact or communication.—Usually used with *with*. *After she moved to another town, she lost touch with her childhood friends.*

lose track *v. phr.* To forget about something; not stay informed; fail to keep a count or record. *What's the score now? I've lost track.*—Usually used with *of*. *Mary lost track of her friends at camp after summer was over. John lost track of the money he spent at the circus.*

loud mouth or **big mouth** *n., slang* A noisy, boastful, or foolish talker. *Fritz is a loud mouth who cannot be trusted with secrets. When he has had a few drinks, Joe will make empty boasts like any other big mouth.*

louse up *v., slang* To throw into confusion; make a mess of; spoil; ruin. *When the man who was considering John's house heard that the basement was wet, that was enough to louse up the sale. Fred's failure in business not only lost him his business but loused him up with his wife. The rain loused up the picnic.*

lovers' lane *n.* A hidden road or walk where lovers walk or park in the evening. *A parked car in a lonely lovers' lane often is a chance for holdup men.*

lowdown *n., slang, informal* The inside facts of a matter; the total truth. *Nixon never* *gave the American people the lowdown on Watergate.*

lower the boom *v. phr., informal* To punish strictly; check or stop fully. *The mayor lowered the boom on outside jobs for city firemen. Father lowered the boom on the girls for staying out after midnight.*

low-key *adj.* Relaxed and easygoing. *Surprisingly, dinner with the governor was a low-key affair.*

luck out *v. phr., slang, informal* **1.** Suddenly to get lucky when in fact the odds are against one's succeeding. *I was sure I was going to miss the train as I was three minutes late, but I lucked out; the train was five minutes late.* **2.** To be extraordinarily fortunate. *Catwallender really lucked out at Las Vegas last month; he came home with $10,000 in cash.* **3.** (By sarcastic opposition) to be extremely unfortunate; to be killed. *Those poor marines sure lucked out in Saigon, didn't they?*

lucky star *n.* A certain star or planet which, by itself or with others, is seriously or jokingly thought to bring a person good luck and success in life. *John was born under a lucky star. Ted was unhurt in the car accident, for which he thanked his lucky stars.*

lump in one's throat *n. phr.* A feeling (as of grief or pride) so strong that you almost sob. *John's mother had a lump in her throat at his college graduation. All during her husband's funeral, Aunt May had a lump in her throat. The bride's mother had a lump in her throat.*

lump sum *n.* The complete amount; a total agreed upon and to be paid at one time. *The case was settled out of court with the plaintiff receiving a lump sum of half a million dollars for damages.*

M

mad as a hornet *or* **mad as hops** *or* **mad as a wet hen** *adj. phr.*, *informal* In a fighting mood; very angry. *When my father sees the dent in his fender, he'll be mad as a hornet. Bill was mad as hops when the fellows went on without him. Mrs. Harris was mad as a wet hen when the rabbits ate her tulips.*

magic carpet *n.* **1.** A rug said to be able to transport a person through the air to any place he wishes. *The caliph of Baghdad flew on his magic carpet to Arabia.* **2.** Any form of transportation that is comfortable and easy enough to seem magical. *Flying the Concord from Dallas to London seemed like boarding the magic carpet. Mr. Smith's new car drove so smoothly it seemed like a magic carpet.*

main drag *n.*, *colloquial* **1.** The most important street or thoroughfare in a town. *Lincoln Avenue is the main drag of our town.* **2.** The street where the dope pushers and the prostitutes are. *Wells Street is the main drag of Chicago, actionwise.*

main squeeze *n.*, *slang* **1.** The top ranking person in an organization or in a neighborhood; an important person, such as one's boss. *Mr. Bronchard is the main squeeze in this office.* **2.** The top person in charge of an illegal operation, such as drug sales, etc. *Before*

we can clean up this part of town, we must arrest the main squeeze. **3.** One's principal romantic or sexual partner. *The singer's main squeeze is a member of the band.*

make a beeline for *v. phr.* To go in a straight line toward. *The runner made a beeline for first base. When the bell rang Ted made a beeline for the door of the classroom.*

make a big deal about *v. phr.*, *informal* To exaggerate an insignificant event. *Jeff said, "I'm sorry I banged into you in the dark. Don't make a big deal out of it."*

make a day of it *v. phr.*, *informal* To do something all day. *When they go to the beach they take a picnic lunch and make a day of it.*

make a dent in *v. phr.*, *informal* To make less by a very small amount; reduce slightly.—Usually used in the negative or with such qualifying words as *hardly* or *barely. John shoveled and shoveled, but he didn't seem to make a dent in the pile of sand. Mary studied all afternoon and only made a dent in her homework.*

make a difference *or* **make the difference** *v. phr.* To change the nature of something or a situation; be important; matter. *John's good score on the test made the difference between his passing or failing the course. It doesn't make a bit of difference* *if you are late to my party. I just want you to come.*

make a go of *v. phr.* To turn into a success. *He is both energetic and highly skilled at trading; he is sure to make a go of any business that holds his interest.*

make a hit *v. phr., informal* To be successful; be well-liked; get along well. *Mary's new red dress made a hit at the party. Alice was so happy that her boyfriend made a hit with her parents.*

make a mountain out of a molehill To think a small problem is a big one; try to make something unimportant seem important. *You're not hurt badly, Johnny. Stop trying to make a mountain out of a molehill with crying. Sarah laughed at a mistake Betty made in class, and Betty won't speak to her; Betty is making a mountain out of a molehill.*

make a move *v. phr.* **1.** To budge; change places. *"If you make a move," the masked gangster said, "I'll start shooting."* **2.** To go home after dinner or a party. *"I guess it's time to make a move," Roy said at the end of the party.*

make a pass at *v. phr., slang, informal* Make advances toward a member of the opposite sex (usually man to a woman) with the goal of seducing the person. *We've been dating for four weeks but Joe has never even made a pass at me.*

make a play for *v. phr., slang* To try to get the interest or liking of; flirt with; attract. *Bob made a play for the pretty new girl. John made a play for the*

other boys' votes for class presi
dent.

make a point *v. phr.* To try hard; make a special effort.— Used with *of* and a verba noun. *He made a point of re membering to get his glasse fixed. He made a point o thanking his hostess before h left the party.*

make away with *v., informa* Take; carry away; cause to dis appear. *The lumberjack mad away with a great stack of pan cakes. Two masked men hel up the clerk and made away with the payroll.*

make-believe *n.* False; untrue created by illusion. *The crea tures of* Star Wars *are all make believe.*

make believe *v.* To act as i something is true while on knows it is not; pretend. *Let' make believe we have a millio dollars. Danny made believe h didn't hear his mother calling.*

make do *v. phr.* To use a poo substitute when one does no have the right thing. *John di not have a hammer, and he ha to make do with a heavy rock This motel isn't what w wanted, but we must make do Many families manage to mak do on very little income.*

make ends meet *v. phr.* T have enough money to pa one's bills; earn what it costs t live. *Both husband and wif had to work to make end meet.*

make eyes at *v. phr., informa* To look at a girl or boy in way that tries to attract him t you; flirt. *The other girls dis liked her way of making eyes a* *their boyfriends instead of find-ing one of her own.*

make for *v.* To go toward; start in the direction of. *The children took their ice skates and made for the frozen pond. The bee got his load of pollen and made for the hive.*

make free with *v.* **1.** To take or use (things) without asking. *Bob makes free with his room-mate's clothes. A student should not make free with his teacher's first name.* **2.** To act toward (someone) in a rude or impolite way. *The girls don't like Ted because he makes free with them.*

make fun of *or* **poke fun at** *v. phr., informal* To joke about; laugh at; tease; mock. *Men like to make fun of the trimmings on women's hats. James poked fun at the new pupil because her speech was not like the other pupils.*

make good *v. phr.* **1.** To do what one promised to do; make something come true. *Mr. Smith borrowed some money. He promised to pay it back on payday. He made good his promise. Joe made good his boast to swim across the lake. John's mother promised to take him and his friends to the zoo on Saturday. She made good her promise.* **2.** To compensate; pay for loss or damage. *The po-liceman told the boy's parents that the boy must make good the money he had stolen or go to jail.*—Often used in the phrase *make it good. The radio was broken while it was being delivered so the store had to make it good and send us a new radio.* **3.** To do good work at

one's job; succeed. *Kate wanted to be a nurse. She studied and worked hard in school. Then she got a job in the hospital and made good as a nurse.*

make hay while the sun shines *v. phr.* To do something at the right time; not wait too long. *Dick had a free hour so he made hay while the sun shone and got his lesson for the next day.*

make head or tail of *v. phr., informal* To see the why of; finding a meaning in; under-stand.—Used in negative, con-ditional, and interrogative sentences. *She could not make head or tail of the directions on the dress pattern. Can you make head or tail of the letter?*

make it with *v. phr., slang, informal* **1.** To be accepted by a group. *Joe finally made it with the in crowd in Hollywood.* **2.** *vulgar* To have sex with (someone). *I wonder if Joe has made it with Sue.*

make light of *v. phr.* To treat an important matter as if it were trivial. *One ought to know which problems to make light of and which ones to han-dle seriously.*

make love *v. phr.* **1.** To be warm, loving, and tender to-ward someone of the opposite sex; try to get him or her to love you too. *There was moon-light on the roses and he made love to her in the porch swing.* **2.** To have sexual relations with (someone). *It is rumored that Alfred makes love to every girl he hires as a secretary.*

make merry *v. phr., literary* To have fun, laugh, and be happy. *In Aesop's fable the* *grasshopper made merry while the ant worked and saved up food. In the Bible story a rich man ate and drank and made merry.*

make no bones *v. phr., informal* **1.** To have no doubts; not to worry about right or wrong; not to be against.—Used with *about. Bill makes no bones about telling a lie to escape punishment. The boss made no bones about hiring extra help for the holidays.* **2.** To make no secret; not keep from talking; admit.—Used with *about* or *of the fact. John thinks being poor is no disgrace and he makes no bones of the fact. Mary made no bones about her love of poetry even after some of her friends laughed at her.*

make of *v. phr.* To interpret; understand. *What do you make of his sudden decision to go to Africa?*

make off *v.* To go away; run away; leave. *When the deer saw the hunter it made off at once. A thief stopped John on a dark street and made off with his wallet.*

make one's bed and lie in it To be responsible for what you have done and so to have to accept the bad results. *Billy smoked one of his father's cigars and now he is sick. He made his bed, now let him lie in it.*

make one's blood boil *or* **make the blood boil** *v. phr., informal* To make someone very angry. *When someone calls me a liar it makes my blood boil. It made Mary's blood boil to see the children make fun of the crippled girl.*

make oneself scarce *v. phr., slang* To leave quickly; go away. *The boys made themselves scarce when they saw the principal coming to stop their noise. A wise mouse makes himself scarce when a cat is nearby.*

make one's mouth water *v. phr.* **1.** To look or smell very good; make you want very much to eat or drink something you see or smell. *The pies in the store window made Dan's mouth water. The picture of the ice cream soda made his mouth water.* **2.** To be attractive; make you want to have something very much. *Judy collects folk song records, and the records in the store window made her mouth water.*

make out *v.* **1.** To write the facts asked for (as in an application blank or a report form); fill out. *The teacher made out the report cards and gave them to the students to take home. Mrs. Smith gave the clerk in the store some money and the clerk made out a receipt.* **2.** To see, hear, or understand by trying hard. *It was dark, and we could not make out who was coming along the road. They could not make out what the child had drawn. The book had many hard words and Anne could not make out what the writer meant. Mr. White does many strange things. No one can make him out.* **3.** *informal* To make someone believe; show; prove. *Charles and Bob had a fight, and Charles tried to make out that Bob started it. The boy said he did not take the money but the teacher found the* money in the boy's desk and it made him out to be a liar. **4.** *informal* Do well enough; succeed. *John's father wanted John to do well in school and asked the teacher how John was making out. The sick woman could not make out alone in her house, so her friend came and helped her.* **5.** To kiss or pet. *What are Jack and Jill up to?—They're making out on the back porch.*

make over *v.* **1.** To change by law something from one owner to another owner; change the name on the title (lawful paper) from one owner to another. *Mr. Brown made over the title to the car to Mr. Jones.* **2.** To make something look different; change the style of. *He asked the tailor to make over his pants. The tailor cut off the cuffs and put a belt across the back.*

make the grade *v. phr., informal* **1.** To make good; succeed. *It was clear that Mr. Baker had made the grade in the insurance business. It takes hard study to make it in school.* **2.** To meet a standard; qualify. *That whole shipment of cattle made the grade as prime beef.*

make time *v. phr., slang* **1.** To be successful in arriving at a designated place in short or good time. *We're supposed to be there at 6 P.M., and it's 5:30—we're making good time.* **2.** To be successful in making sexual advances to someone. *Joe sure is making time with Sue, isn't he?*

makeup *n.* (stress on *make*) **1.** Cosmetics. *All the actors and actresses put on a lot of makeup.* **2.** Attributive auxiliary in lieu of, or belated. *The professor gave a makeup to the sick students.*

make up *v.* (stress on *up*) **1.** To make by putting things or parts together. *A car is made up of many different parts.* **2.** To invent; think and say something that is new or not true. *Jean makes up stories to amuse her little brother.* **3a.** To do or provide (something lacking or needed); do or supply (something not done, lost, or missed); get back; regain; give back; repay. *I have to make up the test I missed last week. I want to go to bed early to make up the sleep I lost last night. We have to drive fast to make up the hour we lost in Boston. Vitamin pills make up what you lack in your diet. The toy cost a dollar and Ted only had fifty cents, so Father made up the difference.*—Often used in the phrase *make it up to. Uncle Fred forgot my birthday present but he made it up to me by taking me to the circus. Mrs. Rich spent so much time away from her children that she tried to make it up to them by giving them things.* **3b.** To do what is lacking or needed; do or give what should be done or given; get or give back what has been lost, missed, or not done; get or give instead; pay back.—Used with *for. We made up for lost time by taking an airplane instead of a train. Saying you are sorry won't make up for the damage of breaking the window. Mary had to make up for the time she missed in school* *when she was sick, by studying very hard. The beautiful view at the top of the mountain makes up for the hard climb to get there.* **4.** To put on lipstick and face paint powder. *Clowns always make up before a circus show. Tom watched his sister make up her face for her date.* **5.** To become friends again after a quarrel. *Mary and Joan quarreled, but made up after a while.* **6.** To try to make friends with someone; to win favor.—Followed by *to*. *The new boy made up to the teacher by sharpening her pencils.*

make up one's mind *v. phr.* To choose what to do; decide. *They made up their minds to sell the house. Tom couldn't decide whether he should tell Mother about the broken window or let her find it herself.*

make waves *v. phr., informal* Make one's influence felt; create a disturbance, a sensation. *Joe Catwallender is the wrong man for the job; he is always trying to make waves.*

make way *v. phr.* To move from in front so someone can go through; stand aside. *The people made way for the king. When older men retire they make way for younger men to take their places.*

man in the street *n. phr.* The man who is just like most other men; the average man; the ordinary man. *The newspaper took a poll of the man in the street.*

mark time *v. phr.* **1.** To move the feet up and down as in marching, but not going forward. *The officer made the soldiers mark time as a punish-*

ment. **2.** To be idle; waiting for something to happen. *The teacher marked time until all the children were ready for the test.* **3.** To seem to be working or doing something, but really not doing it. *It was so hot that the workmen just marked time.*

matter of course *n. phr.* Something always done; the usual way; habit; rule. *It was a matter of course for John to dress carefully when he was meeting his wife. Bank officers ask questions as a matter of course when someone wants to borrow money.*

matter of fact *n. phr.* Something that is really true; something that can be proved. *The town records showed that it was a matter of fact that the two boys were brothers. It is a matter of fact that the American war against England was successful.*—Often used for emphasis in the phrase *as a matter of fact. I didn't go yesterday, and as a matter of fact, I didn't go all week. Mary wasn't wearing a blue dress. As a matter of fact, she hasn't got a blue dress.*

matter-of-fact *adj.* **1.** Simply telling or showing the truth; not explaining or telling more. *The newspaper gave a matter-of-fact account of the murder trial.* **2.** Showing little feeling or excitement or trouble; seeming not to care much. *When Mary's father died she acted in a very matter-of-fact way. He was a very matter-of-fact person.*

mean business *v. phr., informal* To decide strongly to do what you plan to do; really mean it;

be serious. *The boss said he would fire us if we didn't work harder and he means business. When she went to college to study, she meant business. He just liked the company of the other girls he dated, but this time he seems to mean business.*

measure up *v.* To be equal; be of fully high quality; come up. *John didn't measure up to the best catchers but he was a good one. Lois' school work didn't measure up to her ability.*

meet up with *v. phr.* To meet by accident; come upon without planning or expecting to. *When he ran around the tree, Bob suddenly meet up with a large bear. The family would have arrived on time, but they met up with a flat tire.*

melt in one's mouth *v. phr.* **1.** To be so tender as to seem to need no chewing. *The chicken was so tender that it melted in your mouth.* **2.** To taste very good; be delicious. *Mother's apple pie really melts in your mouth.*

mend one's fences *v. phr., informal* To do something to make people like or follow you again; strengthen your friendships or influence. *The senator went home from Washington to mend his fences. John saw that his friends did not like him, so he decided to mend his fences.*

mess around *v. phr.* **1.** To engage in idle or purposeless activity. *Come on, you guys,—start doing some work, don't just mess around all day!* **2.** *vulgar* To be promiscuous; to indulge in sex with little discrimination as to who the part-

ner is. *Allen needs straightening out; he's been messing around with the whole female population of his class.*

mess up *v. phr., slang, informal* **1.** To cause trouble; to spoil something. *What did you have to mess up my accounts for?* **2.** To cause someone emotional trauma. *Sue will never get married; she got messed up when she was a teenager.* **3.** To beat up someone physically. *When Joe came in after the fight with the boys, he was all messed up.*

middle of the road *n. phr.* A way of thinking which does not favor one idea or thing too much; being halfway between two different ideas. *The teacher did not support the boys or the girls in the debate, but stayed in the middle of the road.*

middle-of-the-road *adj.* Favoring action halfway between two opposite movements or ideas; with ideas halfway between two opposite sides; seeing good on both sides. *The men who wrote the Constitution followed a middle-of-the-road plan on whether greater power belonged to the United States government or to the separate states. Senator Jones favors a middle-of-the-road policy in the labor-management dispute.*

mind one's p's and q's *v. phr.* To be very careful what you do or say; not make mistakes. *When the principal of the school visited the class the students all minded their p's and q's. If you wish to succeed you must mind your p's and q's.* [From the old U.S. Navy when sailors marked on a board in the bar how many Pints and

Quarts of liquor they had taken. It was bad manners to cheat.]

mind you *v. phr.*, *informal* I want you to notice and understand. *Mind you, I am not blaming him.*

miss out *v.*, *informal* To fail; lose or not take a good chance; miss something good. *Jim's mother told him he missed out on a chance to go fishing with his father because he came home late. You missed out by not coming with us; we had a great time.*

miss the boat *also* **miss the bus** *v. phr.*, *informal* To fail through slowness; to put something off until too late; do the wrong thing and lose the chance. *Mr. Brown missed the boat when he decided not to buy the house. In college he didn't study enough so he missed the boat and failed to pass. Ted could have married Lena but he put off asking her and missed the boat.*

miss the point *v. phr.* To be unable to comprehend the essence of what was meant. *The student didn't get a passing grade on the exam because, although he wrote three pages, he actually missed the point.*

mixed up *adj. phr.* **1.** *informal* Confused in mind; puzzled. *Bob was all mixed up after the accident.* **2.** Disordered; disarranged; not neat. *The papers on his desk were mixed up.* **3.** *informal* Joined or connected (with someone or something bad). *Harry was mixed up in a fight after the game. Mary's father told her not to get mixed up with the students that always break school rules.*

mix up *v.* To confuse; make a mistake about. *Jimmy doesn't know colors yet; he mixes up purple with blue. Even the twins' mother mixes them up.*

money to burn *n. phr.*, *informal* Very much money, more than is needed. *Dick's uncle died and left him money to burn. When Joe is twenty-one he will have money to burn. Jean is looking for a husband with money to burn.*

monkey business *n.*, *slang*, *informal* **1.** Any unethical, illegitimate, or objectionable activity that is furtive or deceitful, e.g., undercover sexual advances, cheating, misuse of public funds, etc. *There is a lot of monkey business going on in that firm; you'd better watch out who you deal with!* **2.** Comical or silly actions; goofing off. *Come on boys, let's cut out the monkey business and get down to work!*

more the merrier *n. phr.* The more people who join in the fun, the better it will be.— Used in welcoming more people to join others in some pleasant activity. *Come with us on the boat ride; the more the merrier.*

morning after *n.*, *slang* The effects of drinking liquor or staying up late as felt the next morning; a hangover. *One of the troubles of drinking too much liquor is the morning after. Mr. Smith woke up with a big headache and knew it was the morning after.*

move a muscle *v. phr.* To move even a very little.—Used in negative sentences and questions and with *if*. *The deer stood without moving a muscle until the hunter was gone. The girls were so startled that they did not move a muscle. You're sitting right where you were when I left! Have you moved a muscle? The robber said he would shoot the bank worker if he moved a muscle.*

move heaven and earth   *v. phr.* To try every way; do everything you can. *Joe moved heaven and earth to be sent to Washington.*

move in on   *v. phr., slang, colloquial* To take over something that belongs to another. *He moved in on my girlfriend and now we're not talking to each other.*

musical chairs   *n. phr.* (Originally the name of a children's game.) The transfer of a number of officers in an organization into different jobs, especially each other's jobs. *The boss regularly played musical chairs with department heads to keep them fresh on the job.*

music to one's ears   *n. phr.* Something one likes to hear. *When the manager phoned to say I got the job, it was music to my ears.*

my God *or* **my goodness**   *interj.* Used to express surprise, shock, or dismay. *My God! What happened to the car?*

my lips are sealed   *informal sentence* A promise that one will not give away a secret. *"You can tell me what happened,"* Helen said. *"My lips are sealed."*

nail down v. phr., informal To make certain; make sure; settle. *Joe had a hard time selling his car, but he finally nailed the sale down when he got his friend Sam to give him $300. The New York Yankees nailed down the American League Championship when they beat the Red Sox 3 to 0 on September 15.*

name is mud informal (You) are in trouble; a person is blamed or no longer liked.—Used in the possessive. *If you tell your mother I spilled ink on her rug my name will be mud. Your name will be mud if you tell the teacher about the bad thing we did.*

name of the game n., informal The crux of the matter; that which actually occurs under the disguise of something else. *Getting medium income families to support the rest of society—that's the name of the game!*

neck and neck adj. or adv., informal Equal or nearly equal in a race or contest; abreast; tied. *At the end of the race the two horses were neck and neck. For months John and Harry seemed to be neck and neck in Alice's favor.*

neck of the woods n. phr., informal Part of the country; place; neighborhood; vicinity. *We visited Illinois and Iowa last summer; in that neck of the woods the corn really grows tall. We were down in your neck of the woods last week.*

needle in a haystack n. phr., informal Something that will be very hard to find. *"I lost my class ring somewhere in the front yard," said June. Jim answered, "Too bad. That will be like finding a needle in a haystack."*

neither fish nor fowl also **neither fish, flesh, nor fowl** Something or someone that does not belong to a definite group or known class; a strange person or thing; someone or something odd or hard to understand. *The man is neither fish nor fowl; he votes Democrat or Republican according to which will do him the most good. Mrs. Harris bought a piece of furniture that was both a table and a chair. Mr. Harris said it was neither fish nor fowl. The movie is neither fish nor fowl; it is a funny love story.*

neither here nor there adj. phr. Not important to the thing being discussed; off the subject; not mattering. *Perhaps you did stay up late finishing your homework. That's neither here nor there. You still must come to school on time. The boys all like the coach but that's neither here nor there; the question is, "Does he know how to teach football?"*

Nervous Nellie n., informal A timid person who lacks determination and courage. *I say we* *will never win if we don't stop being Nervous Nellies!*

never mind *v. phr.* Don't trouble about it; don't worry about it; forget it; skip it.—Usually used in speaking or when writing dialogue. *Never mind preparing a picnic lunch; we'll find a lunchstand when we get to the beach. "What did you say?" "Oh, never mind." "What about money?" "Never mind that. I'll take care of it."*

new blood *n.* Something or someone that gives new life or vigor, fresh energy or power. *New blood was brought into the company through appointment of younger men to important positions.*

new broom sweeps clean A new person makes many changes.—A proverb. *The new superintendent has changed many of the school rules. A new broom sweeps clean.*

new deal *n., informal* **1.** A complete change; a fresh start. *People had been on the job too long; a new deal was needed to get things out of the old bad habits.* **2.** Another chance. *The boy asked for a new deal after he had been punished for fighting in school.*

new money *n. phr.* People who have become rich recently. *Since Bobby's father invented a new computer component, Bobby and his family are new money.*

night owl *n. phr.* One who sleeps during the day and stays up or works during the night. *Tom hardly ever sleeps at night; he prefers to work by lamp light and has become a regular night owl.*

nip and tuck *adj. or adv., informal* Evenly matched; hard fought to the finish. *The game was nip and tuck until the last minute. It was a nip and tuck race right to the finish line. The two salesmen fought nip and tuck for the contract all the way.*

nip in the bud *v. phr.* To check at the outset; prevent at the start; block or destroy in the beginning. *The police nipped the plot in the bud. The teacher nipped the disorder in the bud.*

nobody home *slang* **1.** Your attention is somewhere else, not on what is being said or done here; you are absent-minded. *The teacher asked him a question three times but he still looked out the window. She gave up, saying, "Nobody home."* **2.** You are feeble-minded or insane. *He pointed to the woman, tapped his head, and said, "Nobody home."*

nobody's fool *n. phr.* A smart person; a person who knows what he is doing; a person who can take care of himself. *In the classroom and on the football field, Henry was nobody's fool.*

no deal *or* **no dice** *or* **no go** *or* **no sale** *or* **no soap** *slang* Not agreed to; refused or useless; without success or result; no; certainly not.—Used in the predicate or to refuse something. *Billy wanted to let Bob join the team, but I said that it was no deal because Bob was too young. "Let me have a dollar." "No dice!" answered Joe. I tried to get Mary on the telephone but it was no go.*

"Let's go to the beach tomorrow." "No sale, I have my music lesson tomorrow." I asked Dad for a new bicycle but it was no soap.

no doubt *adv.* **1.** Without doubt; doubtless; surely; certainly. *No doubt Susan was the smartest girl in her class.* **2.** Probably. *John will no doubt telephone us if he comes to town.*

no end *adv., informal* **1.** Very much; exceedingly. *Jim was no end upset because he couldn't go swimming.* **2.** Almost without stopping; continually. *The baby cried no end.*

no end to *or informal* **no end of** So many, or so much of, as to seem almost endless; very many or very much. *There was no end to the letters pouring into the post office. Bob and Dick became close friends and had no end of fun together.*

no frills *n. phr.* A firm or product that offers no extras; a generic product that carries no expensive label. *We went on a no frills trip to Europe with few luxuries.*

no love lost *n. phr.* Bad feeling; ill will. *Bob and Dick both wanted to be elected captain of the team, and there was no love lost between them. There was no love lost between the sales and the accounting departments.*

no matter **1.** Not anything important. *I wanted to see him before he left but it's no matter.* **2.** It makes no difference; regardless of. *She was going to be a singer no matter what difficulties she met. He had to get the car fixed no matter how much it* cost. *No matter what you try to do, it is important to be able to speak well. You can't go in no matter who you are. Mary wanted to get to school on time, no matter if she went without breakfast.*

nose about *or* **nose around** *v. phr., informal* To look for something kept private or secret; poke about; explore; inquire; pry. *In Grandmother's attic, Sally spent a while nosing about in the old family pictures. The detective was nosing around in the crowd looking for pickpockets.*

nose down *v., of an aircraft* To head down; bring down the nose of. *The big airliner began to nose down for a landing. The pilot nosed the plane down toward the runway.*

nose in^1 *or* **nose into^1** *informal* Prying or pestering interest in; unwelcome interest in; impolite curiosity. *He always had his nose in other people's business.*

nose in^2 *or* **nose into^2** *v.* To move in close; move slowly in with the front first. *The ship nosed into the pier. The car nosed into the curb.*

nose out of *informal* Curious attention; bothering.—Usually used with a possessive and usually used with keep. *When Billy asked his sister where she was going she told him to keep his nose out of her business.*

no-show *n., informal* A person who makes a reservation, e.g., at a hotel or at an airline, and then neither claims nor cancels it. *The airlines were messed up because of a great number of no-show passengers.*

no sweat[1] *adj.*, *slang*, *informal* Easily accomplished, uncomplicated. *That job was no sweat.*

no sweat[2] *adv.* Easily. *We did it no sweat.*

not a leg to stand on *n. phr.*, *informal* No good proof or excuse; no good evidence or defense to offer. *The man with a gun and $300 in his pocket was accused of robbing an oil station. He did not have a leg to stand on.*

not bad *or* **not so bad** *or* **not half bad** *adj.*, *informal* Pretty good; all right; good enough. *The party last night was not bad. It was not so bad, as inexpensive vacations go. The show was not half bad.*

not for the world *or* **not for worlds** *adv. phr.* Not at any price; not for anything. *I wouldn't hurt his feelings for the world. Not for worlds would he let his children go hungry.*

nothing doing *adv. phr.*, *informal* I will not do it; certainly not; no indeed; no. *"Will you lend me a dollar?" "Nothing doing!" "Let's go for a boat ride!" "Nothing doing!"*

nothing if not *adv. phr.* Without doubt; certainly. *With its bright furnishings, flowers, and sunny windows, the new hospital dayroom is nothing if not cheerful.*

not on your life *adv. phr.*, *informal* Certainly not; not ever; not for any reason.— Used for emphasis. *I wouldn't drive a car with brakes like that—not on your life. Did he thank me for my advice? Not on your life.*

not to give one the time of day *v. phr.*, *slang*, *informal* To dislike someone strongly enough so as to totally ignore him. *Sue wouldn't give Helen the time of day.*

not to give quarter *v. phr.* **1.** To be utterly unwilling to show mercy; not to allow a weaker or defeated party the chance to save themselves through escape. *The occupying foreign army gave no quarter—they took no prisoners, shot everyone, and made escape impossible.* **2.** To argue so forcefully during a negotiation or in a court of law as to make any counter-argument or counterproposal impossible. *The District Attorney hammered away at the witnesses and gave no quarter to the attorney for the defense.*

not to know one from Adam *v. phr.* To not know a person; be unable to recognize someone. *I have no idea who that guy is that Jane just walked in with; I don't know him from Adam.*

not to touch (something) with a ten-foot pole *v. phr.* To consider something completely undesirable or uninteresting. *Some people won't touch spinach with a ten-foot pole. Kids who wouldn't touch an encyclopedia with a ten-foot pole love to find information with this computer program.*

number one[1] *or* **Number One[1]** *n. phr.*, *informal* Yourself; your own interests; your private or selfish advantage. Usually used in the phrase *look out for number one*. *He was well known for his habit of always looking out for number one.*

number one[2] *adj. phr.* **1.** Of first rank or importance; foremost; principal. *He is easily America's number one golfer.* **2.** Of first grade; of top quality; best. *That is number one western steer beef.*

nurse a drink *v. phr., informal* To hold a drink in one's hand at a party, pretending to be drinking it or taking extremely small sips only. *John's been nursing that drink all evening.*

nurse a grudge *v. phr.* To keep a feeling of envy or dislike toward some person; remember something bad that a person said or did to you, and dislike the person because of that. *Tom nursed a grudge against John because John took his place on the basketball team. Mary nursed a grudge against her teacher because she thought she deserved a better grade in English.*

nut case *n. phr.* A very silly, crazy, or foolish person. *I am going to be a nut case if I don't go on a vacation pretty soon.*

nutty as a fruitcake *adj. phr. slang* Very crazy; entirely mad. *He looked all right, as we watched him approach, but when he began to talk, we saw that he was as nutty as a fruitcake.*

O

oddball n., slang, informal An eccentric person; one who doesn't act like everyone else. *John is an oddball—he never invites anyone.*

age adj. phr. **1a.** Old enough to be allowed to do or manage something. *Mary will be of driving age on her next birthday.* **1b.** Old enough to vote; having the privileges of adulthood. *The age at which one is considered of age to vote, or of age to buy alcoholic drinks, or of age to be prosecuted as an adult, varies within the United States.* **2.** Fully developed; mature. *Education for the foreign born came of age when bilingual education was accepted as a necessary part of the public school system.*

course adv. phr. **1.** As you would expect; naturally. *Bob hit Herman, and Herman hit him back, of course. The rain came pouring down, and of course the track meet was cancelled.* **2.** Without a doubt; certainly; surely. *Of course you know that girl; she's in your class.*

again, on-again or **on-again, off-again** adj. phr., informal Not settled; changeable; uncertain. *John and Susan had an off-again, on-again romance. I don't like this off-again, on-again business. Are we going to have the party or not?*

and on also **on and off** adv.

Not regularly; occasionally; sometimes. *Joan wrote to a pen pal in England off and on for several years. It rained off and on all day.*—Sometimes used with hyphens like an adjective. *A worn-out cord may make a hearing aid work in an off-and-on way.*

off balance adj. phr. **1.** Not in balance; not able to stand up straight and not fall; not able to keep from turning over or falling; unsteady. *Never stand up in a canoe; it will get off balance and turn over. Paul was speeding along on his bicycle, when an unexpected hole in the road caught him off balance and he fell over.* **2.** Not prepared; not ready; unable to meet something unexpected. *Our quarterback kept the other team off balance by changing often from line plays to passes and tricky end runs. The teacher's surprise test caught the class off balance, and nearly everyone got a poor mark.*

off base adj. phr., informal Not agreeing with fact; wrong. *The idea that touching a toad causes warts is off base. When Tom said that the teacher's explanation did not agree with the book, the teacher was embarrassed at being caught off base.*

offbeat adj., informal Nonconventional; different from the usual; odd. *Linguistics used to be an offbeat field, but nowadays every self-respecting uni-*

versity has a linguistics department.

off center *adv. phr.* Not exactly in the middle. *Mary hung the picture off center, because it was more interesting that way.*

off-center *adj., informal* Different from the usual pattern; not quite like most others; odd. *Roger's sense of humor was a bit off-center.*

off-color or **off-colored** *adj.* **1.** Not of the proper hue or shade; not matching a standard color sample. *The librarian complained that the painter had used an off-color green on the walls.* **2.** *informal* Not of the proper kind for polite society; in bad taste; dirty. *When Joe finished his off-color story, no one was pleased.*

off duty *adj.* Not supposed to be at work; having free time; not working. *Sailors like to go sight-seeing, when they are off duty in a foreign port. It seems that all the taxis in New York are off duty whenever it rains.*—Often used with hyphens, before a noun. *The bank robber was captured by an off-duty policeman.*

off guard *adj.* In a careless attitude; not alert to coming danger; not watching. *In the second that the boxer was off guard, his opponent landed a knockout punch. Timmy's question caught Jean off guard, and she told him the secret before she knew it.*

off one's back *adj. phr.* **1.** *informal* Stopped from bothering one; removed as an annoyance or pest. *"Having a kid brother always following me is a nuisance," Mary told* her mother. *"Can't you get h off my back?" The singer v so popular with teenagers he took a secret vacation, keep them off his back.*

off one's chest *adj. phr., inf mal* Told to someone and not bothering you anymo not making you feel worried upset, because you have talk about it. *After Dave told principal that he had cheated the test, he was glad becaus was off his chest. Father that Tom wasn't help enough around the house, so got it off his chest by giv Tom a list of things to do.*

off one's hands *adv. phr.* longer in your care or poss sion. *Ginny was glad to h the sick dog taken off her ha by the doctor.*

off one's high horse *adj. p informal* **1.** Not acting pro and scornful; humble a agreeable. *The girls were kind to Nancy after her motl died that she came down off high horse and made frie with them.* **2.** Acting frien again; not angry and unple ant any more; agreeable. *Sc wouldn't speak to anyone all ternoon because she couldn't to the movies, but she's off high horse now.*

off one's rocker or **off on trolley** *adj. phr., inform* Not thinking correctly; cra silly; foolish. *Tom is off rocker if he thinks he can r faster than Bob can. If y think you can learn to fig skate in one lesson, you're your trolley.*

off the beam *adv.* or *adj. p* **1.** *(Of an airplane)* Not in radio beam that marks the path to follow between airports; flying in the wrong direction. *A radio signal tells the pilot of an airplane when his plane is off the beam.* **2.** *slang* Wrong; mistaken. *Maud was off the beam when she said that the girls didn't like her.*

off the beaten track *adv. phr.* Not well known or often used; not gone to or seen by many people; unusual. *This theater is off the beaten track. We are looking for a vacation spot that's off the beaten track.*

off the cuff *adv. phr., informal* Without preparing ahead of time what you will say; without preparation. *Some presidents like to speak off the cuff to newspaper reporters but others prefer to think questions over and write their answers.*

off-the-cuff *adj., informal* Not prepared ahead of time.—Used of a speech or remarks. *Jack was made master of ceremonies because he was a good off-the-cuff speaker.*

off the hook *adv. phr.* Out of trouble; out of an awkward or embarrassing situation. *Thelma found she had made two dates for the same night; she asked Sally to get her off the hook by going out with one of the boys.*

off the record[1] *adv. phr.* Confidentially. *"Off the record," the boss said, "you will get a good raise for next year, but you'll have to wait for the official letter."*

off the record[2] *adj. phr.* Not to be published or told; secret; confidential. *The President told the reporters his remarks were strictly off the record.*—Some-

times used with hyphens, before the noun. *The governor was angry when a newspaper printed his off-the-record comments.*

off the top of one's head *adv. or adj. phr., informal* Without thinking hard; quickly. *Vin answered the teacher's question off the top of his head. When Lorraine was asked to recite, she talked off the top of her head.*

off the wagon *adj. phr., slang* No longer refusing to drink whiskey or other alcoholic beverages; drinking liquor again, after stopping for a while. *When a heavy drinker quits he must really quit. One little drink of whiskey is enough to drive him off the wagon.*

off the wall *adj. phr.* Strange; out of the ordinary; stupid. *He has been making off-the-wall remarks all day; something must be the matter with him.*

old as the hills *adj. phr.* Very old; ancient. *"Why didn't you laugh?" she asked. "Because that joke is as old as the hills," he answered.*

old hat *adj., informal* Old-fashioned; not new or different. *By now, putting satellites in orbit is old hat to space scientists. Andrea thought her mother's ideas about dating were old hat.*

old maid *n. phr.* A spinster; a woman who has never married. *Because my old maid aunt is a terrific cook as well as a good-looking woman, nobody understands why she never married.*

on a dime *adv. phr., informal* In a very small space. *Bob can turn that car on a dime. Tom* says his new sports car will stop on a dime.

on an even keel *adv. phr., informal* In a well-ordered way or condition; orderly. *When the football rally seemed almost ready to become a riot, the principal stepped to the platform and got things back on an even keel.*

on a pedestal *adv. phr.* Lovingly honored and cared for. *Mrs. Raymond's children served her breakfast in bed on Mother's Day and later took her out to dinner. She felt on a pedestal. Bill is always waiting on his fiancee and bringing her flowers and candy. He has certainly put her on a pedestal.*

on a shoestring *adv. phr.* With little money to spend; on a very low budget. *The couple was seeing Europe on a shoestring.*

on board[1] *prep.* On (a ship). *Joan was not on board the ship when it sailed.*

on board[2] *adv. or adj. phr.* On a ship. *The captain was not on board when the S.S. Flandre sailed. A ship was leaving the harbor, and we saw the people on board waving.*

on call *adj. phr.* **1.** Having to be paid on demand. *Jim didn't have the money ready even though he knew the bill was on call.* **2.** Ready and available. *This is Dr. Kent's day to be on call at the hospital. The nurse is on call for emergency cases.*

once and for all *adv. phr.* **1.** One time and never again; without any doubt; surely; certainly; definitely. *Let me say, for once and for all, you may not go to the party Saturday.*

For once and for all, I will ne go swimming with you. **2.** Permanently. *Bill and Tom aske the teacher to settle the arg ment once and for all. Th general decided that tw bombs would destroy the e emy and end the war once an for all.*

once in a blue moon *adv. ph* Very rarely; very seldom; a most never. *Coin collecting interesting, but you find a val able coin only once in a blu moon. Once in a blue moo someone grows a very pa marigold, but no truly whi marigolds have been raised.*

once in a while *adv. phr.* N often; not regularly; som times; occasionally. *We go for picnic in the park once in while. Once in a while th puppy would run away, b usually he stayed in the yard.*

once-over *n., slang* **1.** A quic look; a swift examination someone or something.—Us ally used with *give* or *get. Th new boy got the once-ove from the rest of the class whe he came in. Bob gave h paper the once-over befor handing it in.* **2.** *or* **once-ove lightly** A quick or carele job, especially of cleaning straightening; work done has ily for now. *Ann gave her roo a quick once-over-lightly wi the broom and dust cloth. "Ju give my hair the once-over," said to the barber.*

on cloud nine *adj. phr., slan* Too happy to think of anythin else; very happy. *Ada has bee on cloud nine since the maga zine printed the story she wrot We were on cloud nine whe* our team won the state championship.

on easy street *adj. phr., informal* Having enough money to live very comfortably; rather rich. *After years of hard work, the Grants found themselves on easy street. Jim's novel was a success and put him on easy street.*

on edge *adj. phr.* Excited or nervous; impatient. *The magician kept the children on edge all through his show. We were all on edge as we listened to the TV for news of the election results. Father was on edge after driving home through the heavy holiday traffic.*

one eye on *informal* Watching or minding (a person or thing) while doing something else; part of your attention on.—Used after *have*, *keep*, or *with*. *Jane had one eye on the baby as she ironed. Bill kept one eye on his books and the other on the clock. Chris tried to study with one eye on the TV set.*

one foot in the grave *n. phr.* Near to death. *The dog is fourteen years old, blind, and feeble. He has one foot in the grave. Grandfather has never been sick a day in his life, but Mother cares for him as if he had one foot in the grave.*

one for the books *n. phr., informal* Very unusual; a remarkable something. *The newspaper reporter turned in a story that was one for the books. Their trip through the Rocky Mountains was one for the books.*

on end *adj. phr.* Seemingly endless.—Used with plural nouns of time. *Judy spent hours on end writing and re-*

writing her essay. *During July and August there was no rain for weeks on end.*

one on the city *n., slang* A glass of water (which is provided free of charge, as a free gift from the city). *What will you have?—Oh, just give me one on the city.*

one-two *n.* **1.** A succession of two punches, the first a short left, followed by a hard right punch, usually in the jaw. *Ali gave Frazier the one-two.* **2.** Any quick or decisive action which takes the opposition by surprise, thereby ensuring victory. *He gave us the old one-two and won the game.*

one up *adj. phr.* Having an advantage; being one step ahead. *John graduated from high school; he is one up on Bob, who dropped out. The Platters are one up on their neighbors. They own the only color television set in their neighborhood.*

one-upmanship *v., informal* Always keeping ahead of others; trying to keep an advantage. *No matter what I do, I find that Jim has already done it better. He's an expert at one-upmanship. Jack took the news to the principal while we were still talking about it. He's very quick to practice one-upmanship.* [The word one-upmanship was made up by a British humorist, Stephen Potter, on the pattern of such words as sportsmanship and workmanship.]

on faith *adv. phr.* Without question or proof. *He said he was twenty-one years old and the employment agency took him on faith. He looked so hon-*

est that we accepted his story on faith.

on file *adv. phr.* Placed in a written or electronic file; on record. *We are sorry we cannot hire you right now but we will keep your application on file.*

on hand *adv. phr.* **1a.** Nearby; within reach. *Always have your dictionary on hand when you study.* **1b.** Here. *Soon school will end and vacation will be on hand.* **2.** Present. *Mr. Blake's secretary is always on hand when he appears in public.* **3.** In your possession; ready. *The Girl Scouts have plenty of cookies on hand. Tim had no cash on hand to pay for the gas.*

on ice *adv. or adj. phr., slang* **1.** The same as won; sure to be won. *The score was 20–10 in the last inning, and our team had the game on ice.* **2.** Away for safekeeping or later use; aside. *You will have to put your vacation plans on ice until your debts are paid. The senator was voted out of office. He is on ice until the next election.*

on one's back *adj. phr., informal* Making insistent demands of you; being an annoyance or bother. *My wife has been on my back for weeks to fix the front door screen. I can't get any work done with the children on my back from morning until night. Jim could do a better job if his boss weren't on his back so often.*

on one's coattails *adv. phr.* Because of another's merits, success, or popularity. *Bob and Jim are best friends. When Jim was invited to join a fraternity, Bob rode in on his coattails.*

Many people vote straight for all the candidates in the same political party. Most people voted for President K., so Governor B. rode in on K.'s coattails.

on one's feet *adv. phr.* **1.** Standing or walking; not sitting or lying down; up. *Before the teacher finished asking the question, George was on his feet ready to answer it. In a busy gasoline station, the attendant is on his feet all day.* **2.** Recovering; getting better from sickness or trouble. *Jack is back on his feet after a long illness. Susan was on her feet soon after the operation. The bank loaned the store money to get it back on its feet after the fire.*

on one's head *or* **upon one's head** *adv. phr.* On one's self. *When the school board fired the superintendent of schools, they brought the anger of the parents upon their heads. Billy had been naughty all day, but he really brought his parents' anger down on his head by pushing his little sister into a mud puddle.*

on one's high horse *adj. phr., informal* **1.** Acting as if you are better than others; being very proud and scornful. *Martha was chairman of the picnic committee, and at the picnic she was on her high horse, telling everyone what to do. Mrs. Jones asked to see a less expensive hat. The salesgirl got up on her high horse and said the shop did not sell cheap merchandise.* **2.** Refusing to be friendly because you are angry; in a bad temper. *Joe was on his* *high horse because he felt Mary wasn't giving him enough attention.*

on one's last legs *adj. phr.* Failing; near the end. *The blacksmith's business is on its last legs. The dog is old and sick. He is on his last legs.*

on one's toes *adj. phr., informal* Alert; ready to act. *The successful ball player is always on his toes.*

on pins and needles *adj. phr., informal* Worried; nervous. *Jane's mother was on pins and needles because Jane was very late getting home from school. Many famous actors are on pins and needles before the curtain opens for a play.*

on purpose *adv. phr.* For a reason; because you want to; not accidentally. *Jane did not forget her coat; she left it in the locker on purpose. The clown fell down on purpose.*

on sale *adj. phr.* Selling for a special low price. *Tomato soup that is usually sold for sixty cents a can is now on sale for fifty cents. John and Mary couldn't sell all of the lemonade at twenty cents a cup so they have it on sale for ten cents a cup.*

on schedule¹ *adv. phr.* As planned or expected; at the right time. *The school bus arrived at school on schedule. The four seasons arrive on schedule each year.*

on schedule² *adj. phr.* Punctual; as planned. *The new airline claims to have more on schedule arrivals than the competition.*

on the air *adj. or adv. phr.* Broadcasting or being broadcast on radio or TV. *His show is on the air at six o'clock. The ball game is on the air now.*

on the ball *adj. phr., informal* **1.** Paying attention and doing things well.—Used after *is* or *get*. *Ben is really on the ball in school. The coach told Jim he must get on the ball or he cannot stay on the team.* **2.** That is a skill or ability; making you good at things.—Used after *have*. *John will succeed in life; he has a lot on the ball. The coach was eager to try out his new team and see what they had on the ball.*

on the bandwagon *adj. phr., informal* In or into the newest popular group or activity; in or into something that you join just because many others are joining it.—Often used after *climb*, *get*, or *jump*. *When all George's friends decided to vote for Bill, George climbed on the bandwagon too.*

on the beam *adv. or adj. phr.* **1.** (Of an airplane) In the radio beam that marks the path to follow between airports; flying in the right direction. *A radio signal tells the pilot of an airplane when he is flying on the beam.* **2.** *slang* Doing well; just right; good or correct. *Kenneth's answer was right on the beam.*

on the blink *adj. phr.* Faulty; malfunctioning; inoperative. *I need to call a competent repairman because my computer is on the blink again.*

on the block *adj. phr.* To be sold; for sale. *The vacant house was on the block. Young cattle are grown and sent to* *market to be placed on the block.*

on the cuff *adj. or adv. phr., informal* Agreeing to pay later; to be paid for later; on credit. *Peter lost the money that Mother gave him to buy meat, and the store would not let him have meat on the cuff. Many people buy cars and television sets on the cuff.*

on the dot *also* **on the button** *adv. phr., informal* Exactly on time; not early and not late. *Susan arrived at the party at 2:00 P.M. on the dot. Ben's plane arrived on the dot.*

on the double! *adv. phr.* Hurry up! *"Let's go! On the double!" the pilot cried, as he started up the engine of the small plane.*

on the go *adj. phr., informal* Active and busy. *Successful businessmen are on the go most of the time. Healthy, happy people are usually on the go.*

on the house *adj. phr., informal* Paid for by the owner. *At the opening of the new hotel, the champagne was on the house. Oscar was the first customer at the diner, so his lunch was on the house.*

on the level *adj. phr., informal* Honest and fair; telling the whole truth. *Our teacher respects the students who are on the level with her. Joyce wondered if the fortune-teller was on the level.*

on the loose *adj. phr., informal* Free to go; not shut in or stopped by anything. *The zookeeper forgot to close the gate to the monkey cage and the monkeys were on the loose. All*

of the seniors were on the loose on "Senior Skip Day."

on the make *adj., slang* **1.** Promiscuous or aggressive in one's sexual advances. *I can't stand Murray; he's always on the make.* **2.** Pushing to get ahead in one's career; doing anything to succeed. *The new department head is a young man on the make, who expects to be company president in ten years.*

on the mend *adj. phr.* Healing; becoming better. *John's broken leg is on the mend. Mary's relationship with Joan is on the mend.*

on the money *adv. phr.* Exactly right; exactly accurate. *Algernon won the lottery; the numbers he picked were right on the money.*

on the move *adj. or adv. phr.* **1.** Moving around from place to place; in motion. *It was a very cold day, and the teacher watching the playground kept on the move to stay warm. It was vacation time, and the highways were full of families on the move.* **2.** Moving forward; going somewhere. *The candidate promised that if people would make him president, he would get the country on the move.*

on the nose *adv. phr., informal* Just right; exactly. *Stanley hit the ball on the nose. The airplane pilot found the small landing field on the nose.*

on the other hand *adv. phr.* Looking at the other side; from another point of view.—Used to introduce an opposite or different fact or idea. *Jim wanted to go to the movies; his wife, on* *the other hand, wanted to stay home and read. Mr. Harris may still want a boy to mow his lawn; on the other hand, he may have found someone to do it.*

on the Q.T. *adv. phr., informal* Secretly; without anyone's knowing. *George and Paul formed a club on the Q.T. The teachers got the principal a pres-ent strictly on the Q.T.* [from quiet.]

on the road *adv. or adj. phr.* **1.** Traveling; moving from one place to another. *When we go on vacation, we take a lunch to eat while on the road. Mr. Smith is on the road for his insurance company.* **2.** Changing; going from one condition to another. *Mary was very sick for several weeks, but now she is on the road to recovery. Hard study in school put John on the road to success.*

on the rocks *adj. phr.* **1.** *informal* Wrecked or ruined. *Mr. Jones' business and marriage were both on the rocks.* **2.** With ice only. *At the restaurant, Sally ordered orange juice on the rocks.*

on the run *adv. or adj. phr.* **1.** In a hurry; hurrying. *Jane called "Help!" and Tom came on the run. Modern mothers are usually on the run.* **2.** Going away from a fight; in retreat; retreating. *The enemy soldiers were on the run.*

on the safe side *adv. phr.* Provided for against a possible emergency; well prepared. *"Please double-check these proofs, Mr. Brown," the printer said, "just to be on the safe side."*

on the sly *adv. phr.* So that other people won't know; secretly. *The boys smoked on the sly. Mary's mother did not approve of lipstick, but Mary used it on the sly.*

on the spot *adv. or adj. phr.* **1.** *or* **upon the spot** At that exact time and at the same time or place; without waiting or leaving. *The news of important events is often broadcast on the spot over television. When Tom ruined an expensive machine, his boss fired him on the spot.* **2.** *informal* also **in a spot** In trouble, difficulty, or embarrassment. *Mr. Jones is on the spot because he cannot pay back the money he borrowed. Bill is on the spot; he invited George to visit him, but Bill's parents said no.* **3.** *slang* In danger of murder; named or listed for death. *After he talked to the police, the gangsters put him on the spot.*

on the spur of the moment *adv. phr.* On a sudden wish or decision; suddenly; without thought or preparation." *John had not planned to take the trip; he just left on the spur of the moment. Mary saw a help-wanted advertisement and applied for the job on the spur of the moment.*

on the tip of one's tongue *adv. phr.* About to say something, such as a name, a telephone number, etc., but unable to remember it for the moment. *"His name is on the tip of my tongue,"* Tom said. *"It will come to me in a minute."*

on the up and up *adj. phr., informal* Honest; trustworthy; sincere. *We felt that he was* *honest and could be trusted. This information is on the up and up.*

on time *adv. or adj. phr.* **1.** At the time arranged; not late; promptly. *The train left on time. Mary is always on time for an appointment.* **2.** On the installment plan; on credit, paying a little at a time. *John bought a car on time. You can buy things at the department store on time.*

on top *adv. or adj. phr., informal* In the lead; with success; with victory. *The horse that everyone had expected would be on top actually came in third. Although John had been afraid that he was not prepared for the exam, he came out on top.*

on top of *prep.* **1.** On the top of; standing or lying on; on. *When the player on the other team dropped the ball, Bill fell on top of it. That high hill has a tower on top of it.* **2.** *informal* Very close to. *The elevator was so crowded that everybody was on top of each other. I couldn't find my umbrella and then I realized I was almost on top of it.* **3.** *informal* In addition to; along with. *Mrs. Lane had many expenses and on top of everything else, her baby became ill. Mary worked at the store all day and on top of that she had to baby-sit with her brother.* **4.** *informal* Managing very well; in control of. *Although his new job was very complicated, John was on top of it within a few weeks. No matter what goes wrong, Mary always stays on top of it.* **5.** Knowing all about; not falling behind in information about; up-to-date on. *Mary stays on top of the news by reading newspapers and magazines. When he was in California, Mr. Jones kept on top of things in his office by telephoning every day.*

open heart *n.* **1.** No hiding of your feelings; frankness; freedom. *She spoke with an open heart of her warm feelings for her pupils. She told her troubles with an open heart.* **2.** Kindness; generosity. *She contributed to the fund with an open heart. Mr. Jones has an open heart for underprivileged children.*

open one's heart *v. phr.* **1.** To talk about your feelings honestly; confide in someone. *After going around worrying, Mary opened her heart to her mother. John felt much better after he opened his heart to Betty.* **2.** To be sympathetic to; give love or help generously. *Mrs. Smith opened her heart to the poor little boy. After the moving speech by the UN official, the people opened their hearts to the poor people of India.*

open secret *n.* Something that is supposed to be a secret but that everyone knows. *It is an open secret that Mary and John are engaged. Who will be appointed as the next president of the college is an open secret.*

out cold *adv. or adj., informal* Unconscious; in a faint. *The ball hit Dick in the head and knocked him out cold for ten minutes. They tried to lift Mary when she fell down, but she was out cold.*

out for *prep.* Joining, or planning to join; taking part in; competing for a place in. *John is out for the basketball team. Mary is going out for the school newspaper.*

out from under *adj. phr., informal* Free from something that worries you; seeing the end; finished.—Usually used with *be* or *get. Mary had so much to do in the new house she felt as though she would never be out from under. John had so many debts, he couldn't get out from under.*

out in force *adv. phr.* Present in very large numbers; en masse. *On the Fourth of July the police cars are out in force in the Chicago area.*

out in left field *adj. phr., informal* Far from the right answer; wrong; astray. *Johnny tried to answer the teacher's question but he was way out in left field. Susan tried to guess what the surprise was but she was way out in left field.* **2.** Speaking or acting very queerly; crazy. *The girl next door was always queer, but after her father died, she was really out in left field and had to go to a hospital.*

out in the cold *adj. phr., informal* Alone; not included. *All the other children were chosen for parts in the play, but Johnny was left out in the cold. Everybody made plans for Christmas Day and Mary found herself out in the cold.*

out in the open See come out in the open.

out like a light *adj. phr., informal* **1.** Fast asleep; to sleep very quickly. *Tom got so much fresh air and exercise that he went out like a light as soon as he lay down. As soon as the lights were turned off, Johnny was out like a light.* **2.** In a faint; unconscious. *Johnny was hit by a ball and went out like a light. After she read that Tom had married another girl Jean was out like a light for several minutes.*

out of circulation *adj. phr., informal* Not out in the company of friends, other people, and groups; not active; not joining in what others are doing. *John has a job after school and is out of circulation with his friends.*

out of kilter *adj. phr., informal* **1.** Not balanced right; not in a straight line or lined up right. *The scale must be out of kilter because when I weighed myself on it, it said 300 pounds. The wheels of my bicycle were out of kilter after it hit the tree.* **2.** Needing repair; not working right. *My watch runs too slowly; it must be out of kilter.*

out of line[1] *adv. phr.* Not in a straight line; away from a true line. *The two edges were out of line and there was a space between them. The sergeant ordered the soldier who was out of line to get properly lined up.*

out of line[2] *adj. phr.* Not obeying or agreeing with what is right or usual; doing or being what people do not expect or accept; outside ordinary or proper limits; not usual, right, or proper. *Little Mary got out of line and was rude to Aunt Elizabeth. The teacher asked Charlie not to tell one of the*

226 OUT OF ONE'S ELEMENT

jokes because it was out of line. Mrs. Green thought the repair man's charge was out of line.

out of one's element *adv. phr.* Outside of your natural surroundings; where you do not belong or fit in. *Wild animals are out of their element in cages. Chris is out of his element in singing class.*

out of one's hair *adj. phr., informal* Rid of as a nuisance; relieved of as an annoyance. *Harry got the boys out of his hair so he could study.*

out of one's shell *adv. phr., informal* Out of one's bashfulness or silence; into friendly conversation—Usually used after *come. John wouldn't come out of his shell and talk to the boys and girls at the party. The other girls tried to draw Ella out of her shell, but without success.*

out of order *adv. or adj. phr.* **1.** In the wrong order; not coming after one another in the right way. *Peter wrote the words of the sentence out of order. Don't get out of order, children. Stay in your places in line.* **2.** In poor condition; not working properly. *Our television set is out of order.* **3.** Against the rules; not suitable. *The judge told the people in the courtroom that they were out of order because they were so noisy. The children's whispering was out of order in the church.*

out of place[1] *adv. phr.* Not in the right or usual place or position. *Harry fell and knocked one of his teeth out of place.*

The teacher lined up the class and told them not to get out of place.

out of place[2] *adj. phr.* In the wrong place or at the wrong time; not suitable; improper. *Joan was the only girl who wore a formal at the party, and she felt out of place. It was out of place for Russell to laugh at the old lady.*

out of print *adj. phr.* No longer obtainable from the publisher because the printed copies have been sold out; no longer printed. *The book is out of print. An edition of one thousand copies was sold and no more copies were printed.*

out of sorts *adj. phr.* In an angry or unhappy mood; in a bad temper; grouchy. *Mary was out of sorts and wouldn't say good morning. Bob was out of sorts because he didn't get a bicycle for his birthday.*

out of step *adv. or adj. phr.* **1.** Not in step; not matching strides or keeping pace with another or others. *George always marches out of step with the music.* **2.** Out of harmony; not keeping up—Often followed by *with. Just because you don't smoke, it doesn't mean you are out of step with other boys and girls your age.*

out of stock *adj. phr.* Having none for sale or use; no longer in supply; sold out. *When Father tried to get tires for an old car, the man in the store said that size was out of stock and were not sold anymore. So many children have bought bal-*

loons that the store is now out of stock.

out of the blue *or* **out of a clear sky** *or* **out of a clear blue sky** *adv. phr., informal* Without any warning; by surprise; unexpectedly. *At the last minute Johnny came out of the blue to catch the pass and score a touchdown. The cowboy thought he was alone but suddenly out of a clear sky there were bandits all around him.*

out of the frying pan into the fire Out of one trouble into worse trouble; from something bad to something worse.—A proverb. *The movie cowboy was out of the frying pan into the fire. After he escaped from the robbers, he was captured by Indians.*

out of thin air *adv. phr.* Out of nothing or from nowhere. *The teacher scolded Dick because his story was made out of thin air. On the way home from town, Tom saw a house standing on the lot that had been empty that morning; it seemed to have appeared out of thin air.*

out of this world *adj. phr., slang* Wonderfully good or satisfying; terrific; super. *The dress in the store window was out of this world! Mother was on TV last night. Isn't that out of this world?*

out of touch *adj. phr.* Not writing or talking with each other; not getting news anymore. *Fred had got out of touch with people in his hometown. On his island Robinson Crusoe was out of touch with world news.*

out of tune *adv. or adj. phr.* **1.** Out of proper musical pitch; too low or high in sound. *The band sounded terrible, because the instruments were out of tune.* **2.** Not in agreement; in disagreement; not going well together.—Often used with *with*. *What Jack said was out of tune with how he looked; he said he was happy, but he looked unhappy.*

out of turn *adv. phr.* **1.** Not in regular order; at the wrong time. *John played out of turn. By taking a day off out of turn, Bob got the schedule mixed up.* **2.** Too hastily or wrongly; at the wrong time or place; so as to annoy others. *Dick loses friends by speaking out of turn.*

out to lunch *adj., slang, informal* **1.** Gone for the midday meal. **2.** Inattentive; daydreaming; inefficient; stupid. *Neil Bender is just out to lunch today.*

over one's head *adv. or adj. phr.* **1.** Not understandable; beyond your ability to understand; too hard or strange for you to understand. *Mary laughed just to be polite, but the joke was really over her head. The lesson today was hard; it went over my head.* **2.** To a more important person in charge; to a higher official. *When Mary's supervisor said no, Mary went over her head to the person in charge of the whole department. If Johnny can't get what he wants from his big sister, he goes over her head and asks his mother.*

over the hill *adj., informal* Past one's prime; unable to function as one used to; senile. *Poor Mr. Jones is sure not like he used to be; well, he's over the hill.*

over with *adj., informal* At an end; finished. *John knew his mother would scold him for losing the money, and he wanted to get it over with. After the hard test, Jerry said, "I'm glad that's over with!"*

P

pack rat *n., informal* A person who cannot part with old, useless objects; an avid collector of useless things; a junk hoarder. *"Why are there so many things in this room?" John asked. "It is my brother's room, and he is a pack rat; he is unable to throw stuff away."*

pack of lies *n. phr.* An unbelievable story; unprovable allegations. *What Al told us about his new girlfriend was nothing but a pack of lies.*

paddy wagon *n., informal* A police van used for transporting prisoners to jail or the police station. *The police threw the demonstrators into the paddy wagon.*

pain in the ass *or* **pain in the neck** *n., slang, vulgar with ass* An obnoxious or bothersome person or event. *Phoebe Hochrichter is a regular pain in the neck/ass.*

paint oneself into a corner *v. phr.* To get oneself into a bad situation that is difficult or impossible to get out of. *By promising to both lower taxes and raise the defense budget, the President has painted himself into a corner.*

palm off *v., informal* **1.** To sell or give (something) by pretending it is something more valuable; to sell or give by trickery. *He palmed off his own painting as a Rembrandt. The salesman palmed off pine wood floors as oak.* **2.** To deceive

(someone) by a trick or lie. *He palmed his creditors off with a great show of prosperity.* **3.** To introduce someone as a person he isn't; present in a false pretense. *He palmed the girl off as a real Broadway actress.*

pan out *v., informal* To have a result, especially a good result; result favorably; succeed. *Suppose the class tried to make money by selling candy. How would that pan out? Edison's efforts to invent an electric light bulb did not pan out until he used tungsten wires.*

par for the course *n. phr., informal* Just what was expected; nothing unusual; a typical happening.—Usually refers to things going wrong. *Mary is very clumsy so it was par for the course when she bumped into the table and broke the vase. When John came late again, Mary said, "That's par for the course."*

part and parcel *n. phr.* A necessary or important part; something necessary to a larger thing.—Usually followed by *of*. *Freedom of speech is part and parcel of the liberty of a free man.*

pass away *v.* **1.** To slip by; go by; pass. *We had so much fun that the weekend passed away before we realized it. Forty years had passed away since they had met.* **2.** To cease to exist; end; disappear; vanish *When automobiles became*

229

popular, the use of the horse and buggy passed away. **3.** To have your life stop; die. *He passed away at eighty.*

pass muster *v. phr., informal* To pass a test or check-up; be good enough. *After a practice period, Sam found that he was able to pass muster as a lathe operator. His work was done carefully, so it always passed muster.*

pass off *v.* **1.** To sell or give (something) by false claims; offer (something fake) as genuine. *The dishonest builder passed off a poorly built house by pretending it was well constructed.* **2.** To claim to be someone you are not; pretend to be someone else. *He passed himself off as a doctor until someone checked his record.* **3.** To go away gradually; disappear. *Mrs. White's morning headache had passed off by that night.* **4.** To reach an end; run its course from beginning to end. *The party passed off well.*

pass on *v.* **1.** To give an opinion about; judge; settle. *The college passed on his application and found him acceptable. The committee recommended three people for the job and the president passed on them.* **2.** To give away (something that has been outgrown.) *As he grew up, he passed on his clothes to his younger brother.* **3.** To die. *Mary was very sorry to hear that her first grade teacher had passed on.*

pass out *v., informal* **1.** To lose consciousness; faint. *She went back to work while she was still sick, and finally she just passed out. Compare give*

out **2.** or slang **pass out cold** To drop into a drunken stupor; become unconscious from drink. *After three drinks, the man passed out.* **3.** To die. *Life came and went weakly in him for hours after surgery; then he passed out.*

pass the buck *v. phr., informal* To make another person decide something or accept a responsibility or give orders instead of doing it yourself; shift or escape responsibility or blame; put the duty or blame on someone else. *Mrs. Brown complained to the man who sold her the bad meat, but he only passed the buck and told her to see the manager. If you break a window, do not pass the buck; admit that you did it.*—**buck-passer** *n. phr.* A person who passes the buck. *Mr. Jones was a buck-passer even at home, and tried to make his wife make all the decisions.*—**buck-passing** *n. or adj.* *Buck-passing clerks in stores make customers angry.*

pay dirt *n., slang* **1.** The dirt in which much gold is found. *The man searched for gold many years before he found pay dirt.* **2.** *informal* A valuable discovery.—Often used in the phrase *strike pay dirt. When Bill joined the team, the coach struck pay dirt. Jean looked in many books for facts about her hometown, and finally she struck pay dirt.*

pay off *v. phr.* **1.** To pay the wages of. *The men were paid off just before quitting time, the last day before the holiday.* **2.** To pay and discharge from a job. *When the building was*

completed he paid off the labor-
ers. **3.** To hurt (someone) who
has done wrong to you; get revenge on. *When Bob tripped
Dick, Dick paid Bob off by
punching him in the nose.* **4.** informal To bring a return;
make profit. *At first Mr. Harri-
son lost money on his invest-
ments, but finally one paid off.
. informal* To prove successful, rewarding, or worthwhile.
*Ben's friendship with the old
man who lived beside him paid
off in pleasant hours and
broadened interests. John studied hard before the examination, and it paid off. He made
an A.*

pay through the nose *v. phr.,
informal* To pay at a very
high rate; pay too much. *He
had wanted experience, but this
job seemed like paying through
the nose for it. There was a
shortage of cars; if you found
one for sale, you had to pay
through the nose.*

pecking order *n.* The way
people are ranked in relation
to each other (for honor, privilege, or power); status classifi-
cation; hierarchy. *After the
president was in office several
months, his staff developed a
pecking order.*

peeping Tom *n.* A man or boy
who likes sly peeping. *He was
picked up by the police as a
peeping Tom.*

penny for one's thoughts
Please tell me what you are
thinking about; what's your
daydream. *"A penny for your
thoughts!" he exclaimed.*

penny wise and pound foolish
Wise or careful in small things
but not careful enough in im-

portant things.—A proverb.
*Mr. Smith's fence is rotting and
falling down because he
wouldn't spend money to paint
it. He is penny wise and pound
foolish.*

pen pal *n.* A friend who is
known to someone through an
exchange of letters. *John's pen
pal writes him letters about
school in Alaska.*

**people who live in glass houses
should not throw stones** Do
not complain about other
people if you are as bad as they
are.—A proverb. *Mary says
that Betty is jealous, but Mary
is more jealous herself. People
who live in glass houses should
not throw stones.*

pep talk *n., informal* A speech
that makes people feel good so
they will try harder and not
give up. *The football coach
gave the team a pep talk. Mary
was worried about her exams,
but felt better after the teacher's
pep talk.*

peter out *v., informal* To fail
or die down gradually; grow
less; become exhausted. *After
the factory closed, the town
pretty well petered out. The
mine once had a rich vein of
silver, but it petered out. But
as he thought of her, his anger
slowly petered out.*

pick-me-up *n. phr.* Something
you take when you feel tired or
weak. *John stopped at a drugstore for a pick-me-up after
working three hours overtime.
Mary always carried a bar of
chocolate in her pocketbook for
a pick-me-up.*

pickpocket *n.* A thief; a petty
criminal who steals things and
money out of people's pockets

on a bus, train, etc. *In some big cities many poor children become pickpockets out of poverty.*

pick on v. **1.** *informal* To make a habit of annoying or bothering (someone); do or say bad things to (someone). *Other boys picked on him until he decided to fight them.* **2.** To single out; choose; select. *He visited a lot of colleges, and finally picked on Stanford.*

pick out v. **1.** To choose. *It took Mary a long time to pick out a dress at the store.* **2.** To see among others; recognize; tell from others. *We could pick out different places in the city from the airplane. We could not pick Bob out in the big crowd.* **3.** To find by examining or trying; tell the meaning. *The box was so dirty we couldn't pick out the directions on the label.*

pick the brains of v. phr. To get ideas or information about a particular subject by asking an expert. *If you have time, I'd like to pick your brains about home computers.*

pickup n., (stress on *pick*) **1.** A rugged, small truck. *When he got into the lumber business, Max traded in his comfortable two-door sedan for a pickup.* **2.** Scheduled meeting in order to transfer merchandise or stolen goods. *The pickup goes down at 7 A.M. every day by the loading dock. The dope pushers usually make their pickup on Rush Street.* **3.** A person who is easy to persuade to go home with the suitor. *Sue is said to be an easy pickup.*

pick up v. **1.** To take up; lift. *During the morning Mrs. Car-*

ter picked up sticks in the ya[rd] **2.** *informal* To pay for som[e]one else. *After lunch, in the re[s]taurant, Uncle Bob picked [up]the check.* **3.** To take on[e]away; receive; get. *At the ne[xt]corner the bus stopped a[nd]picked up three people.* **4.** [To]get from different places at d[if]ferent times; a little at a tim[e];collect. *He had picked up r[are]coins in seaports all over [the]world.* **5.** To get without tryin[g];get accidentally. *He picked [up]knowledge of radio just by sta[y]ing around the radio statio[n].Billy picked up a cold [at]school.* **6a.** To gather [to]gether; collect. *When the ca[r]penter finished making [a]cabinet, he began picking up [his]tools.* **6b.** To make neat a[nd]tidy; tidy up; put in order. *P[ick]up your room before Moth[er]sees it.* **6c.** To gather things [to]gether; tidy a place up. *It's [al]most dinner time, childre[n].Time to pick up and get rea[dy].* **7.** To catch the sound of. *[He]picked up Chicago on the [ra]dio.* **8.** To get acquainted wi[th](someone) without an intr[o]duction; make friends with [a]person of the other se[x].Mother told Mary not to wa[lk]home by herself from the pa[rty]because some stranger might [try]to pick her up.* **9.** *informal*take to the police station [or]jail; arrest. *Police picked [the]man up for burglary.* **10.** [To]recognize the trail of a hunt[ed]person or animal; find. *St[ate]police picked up the bandi[t's]trail. The dogs picked up t[he]fox's smell.* **11.** To ma[ke](someone) feel better; refres[h].A little food will pick you u[p].*

12a. To increase (the speed); make (the speed) faster. *The teacher told her singing class to pick up the tempo. The car picked up speed.* **12b.** To become faster; become livelier. *The speed of the train began to pick up. After the band practiced for a while, the music began to pick up.* **13.** To start again after interruption; go on with. *The class picked up the story where they had left it before the holiday. They met after five years, and picked up their friendship as if there had been no interruption.* **14.** *informal* To become better; recover; gain. *She picked up in her schoolwork. He picked up gradually after a long illness. His spirits picked up as he came near home.*

piece of cake *adj., slang* Easy. *The final exam was a piece of cake.*

piggy-back *adj. or adv.* Sitting or being carried on the shoulders. *Little John loved to go for a piggy-back ride on his father's shoulders. When Mary sprained her ankle, John carried her piggy-back to the doctor.*

piggy bank *n.* A small bank, sometimes in the shape of a pig, for saving coins. *John's father gave him a piggy bank.*

pigheaded *adj.* Stubborn; unwilling to compromise. *"Stop being so pigheaded!" she cried. "I, too, can be right sometimes!"*

pig in a poke *n. phr.* An unseen bargain; something accepted or bought without looking at it carefully. *Buying land by mail is buying a pig in a poke: sometimes the land turns out to be under water.*

pin down *v.* **1a.** To keep (someone) from moving; make stay in a place or position; trap. *Mr. Jones' leg was pinned down under the car after the accident. The soldier was pinned down in the hole because rifle bullets were flying over his head.* **1b.** To keep (someone) from changing what (he) says or means; make (someone) admit the truth; make (someone) agree to something. *Mary didn't like the book but I couldn't pin her down to say what she didn't like about it. I tried to pin Bob down to fix my bicycle tomorrow, but he wouldn't say that he could.* **2.** To tell clearly and exactly; explain so that there is no doubt. *The police tried to pin down the blame for the fire in the school.*

pipe dream *n., informal* An unrealizable, financially unsound, wishful way of thinking; an unrealistic plan. *Joe went through the motions of pretending that he wanted to buy that $250,000 house, but his wife candidly told the real estate lady that it was just a pipe dream.*

pipe up *v., informal* To speak up; to be heard. *Mary is so shy, everyone was surprised when she piped up with a complaint at the club meeting. Everyone was afraid to talk to the police, but a small child piped up.*

pip-squeak *n., informal* A small, unimportant person. *If the club is really democratic, then every little pip-squeak has the right to say what he thinks.*

When the smallest boy was chosen to be the monitor, the class bully said he would not obey a little pip-squeak.

piss off v., slang, vulgar, avoidable To bother; annoy; irritate. You really piss me off when you talk like that.—**pissed off** adj. Why act so pissed off just because I made a pass at you?

pitch in v., informal **1.** To begin something with much energy; start work eagerly. Pitch in and we will finish the job as soon as possible. **2.** To give help or money for something; contribute. Everyone must pitch in and work together. We all pitched in a quarter to buy Nancy a present.

play ball v. phr. **1.** To begin play in a ball game. When the umpire calls "Play ball," the game begins. **2.** informal To join in an effort with others; cooperate. To get along during Prohibition, many men felt that they had to play ball with gangsters. It is often good business to play ball with a political machine.

play by ear v. phr. **1.** To play a musical instrument by remembering the tune, not by reading music. Mary does not know how to read music. She plays the piano by ear. Joe doesn't need any music sheets when he plays his guitar; he knows many songs well and can play them by ear. **2.** informal To decide what to do as you go along; to fit the situation.—Used with it. John decided to play it by ear when he went for his interview. It was her first job and she

didn't know what to expect, s she had to play it by ear.

play cat and mouse with v. ph To tease or fool (someone) b pretending to let him go fre and then catching him agai Joe's uncle had fun playing c and mouse with him. The p liceman decided to play cat an mouse when he saw the woma steal the dress in the store.

play down v. To give less em phasis to; make (something seem less important; divert a tention from; draw notice awa from. The newspaper storie played down the actor's una tractive past. A salesman's jo is to emphasize the good poin of his merchandise; he mu: play down any faults it has.

played out adj. phr. Tired ou worn out; finished; exhauste It had been a hard day, and b night he was played out. For while, at least, it seemed the in terest in great speed was playe out.

play footsie v. phr., slang, in formal **1.** Touch the feet of member of the opposite se under the table as an act of fli tation. Have you at least playe footsie with her? **2.** To engag in any sort of flirtation or co laboration, especially in a po litical situation. The mayor wa suspected of playing footsi with the Syndicate.

play hooky v. phr., informe To stay out of school to play Carl is failing in school becaus he has played hooky so mar times during the year.

play into one's hands v. ph To be or do something that an other person can use agains you; help an opponent against yourself. *In the basketball game, Jerry's foul played into the opponents' hands. Mary and Bobby both wanted the last piece of cake, but Bobby played into Mary's hands by trying to grab it.*

play off *v.* **1.** To match opposing persons, forces, or interests so that they balance each other. *The girl played off her admirers against each other. Britain tried to play off European nations against each other so that she would have a balance of power.* **2.** To finish the playing of (an interrupted contest.) *The visitors came back the next Saturday to play off the game stopped by rain.* **3.** To settle (a tie score) between contestants by more play. *When each player had won two matches, the championship was decided by playing off the tie.*

play on *or* **play upon** *v.* **1.** To cause an effect on; influence. *A heavy diet of television drama played on his feelings.* **2.** To work upon for a planned effect; excite to a desired action by cunning plans; manage. *The makeup salesman played on the woman's wish to look beautiful. In some places, leaders play upon people's superstitious fears. He played on the man's ambition and love of honor.*

play one's cards right *or* **play one's cards well** *v. phr., informal* To use abilities and opportunities so as to be successful; act cleverly; make the best use of your place or skills. *That millionaire started with very little but showed a*

skill in playing his cards right. People liked Harold, and he played his cards well—and soon he began to get ahead rapidly.

play the field *v. phr., informal* To date many different people; not always have dates with the same person. *Al had a steady girlfriend, but John was playing the field. Jim was crazy about Mary, but she was still playing the field.*

play up *v.* To call attention to; talk more about; emphasize. *The coach played up the possibilities, and kept our minds off our weaknesses. The director played up the woman's glamor to conceal her lack of acting ability.*

play up to *v. phr., slang* **1.** To try to gain the favor of, especially for selfish reasons; act to win the approval of; try to please. *He played up to the boss.* **2.** To use (something) to gain an end; to attend to (a weakness). *He played up to the old lady's vanity to get her support.*

play with fire *v. phr.* To put oneself in danger; to take risks. *Leaving your door unlocked in New York City is playing with fire. The doctor told Mr. Smith that he must watch his diet if he doesn't want to play with fire.*

plow into *v.* **1.** To attack vigorously. *He plowed into his work and finished it in a few hours.* **2.** To crash into with force. *A truck plowed into my car and smashed the fender.*

pluck up *v.* **1.** To have (courage) by your own effort; make yourself have (courage). *In* *spite of failure, he plucked up heart to continue. He plucked up courage when he saw a glimmer of hope.* **2.** To become happier; feel better; cheer up. *He plucked up when his wife recovered.*

point out *v.* **1.** To show by pointing with the finger; point to; make clear the location of. *The guide pointed out the principal sights of the city.* **2.** To bring to notice; call to attention; explain. *The policeman pointed out that the law forbids public sale of firecrackers. The school secretary pointed out that the closing date for making applications had passed.*

point up *v.* To show clearly; emphasize. *The increase in crime points up the need for greater police protection. Johnny's report card points up his talent for math.*

polish off *v., informal* **1.** To defeat easily. *The Dodgers polished off the Yankees in four straight games in the 1963 World Series.* **2.** To finish completely; finish doing quickly, often in order to do something else. *The boys were hungry and polished off a big steak. Mary polished off her homework early so that she could watch TV.*

polish the apple *v. phr., slang* To try to make someone like you; to try to win favor by flattery.—*Mary polished the apple at work because she wanted a day off. Susan is the teacher's pet because she always polishes the apple.*—**apple polisher** *n., slang* A person who is nice to the one in

charge in order to be liked or treated better; a person who does favors for a superior. *Jane is an apple polisher. She is always helping the teacher and talking to him. Joe is an apple-polisher. He will do anything for the boss.*—**apple polishing** *n., slang* Trying to win someone's good-will by small acts currying favor; the behavior of an apple polisher. *When John brought his teacher flowers, everyone thought he was apple polishing.*

pooped out *adj., slang* Worn out; exhausted. *Everyone was pooped out after the hike. The heat made them feel pooped out.*

pop in *v. phr.* To suddenly appear without announcement. *"Just pop into my office any time you're on campus," Professor Brown said.*

pop up *v.* **1.** *or* **bob up** To appear suddenly or unexpectedly; show up; come out. *Just when the coach thought he had everything under control, a new problem bobbed up. After no one had heard from him for years, John popped up in town again.* **2.** To hit a pop fly in baseball. *Jim popped the pitch up.*

pot call the kettle black *informal* The person who is criticizing someone else is as guilty as the person he accuses; the charge is as true of the person who makes it as of the one he makes it against. *When the commissioner accused the road builder of bribery, the contractor said the pot was calling the kettle black. Bill said John was* cheating at a game but John replied that the pot was calling the kettle black.

pour oil on troubled waters *v. phr.* To quiet a quarrel; say something to lessen anger and bring peace. *The troops were nearing a bitter quarrel until the leader poured oil on the troubled waters.*

pour out *v.* **1.** To tell everything about; talk all about. *Mary poured out her troubles to her pal.* **2.** To come out in great quantity; stream out. *The people poured out of the building when they heard the fire alarm.*

powder room *n.* The ladies' rest room. *When they got to the restaurant, Mary went to the powder room to wash up.*

press one's luck *or* **push one's luck** *v. phr.* To depend too much on luck; expect to continue to be lucky. *When John won his first two bets at the race track, he pressed his luck and increased his bets. If you're lucky at first, don't press your luck.*

prey on *or* **prey upon** *v.* **1.** To habitually kill and eat; catch for food. *Cats prey on mice.* **2.** To capture or take in spoils of war or robbery. *Pirates preyed on American ships in the years just after the Revolutionary War.* **3.** To cheat; rob. *Gangsters preyed on businesses of many kinds while the sale of liquor was prohibited.* **4.** To have a tiring and weakening effect on; weaken. *Ill health had preyed on him for years. Business worries preyed on his mind.*

promise the moon *v. phr.* To promise something impossible. *A politician who promises the moon during a campaign loses the voters' respect. I can't promise you the moon, but I'll do the best job I can.*

psyched up *adj., informal* Mentally alert; ready to do something. *The students were all psyched up for their final exams.*

psych out *v. phr., slang, informal* **1.** To find out the real motives of (someone). *Sue sure has got Joe psyched out.* **2.** To go berserk; to lose one's nerve. *Joe says he doesn't ride his motorcycle on the highway anymore because he's psyched out. Jim psyched out and robbed a liquor store, when he has all he needs and wants!*

pull a fast one *v. phr.* To gain the advantage over one's opponent unfairly; deceive; trick. *When Smith was told by his boss that he might be fired, he called the company president, his father-in-law, and pulled a fast one by having his boss demoted.*

pull off *v., informal* To succeed in (something thought difficult or impossible); do. *Ben Hogan pulled off the impossible by winning three golf tournaments in one year. The bandits pulled off a daring bank robbery.*

pull one's leg *v. phr., informal* To get someone to accept a ridiculous story as true; fool someone with a humorous account of something; trick. *For a moment, I actually believed that his wife had royal blood.*

Then I realized he was pulling my leg. Western cowboys loved to pull a stranger's leg.—**leg-pulling** *n. Strangers were often fooled by the cowboys' leg-pulling.*

pull one's punches *v. phr., informal* **1.** Not to hit as hard as you can. *Jimmy pulled his punches and let Paul win the boxing match.* **2.** To hide unpleasant facts or make them seem good.—*Usually used in the negative. The mayor spoke bluntly; he didn't pull any punches.*

pull one's weight *v. phr.* To do your full share of work; do your part. *In a small shop, it is important that each man pull his weight. When Mother was sick in the hospital, Father said each child must pull his own weight.*

pull out of a hat *v. phr., informal* To get as if by magic; invent; imagine. *When the introduction to a dictionary tells you how many hours went into its making, these figures were not pulled out of a hat. Let's see you pull an excuse out of your hat.*

pull over *v.* To drive to the side of the road and stop. *The policeman told the speeder to pull over. Everyone pulled over to let the ambulance pass.*

pull rank *v. phr., slang, informal* To assert one's superior position or authority on a person of lower rank as in exacting a privilege or a favor. *How come you always get the night duty?—Phineas Leman pulled rank on me.*

pull strings or **pull wires** *v. phr., informal* To secretly use influence and power, especially with people in charge or in important jobs to do or get something; make use of friends to gain your wishes. *If you want to see the governor, Mr. Root can pull strings for you. Jack pulled wires and got us a room at the crowded hotel.*—**wire-puller** *n. Bill got a ticket for speeding, but his father is a wire-puller and got it fixed.*—**wire-pulling** *n. It took some wire-pulling to get the mayor to come to the party.*

pull the plug on *v. phr., slang* To expose (someone's) secret activities. *The citizens' committee pulled the plug on the mayor, and he lost his election.*

pull the rug out from under *v. phr., informal* To withdraw support unexpectedly from; to spoil the plans of. *Bill thought he would be elected, but his friends pulled the rug out from under him and voted for Vin. We were planning a vacation, but the baby's illness pulled the rug out from under us.*

pull the wool over one's eyes *v. phr., informal* To fool someone into thinking well of you; deceive. *The businessman had pulled the wool over his partner's eyes about their financial position. Bob tried to pull the wool over his teacher's eyes, but she was too smart for him.*

pull through *v.* **1.** To help through; bring safely through a difficulty or sudden trouble; save. *A generous loan showed the bank's faith in Father and pulled him through the business trouble.* **2.** To recover from an illness or misfortune; conquer a disaster; escape death or failure. *By a near-miracle, he pulled through after the smashup.*

push around *v., informal* To be bossy with; bully. *Don't try to push me around! Paul is always pushing the smaller children around.*

push off or **shove off** *v.* **1.** To push a boat away from the shore. *Before Tom could reach the boat, Jake had shoved off.* **2.** *slang* To start; leave. *We were ready to push off at ten o'clock, but had to wait for Jill. Jim was planning to stay at the beach all day, but when the crowds arrived he shoved off.*

pushover *n.* **1.** Something easy to accomplish or overcome. *For Howard steering a boat is a pushover as he was raised on a tropical island.* **2.** A person easily seduced. *It is rumored that she is a pushover when she has a bit to drink.*

push over *v. phr.* To upset; overthrow. *She is standing on her feet very solidly; a little criticism from you certainly won't push her over. The wind in Chicago can be so strong that sometimes I'm afraid I'll get pushed over.*

push the panic button *v. phr., slang* To become very much frightened; nervous or excited, especially at a time of danger or worry. *John thought he saw a ghost and pushed the panic button. Keep cool; don't hit the panic button!*

put across *v.* **1.** To explain clearly; make yourself understood; communicate. *He knew how to put his ideas across.* **2.** *informal* To get (something) done successfully; bring to suc-

cess; make real. *He put across a big sales campaign. The new librarian put across a fine new library building.*

put all one's eggs in one basket *v. phr.* To place all your efforts, interests, or hopes in a single person or thing. *Going steady in high school is putting all your eggs in one basket too soon. To buy stock in a single company is to put all your eggs in one basket. He has decided to specialize in lathe work, although he knows it is risky to put all his eggs in one basket.*

put away *v.* **1.** To put in the right place or out of sight. *She put away the towels.* **2.** To lay aside; stop thinking about. *He put his worries away for the weekend.* **3.** *informal* To eat or drink. *He put away a big supper and three cups of coffee.* **4.** *informal* To put in a mental hospital. *He had to put his wife away when she became mentally ill.* **5.** To put to death for a reason; kill. *He had his dog put away when it became too old and unhappy.*

putdown *n.* An insult. *It was a nasty putdown when John called his sister a fat cow.*

put down *v. phr.* **1.** To stop by force; crush. *In 24 hours the general had entirely put down the rebellion.* **2.** To put a stop to; check. *She had patiently put down unkind talk by living a good life.* **3.** To write a record of; write down. *He put down the story while it was fresh in his mind.* **4.** To write a name in a list as agreeing to do something. *The banker put himself down for $1000. Sheila put*

Barbara down for the decorations. **5.** To decide the kind or class of; characterize. *He put the man down as a bum. He put it down as a piece of bad luck.* **6.** To name as a cause; attribute. *He put the odd weather down to nuclear explosions.* **7.** To dig; drill; sink. *He put down a new well.*

put in *v.* **1.** To add to what has been said; say (something) in addition to what others say. *While the boys were discussing the car accident, Ben put in that the road was icy. My father put in a word for me and I got the job.* **2.** To buy and keep in a store to sell. *He put in a full stock of drugs.* **3.** To spend (time). *He put in many years as a printer. He put in an hour a day reading.* **4.** To plant. *He put in a row of radishes.* **5.** To stop at a port on a journey by water. *After the fire, the ship put in for repairs.* **6.** To apply; ask.—Used with *for.* *When a better job was open, he put in for it. The sailor put in for time to visit his family before the ship went to sea.*

put in a word for *v. phr.* To speak in favor of someone; recommend someone. *"Don't worry about your job application,"* Sam said to Tim. *"I'll put in a word for you with the selection committee."*

put off *v.* **1.** *informal* To cause confusion in; embarrass; displease. *I was rather put off by the shamelessness of his proposal. The man's slovenliness put me off.* **2.** To wait and have (something) at a later time; postpone. *They put off the pic-*

nic because of the rain. **3.** To make (someone) wait; turn aside. *When he asked her to name a day for their wedding, she put him off. When the bill collector called, Mrs. Smith managed to put him off.* **4.** To draw away the attention; turn aside; distract. *Little Jeannie began to tell the guests some family secrets, but Father was able to put her off.* **5.** To move out to sea; leave shore. *They put off in small boats to meet the coming ship.*

put on *v. phr.* **1.** To dress in. *The boy took off his clothes and put on his pajamas. Mother put a coat on the baby.* **2a.** To pretend; assume; show. *Mary isn't really sick; she's only putting on. He put on a smile. The child was putting on airs.* **2b.** To exaggerate; make too much of. *That's rather putting it on.* **3.** To begin to have more (body) weight; gain (weight). *Mary was thin from sickness, and the doctor said she must put on ten pounds. Too many sweets and not enough exercise will make you put on weight.* **4a.** To plan and prepare; produce; arrange; give; stage. *The senior class put on a dance. The actor put on a fine performance.* **4b.** To make (an effort). *The runner put on an extra burst of speed and won the race.* **5.** To choose to send; employ on a job. *The school put on extra men to get the new building ready.*

put-on *n.* An act of teasing; the playing of a practical joke on someone. *Eric didn't realize that it was a put-on when his friends phoned him that he won the lottery.*

put one's foot in it *or* **put one's foot in one's mouth** *v. phr.*, *informal* To speak carelessly and rudely; hurt another's feelings without intending to; make a rude mistake. *He put his foot in it with his remark about self-made men because Jones was one of them. She put her foot in her mouth with her joke about that church, not knowing that one of the guests belonged to it.*

put on one's thinking cap *v. phr.* To think hard and long about some problem or question. *Miss Stone told her pupils to put on their thinking caps before answering the question.*

put on the map *v. phr.* To make (a place) well known. *The first successful climb of Mount Matterhorn put Zermatt, Switzerland, on the map. Shakespeare put his hometown of Stratford-on-Avon on the map.*

put out *v.* **1.** To make a flame or light stop burning; extinguish; turn off. *Please put the light out when you leave the room. The firemen put out the blaze.* **2.** To prepare for the public; produce; make. *For years he had put out a weekly newspaper. It is a small restaurant, which puts out an excellent dinner.* **3.** To invest or loan money. *He put out all his spare money at 4 percent or better.* **4.** To make angry; irritate; annoy. *It puts the teacher out to be lied to. Father was put out when Jane spilled grape juice on his new suit.* **5.** *informal* To cause inconvenience to; bother. *He put himself out to make things pleasant for us. Will it put you*

out *if I borrow your pen?* **6.** To retire from play in baseball. *The runner was put out at first base.* **7.** To go from shore; leave. *A Coast Guard boat put out through the waves.* **8.** *vulgar, avoidable* Said of women easy and ready to engage in sexual intercourse. *It is rumored that Hermione gets her promotions as fast as she does because she puts out.*

put over *v.* **1.** To wait to a later time; postpone. *They put over the meeting to the following Tuesday.* **2.** *informal* To make a success of; complete. *He put over a complex and difficult business deal.* **3.** *informal* To practice deception; trick; fool.—Used with *on*. *George thought he was putting something over on the teacher when he said he was absent the day before because his mother was sick and needed him. Tom really slipped one over on us when he came to the Halloween party dressed as a witch.*

put the bite on *v. phr.*, *slang* To ask (for money, favors, etc.) *John put the bite on his friend for several tickets to the dance. Willie Mays put the bite on the Giants for a large raise.*

put two and two together *v. phr.* To make decisions based on available proofs; reason from the known facts; conclude; decide. *He had put two and two together and decided where they had probably gone. It was just a mater of putting two and two together: the facts seemed to permit only one decision.*

put up *v.* **1a.** To make and pack (especially a lunch or medicine); get ready; prepare. *Every morning Mother puts up lunches for the three children. The druggist put up the medicine that the doctor had prescribed.* **1b.** To put food into jars or cans to save; can. *Mother is putting up peaches in jars.* **1c.** To store away for later use. *The farmer put up three tons of hay for the winter.* **2.** To put in place; put (something) where it belongs. *After he unpacked the car, John put it up. After the hard ride, the doctor gave the horse to the stable boy to put up. After the battle, the knight put up his sword.* **3.** To suggest that (someone) be chosen a member, officer, or official. *The club decided to take in another member, and Bill put up Charles.*—Often used with *for. The Republicans put Mr. Williams up for mayor.* **4.** To put (hair) a special way; arrange. *Aunt May puts up her hair in curlers every night.* **5.** To place on sale; offer for sale. *She put the house up for sale.* **6a.** To provide lodging for; furnish a room to. *The visitor was put up in the home of Mr. Wilson. They put Frank up at a good hotel.* **6b.** To rent or get shelter; take lodging; stay in a place to sleep. *The traveler put up at a motel. We put up with friends on our trip to Canada.* **7.** To make; engage in. *He put up a good fight against his sickness.* **8.** To furnish (money) or something needed; pay for. *He put up the money to build a hotel.*

put-up *adj.* Artificially arranged; plotted; phony; illegal *The FBI was sure that the bank robbers worked together with an insider and that the whole affair was a put-up job.*

put up or shut up *v. phr. informal* **1.** To bet your money on what you say or stop saying it.—Often used as a command, often considered rude. *The man from out of town kept saying their team would beat ours and finally John told him "Put up or shut up."* **2.** To prove something or stop saying it.—Often used as a command; often considered rude. *George told Al that he could run faster than the school champion and Al told George to put up or shut up.*

put up to *v. phr., informal* To talk to and make do; persuade to; get to do. *Older boys put us up to painting the statue red.*

put up with *v.* To accept patiently; bear. *We had to put up with Jim's poor table manners because he refused to change. The mother told her children, "I refuse to put up with your tracking in mud!"*

put wise *v., slang* To tell (someone) facts that will give him an advantage over others or make him alert to opportunity or danger. *The new boy did not know that Jim was playing a trick on him, so I put him wise.* Often used with to. *Someone put the police wise to the plan of the bank robbers, and when the robbers went into the bank, the police were waiting to catch them.*

put words into one's mouth *v. phr.* To say without proof that another person has certain feelings or opinions; claim a stand or an idea is another's without asking; speak for another without right. *When he said "John here is in favor of the idea." I told him not to put words in my mouth.*

Q

queer fish *n.* A strange or unusual person who does odd things. *Uncle Algernon dresses in heavy furs in the summer and short-sleeved shirts in the winter. No wonder everyone considers him a queer fish.*

queer oneself *v. phr.* To act in such a manner as to offend others and thus one's own chances or position. *Phil has queered himself with many girls by his erratic behavior.*

quick on the trigger *or* **trigger happy** *adj. phr.* **1.** Ready to shoot without warning; fast with a gun. *He's a dangerous criminal quick on the trigger.* **2.** *informal* Fast at answering questions or solving problems. *In class discussions John is always quick on the trigger.*

quick on the uptake *adj. phr.* Smart; intelligent. *Eleanor is very witty and quick on the uptake.*

quick study *n. phr.* One who acquires new skills and habits in record time. *Sue is new a her job but people have confi dence in her because she is a quick study.*

quite a few *or* **quite a number** *also formal* **not a few** *n. o adj. phr.* Rather a large number; more than a few. *Quite a few went to the game. The bas ket had quite a few rotten ap ples in it.*—The phrase *quite a number* is used like an adjec tive only before *less, more. Few people saw the play on the firs night but quite a number more came on the second night.*— Sometimes used like an ad verb. *We still have quite a few more miles to go before we reach New York.*

quite the thing *n. phr.* The so cially proper thing to do. *In po lite society it is quite the thing to send a written thank you note to one's host or hostess after a din ner party.*

R

rack one's brain *v. phr.* To try your best to think; make a great mental effort; especially: to try to remember something you have known. *Bob racked his brain trying to remember where he left the book. Susan racked her brain trying to guess whom the valentine came from. John racked his brain during the test trying to solve the problem.*

rain cats and dogs *or* **rain buckets** *or* **rain pitchforks** *v. phr.*, *informal* To rain very hard; come down in torrents. *In the middle of the picnic it started to rain cats and dogs, and everybody got soaked. Terry looked out of the window and said, "It's raining pitchforks, so we can't go out to play right now."*

rain check *n.* **1.** A special free ticket to another game or show which will be given in place of one canceled because of rain. *When the drizzle turned into a heavy rain the manager announced that the baseball game would be replayed the next day. He told the crowd that they would be given rain checks for tomorrow's game as they went out through the gates.* **2.** *informal* A promise to repeat an invitation at a later time. *Bob said, "I'm sorry you can't come to dinner this evening, Dave. I'll give you a rain check."*

rained out *adj.* Stopped by rain. *The ball game was rained out in the seventh inning. The*

Friday night rally in the stadium was rained out.

rain or shine *adv. phr.* **1.** If the weather is stormy or if it is fair. *The parade will start promptly, rain or shine.* **2.** No matter; if your luck is good or bad. *Sam knows he can depend on his family, rain or shine.*

raise Cain *v. phr.*, *slang* To be noisy; cause trouble. *When John couldn't go on the basketball trip with the team he raised Cain. The children raised Cain in the living room.*

raise eyebrows *v. phr.* To shock people; cause surprise or disapproval. *The news that the princess was engaged to a commoner raised eyebrows all over the kingdom.*

rat out *or* **rat out on** *v. phr.*, *slang* To desert; to leave at a critical time. *Joe ratted out on Sue when she was seven months pregnant.*

rat race *n.*, *slang* A very confusing, crowded, or disorderly rush; a confusing scramble, struggle, or way of living that does not seem to have a purpose. *The dance last night was a rat race. It was too noisy and crowded. School can be a rat race if you don't keep up with your studies. This job is a rat race. The faster you work, the faster the boss wants you to work.*

reach for the sky *v. phr.*, *slang* **1.** To put your hands high above your head or be shot.—

Usually used as a command. *A holdup man walked into a gas station last night and told the attendant "Reach for the sky!"* **2.** To set one's aims high. *"Why medical technician?" asked her father. "Reach for the sky! Become a physician!"*

read between the lines *v. phr.* To understand all of a writer's meaning by guessing at what he has left unsaid. *Some kinds of poetry make you read between the lines. A clever foreign correspondent can often avoid censorship by careful wording, leaving his audience to read between the lines.*

read one one's rights *v. phr.* To give to an arrested person the legally required statement regarding the rights of such a person. *"Read him his rights," Sergeant," the captain said, "and book him for breaking and entering."*

read one's mind *v. phr.* To know what someone else is thinking. *I have known John so long that I can read his mind.—* **mind reader** *n.* *That's exactly what I was going to say. You must be a mind reader!*

read the riot act *v. phr.* To give someone a strong warning or scolding. *Three boys were late to class and the teacher read the riot act to them.*

ready money *n. phr.* Cash on hand. *Frank refuses to buy things on credit, but, if he had the ready money, he would buy that lovely old house.*

redcap *n.* A porter at an airport or at a railroad station.

Mr. Smith works as a redcap (Chicago's O'Hare Airport.

red eye *adj. phr.* Bloodsho eyes that are strained from to much reading. *Poor Tim has red eye; he must have bee studying too late again.*

red eye *n. phr., informal A night flight. The company re fused to pay for him to take more expensive daytime fligh so he had to come in on the re eye.*

red-handed *adj.* In the ver act; while committing a crim or evil action. *The criminal wa caught red-handed while hold ing up the neighborhood ban at gunpoint.*

red herring *n. phr.* A fals scent laid down in order to de ceive; a phony or misleadin story designed to cause confu sion. *That story about the presi dent having an affair was a re herring created by the oppos tion in order to discredit him.*

red tape *n. phr.* Unnecessar bureaucratic routine; needles but official delays. *If you wan to get anything accomplished i a hurry, you have to find some one in power who can cu through all that red tape.*

regular guy or **regular fellow** *n., informal* A friendly perso who is easy to get along with; good sport. *You'll like Tom He's a regular guy.*

rest on one's laurels *v. phr.* T be satisfied with the succes you have already won; sto trying to win new honors. Ge ting an A in chemistry almos caused Mike to rest on hi laurels.*

t room n. A room or series f rooms in a public building hich has things for personal >mfort and grooming, such as ilets, washbowls, mirrors, id often chairs or couches. *lly went to the rest room to >wder her nose.*

me or reason n. phr. A >od plan or reason; a reason->le purpose or explanation. sed in negative, interroga-ve, or conditional sentences. *on could see no rhyme or rea->n to the plot of the play. It emed to Ruth that her little rother had temper tantrums ithout rhyme or reason.*

e herd on v. phr. **1.** To atrol on horseback around a :rd of animals to see that >ne of them wanders away. *wo cowboys rode herd on the ttle being driven to market.* **2.** formal To watch closely and >ntrol; take care of. *A special gislative assistant rides herd 1 the bills the President is ixious to have congress pass. 'ary rode herd on the small iildren walking home from :hool to keep them from run-ng into the street.*

e out v. To survive safely; idure. *The captain ordered all ils lowered so the ship could ide out the storm. Jack decided ride out his troubles by say-g that he had made a mistake ut that he had learned his sson.*

ing high adj. Attracting at-ntion; enjoying great popu-rity. *After scoring the winning uchdown, John is riding high ith his classmates.*

rid of Free of; away from; with-out the care or trouble. *The puppy is finally rid of worms. If I could be rid of the children for the day, I would go. I wish you'd get rid of that cat!*

right on adj., interj., slang, in-formal **1.** Exclamation of ani-mated approval "Yes," "That's correct," "You're telling the truth," "we believe you," etc. *Orator: And we shall see the promised land! Crowd: Right on!* **2.** Correct; to the point; ac-curate. *The reverend's remark was right on!*

right out or **straight out** adv. Plainly; in a way that hides nothing; without waiting or keeping back anything. *When Mother asked who broke the window, Jimmie told her right out that he did it. When Ann entered the beauty contest her little brother told her straight out that she was crazy.*

ring a bell v. phr. To make you remember something; sound familiar. *Not even the cat's meowing seemed to ring a bell with Judy. She still forgot to feed him. When Ann told Jim the name of the new teacher it rang a bell, and Jim said, "I went to school with a James Carson."*

ring up v. **1.** To add and re-cord on a cash register. *The supermarket clerk rang up Mrs. Smith's purchases and told her she owed $33. Busi-ness was bad Tuesday; we didn't ring up a sale all morn-ing.* **2.** informal To telephone. *Sally rang up Sue and told her the news.*

rip off v., slang (Stress on off) Steal. *The hippies ripped off the grocery store.*

rip-off n., slang (Stress on rip) An act of stealing or burglary. *Those food prices are so high, it's almost a rip-off.*

road hog n., informal A car driver who takes more than his share of the road. *A road hog forced John's car into the ditch.*

rob Peter to pay Paul v. phr. To change one duty or need for another; take from one person or thing to pay another. *Bill owed Sam a dollar, so he borrowed another from Joe to pay Sam back. He robbed Peter to pay Paul. Trying to study a lesson for one class during another class is like robbing Peter to pay Paul.*

rob the cradle v. phr., informal To have dates with or marry a person much younger than yourself. *When the old woman married a young man, everyone said she was robbing the cradle.*—**cradle-robber** n. *The judge died when he was seventy. He was a real cradle-robber because he left a thirty-year-old widow.*—**cradle-robbing** adj. or n. *Bob is seventeen and I just saw him with a girl about twelve years old. Has he started cradle-robbing? No, that girl was his sister, not his date!*

rock the boat v. phr., informal To make trouble and risk losing or upsetting something; cause a disturbance that may spoil a plan. *The other boys said that Henry was rocking the boat by wanting to let girls in their club. Politicians don't li to rock the boat around electi time.*

roll around v., informal To r turn at a regular or usual tim come back. *When winter ro around, out come the skis a skates.*

rolling stone gathers no mo A person who changes jobs where he lives often will not able to save money or things his own.—A proverb. *Unc Willie was a rolling stone th gathered no moss. He work in different jobs all over t country.*

roll out the red carpet v. ph 1. To welcome an importa guest by putting a red carp down for him to walk on. *Th rolled out the red carpet for t Queen when she arrived Australia.* 2. To greet a pers with great respect and hon give a hearty welcom *Margaret's family rolled out t red carpet for her teacher wh she came to dinner.*—**re carpet** adj. *When the pre dent visited the foreign cou try, he was given the re carpet treatment and w comed by a great crowd. V gave Uncle Willie the re carpet treatment when he r turned from Hong Kong.*

roll up one's sleeves To g ready for a hard job; prepa to work hard or serious *When Paul took his science e amination, he saw how little knew about science. He roll up his sleeves and went work.*

rope into v., *informal* **1.** To trick into; persuade dishonestly. *Jerry let the big boys rope him into stealing some apples.* **2.** To get (someone) to join in; persuade to work at. *It was Sue's job to bathe the dog but she roped Sam into helping her. Mother did not go to the first meeting of the club because she was afraid she would be roped into something.*

rough-and-ready *adj.* **1.** Not finished in detail; not perfected; rough but ready for use now. *We asked Mr. Brown how long it would take to drive to Chicago and his rough-and-ready answer was two days.* **2.** Not having nice manners but full of energy and ability. *Jim is a rough-and-ready character; he'd rather fight than talk things over.*

rough-and-tumble **1.** *n.* Very rough, hard fighting or arguing that does not follow any rules. *There was a rough-and-tumble on the street last night between some soldiers and sailors. Many people don't like the rough-and-tumble of politics.* **2.** *adj.* Fighting or arguing in a very rough and reckless way; struggling hard; not following rules or laws. *It took strong men to stay alive in the rough-and-tumble life of the western frontier.*

rough up v. To attack or hurt physically; treat roughly; beat. *Three boys were sent home for a week because they roughed up a player on the visiting team. While Pete was walking in a strange part of town some boys*

roughed him up and told him to stay out of their territory.

round off v. **1.** To make round or curved. *John decided to round off the corners of the table he was making so that no one would be hurt by bumping them.* **2.** To change to the nearest whole number. *The teacher said to round off the averages.* **3.** To end in a satisfactory way; put a finishing touch on; finish nicely. *We rounded off the dinner with mixed nuts. A boat ride in the moonlight rounded off the day at the lake.*

round robin *n. phr.* **1.** Something written, especially a request or protest that is signed by a group of people.—Often used like an adjective. *The people in our neighborhood are sending a round robin to the Air Force to protest the noise the jet planes make flying over our houses.* **2.** A letter written by a group of people each writing one or two paragraphs and then sending the letter to another person, who adds a paragraph, and so on. *The class sent a round-robin letter to Bill in the hospital.* **3.** A meeting in which each one in a group of people takes part; a talk between various members of a group.—Often used like an adjective. *There is a round-robin meeting of expert fishermen on the radio, giving advice on how to catch fish.* **4.** A contest or games in which each player or team plays every other player or team in turn.—Often used like an adjective. *The tournament will be a round robin for*

all the high school teams in the
city.

round up v. **1.** To bring together (cattle or horses). *Cowboys round up their cattle in the springtime to brand the new calves.* **2.** *informal* To collect; gather. *Dave rounded up many names for his petition.*

rub elbows also **rub shoulders** v. phr. To be in the same place (with others); meet and mix. *City people and country people, old and young, rub elbows at the horse show. On a visit to the United Nations Building in New York, you may rub elbows with people from faraway lands.*

rub it in v. phr., slang To remind a person again and again of an error or short-coming; tease; nag. *Jerry was already unhappy because he fumbled the ball, but his teammates kept rubbing it in. I know my black eye looks funny. You don't need to rub it in.*

rub off v. **1.** To remove or be removed by rubbing; erase. *The teacher rubs the problem off the chalkboard. After Ann shook hands with the President, she would not shake hands with anyone else because she thought that the good luck would rub off.* **2.** To stick to something touched; come off. *Don't touch that charcoal, it will rub off. Mary's dress touched the door that Father was painting, and some paint rubbed off on her dress.* **3.** To pass to someone near as if by touching. *Jimmy is very lucky; I wish some of his luck would rub off on me.*

rub out v. slang To destroy completely; kill; eliminate. *The gangsters rubbed out four po- licemen before they were caught. The gangsters told th storekeeper that if he did no pay them to protect him, some one would rub him out.*

rub the wrong way v. phr., in formal To make (someone) little angry; do something no liked by (someone); anno bother. *John's braggin rubbed the other boys th wrong way. Mother's frien called Harold a little boy, an that rubbed Harold the wron way.*

rule out v. **1.** To say tha (something) must not be don not allow; also: decide agains *The principal ruled out danc on school nights. The play w ruled out by the referee. Jea probably will not go to colleg but she has not ruled that out. .* To show that (someone o something) is not a possibilit make it unnecessary to thin about; remove (a chance). W have to find a baby-sitter for t night; Betsy has a date, so th rules her out. The doctor too X rays to rule out the chance broken bones.* **3.** To make im possible; prevent. *Father death seems to rule out colleg for Jean. Betsy's date for th dance ruled out any baby-si ting that evening.*

run a risk or **take a risk** v. ph To be open to danger or los put yourself in danger; be u protected. *A baseball umpi wears a mask and chest prote tor so he won't run the risk being hit by the ball. Billy tak* *a risk of being hit by a car when he runs into the street without looking. I was afraid to run the risk of betting on the game.*

run around in circles *v. phr.* To waste time in repetitious movements; be confused. *There was such a crowd in the lobby that I ran around in circles trying to find my group.*

run around *or* **chase around** *v., informal* To go to different places for company and pleasure; be friends. *Tim hasn't been to a dance all year; with school work and his job, he hasn't time to run around. Chuck and Jim chase around a lot together.*— Often used with *with. Ruth runs around with girls who like to go dancing.*

run away with *v.* **1a.** To take quickly and secretly, especially without permission; steal. *A thief ran away with Grandma's silver teapot.* **1b.** To go away with; elope. *Mary said that if her parents wouldn't let her marry Phil, she would run away with him.* **1c.** To take hold of; seize. *The boys thought they saw a ghost in the old house last night; they let their imagination run away with them.* **2.** To be much better or more noticeable than others in; win easily. *Our team ran away with the game in the last half. The fat comedian ran away with the TV show.*

run down *v.* (stress on *down*) **1.** To crash against and knock down or sink. *Jack rode his bicycle too fast and almost ran down his little brother. It was so foggy that the steamship*

almost ran down a small boat leaving port. **2a.** To chase until exhausted or caught. *The dogs ran down the wounded deer.* **2b.** To find by hard and thorough search; *also:* trace to its cause or beginning. *The policeman ran down proof that the burglar had robbed the store.* **2c.** To catch (a base runner) between bases and tag out in baseball. *The pitcher saw that the base runner was not on base, so he surprised him by throwing the ball to the first baseman, who ran him down before he reached second base.* **3.** *informal* To say bad things about; criticize. *Suzy ran down the club because the girls wouldn't let her join.* **4.** To stop working; not run or go. *The battery in Father's car ran down this morning. The kitchen clock ran down because we forgot to wind it.* **5.** To get into poor condition; look bad. *A neighborhood runs down when the people don't take care of their houses.*

run-down *adj.* (stress on *run*) In poor health or condition; weak or needing much work. *Grandma caught a cold because she was very run-down from loss of sleep. The houses near the center of the city get more run-down every year.*

run for it *or* **make a run for it** *v. phr.* To dash for safety; make a speedy escape. *The bridge the soldiers were on started to fall down and they had to run for it. The policeman shouted for the robber to stop, but the robber made a run for it.*

run in *v. phr.* **1.** *informal* To take to jail; arrest. *The policeman ran the man in for peddling without a license.* **2.** To make a brief visit. *The neighbor boy ran in for a minute to see Bob's newest model rocket.*

run-in *n.* **1.** A traffic accident. *My car was wrecked when I had a run-in with a small truck.* **2.** A violent quarrel. *John had a nasty run-in with his boss and was fired.*

run in the blood *or* **run in the family** *v. phr.* To be a common family characteristic; be learned or inherited from your family. *A great interest in gardening runs in his family. Red hair runs in the family.*

run into *v.* **1.** To mix with; join with. *If the paint brush is too wet, the red paint will run into the white on the house. This small brook runs into a big river in the valley below.* **2.** To add up to; reach; total. *Car repairs can run into a lot of money. The number of people killed on the highways during holidays runs into hundreds. A good dictionary may run into several editions.* **3a.** Bump; crash into; hit. *Joe lost control of his bike and ran into a tree.* **3b.** To meet by chance. *I ran into Joe yesterday on Main Street.* **3c.** Be affected by; get into. *I ran into trouble on the last problem on the test. When I ran into a problem while making my model airplane, I asked Uncle Mark for help.*

run into the ground *v. phr., informal* **1.** To do or use (something) more than is wanted or needed. *It's all right to borrow my hammer once in a while, but don't run it into the ground.* **2.** To win over or defeat (someone) completely. *We lost the game today, but tomorrow we'll run them into the ground.*

run its course *v. phr.* To fulfill a normal development; terminate a normal period. *Your flu will run its course; in a few days you'll be back on your feet.*

run off *v., phr.* **1.** To produce with a printing press or duplicating machine. *The print shop ran off a thousand copies of the newspaper.* **2.** To drive away. *The boys saw a dog digging in Mother's flower bed, and they ran him off. When the salesman tried to cheat the farmer, the farmer ran him off the farm with a shotgun.*

run-off *n.* A second election held to determine the winner when the results of the first one were inconclusive. *The senatorial race was so close that the candidates will have to hold a run-off.*

run-of-the-mill *or* **run-of-the-mine** *adj.* Of a common kind; ordinary; usual. *Frank is a very good bowler, but Joe is just run-of-the-mill. It was just a run-of-the-mine movie.*

runner-up *n.* The person who finishes second in a race or contest; the one next after the winner. *Tom won the race and Jack was runner-up. Joan was runner-up in the contest for class secretary.*

run out *v.* **1a.** To come to an end; be used up. *Jerry almost* got across the brook on the slippery stones but his luck ran out and he slipped and fell. *We'd better do our Christmas shopping; time is running out.* **1b.** To use all of the supply; be troubled by not having enough. *The car ran out of gas three miles from town. Millie never runs out of ideas for clever party decorations.* **2.** *informal* To force to leave; expel. *Federal agents ran the spies out of the country.*

run over *v.* **1.** To be too full and flow over the edge; spill over. *Billy forgot he had left the water on, and the tub ran over.* **2.** To try or go over (something) quickly; practice briefly. *During the lunch hour, Mary ran over her history facts so she would remember them for the test. The coach ran over the signals for the trick play with the team just before game time.* **3.** To drive on top of; ride over. *At night cars often run over small animals that are blinded by the headlights.*

run scared *v. phr.* To expect defeat, as in a political campaign. *The one-vote defeat caused him to run scared in every race thereafter.*

run short *v. phr.* **1.** To not have enough. *Bob asked Jack to lend him five dollars because he was running short. We are running short of sugar.* **2.** To be not enough in quantity. *We are out of potatoes and the flour is running short.*

run that by me again! *v. phr., informal command* Repeat what you just said, as I couldn't

understand you. *"Run that by me again,"* he cried. *"This telephone connection is very bad."*

run the gauntlet *also* **gantlet** *v. phr.* **1.** To be made to run between two lines of people facing each other and be hit by them with clubs or other weapons. *Joe had to run the gauntlet as part of his initiation into the club.* **2.** To face a hard test; bear a painful experience. *Ginny had to run the gauntlet of her mother's questions about how the ink spot got on the dining room rug.*

run through *v.* **1.** To make a hole through, especially with a sword; pierce. *The pirate was a good swordsman, but the hero finally ran him through.* **2.** To spend recklessly; use up wastefully. *The rich man's son quickly ran through his money.* **3.** To read or practice from beginning to end without stopping. *The visiting singer ran through his numbers with the orchestra just before the program.*

run up *v. phr.* **1.** To add to the amount of; increase. *Karl ran up a big bill at the bookstore.* **2.** To put together or make hastily; sew quickly together. *Jill ran up a costume for the party on her sewing machine.* **3.** To pull (something) upward on a rope; put (something) up quickly. *The pirates ran up the black flag.*

run wild *v. phr.* To be or go out of control. *The students ran wild during spring vacation. The new supervisor lets the chil-*

dren run wild. *The violets are running wild in the flower bed.*

Russian roulette *n.* A game of chance in which one bullet is placed in a revolver, the cartridge cylinder is spun, and the player aims the gun at his own head and pulls the trigger. *Only a fool would risk playing Russian roulette.*

S

sack in/out v., slang To go to sleep for a prolonged period (as in from night to morning). *Where are you guys going to sack in/sack out?*

sacred cow n. A person or thing that is never criticized, laughed at, or insulted even if it deserves such treatment. *Motherhood is a sacred cow to most politicians. The bold young governor had no respect for the state's sacred cows. Television respects too many sacred cows.*

sail into v., informal **1.** To attack with great strength; begin hitting hard. *George grabbed a stick and sailed into the dog.* **2.** To scold or criticize very hard. *The coach really sailed into Bob for dropping the pass.*

save face v. phr. To save your good reputation, popularity, or dignity when something has happened or may happen to hurt you; hide something that may cause you shame. *The policeman was caught accepting a bribe; he tried to save face by claiming it was money owed to him. Bill would not play in the game because he knew he could not do well and he wanted to save face. The colonel who lost the battle saved face by showing his orders from the general.*—**face-saver** n. *The shop teacher's note was a face-saver when another teacher thought John and Bill were playing hookey in town.*

—**face-saving** adj. *The note was a face-saving idea.*—**face-saving** n. *Face-saving is not helped by too many invented excuses.*

save one's breath v. phr., informal To keep silent because talking will not help; not talk because it will do no good. *Save your breath; the boss will never give you the day off.*

save one's neck or **save one's skin** v. phr., slang To save from danger or trouble. *The fighter planes saved our skins while the army was landing from the ships. Betty saved Tim's neck by typing his report for him; without her help he could not have finished on time.*

save the day v. phr. To bring about victory or success, especially when defeat is likely. *The forest fire was nearly out of control when suddenly it rained heavily and saved the day. The team was behind, but at the last minute Sam saved the day with a touchdown.*

say a mouthful 1. v. phr., slang To say something of great importance or meaning; say more by a sentence than the words usually mean.—Usually in past tense. *Tom said a mouthful when he guessed that company was coming to visit. A dozen people came.* **2.** v. phr., informal To vent one's honest opinion, even in anger. *He sure said a mouthful when he told*

255

his boss what was wrong with our business.

say one's piece or **speak one's piece** *v. phr.* To say openly what you think; say, especially in public, what you usually say or are expected to say. *John told the boss that he thought he was wrong and the boss got angry. He said, "You've said your little piece, so go on home." Every politician got up and said his piece about how good the mayor was and then sat down.*

say the word *v. phr., informal* To say or show that you want something; agree to something; show a wish, willingness, or readiness; give a sign; say yes; say so. *Just say the word and I will lend you the money. I will do anything you want; just say the word. If you get tired of those pictures, say the word.*

say uncle also **cry uncle** *v. phr., informal* To say that you surrender; admit that you have lost; admit a defeat; give up. *Bob fought for five minutes, but he had to say uncle. The bully twisted Jerry's arm and said, "Cry uncle." The other team was beating us, but we wouldn't say uncle.*

scare out of one's wits or **scare stiff** or **scare the daylights out of** *v. phr., informal* To frighten very much. *The owl's hooting scared him out of his wits. The child was scared stiff in the dentist's chair. Pete's ghost story scared the daylights out of the smaller boys.*

scare up or **scrape up** *v., informal* To find, collect, or get together with some effort when needed. *The boy scared up enough money to go to college.*

"Will you stay for supper?" she asked. "I can scare up enough for us all." He managed to scrape up the money for his speeding fine.

school of hard knocks *n. phr.* Life outside of school or college; life out in the world; the ordinary experience of learning from work and troubles. *He never went to high school; he was educated in the school of hard knocks.*

scot-free *adj. phr.* Without punishment; completely free. *In spite of his obvious guilt, the jury acquitted him and he got off scot-free.*

scrape the bottom of the barrel *v. phr., informal* To use or take whatever is left after the most or the best has been taken; accept the leftovers. *At first they took out quarters, but they had so little money that they had to scrape the bottom of the barrel and paid with nickels and pennies for their lunch. The garage owner had to scrape the bottom of the barrel to find a qualified mechanic to work for him.*

scratch one's back *v. phr., informal* To do something kind and helpful for someone or to flatter him in the hope that he will do something for you. Usually used in the expression "You scratch my back and I'll scratch yours." *Mary asked Jean to introduce her to her brother. Jean said, "You scratch my back and I'll scratch yours."*

scratch the surface *v. phr.* To learn or understand very little about something.—Usually used with a limiting adverb (as *only, hardly).* We thought we understood Africa but when we made a trip there we found we had only scratched the surface. High school students have only scratched the surface of their subjects, and even after college graduation, they still find there is much more to learn.

scream bloody murder *v. phr.,* *informal* To yell or protest as strongly as one can. *When the thief grabbed her purse, the woman screamed bloody murder. When the city doubled property taxes, home owners screamed bloody murder.*

screw around *v. phr., vulgar, avoidable* To hang around idly without accomplishing anything, to loaf about, to beat or hack around. *You guys are no longer welcome here; all you do is screw around all day.*

screw up *v. phr., slang, semi-vulgar, best avoided* **1.** To make a mess of, to make an error which causes confusion. *The treasurer screwed up the accounts of the Society so badly that he had to be fired.* **2.** To cause someone to be neurotic or maladjusted. *Her divorce screwed her up so badly that she had to go to a shrink.*

screw-up *n.* A mistake; an error; a confusing mess. *"What a screw-up!" the manager cried, when he realized that the bills were sent to the wrong customers.*

search me *informal* I don't know; how should I know?— May be considered rude. *When I asked her what time it was, she said, "Search me, I have no watch."*

search one's heart *or* **search one's soul** *v. phr.,* formal To study your reasons and acts; try to discover if you have been fair and honest. *The teacher searched his heart trying to decide if he had been unfair in failing Tom.*—**heart-searching** *or* **soul-searching** *n. or adj. After much heart-searching, Jean told Beth she was sorry for the unkind things she had said. The minister preached a soul-searching sermon about the thoughtless ways people hurt each other.*

second-guess *v. phr.* **1.** To criticize another's decision with advantage of hindsight. *The losing team's coach is always second-guessed.* **2.** To guess what someone else intends or would think or do. *Television planners try to second-guess the public.*

second thought *n.* A change of ideas or opinions resulting from more thought or study. *Your second thoughts are very often wiser than your first ideas. We decided to climb the mountain, but on second thought realized that it was too dangerous.*

second wind *also* **second breath** *n.* **1.** The easier breathing that follows difficult breathing when one makes a severe physical effort, as in running or swimming. *After the first quarter mile, a mile runner usually gets his second wind and can breathe better. We climbed with labored breathing for half an hour, but then got our second wind and went up more easily.* **2.** *informal* The refreshed feeling you get after first becoming tired while doing something and then becoming used to it. *Tom became very tired of working at his algebra, but after a while he got his second wind and began to enjoy it.*

security blanket *n.*, slang, colloquial An idea, person, or object that one holds on to for psychological reassurance or comfort as infants usually hang on to the edge of a pillow, a towel, or a blanket. *Sue has gone to Aunt Mathilda for a chat; she is her security blanket.*

see about *v.* **1.** To find out about; attend to. *If you are too busy, I'll see about the train tickets.* **2.** *informal* To consider; study. *I cannot take time now but I'll see about your plan when I have time.*

see eye to eye *v. phr.* To agree fully; hold exactly the same opinion. *Though we did not usually agree, we saw eye to eye in the matter of reducing taxes. Jim did not see eye to eye with Sally on where they would go for their vacation.*

see fit or **think fit** *v. phr.* To decide that an action is necessary, wise, or advisable; choose. *Jim asked "Dad, what time should I come home after the dance?" His father answered, "You may do as you see fit."*—Often used with an infinitive. *After much thought, we did not see fit to join the Smiths on their Caribbean cruise. The boys were angry because Ed thought fit to report the fight to the principal.*

see off *v.* To go to say or wave goodbye to. *His brother went to the train with him to see him off. When Marsha flew to Paris, Flo saw her off at the airport.*

see out *v.* **1.** To go with to an outer door. *A polite man sees his company out after a party.* **2.** To stay with and finish; not quit. *Pete's assignment was hard but he saw it out to the end.*

see red *v. phr.*, *informal* To become very angry. *Whenever anyone teased John about his weight, he saw red.*

see stars *v. phr.*, *informal* To imagine you are seeing stars as a result of being hit on the head. *When Ted was hit on the head by the ball, he saw stars. The boxer's head hit the floor, making him see stars.*

see the light *v. phr.*, *informal* To understand or agree, often suddenly; accept another's explanation or decision. *I did not approve of his action, but he explained his reason and then I saw the light. Bill wanted Harry to help him, but Harry wasn't in the mood until Bill offered to pay him. Then Harry saw the light. Mary thought it was fun to date older boys but when they started drinking, she saw the light.*

see the light at the end of the tunnel *v. phr.*, *informal* To anticipate the happy resolution of a prolonged period of problems. *We've been paying on our house mortgage for many years, but at long last we can see the light at the end of the tunnel.*

see the light of day *v. phr.* To be born or begun. *The children visited the old house where their great-grandfather first saw the light of day. The party was a failure, and Mathilda wished* *her plan had never seen the light of day.*

see things *v. phr., informal* To imagine sights which are not real; think you see what is not there. *I had not seen him for twenty years and when we met on the street I thought I was seeing things. She woke her husband to tell him she had seen a face at the window, but he told her she was seeing things.*

see to *also* **look to** *v.* To attend to; take care of; do whatever needs to be done about. *While Donna bought the theatre tickets, I saw to the parking of the car.*

see to it *v. phr.* To take care; take the responsibility; make sure.—Usually used with a noun clause. *We saw to it that the child was fed and bathed.*

sellout *n.* A betrayal or act of treason. *The spy's behavior during the Cold War was a classical sellout.*

sell out *v.* **1a.** To sell all of a certain thing which a store has in stock. *In the store's January white sale the sheets and pillowcases were sold out in two days.* **1b.** To sell all the stock and close the store; go out of business. *The local hardware store sold out last month and was replaced by a cafe.* **2.** *informal* To be unfaithful to your country for money or other reward; be disloyal; sell a secret; accept a bribe. *In the Revolutionary War, Benedict Arnold sold out to the British. The dishonest wrestler sold out to his opponent for a hundred dollars.*

sell short *v.* To think (a person or thing) less good or valu-

able than is true; underestimate. *Don't sell the team short; the players are better than you think. Some teachers sold John short.*

send up *v. phr., colloquial* To sentence (someone) to prison. *Did you know that Milton Shaeffer was sent up for fifteen years?*

senior citizen *n.* An older person, often one who has retired from active work or employment. *Mrs. North, the history teacher, is a senior citizen.*

serve one right *v. phr.* To be what (someone) really deserves as a punishment; be a fair exchange for what (someone) has done or said or failed to do or say. *He failed his exam; it served him right because he had not studied. Bob said it served Sally right when she cut her finger; she had taken his knife without asking him.*

set about *v.* To begin; start. *Benjamin Franklin set about learning the printer's trade at an early age. After breakfast, Mother set about her household duties.*

setback *n.* A disadvantage; a delay. *We suffered a major setback when my wife lost her job.*

set back *v.* **1.** To cause to put off or get behind schedule; slow up; check. *The cold weather set back the planting by two weeks.* **2.** *informal* To cause to pay out or to lose (a sum of money); cost. *His new car set him back over $3000.*

set foot *v. phr.* To step; walk; go.—Used with a negative. *She would not let him set foot* *across her threshold. She told the boy not to set foot out of the house until he had finished supper.*

set forth *v., formal* **1.** To explain exactly or clearly. *The President set forth his plans in a television talk.* **2.** To start to go somewhere; begin a trip. *The troop set forth on their ten-mile hike early.*

set in *v.* To begin; start; develop. *Before the boat could reach shore, a storm had set in. He did not keep the cut clean and infection set in. The wind set in from the east.*

set in one's ways *adj. phr.* Stubborn; opinionated; unchangeable. *My grandfather is so old and set in his ways that he'll eat nothing new.*

set off *v.* **1.** To decorate through contrast; balance by difference. *The bright colors of the birds were set off by the white snow. A small gold pin set off her plain dark dress.* **2.** To balance; make somewhat equal. *Her great wealth, as he thought, set off her plain face.* **3a.** To begin to go. *They set off for the West in a covered wagon.* **3b.** To cause to begin. *A letter from home set off an attack of homesickness. An atomic explosion is created by setting off a chain reaction in the atom.* **3c.** To cause to explode. *On July 4 we set off firecrackers in many places.*

set one's heart on *v. phr.* To want very much. *He set his heart on that bike. also:* To be very desirous of; hope very much to succeed in.—Used with a verbal noun. *He set his heart on winning the race.*

set out *v.* **1.** To leave on a journey or voyage. *The Pilgrims set out for the New World.* **2.** To decide and begin to try; attempt. *George set out to improve his pitching.* **3.** To plant in the ground. *The gardener set out some tomato seedlings.*

set sail *v. phr.* To begin a sea voyage; start sailing. *The ship set sail for Europe.*

set store by *v. phr., informal* To like or value; want to keep. Used with a qualifying word between *set* and *store*. *George sets great store by that old tennis racket. Pat doesn't set much store by Mike's advice.*

set the pace *v. phr.* To decide on a rate of speed of travel or rules that are followed by others. *The scoutmaster set the pace so that the shorter boys would not get tired trying to keep up. Louise set the pace in selling tickets for the school play.*—**pace-setter** *n.* *John is the pace-setter of the class.*—**pace-setting** *adj.* *Bob's time in the cross-country race was pace-setting. The country is growing at a pace-setting rate.*

set the world on fire *v. phr., informal* To do something outstanding; act in a way that attracts much attention or makes you famous. *John works hard, but he will never set the world on fire. Mary could set the world on fire with her piano playing.*

settle a score *also* **wipe out an old score** To hurt (someone) in return for a wrong or loss. *John settled an old score with Bob by beating him.*

settle down *v.* **1.** To live more quietly and sensibly; have a regular place to live and a regular job; stop acting wildly or carelessly, especially by growing up. *John will settle down after he gets a job and gets married.* **2.** To become quiet, calm, or comfortable. *Father settled down with the newspaper. The house settled down for the night after the children were put to bed. The teacher told the students to settle down and study the lesson.*

settle for *v.* To be satisfied with (less) agree to; accept. *Jim wanted $200 for his old car, but he settled for $100.*

set up *v.* **1.** To provide the money for the necessities for. *When he was twenty-one, his father set him up in the clothing business.* **2.** To establish; start. *The government has set up many hospitals for veterans of the armed forces.* **3.** To make ready for use by putting the parts together or into their right place. *The men set up the new printing press.* **4.** To bring into being; cause. *Ocean tides are set up by the pull between earth and the moon.* **5.** To claim; pretend. *He set himself up to be a graduate of a medical school, but he was not.* **6.** To harm someone by entrapment or some other ruse. *Joe was actually innocent of the robbery, but his "trusted friends" set him up, so the police found the gun in his car.*

setup *n. phr.* (stress on *set*) **1.** Arrangement, management, circumstances. *Boy, you really have a wonderful setup in your office! I just can't do my work in such a messy setup!* **2.** Financial arrangement. *It is a fairly generous setup sending your uncle $1,000 a month.*

sewed up *adj. phr., informal* Won or arranged as you wish; decided. *They thought they had the game sewed up, but the other team won it with a touchdown in the last quarter. Dick thought he had the job sewed up, but another boy got it.*

sexual harassment *n. phr.* The act of constantly making unwanted advances of a sexual nature for which the offended party may seek legal redress. *The court fined Wilbur Catwallender $750,000 for sexual harassment of two of his female employees.*

shack up with *v. phr., slang* To move in with (someone) of the opposite sex without marrying the person. *Did you know that Ollie and Sue aren't married? They just decided to shack up for a while.*

shaggy dog (story) *n. phr.* A special kind of joke whose long and often convoluted introduction and development delay the effect of the punch line. *Uncle Joe only seems to bore his audiences with his long shaggy dog jokes, for when he comes to the long-awaited punch line, he gets very few laughs.*

shake a leg *v. phr., slang* To go fast; hurry. *Shake a leg! The bus won't wait.*

shakedown *n.* **1.** A test. *Let's take the new car out and give it a shakedown.* **2.** An act of extorting money by threatening. *It was a nasty shakedown, to get $500 from the old man, promising to protect him.*

shake down v. phr. **1.** To cause to fall by shaking. *He shook some pears down from the tree.* **2.** *informal* To test, practice, get running smoothly (a ship or ship's crew). *The captain shook down his new ship on a voyage to the Mediterranean Sea.* **3.** *slang* To get money from by threats. *The gangsters shook the store owner down every month.*

shake up v., *informal* To bother; worry; disturb. *The notice about a cut in pay shook up everybody in the office.*

shake-up n. A change; a reorganization. *After the scandal there was a major shake-up in the Cabinet.*

shape up v. phr., *informal* **1.** To begin to act or work right; get along satisfactorily. *If the new boy doesn't begin to shape up soon, he'll have to leave school. "How is the building of the new gym coming along?" "Fine. It's shaping up very well."* **2.** To show promise. *Plans for our picnic are shaping up very well.*

shell out v., *informal* To pay or spend. *Dick had to shell out a lot of money for his new car.*

shine up to v., *slang* To try to please; try to make friends with. *Smedley shines up to all the pretty girls.*

shoe on the other foot The opposite is true; places are changed. *He was my captain in the army but now the shoe is on the other foot.*

shoo-in n., *informal* Someone or something that is expected to win; a favorite; sure winner. *Chris is a shoo-in to win a scholarship. Do you think he will win the election? He's a shoo-in. This horse is a shoo-in. He can't miss winning.*

shoot one's wad v. phr. slang colloquial **1.** To spend all of one's money. *We've shot our wad for the summer and can't buy any new garden furniture.* **2.** To say everything that is on one's mind. *Joe feels a lot better now that he's shot his wad at the meeting.*

shoot straight or **shoot square** v., *informal* To act fairly; deal honestly. *You can trust that salesman; he shoots straight with his customers. We get along well because we always shoot square with each other.*—**straight shooter** or **square shooter** n., *informal* Bill is a square-shooter.—**straight-shooting** adj. *The boys all liked the straight-shooting coach.*

shoot the breeze or **bat the breeze** or **fan the breeze** or **shoot the bull** v. phr., *slang* To talk. *Jim shot the breeze with his neighbor while the children were playing. Come into the kitchen and we'll bat the breeze over a cup of coffee. The women were shooting the breeze about Jim's latest trouble with the police. The fishermen were shooting the bull about the school of sailfish they had seen.*

shoot the works v. phr., *slang* **1.** To spare no expense or effort; get or give everything. *Billy shot the works when he bought his bicycle; he got a bell, a light, a basket, and chrome trimmings on it, too. The Greens shot the works on their daughter's wedding reception.*

, To go the limit; take a risk. *he motor of Tom's boat was angerously hot, but he decided shoot the works and try to in the race.*

ot up *v.* **1.** To grow quickly. *illy had always been a small oy, but when he was thirteen ears old he began to shoot p.* **2.** To arise suddenly. *As we atched, flames shot up from ie roof of the barn.* **3.** *informal* To shoot or shoot at reckssly; shoot and hurt badly. *he cowboys got drunk and ot up the bar room. The soliier was shot up very badly.* **4.** o take drugs by injection. *A eroin addict will shoot up as ften as he can.*

ore up *v.* To add support to something) where weakness shown; make (something) ronger where support is eeded; support. *When the ood waters weakened the ridge, it was shored up with eel beams and sandbags until could be rebuilt. The coach nt in a substitute guard to iore up the line when itchburg began to break rough.*

ort end *n.* The worst or iost unpleasant part. *The new oy got the short end of it beiuse all the comfortable beds the dormitory had been taken efore he arrived. The girls who rved refreshments at the party ot the short end of it. When verybody had been served, iere was no cake left for them.*

ot in the arm *n. phr.*, *informal* Something inspiring or ncouraging. *The general's apearance was a shot in the arm r the weary soldiers. We were*

ready to quit, but the coach's talk was a shot in the arm.

shot in the dark *n. phr.* An attempt without much hope or chance of succeeding; a wild guess. *It was just a shot in the dark, but I got the right answer to the teacher's question.*

shove down one's throat *or* **ram down one's throat** *v. phr.*, *informal* To force you to do or agree to (something not wanted or liked.) *We didn't want Mr. Bly to speak at our banquet, but the planning committee shoved him down our throats. The president was against the idea, but the club members rammed it down his throat.*

showoff *n.* A boastful person. *Jim always has to be the center of attention; he is an insufferable showoff.*

show off *v. phr.* **1.** To put out nicely for people to see; display; exhibit. *The Science Fair gave Julia a chance to show off her shell collection. The girls couldn't wait to show off their fine needlework to our visitors.* **2.** *informal* To try to attract attention; also, try to attract attention to. *The children always show off when we have company. Joe hasn't missed a chance to show off his muscles since that pretty girl moved in next door.*

show of hands *n. phr.* An open vote during a meeting when those who vote "yes" and those who vote "no" hold up their hands to be counted. *The chairman said, "I'd like to see a show of hands if we're ready for the vote."*

show one's colors *v. phr.* **1.** To

show what you are really like. *We thought Toby was timid, but he showed his colors when he rescued the ponies from the burning barn.* **2.** To make known what you think or plan to do. *Mr. Ryder is afraid that he will lose the election if he shows his colors on civil rights. We would not help Jim until he showed his colors.*

show the door *v. phr.* To ask (someone) to go away. *Ruth was upsetting the other children, so I showed her the door. Our neighbors invited themselves to the party and stayed until Harry showed them the door.*

show up *v.* **1.** To make known the real truth about (someone). *The man said he was a mind reader, but he was shown up as a fake.* **2.** To come or bring out; become or make easy to see. *The detective put a chemical on the paper, and the fingertips showed up. This test shows up your weaknesses in arithmetic.* **3.** *informal* To come; appear. *We had agreed to meet at the gym, but Larry didn't show up. Only five students showed up for the class meeting.*

shut off *v.* **1.** To make (something like water or electricity) stop coming. *Please shut off the hose before the grass gets too wet.* **2.** To be apart; be separated from; also to separate from. *Our camp is so far from the highway we feel shut off from the world when we are there. The sow is so bad tempered we had to shut it off from its piglets.*

shut out *v.* **1.** To prevent from coming in; block. *During* World War II, Malta manage to shut out most of the Italia and German bombers t throwing up an effective an aircraft screen. The boys we annoyed by Tom's telling clu secrets and shut him out of the meeting.* **2.** To prevent (an o posing team) from scorin throughout an entire gam *The Dodgers shut out the Red 5–0.*

shut up *v.* **1.** *informal* T stop talking. *Little Ruthie to Father about his birthday su prise before Mother could sh her up.*—Often used as a com mand; usually considered rud *Shut up and let Joe say som thing. If you'll shut up for minute, I'll tell you our plan.* To close the doors and win dows of. *We got the house sh up only minutes before th storm hit.* **3.** To close and lo for a definite period of tim *The Smiths always spend L bor Day shutting up their sur mer home for the year. We g to the store only to find that t owner had shut up shop for th weekend.* **4.** To confine. *Th dog bites. It should be shut u John has been shut up with cold all week.*

sick and tired *adj.* Feelin strong dislike for something r peated or continued too lon exasperated; annoyed. *Jar was sick and tired of alwa having to wait for Bill, s when he didn't arrive on tin she left without him. John sick and tired of having h studies interrupted. I've bee studying all day, and I'm si and tired of it.*

side with *v.* To agree wit

help. Alan always sides with Johnny in an argument. Gerald sided with the plan to move the club.

ght unseen *adv. phr.* Before seeing it; before seeing her, him, or them. *Tom read an ad about a car and sent the money for it sight unseen.*

gn over *v.* To give legally by signing your name. *He signed his house over to his wife.*

gn up *v.* **1.** To promise to do something by signing your name; join; sign agreement. *We will not have the picnic unless more people sign up. John wants to sign up for the contest. Miss Carter has signed up to be the chaperone at the dance.* **2.** To write the name of (a person or thing) to be in an activity; also, to persuade (someone) to do something. *Betty decided to sign up her dog for obedience training. The superintendent has signed up three new teachers for next year.*

lver anniversary *or* **wedding** *n. phr.* The twenty-fifth wedding anniversary of a couple; the twenty-fifth anniversary of a business or an association, etc. "*The day after tomorrow is Mom and Dad's silver anniversary,*" *Sue said to her brother. "I hope you have a nice present picked out.*"

mmer down *v., informal* To become less angry or excited; become calmer. *Tom got mad, but soon simmered down.*

ng a different tune *or* **whistle a different tune** *also* **sing a new tune** *v. phr., informal* To talk or act in the opposite way; contradict something said before. *Charles said that all smokers*

should be expelled from the team but he sang a different tune after the coach caught him smoking.

sink in *or* **soak in** *v., informal* To be completely understood; be fully realized or felt. *Everybody laughed at the joke but Joe; it took a moment for it to sink in before he laughed too. When Frank heard that war had started, it didn't sink in for a long time until his father was drafted into the army.*

sit back *v.* **1.** To be built a distance away; stand away (as from a street). *Our house sits back from the road.* **2.** To relax; rest, often while others are working; take time out. *Sit back for a minute and think about what you have done.*

sit by *v.* **1.** To stay near; watch and care for. *The nurse was told to sit by the patient until he woke up. Mother sat by her sick baby all night.* **2.** To sit and watch or rest especially while others work *Don't just sit idly by while the other children are all busy.*

sit in *v.* **1.** To be a member; participate. *We're having a conference and we'd like you to sit in.* also **sit in on:** To be a member of; participate in. *We want you to sit in on the meeting.* **2.** To attend but not participate. Often used with *on. Our teacher was invited to sit in on the conference.*

sit on *v.* **1.** To be a member of (a jury, board, commission), etc. *Mr. Brown sat on the jury at the trial.* **2.** *informal* To prevent from starting or doing something; squelch. *The teacher sat on Fred before he* could get started with the long story. The teacher sat on Joe as soon as he began showing off.

sit out *v.* To not take part in. *The next dance is a polka. Let's sit it out. Toby had to sit out the last half of the game because his knee hurt.*

sit tight *v. phr., informal* To make no move or change; stay where you are.—Often used as a command. *Sit tight; I'll be ready to go in a few minutes. The doctor said to sit tight until he arrived. The gangsters sat tight in the mountains while the police looked for them.*

sit up *v.* **1.** To move into a sitting position. *Joe sat up when he heard the knock on his bedroom door.* **2.** To stay awake instead of going to bed. *Mrs. Jones will sit up until both of her daughters get home from the dance. We sat up until two A.M. hoping for news from Alaska.* **3.** *informal* To be surprised. *Janice really sat up when I told her the gossip about Tom.*

sit-up *n.* A vigorous exercise in which the abdominal muscles are strengthened by locking one's feet in a fastening device and sitting up numerous times. *Do a few sit-ups if you want to reduce your waist.*

sit well (with) *v.* Find favor with; please. *The reduced school budget did not sit well with the teachers.*

six of one and half-a-dozen of the other *n,. phr.* Two things the same; not a real choice; no difference. *Which coat do you like better, the brown or the blue? It's six of one and half-a-dozen of the other. Johnny says*

it's six of one and half-a-dozen of the other whether he does th... job tonight or tomorrow night.

size up *v., informal* To decid... what one thinks about (some thing); to form an opinio... about (something). *Give Jo... an hour to size up the situ ation and he'll tell you what t... do next. Our coach went t... New York to size up the tea... we'll face in our homecomin... game.*

skate on thin ice *v. phr.* T... take a chance; risk danger, dis... approval or anger. *You'll b... skating on thin ice if you as... Dad to increase your allowanc... again. John knew he was ska... ing on thin ice, but he could n... resist teasing his sister abo... her boyfriend.*

skeleton in the closet *n. ph...* A shameful secret; someone o... something kept hidden, espe... cially by a family. *The skeleto... in our family closet was Unc... Willie. No one mentioned hi... because he drank too much.*

skid row *n.* The poor part of... city where men live who hav... no jobs and drink too much li... uor. *That man was once ric... but he drank and gambled to... much, and ended his life livin... on skid row. The Bowery... New York City's skid row.*

skim the surface *v. phr.* To d... something very superficiall... *He seems knowledgeable i... many different areas but his f... miliarity is very superficia... since he only skims the surfac... of everything he touches.*

skin alive *v. phr.* **1.** *inform...* To scold angrily. *Mother w... skin you alive when she se... your torn pants.* **2.** *inform...*

To spank or beat. *Dad was ready to skin us alive when he found we had ruined his saw.* **3.** *slang* To defeat. *We all did our best, but the visiting gymnastic team skinned us alive.*

skin and bones *n.* A person or animal that is very thin; someone very skinny. *The puppy is healthy now, but when we found him he was just skin and bones. Have you been dieting? You're nothing but skin and bones!*

skin-deep *adj.* Only on the surface; not having any deep or honest meaning; not really or closely connected with what it seems to belong to. *Mary's friendliness with Joan is only skin-deep. Ralph crammed for the test and got a good grade, but his knowledge of the lesson is only skin-deep.*

skin off one's nose *n. phr., slang* Matter of interest, concern, or trouble to you. Normally used in the negative. *Go to Jake's party if you wish. It's no skin off my nose. Grace didn't pay any attention to our argument. It wasn't any skin off her nose. You could at least say hello to our visitor. It's no skin off your nose.*

skip it *v. phr., informal* To forget all about it. *When Jack tried to reward him for returning his lost dog, the man said to skip it. I asked what the fight was about, but the boys said to skip it.*

sky is the limit There is no upper limit to something. *"Buy me the fastest racehorse in Hong Kong," Mr. Lee instructed his broker. "Spend whatever is necessary; the sky is the limit."*

slack off *v. phr.* **1.** To become less active; grow lazy. *Since construction work has been slacking off toward the end of the summer, many workers were dismissed.* **2.** To gradually reduce; taper off. *The snowstorms tend to slack off over the Great Lakes by the first of April.*

slap one's wrist *v. phr.* To receive a light punishment. *She could have been fired for contradicting the company president in public, but all she got was a slap on the wrist.*

sleep around *v. phr., slang, vulgar, avoidable* To be free with one's sexual favors; to behave promiscuously. *Sue Catwallender is a nice girl but she sleeps around an awful lot with all sorts of guys.*

sleep a wink *v. phr.* To get a moment's sleep; enjoy a bit of sleep.—Used in negative and conditional statements and in questions. *I didn't sleep a wink all night.*

sleep like a log *v. phr.* To sleep very deeply and soundly. *Although I am usually a light sleeper, I was so exhausted from the sixteen-hour transpacific flight that, once we got home, I slept like a log for twelve hours.*

sleep off *v. phr.* To sleep until the effect of too much alcohol or drugs passes. *George had too many beers last night and he is now sleeping off the effects.*

sleep on *v.* To postpone a decision about. *We asked Judy if she would join our club and she* answered that she would sleep on it. *We will have to sleep on your invitation until we know whether we will be free Monday night.*

slip of the pen *n. phr.* The mistake of writing something different from what you should or what you planned. *That was a slip of the pen. I meant to write September, not November. I wish you would forget it. That was a slip of the pen.*

slip of the tongue *also* **slip of the lip** *n. phr.* The mistake of saying something you had not wanted or planned to say; an error of speech. *No one would have known our plans if Kay hadn't made a slip of the tongue. She didn't mean to tell our secret; it was a slip of the lip.*

slip one's mind *v. phr.* To forget something. *I meant to mail those letters but it entirely slipped my mind.*

slipup *n.* A mistake. *"I'm sorry, sir. That was an unfortunate slipup," the barber said when he scratched the client's face.*

slip up *v. phr.* To make a mistake. *Someone at the bank slipped up. There are only 48 pennies in this 50¢ roll of coins. If he hadn't slipped up on the last questions, his score on the test would have been perfect.*

slowdown *n.* A period of lesser activity, usually in the economic sphere. *We all hope the current slowdown in the economy will soon be over.*

slow down *v. phr.* To go more slowly than usual. *The road was slippery, so Mr. Jones slowed down the car. Pat once*

could run a mile in five minutes, but now that he's older he's slowing down.

small fry *n.* **1.** Young children. *In the park, a sandbox is provided for the small fry.* **2.** Something or someone of little importance. *Large dairies ignore the competition from the small fry who make only a few hundred pounds of cheese a year.*

smash hit *n., informal* A very successful play, movie or opera. *The school play was a smash hit.*

smell a rat *v. phr., informal* To be suspicious; feel that something is wrong. *Every time Tom visits me, one of my ashtrays disappears. I'm beginning to smell a rat. When the policeman saw a light go on in the store at midnight, he smelled a rat.*

smoke out *v. phr.* **1.** To force out with smoke. *The boys smoked a squirrel out of a hollow tree. The farmer tried to smoke some gophers out of their burrows.* **2.** *informal* To find out the facts about. *It took the reporter three weeks to smoke out the whole story.*

smoke-out *n.* A successful conclusion of an act of investigative journalism revealing some long-kept secrets. *Journalist Bob Woodward was the hero of the Watergate smoke-out.*

smooth over *v.* To make something seem better or more pleasant; try to excuse. *Bill tried to smooth over his argument with Mary by making her laugh.*

snail's pace *n.* A very slow

movement forward. *Time moved at a snail's pace before the holidays. The donkey on which he was riding moved at a snail's pace.*

snap up *v., informal* To take or accept eagerly. *Eggs were on sale cheap, and the shoppers snapped up the bargain. Mr. Hayes told Bob that he would take him skiing, and Bob snapped up the offer.*

sneeze at *v., informal* To think of as not important; not take seriously.—Used with negative or limiting words and in questions. *Mr. Jones was chosen by his party to run for President. He was not elected, but to be chosen to run is not to be sneezed at. If you think Mrs. Green's tests are things to be sneezed at, you have a surprise coming. Is a thousand dollars anything to sneeze at? John finished third in a race with twenty other runners. That is nothing to sneeze at.*

snow job *n., slang, informal* **1.** Insincere or exaggerated talk designed to gain the favors of someone. *Joe gave Sue a snow job and she believed every word of it.* **2.** The skillful display of technical vocabulary and prestige terminology in order to pass oneself off as an expert in a specialized field without really being a knowledgeable worker in that area. *That talk by Nielsen on pharmaceuticals sounded very impressive, but I will not hire him because it was essentially a snow job.*

snow under *v.* **1.** To cover over with snow. *The doghouse was snowed under during the bliz-*

zard. **2.** *informal* To give so much of something that cannot be taken care of; to weigh down by so much of something that you cannot do anything about it.—Usually used in the passive. *The factory received so many orders that it was snowed under with work. The disabled girl was snowed under with Christmas letters.*

soak up *v.* **1.** To take up water or other liquid as a sponge does. *The rag soaked up the water that I spilled.* **2.** To use a sponge or something like a sponge to take up liquid. *John soaked up the water with the rag.* **3.** *informal* To take up into yourself in the way a sponge takes up water. *Mary was lying on the beach soaking up the sun. Charles soaks up facts as fast as the teacher gives them.*

sob story *n.* A story that makes you feel pity or sorrow; a tale that makes you tearful. *The beggar told us a long sob story before he asked for money. The movie is based on a sob story, but people love it.*

sock it *v. phr., also interj., slang, informal* To give one's utmost; everything one is capable of; to give all one is capable of. *Right on, Joe, sock it to 'em! I was watching the debate on television and more than once Bill Buckley really socked it to them.*

so far, so good *informal* Until now things have gone well. *So far, so good; I hope we keep on with such good luck.*

so help me *interj., informal* I promise; I swear; may I be punished if I lie. *I've told you* the truth, so help me. So help me, there was nothing else I could do.

so long interj., informal Goodbye.—Used when you are leaving someone or he is leaving you. So long, I will be back tomorrow.

somebody up there loves/hates me slang An expression intimating that an unseen power in heaven, such as God, has been favorable or unfavorable to the one making the exclamation. Look at all the money I won! I say somebody up there sure loves me! Look at all the money I've lost! I say somebody up there sure hates me!

something else adj., slang, informal So good as to be beyond description; the ultimate; stupendous. Janet Hopper is really something else.

song and dance n., informal **1.** Foolish or uninteresting talk; dull nonsense. Usually used with give. I met Nancy today and she gave me a long song and dance about her family. **2.** A long lie or excuse, often meant to get pity. Usually used with give. Billy gave the teacher a song and dance about his mother being sick as an excuse for being late. The tramp asked us for money and tried to give us a big song and dance about having to buy a bus ticket to Chicago.

son of a bitch or **sunuvabitch** also **S.O.B.** n. phr., vulgar, avoidable (but becoming more and more acceptable, especially if said with a positive or loving intonation). Fellow, character, guy, individual. Negatively: Get out of here you filthy, miserable sunuvabitch! Positively: So you won ten million dollars at the lottery, you lucky son of a bitch (or sunuvabitch)!

son of a gun n. phr., slang **1.** A bad person; a person not liked. I don't like Charley; keep that son of a gun out of here. **2.** A mischievous rascal; a lively guy.—Often used in a joking way. The farmer said he would catch the son of a gun who let the cows out of the barn. Hello Bill, you old son of a gun! **3.** Something troublesome; a hard job. The test today was a son of a gun. Used as an exclamation, usually to show surprise or disappointment. Son of a gun! I lost my car keys.

sound off v. **1.** To say your name or count "One! Two! Three! Four!" as you march.—Used as orders in U.S. military service. "Sound off!" said the sergeant, and the soldiers shouted, "One! Two! Three! Four!" with each step as they marched. **2.** informal To tell what you know or think in a loud clear voice, especially to brag or complain. If you don't like the way we're doing the job, sound off! George sounded off about how the game should have been played. The teacher is always sounding off about the students not doing their homework.

sound out v. To try to find out how a person feels about something usually by careful questions. Alfred sounded out his boss about a day off from his job. When you see the coach, sound him out about my chances of getting on the basketball team.

ouped-up *adj.,* *informal* More powerful or faster because of changes and additions. *Many teen-aged boys like to drive souped-up cars. The basketball team won the last five games with souped-up plays.*

paced out *adj., slang, informal* Having gaps in one's train of thought, confused, incoherent; resembling the behavior of someone who is under the influence of drugs. *Joe's been acting funny lately—spaced out, you might say.*

peak for *v.* **1.** To speak in favor of or in support of. *At the meeting John spoke for the change in the rules. The other girls made jokes about Jane, but Mary spoke for her.* **2.** To make a request for; to ask for. *The teacher was giving away some books. Fred and Charlie spoke for the same one.* **3.** To give an impression of; be evidence that (something) is or will be said.—Used with the words *well* or *ill. It seems that it will rain today. That speaks ill for the picnic this afternoon. Who robbed the cookie jar? The crumbs on your shirt speak ill for you, Billy. John wore a clean shirt and a tie when he went to ask for a job, and that spoke well for him. It speaks well for Mary that she always does her homework.*

peak of the devil and he appears A person comes just when you are talking about him.—A proverb. *We were just talking about Bill when he came in the door. Speak of the devil and he appears.*

peak out *or* **speak up** *v.* **1.** To peak in a loud or clear voice.

The trucker told the shy boy to speak up. **2.** To speak in support of or against someone or something. *Willie spoke up for Dan as club president. Ed spoke up against letting girls join the club.*

speed up *v.* To go faster than before; also, to make go faster. *The car speeded up when it reached the country. Push in the throttle to speed up the engine.*

spell out *v.* **1.** To say or read aloud the letters of a word, one by one; spell. *John could not understand the word the teacher was saying, so she spelled it out on the blackboard.* **2.** To read slowly, have trouble in understanding. *The little boy spelled out the printed words.* **3.** *informal* To explain something in very simple words; explain very clearly. *The class could not understand the problem, so the teacher spelled it out for them. Before the game the coach spelled out to the players what he wanted them to do.*

spill the beans *v. phr., informal* To tell a secret to someone who is not supposed to know about it. *John's friends were going to have a surprise party for him, but Tom spilled the beans.*

spitting image *n.* **spit and image** *informal* An exact likeness; a duplicate. *John is the spitting image of his grandfather. That vase is the spitting image of one I wanted to buy in Boston.*

split hairs *v. phr.* To find and argue about small and unimportant differences as if the differences are important. *John* is always splitting hairs; he often starts an argument about something small and unimportant. Don't split hairs about whose turn it is to wash the dishes and make the beds; let's work together and finish sooner.

split the difference v. phr., informal To settle a money disagreement by dividing the difference, each person giving up half. Bob offered $25 for Bill's bicycle and Bill wanted $35; they split the difference.

split ticket n. A vote for candidates from more than one party. Mr. Jones voted a split ticket. An independent voter likes a split ticket.

split up v. phr. 1. To separate; get a divorce. After three years of marriage, the unhappy couple finally split up. 2. To separate something; divide into portions. The brothers split up their father's fortune among themselves after his death.

split-up n. A separation or division into two or many smaller parts. The split-up of our company was due to the founder's untimely death.

spoken for adj. Occupied; reserved; taken; already engaged or married. "Sorry, my boy," Mr. Jones said condescendingly, "but my daughter is already spoken for. She will marry Fred Wilcox next month."

spoon-feed v. 1. To feed with a spoon. Mothers spoon-feed their babies. 2a. To make something too easy for (a person). Bill's mother spoon-fed him and never let him think for himself. Alice depended on her mother for all decisions becaus[e] she had been spoon-fed. 2b. T[o] make (something) too easy fo[r] someone. Some students wan[t] the teacher to spoon-feed th[e] lessons.

spread oneself too thin v. ph[r.] To try to do too many things a[t] one time. As the owner, che[f,] waiter, and dishwasher of h[is] restaurant, Pierre was spread[ing himself too thin.

spring chicken n., slang [A] young person.—Usually use[d] with no. Mr. Brown is n[o] spring chicken, but he can sti[ll] play tennis well. The coach [is] no spring chicken, but he ca[n] show the players what to do.

square away v. phr. 1. To a[r]range the sails of a ship so tha[t] the wind blows from behind[.] The captain ordered the crew t[o] square away and sail before th[e] wind. 2. informal To put righ[t] for use or action.—Often use[d] in the passive or participle. Th[e] living room was squared awa[y] for the guests. Harry got int[o] trouble, but his scoutmaste[r] talked with him and got hi[m] squared away. 3. informal T[o] stand ready to fight; put u[p] your fists. Jack and Le[e] squared away.

square peg in a round hole n[.] informal A person who doe[s] not fit into a job or positio[n;] someone who does not belon[g] where he is. Arthur is a squar[e] peg in a round hole when he[is] playing ball. George likes t[o] work with his hands. When [it] comes to books, he's a squar[e] peg in a round hole.—Some[-]times used in a short form [:] **square peg.**

stab in the back[1] v. phr., slan[g]

o say or do something unfair hat harms (a friend or some-ne who trusts you). *Owen tabbed his friend Max in the ack by telling lies about him.*

ab in the back[2] *n. phr., slang* An act or a lie that hurts a riend or trusting person; a romise not kept, especially to friend. *John stabbed his own riend in the back by stealing rom his store. My friend tabbed me in the back by tell-ng the teacher I was playing ooky when I was home sick.*

ab in the dark *n. phr.* A ran-om attempt or guess at some-hing without previous xperience or knowledge of he subject. *"You're asking me ho could have hidden randpa's will," Fred said. "I eally have no idea, but let me take a stab in the dark—I hink my sister Hermione has ."*

ack the cards *v. phr.* **1.** To ar-ange cards secretly and dis-onestly for the purpose of heating. *The gambler had tacked the cards against Bill.* **2.** o arrange things unfairly for r against a person; have things o that a person has an unfair dvantage or disadvantage; take sure in an unfair way hat things will happen.—Usu-lly used in the passive with *in one's favor* or *"against ne."* *A tall basketball player as the cards stacked in his fa-or. The cards are stacked gainst a poor boy who wants o go to college.*

mping ground *n., informal* place where a person spends uch of his time. *Pete's soda untain is an after-school*

stamping ground. When John returned to his hometown many years later, he visited all of his old stamping grounds.

stamp out *v.* To destroy com-pletely and make disappear. *In the last few years, we have nearly stamped out polio by us-ing vaccine. The police and judges are trying to stamp out crime.*

stand by *v.* **1.** To be close be-side or near. *Mary could not tell Jane the secret with her little brother standing by. Would you just stand by and watch the big boys beat your little brother?* **2.** To be near, waiting to do something when needed. *The policeman in the patrol car ra-dioed the station about the rob-bery, and then stood by for orders. Lee stood by with a fire extinguisher while the trash was burning.* **3.** To follow or keep (one's promise). *He is a boy who always stands by his prom-ises.* **4.** To be loyal to; support; help. *When three big boys at-tacked Bill, Ed stood by him. Some people blamed Harry when he got into trouble, but Joe stood by him.*

stand for *v.* **1.** To be a sign of; make you think of; mean. *The letters "U.S.A." stand for "United States of America." The written sign "=" in an arithmetic problem stands for "equals." Our flag stands for our country. The owl stands for wisdom.* **2.** To speak in favor of something, or show that you support it. *The new President stood for honest government. John always stands for what is right.* **3.** *Chiefly British* To try to be elected for. *Three men* *from London are standing for parliament. The governor did not stand for reelection.* **4.** *informal* To allow to happen or to be done; permit.—Usually used in the negative. *The teacher will not stand for fooling in the classroom.*

stand in awe of *v. phr.* To look upon with wonder; feel very respectful to. *Janet always stands in awe of the superintendent. The soldier stood in awe to his officers.*

stand in for *v. phr.* To substitute for someone. *The famous brain surgeon was called out of town so his assistant had to stand in for him during the operation.*

stand off *v.* **1.** To stay at a distance; stay apart. *At parties, Mr. Jones goes around talking to everyone, but Mrs. Jones is shy and stands off.* **2.** To keep (someone or something) from coming near or winning. *The soldiers defending the fort stood off a large band of Indians. The other schools wanted to beat our team and win the championship, but our boys stood them all off.*

standoffish *adj.* Stiff; aloof; reserved in manner. *The famous chess player is hard to get to know because he is so standoffish.*

stand out *v.* **1.** To go farther out than a nearby surface; project. *A mole stood out on her cheek.* **2.** To be more noticeable in some way than those around you; be higher, bigger, or better. *Fred was very tall and stood out in the crowd. John stood out as a track star.*

stand over *v.* **1.** To watch

closely; keep checking all th time. *Ted's mother had to stan over him to get him to do h homework.* **2.** To be held ove for later action; be postpone wait. *The committee decided let the proposal stand over unt its next meeting.*

stand pat *v., informal* To b satisfied with things and b against a change. *Bill ha made up his mind on the que tion and when his friends trie to change his mind, he stoo pat.*

stand to reason *v. phr.* T seem very likely from th known facts. *If you have driver's license, it stands to re son you can drive. Joe is intell gent and studies hard; it stand to reason that he will pass th examination.*

stand trial *v. phr.* To subm to a trial by court. *The case h been postponed and he may n have to stand trial until ne April.*

stand up *v.* **1.** To rise to standing position; get up o your feet. *A gentleman stan up when a lady enters a room* **2.** To be strong enough to us hard or for a long time. * rocket must be built strongly stand up under the blast-oj The old car has already stoo up for twenty years.* **3.** *inform* To make a date and then fail keep it. *June cried when B stood her up on their first date.*

stand up and be counted *v. ph* To be willing to say what yo think in public; let peop know that you are for against something. *The equ rights movement needs peop who are willing to stand up an*

*e counted. If you disagree with
ie group, you should be ready
> stand up and be counted.*

nd up for *or informal* **stick
p for** *v.* To defend against
ttack; fight for. *John always
'ands up for his rights. When
dary was being criticized, Jane
uck up for her.*

nd up to *v.* To meet with
ourage. *Mary stood up to the
narling dog that leaped toward
er. A soldier must stand up to
anger.*

nd up with *v., informal* To
e best man or maid of honor
t a wedding. *A groom often
hooses his brother to stand up
'ith him.*

rs in one's eyes *n. phr.* **1.** An
ppearance or feeling of very
reat happiness or expectation
f happiness. *Mary gets stars in
er eyes when she thinks of her
oyfriend.* **2.** A belief in the
ossibility of quick and lasting
eforms in people and life and
n eagerness to make such
hanges. *Some inexperienced
eople get stars in their eyes
hen they think of improving
ie world.*—**starry-eyed** *adj.*
'ery happy and excited, per-
aps with little reason; eager
nd self-confident about im-
roving human nature and gen-
ral conditions of life. *Young
eople are often starry-eyed
nd eager to improve the world;
iey do not know how hard it
.*

rt in *v., informal* **1.** To be-
in to do something; start. *Fred
'arted in weeding the garden.
'he family started in eating
upper.* **2.** To begin a career.
'ob started in as an office boy
nd became president.* **3.** To

give a first job to. *The bank
started him in as a clerk.*

start up *v.* **1.** To begin operating. *The driver started up the
motor of the car. The engine
started up with a roar.* **2.** To begin to play (music). *The conductor waved his baton, and the
band started up. The orchestra
started up a waltz.* **3.** To rise or
stand suddenly. *When he heard
the bell, he started up from his
chair.*

stay put *v. phr.* To stay in
place; not leave. *Harry's father
told him to stay put until he
came back. The rocks can be
glued to the bulletin board to
make them stay put. After
Grandmother came home from
her trip to visit Aunt May, she
said she wanted to stay put for a
while.*

steal a march on *v. phr.* To
get ahead of someone by doing
a thing unnoticed; get an advantage over. *The army stole a
march on the enemy by
marching at night and attacking them in the morning. Jack
got the job by getting up earlier than Bill. He stole a
march on him.*

steal one's thunder *v. phr.* To
do or say something, intention-
ally or not, that another person
has planned to say or do. *Fred
intended to nominate Bill for
president, but John got up first
and stole Fred's thunder. Mary
was going to sing "Oh!
Susanna," but Ellen did it first
and Mary said Ellen had stolen
her thunder. Smith heard that
Jones was going to offer a new
law which people wanted, so he
himself proposed the law first,
stealing Jones' thunder.*

steal the show v. phr. To act or do so well in a performance that you get most of the attention and the other performers are unnoticed. *Mary was in only one scene of the play, but she stole the show from the stars.*

steal the spotlight v. phr. To attract attention away from a person or thing that people should be watching. *When the maid walked on the stage and tripped over a rug, she stole the spotlight from the leading players. Just as the speaker began, a little dog ran up the aisle, and stole the spotlight from him.*

steer clear of v. **1.** To steer a safe distance from; go around without touching. *A ship steers clear of a rocky shore in stormy weather.* **2.** *informal* To stay away from; keep from staying near. *Fred was angry at Bill, and Bill was steering clear of him. Some words Martha always spells wrong. She tries to steer clear of them.*

step down v. **1.** To come down in one move from a higher position to a lower. *As soon as the train stopped, the conductor stepped down to help the passengers off.* **2.** To make go slower little by little. *The train was approaching the station, so the engineer stepped it down.* **3.** To leave a job as an official or some other important position. *When the judge became ill, he had to step down.*

step on it or **step on the gas** v. phr. **1.** To push down on the gas pedal to make a car go faster. *Be very careful when you step on the gas. Don't go too fast.* **2.** *informal* To go

faster; hurry. *Step on it, o we'll be late for school. Joh is a slow starter, but he ca step on the gas when it look as if he might lose the rac Lee was wasting time breakfast and his father tol him to step on it or the would miss the bus.*

step on one's toes or **tread o one's toes** v. phr. To d something that embarrasses offends someone else. *If yo break in when other peop are talking, you may step o their toes. Mary is pretty, an she often treads on the toes the girls by stealing their boy friends.*

step up v. **1.** To go from lower to a higher place. *Joh stepped up onto the platfor and began to speak.* **2.** To com towards or near; approach. *Th sergeant called for volunteer and Private Jones stepped up volunteer. John waited until th teacher had finished speakir to Mary, and then he steppe up.* **3.** To go or to make (some thing) go faster or more ac tively. *When John found h was going to be late, he steppe up his pace. After we ha reached the outskirts of tow we stepped up the engine. Th enemy was near, and the arm stepped up its patrols to fin them before they got too clos.* **4.** To rise to a higher or mo important position; be pr moted. *This year Mary is secre tary of the club, but I am sur she will step up to presiden next year.*

stew in one's own juice v. phr informal To suffer fro something that you hav caused to happen yourself. *John lied to Tom, but Tom found out. Now Tom is making John stew in his own juice. I warned you not to steal those apples. You got caught, and you can stew in your own juice.*

tick around *v., informal* To stay or wait nearby. *John's father told him to stick around and they would go fishing. After work Mr. Harris stuck around to ride home with his friend.*

tick-in-the-mud *n., informal* An over-careful person; someone who is old-fashioned and fights change. *Mabel said her mother was a real stick-in-the-mud to make a rule that she must be home by 10 o'clock on weeknights and 11:30 Saturdays. Mr. Thomas is a stick-in-the-mud who plows with mules; he won't buy a tractor.*

tick one's neck out *or* **stick one's chin out** *v. phr., informal* To do something dangerous or risky. *When I was in trouble, Paul was the only one who would stick his neck out to help me. John is always sticking his chin out by saying something he shouldn't.*

tick to one's guns *or* **stand by one's guns** *v. phr.* To hold to an aim or an opinion even though people try to stop you or say you are wrong. *People laughed at Columbus when he said the world was round. He stuck to his guns and proved he was right. At first the boss would not give Jane the raise in pay she wanted, but she stood by her guns and he gave it to her.*

stick up *v., informal* To rob with a gun. *When the messenger left the bank, a man jumped out of an alley and stuck him up. In the old West, outlaws sometimes stuck up the stagecoaches.*

stick-up *n., informal* A robbery by a man with a gun. *Mr. Smith was the victim of a stick-up last night.*

stick with *v., informal* **1.** *or* **stay with** To continue doing; not quit. *Fred stayed with his homework until it was done. Practicing is tiresome, but stick with it and some day you will be a good pianist.* **2.** To stay with; not leave. *Stick with me until we get out of the crowd. For two months Bill's boss could not pay his salary, but Bill stuck with him because he thought the company would soon succeed.* **3.** To sell (someone) something poor or worthless; cheat. *Father said that the man in the store tried to stick him with a bad TV set.* **4.** To leave (someone) with (something unpleasant); force to do or keep something because others cannot or will not.— Usually used in the passive. *When Harry and I went to the store to buy ice cream cones, Harry ran out with his cone without paying and I was stuck with paying for it. Mary didn't wash the dishes before she left so I'm stuck with it. Mr. Jones bought a house that is too big and expensive, but now he's stuck with it.*

stick with *v. phr.* To unfairly thrust upon; encumber one with. *In the restaurant my* friends stuck me with the bill although it was supposed to be Dutch treat.

sticky fingers *n. phr.*, *slang* **1.** The habit of stealing things you see and want. *Don't leave money in your locker; some of the boys have sticky fingers. Don't leave that girl alone in the room with so many valuable objects around, because she has sticky fingers.* **2.** Ability to catch a ball, especially football forward passes. *Jack is very tall and has sticky fingers. He is an end on the football team.*

stir up *v.* **1.** To bring (something) into being, often by great exertion or activity; cause. *It was a quiet afternoon, and John tried to stir up some excitement. Bob stirred up a fight between Tom and Bill.* **2.** To cause (someone) to act; incite to action or movement; rouse. *The coach's pep talk stirred up the team to win. When Mary heard what Betty said about her, she became stirred up.*

stir up a hornet's nest *v. phr.* To make many people angry; do something that many people don't like. *The principal stirred up a hornet's nest by changing the rules at school.*

stone-broke *or* **dead broke** *or* **flat broke** *adj.*, *informal* having no money; penniless. *Jill wanted to go to the movies but she was stone-broke. The man gambled and was soon flat broke.*

stop cold *or* **stop dead** *or* **stop in one's tracks** *v. phr.*, *informal* To stop very quickly or with great force. *The hunter pulled* the trigger and stopped the deer cold. When I saw Mary on the street, I was so surprised I stopped dead. The deer heard a noise and he stopped in his tracks.

stop off *v.* To stop at a place for a short time while going somewhere. *We stopped off after school at the soda fountain before going home. On our trip to California we stopped off in Las Vegas for two days.*

stop over *v.* To stay at a place overnight or for some other short time while on a trip else where. *When we came back from California, we stopped over one night near the Grand Canyon.*

straight from the horse's mouth *slang* Directly from the person or place where it began, from a reliable source or a person that cannot be doubted. *They are going to be married. I got the news straight from the horse's mouth—their minister. John found out about the painting straight from the horse's mouth, from the painter himself.*

straw in the wind *n. phr.* A small sign of what may happen. *The doctor's worried face was a straw in the wind. The quickly called meeting of the President and his cabinet was a straw in the wind.*

straw poll *n. phr.* An informal survey taken in order to get an opinion. *The results of our straw poll show that most faculty members prefer to teach between 9 and 11 A.M.*

strike it rich *v. phr.*, *informal* **1.** To discover oil, or a large vein minerals to be mined, or a buried treasure. *The old prospector panned gold for years before he struck it rich.* **2.** To become rich or successful suddenly or without expecting to. *Everyone wanted to buy one of the new gadgets, and their inventor struck it rich. John did not know that he had a rich Uncle John in Australia. John struck it rich when his uncle left the money to John.*

strike one funny *v. phr.* To appear or seem laughable, curious, ironic, or entertaining. *"It strikes me funny," he said, "that you should refuse my invitation to visit my chateau in France. After all, you love both red wine and old castles."*

strike out *v.* **1.** To destroy something that has been written or drawn by drawing a line across through it or by erasing it. *John misspelled "corolly." He struck it out and wrote it correctly.* **2.** To begin to follow a new path or a course of action that you have never tried. *The boy scouts struck out at daybreak over the mountain pass. John quit his job and struck out on his own as a traveling salesman.* **3.** To put (a batter) out of play by making him miss the ball three times; *also:* To be put out of play by missing the ball three times. *The pitcher struck out three men in the game. The batter struck out twice.* **4.** To push out an arm suddenly in a hitting motion. *The boxer saw his chance and struck out at his opponent's jaw.*

string along *v., informal* **1.** To deceive; fool; lead on dishon-

estly. *Mary was stringing John along for years but she didn't mean to marry him. George told the new boy that he must always call the teacher "Sir," but the new boy soon saw that George was stringing him along.* **2.** To follow someone's leadership; join his group. *Those of you who want to learn about wild flowers, string along with Jake.*

string out *v.* To make (something) extend over a great distance or a long stretch of time. *The telephone poles were strung out along the road as far as we could see. Mary and Ann did not have much to say but they did not want to go home. They strung out their gossip for a long time.*

stuck on *slang* Very much in love with; crazy about. *Judy thinks she is very pretty and very smart. She is stuck on herself. Lucy is stuck on the football captain.*

stuck-up *adj., informal* Acting as if other people are not as good as you are; conceited; snobbish. *Mary is very stuck-up, and will not speak to the poor children in her class.*

stuck with *adj. phr.* Left in a predicament; left having to take care of a problem caused by another. *Our neighbors vanished without a trace and we got stuck with their cat and dog.*

sucker list *n., slang* A list of easily fooled people, especially people who are easily persuaded to buy things or give money. *The crook got hold of a sucker list and started out to sell his worthless stock. Mr. Smith gets so many advertise-*

ments in his mail that he says he is on every sucker list in the country.

sugar daddy *n.*, *slang*, *semi-vulgar*, *avoidable* An older, well-to-do man, who gives money and gifts to a younger woman or girls usually in exchange for sexual favors. *Betty Morgan got a mink coat from her sugar daddy.*

sum up *v.* To put something into a few words; shorten into a brief summary; summarize. *The teacher summed up the lesson in three rules. The mailman's job, in all kinds of weather, is summed up in the phrase "Deliver the mail."*

sunbelt *n.*, *informal* A portion of the southern United States where the winter is very mild in comparison to other states. *The Simpsons left Chicago for the sunbelt because of Jeff's rheumatism.*

sunny-side up *adj.* Fried on one side only. *Barbara likes her eggs sunny-side up.*

sure thing 1. *n.*, *informal* Something sure to happen; something about which there is no doubt. *It's no fun betting on a sure thing.*—**sure thing 2.** *adv.* Of course; certainly. *Sure thing, I'll be glad to do it for you.*

swallow one's pride *v. phr.* To bring your pride under control; humble yourself. *After Bill lost the race, he swallowed his pride and shook hands with the winner.*

swallow one's words To speak unclearly; fail to put enough breath into your words. *Phyllis was hard to understand because she swallowed her words.*

swear by *v.* **1.** To use as support or authority that wh you are saying is truthful; ta an oath upon. *A witness swe by the Bible that he will tell truth. In ancient Greece a d tor swore by Apollo, the god healing, that he would be good doctor. John swore by honor he would return the bi* **2.** To have complete cor dence in; be sure of; trust co pletely. *When John has to somewhere fast, he swears his bike to get there. We can sure that Fred will come time, since his friend T swears by him.*

swear in or **swear into** *v.* have a person swear or pro ise to do his duty as a memb or an officer of an organi tion, government departme or similar group.—*Swear i is used when the name of group is given. Mary and A will be sworn into the cl tonight. Fred was sworn in class president. Many new m were sworn into the army l month. At the inaugurati the Chief Justice of the preme Court swore in the n President.*

swear off *v.*, *informal* To g up something you like or y have got in the habit of us by making a promise. *M swore off candy until she ten pounds. John has sworn dessert for Lent.*

swear out *v.* To get (a writ order to do something) swearing that a person has b ken the law. *The policem swore out a warrant for the s pect's arrest. The detecti swore out a search warrant.*

sweat blood v. phr., slang **1.** To be very much worried. *The engine of the airplane stopped, and the pilot sweated blood as he glided to a safe landing.* **2.** To work very hard. *Jim sweated blood to finish his composition on time.*

sweat out v., informal To wait anxiously; worry while waiting. *Karl was sweating out the results of the college exams. The search plane signaled that help was on the way. The men in the lifeboat just had to sweat it out.*

sweep off one's feet v. phr. To make (someone) have feelings as love or happiness) too strong to control; overcome with strong feeling; win sudden and complete acceptance by (someone) through the feelings. *The handsome football captain swept Joan off her feet when he said so many things to her at the dance. Joan was swept off her feet when the football captain started flirting with her. Mary is swept off her feet whenever she hears a band start playing. John was swept off his feet when he won the contest.*

sweep under the rug v. phr. To hide or dismiss casually (something one is ashamed of or does not know what to do about). *In many places, drug abuse by school children is swept under the rug.*

sweetie pie n., informal A person who is loved; darling; sweetheart. *Arnold blushed with pleasure when Annie* called him her sweetie pie. Nancy is Bill's sweetie pie.

sweet on adj. phr., informal In love with; very fond of. *John is sweet on Alice.*

sweet talk 1. n., informal Too much praise; flattery. *Sometimes a girl's better judgment is overcome by sweet talk.* **2.** v., informal To get what you want by great praise; flatter. *Polly could sweet talk her husband into anything.*

sweet tooth n. phr. A great weakness or predilection for sweets. *Sue has such a sweet tooth that she hardly eats anything else but cake.*

swelled head n., informal A feeling that you are very important or more important than you really are. *When John won the race, he got a swelled head. Pretty girls shouldn't get a swelled head about it.*—**swelled-headed** adj. phr. *After he was elected captain of the team, Bob became swell-headed.*

swim against the current or **swim against the stream** v. phr. To do the opposite of what most people want to do; go against the way things are happening; struggle upstream. *The boy who tries to succeed today without an education is swimming against the stream.*

switched on adj., slang **1.** In tune with the latest fads, ideas, and fashions. *I dig Sarah, she is really switched on.* **2.** Stimulated; as if under the influence of alcohol or drugs. *How come you're talking so fast? Are you switched on or something?*

T

tail between one's legs *n. phr.* State of feeling beaten, ashamed, or very obedient, as after a scolding or a whipping. *The army sent the enemy home with their tails between their legs. The boys on the team had boasted they would win the tournament, but they went home with their tails between their legs.* [So called because a beaten dog usually puts his tail down between his legs and slinks away.]

take a back seat *v. phr., informal* To accept a poorer or lower position; be second to something or someone else. *During the war all manufacturing had to take a back seat to military needs. She does not have to take a back seat to any singer alive.*

take a bath *v. phr., informal* To come to financial ruin. *Boy, did we ever take a bath on that merger with Brown & Brown, Inc.*

take a dim view of *v. phr.* **1.** To have doubts about; feel unsure or anxious about. *Tom took a dim view of his chances of passing the exam. Betty hoped to go on a picnic, but she took a dim view of the weather.* **2.** To be against; disapprove. *John's father took a dim view of his wanting to borrow the car. The teacher took a dim view of the class's behavior.*

take advantage of *v. phr.* **1.** To make good use of. *The cat took advantage of the high grass t creep up on the bird. Jean too advantage of the lunch hour t finish her homework.* **2.** T treat (someone) unfairly fo your own gain or help; mak unfair use of. *He took advan tage of his friend's kindnes The little children did not kno how much to pay for the cand and Ralph took advantage them.*

take after *v.* To be like be cause of family relationship; t have the same looks or ways a (a parent or ancestor). *H takes after his father in mathe matical ability. She takes afte her father's side of the family i looks.*

take a shine to *v. phr., slan* To have or show a quick likin for. *He took a shine to his ne teacher the very first day.*

take a shot at *v. phr.* To tr casually; attempt to do. *"Ca you handle all these new boo orders?" Tom asked. "I haven done it before," Sally replie "but I can sure take a shot it."*

take back *v.* To change o deny something offered, prom ised, or stated; admit to mak ing a wrong statement. *I tak back my offer to buy the hou now that I've had a good loo at it. I want you to take back th unkind things you said abo Kenneth.*

take by storm *v. phr.* **1.** To ca ture by a sudden or very bo

282

attack. *The army did not hesitate. They took the town by storm.* **2.** To win the favor or liking of; make (a group of people) like or believe you. *The comic took the audience by storm. John gave Jane so much attention that he took her by storm, and she said she would marry him.*

take care of *v. phr.* **1.** To attend to; supply the needs of. *She stayed home to take care of the baby.* **2.** *informal* To deal with; do what is needed with. *I will take care of that letter. The coach told Jim to take care of the opposing player.*

take down *v.* **1.** To write or record (what is said). *I will tell you how to get to the place; you had better take it down.* **2.** To pull to pieces; take apart. *It will be a big job to take that tree down. In the evening the campers put up a tent, and the next morning they took it down.* **3.** *informal* To reduce the pride or spirit of; humble. *Bob thought he was a good wrestler, but Henry took him down.*

take down a notch or **take down a peg** *v. phr.*, *informal* To make (someone) less proud or sure of himself. *The team was feeling proud of its record, but last week the boys were taken down a peg by a bad defeat.*

take effect *v. phr.* **1.** To have an unexpected or intended result; cause a change. *It was nearly an hour before the sleeping pill took effect.* **2.** To become lawfully right, or operative. *The new tax law will not take effect until January.*

take exception to *v. phr.* To speak against; find fault with;

be displeased or angered by; criticize. *There was nothing in the speech that you could take exception to. Did she take exception to my remarks about her cooking.*

take for *v.* To suppose to be; mistake for. *Do you take me for a fool? At first sight you would take him for a football player, not a poet.*

take for a ride *v. phr.*, *slang* **1.** To take out in a car intending to murder. *The gang leader decided that the informer must be taken for a ride.* **2.** To play a trick on; fool. *The girls told Linda that a movie star was visiting the school, but she did not believe them; she thought they were taking her for a ride.* **3.** To take unfair advantage of; fool for your own gain. *His girlfriend really took him for a ride before he stopped dating her.*

take for granted *v. phr.* **1.** To suppose or understand to be true. *Mr. Harper took for granted that the invitation included his wife. A teacher cannot take it for granted that students always do their homework.* **2.** To accept or become used to (something) without noticing especially or saying anything. *George took for granted all that his parents did for him. No girl likes to have her boyfriend take her for granted; instead, he should always try to make her like him better.*

take heart *v. phr.* To be encouraged; feel braver and want to try. *The men took heart from their leader's words and went on to win the battle. When we* *are in trouble we can take heart from the fact that things often seem worse than they are.*

take ill *or* **take sick** *v.* To become sick. *Father took sick just before his birthday.*—Used in the passive with the same meaning. *The man was taken ill on the train.*

take in *v.* **1.** To include. *The country's boundaries were changed to take in a piece of land beyond the river. The class of mammals takes in nearly all warm-blooded animals except the birds.* **2.** To go and see; visit. *The students decided to take in a movie while they were in town. We planned to take in Niagara Falls and Yellowstone Park on our trip.* **3.** To make smaller. *This waistband is too big; it must be taken in about an inch. They had to take in some sail to keep the ship from turning over in the storm.* **4.** To grasp with the mind; understand. *He didn't take in what he read because his mind was on something else. He took in the situation at a glance.* **5a.** To deceive; cheat; fool. *The teacher was taken in by the boy's innocent manner.* **5b.** To accept without question; believe. *The magician did many tricks, and the children took it all in.* **6a.** To receive; get. *The senior class held a dance to make money and took in over a hundred dollars.* **6b.** Let come in; admit. *The farmer took in the lost travelers for the night. When her husband died, Mrs. Smith took in boarders.* **7.** To see or hear with interest; pay close attention to. *When Bill told about his adventures, the other boys took it all in.*

take in stride *v. phr.* To meet happenings without too much surprise; accept good or bad luck and go on. *He learned to take disappointments in stride.*

take it *v. phr.* **1.** To get an idea or impression; understand from what is said or done.—Usually used with *I. I take it from your silence that you don't want to go.* **2.** *informal* To bear trouble, hard work, criticism; not give up or weaken. *Henry could criticize and tease other boys, but he couldn't take it himself. Bob lost his job and his girl in the same week, and we all admired the way he took it.*

take it easy *v. phr., informal* **1.** *or* **go easy** *or* **take things easy** To go or act slowly, carefully, and gently.—Often used with *on. Take it easy. The roads are icy. "Go easy," said Billy to the other boys carrying the table down the stairs. "Take it easy on John and don't scold him too much," said Mrs. Jones to Mr. Jones. Go easy on the cake. There isn't much left.* **2.** *or* **take things easy** To avoid hard work or worry; have an easy time; live in comfort. *The doctor said that Bob would have to take things easy for awhile after he had his tonsils out. Barbara likes to take it easy. Grandfather will retire from his job next year and take things easy. Mr. Wilson has just made a lot of money and can take things easy now.*

take it on the chin *v. phr., informal* **1.** To be badly beaten or hurt. *Our football team* *really took it on the chin today. They are all bumps and bruises. Mother and I took it on the chin in the card game.* **2.** To accept without complaint something bad that happens to you; accept trouble or defeat calmly. *A good football player can take it on the chin when his team loses.*

take it out on *v. phr., informal* To be unpleasant or unkind to (someone) because you are angry or upset; get rid of upset feelings by being mean to.—Often used with the name of the feeling instead of "it." *The teacher was angry and took it out on the class. Bob was angry because Father would not let him use the car, and he took it out on his little brother.*

take its toll *v. phr.* To cause loss or damage. *The bombs had taken their toll on the little town. The budget cut took its toll of teachers.*

take kindly to *v.* To be pleased by; like.—Usually used in negative, interrogative, and conditional sentences. *He doesn't take kindly to any suggestions about running his business. Will your father take kindly to the idea of your leaving college?*

take leave of *v. phr.* To abandon, go away from, or become separated from.—Usually used in the phrase *take leave of one's senses. Come down from the roof, Billy! Have you taken leave of your senses?*

take liberties *v. phr.* To act toward in too close or friendly a manner; use as you would use a close friend or something of

your own. *Mary would not let any boy take liberties with her. Bill took liberties with Tom's bicycle.*

taken aback *also* **taken back** *adj.* Unpleasantly surprised; suddenly puzzled or shocked. *When he came to pay for his dinner he was taken aback to find that he had left his wallet at home.*

takeoff *n.* **1.** Departure of an airplane; the act of becoming airborne. *The nervous passenger was relieved that we had such a wonderfully smooth takeoff.* **2.** Imitation; a parody. *Vaughn Meader used to do a wonderful takeoff on President Kennedy's speech.*

take off *v. phr.* **1a.** To leave fast; depart suddenly; run away. *The dog took off after a rabbit.* **1b.** *informal* To go away; leave. *The six boys got into the car and took off for the drug store.* **2.** To leave on a flight, begin going up. *A helicopter is able to take off and land straight up or down.* **3.** *informal* To imitate amusingly; copy another person's habitual actions or speech. *He made a career of taking off famous people for nightclub audiences. At the party, Charlie took off the principal and some of the teachers.* **4.** To take (time) to be absent from work. *When his wife was sick he took off from work. Bill was tired out so he took the day off.*

take off one's hat to *v. phr.* To give honor, praise, and respect to. *He is my enemy, but I take off my hat to him for his courage.*

take on v. **1.** To receive for carrying; be loaded with. *A big ship was at the dock taking on automobiles in crates to carry overseas for sale. The bus driver stopped at the curb to take the woman on.* **2.** To begin to have (the look of); take (the appearance of). *Others joined the fistfight until it took on the look of a riot. After the students put up Christmas decorations, the classroom took on a holiday appearance.* **3a.** To give a job to; hire; employ. *The factory has opened and is beginning to take on new workers.* **3b.** To accept in business or a contest. *The big man took on two opponents at once. After his father died, Bill took on the management of the factory. We knew their football team was bigger and stronger, but we took them on anyway and beat them.* **4.** *informal* To show great excitement, grief, or anger. *At the news of her husband's death she took on like a madwoman.*

take one's medicine v. phr. To accept punishment without complaining. *The boy said he was sorry he broke the window and was ready to take his medicine.*

take one's time v. phr. To avoid haste; act in an unhurried way. *He liked to take his time over breakfast. It is better to take your time at this job than to hurry and make mistakes.*

take out v. phr. **1.** To ask for and fill in. *Mary and John took out a marriage license.* **2.** To

begin to run. *When the window broke, the boys took out in all directions. When the wind blew the man's hat off, Charlie took out after it.*

take over v. **1a.** To take control or possession of. *He expects to take over the business when his father retires.* **1b.** To take charge or responsibility. *The airplane pilot fainted and his co-pilot had to take over.* **2.** To borrow, imitate, or adopt. *The Japanese have taken over many European ways of life.*

take place v. phr. To happen; occur. *The accident took place only a block from his home. The action of the play takes place in ancient Rome. The dance will take place after the graduation exercises.*

take sides v. phr. To join one group against another in a debate or quarrel. *Switzerland refused to take sides in the two World Wars. Tom wanted to go fishing. Dick wanted to take a hike. Bob took sides with Tom so they all went fishing.*

take steps v. phr. To begin to make plans or arrangements; make preparations; give orders.—Usually used with *to* and an infinitive. *The city is taking steps to replace its streetcars with busses.*

take stock v. phr. **1.** To count exactly the items of merchandise or supplies in stock; take inventory. *The grocery store took stock every week on Monday mornings.* **2.** To study carefully a situation, or a number of possibilities or opportunities. *During the battle the* commander paused to take stock of the situation.

take stock in v. phr., informal To have faith in; trust; believe.—Usually used in the negative. *He took no stock in the idea that women were better cooks than men. They took little or no stock in the boy's story that he had lost the money. Do you take any stock in the gossip about Joan?*

take the bull by the horns v. phr., informal To take definite action and not care about risks; act bravely in a difficulty. *He decided to take the bull by the horns and raise in salary even though it might cost him his job.*

take the edge off also **take off the edge** v. phr. To lessen, weaken, soften or make dull. *Eating a candy bar before dinner has taken the edge off Becky's appetite. Bob was sorry for hurting Tom and that took the edge off Tom's anger. A headache took the edge off Dick's pleasure in the movie.*

take the fifth v. phr., informal 1. Taking refuge behind the Fifth Amendment of the Constitution of the United States which guarantees any witness the right not to incriminate himself while testifying at a trial. *Alger Hiss took the Fifth when asked whether he was a member of the Communist Party.* 2. Not to answer any question in an informal setting. *Have you been married before?—I take the Fifth.*

take the rap v. phr., slang To receive punishment; to be ac-

cused and punished. *All of the boys took apples, but only John took the rap. Joe took the burglary rap for his brother and went to prison for two years.*

take the words out of one's mouth v. phr. To say what another is just going to say; to put another's thought into words.—*"Let's go to the beach tomorrow." "You took the words right out of my mouth; I was thinking of that." I was going to suggest a movie, but she took the words out of my mouth and said she would like to see one.*

take to v. 1. To go to or into; get yourself quickly to.—Often used in the imperative. *Take to the hills! The bandits are coming! We took to the woods during the day so no one would see us. Take to the boats! The ship is sinking. We stopped at a hotel for the night but took to the road again the next morning.* 2. To begin the work or job of; make a habit of. *He took to repairing watches in his spare time. She took to knitting when she got older. Grandfather took to smoking cigars when he was young and he still smokes them. Uncle Willie took to drink while he was a sailor. The cat took to jumping on the table at mealtime.* 3. To learn easily; do well at. *Father tried to teach John to swim, but John didn't take to it. Mary takes to mathematics like a duck takes to water.* 4. To like at first meeting; be pleased by or attracted to; accept quickly. *Our dog always takes to children* *quickly. Mary didn't take kindly to the new rule that her mother made of being home at 6 o'clock.*

take to task *v. phr.* To reprove or scold for a fault or error. *He took his wife to task for her foolish wastefulness. The principal took Bill to task for breaking the window.*

take to the cleaners *v. phr., slang* **1.** To win all the money another person has (as in poker). *Watch out if you play poker with Joe; he'll take you to the cleaners.* **2.** To cheat a person out of his money and possessions by means of a crooked business transaction or other means of dishonest conduct. *I'll never forgive myself for becoming associated with Joe; he took me to the cleaners.*

take to the woods *v. phr., informal* To run away and hide. *When John saw the girls coming, he took to the woods. Bob took to the woods so he would not have to mow the grass.*

take turns *v. phr.* To do something one after another instead of doing it all at the same time. *In class we should not talk all at the same time; we should take turns. Jean and Beth took turns on the swing. The two boys took turns at digging the hole. The three men took turns driving so one would not be too tired.*

take up *v.* **1.** To remove by taking in. *Use a blotter to take up the spilled ink. When the vacuum cleaner bag is full, it will not take up dirt from the rug.* **2.** To fill or to occupy. *All his evenings were taken up with study. The oceans take up the greater*

part of the earth's surface. The mayor has taken up residence on State Street. **3.** To gather together; collect. *We are taking up a collection to buy flowers for John because he is in the hospital.* **4.** To take away. *John had his driver's license taken up for speeding.* **5a.** To begin; start. *The teacher took up the lesson where she left off yesterday.* **5b.** To begin to do or learn; go into as a job or hobby. *He recently took up gardening. He took up the carpenter's trade as a boy.* **6.** To pull and make tight or shorter; shorten. *The tailor took up the legs of the trousers. Take up the slack on the rope!* **7.** To take or accept something that is offered. *The boss offered me a $5 raise and I took him up. I took John up on his bet.*

take up arms *v. phr., literary.* To get ready to fight; fight or make war. *The people were quick to take up arms to defend their freedom. The President called on people to take up arms against poverty.*

take with a grain of salt *also* **take with a pinch of salt** *v. phr.* To accept or believe only in part; not accept too much. *A man who says he is not a candidate for President should usually have his statement taken with a grain of salt. We took Uncle George's stories of the war with a pinch of salt.*

talk back *also* **answer back** *v., informal* To answer rudely; reply in a disrespectful way; be fresh. *When the teacher told the boy to sit down, he talked back to her and said she couldn't make him. Mary talked back* when her mother told her to stop watching television; she said, "I don't have to if I don't want to." Russell was going somewhere with some bad boys, when his father told him it was wrong, Russell answered him back, "Mind your own business."

talk big v., informal To talk boastfully; brag. He talks big about his pitching, but he hasn't won a game.

talk down v. 1. To make (someone) silent by talking louder or longer. Sue tried to give her ideas, but the other girls talked her down. 2. To use words or ideas that are too easy. The speaker talked down to the students, and they were bored.

talk into v. 1. To get (someone) to agree to; make (someone) decide on (doing something) by talking; persuade to.—Used with a verbal noun. Bob talked us into walking home with him. 2. To cause to be in or to get into by talking. You talked us into this mess. Now get us out! Mr. Jones lost the customer in his store by arguing with him. "You'll talk us into the poor house yet!" said Mrs. Jones.

talk out v. To talk all about and leave nothing out; discuss until everything is agreed on; settle. After their quarrel, Jill and John talked things out and reached full agreement.

talk out of v. 1. To persuade not to; make agree or decide not to.—Used with a verbal noun. Mary's mother talked her out of quitting school. 2. To allow to go or get out by talking; let escape by talking.

Johnny is good at talking his way out of trouble.

talk over v. 1. To talk together about; try to agree about or decide by talking; discuss. Tom talked his plan over with his father before he bought the car. The boys settled their argument by talking it over. 2. To persuade; make agree or willing; talk and change the mind of. Fred is trying to talk Bill over to our side.

talk shop v. phr., informal To talk about things in your work or trade. Two chemists were talking shop, and I hardly understood a word they said.

talk through one's hat v. phr., informal To say something without knowing or understanding the facts; talk foolishly or ignorantly. John said that the earth is nearer the sun in summer, but the teacher said he was talking through his hat.

talk up v. 1. To speak in favor or support of. Let's talk up the game and get a big crowd. 2. To speak plainly or clearly. The teacher asked the student to talk up. 3. informal To say what you want or think; say what someone may not like. Talk up if you want more pie. George isn't afraid to talk up when he disagrees with the teacher.

tan one's hide v. phr., informal To give a beating to; spank hard. Bob's father tanned his hide for staying out too late.

taper off v. 1. To come to an end little by little; become smaller toward the end. The river tapers off here and becomes a brook. 2. To stop a habit gradually; do something less and less often. Robert gave *up smoking all at once instead of tapering off.*

tar and feather *v.* To pour heated tar on and cover with feathers as a punishment. *In the Old West bad men were sometimes tarred and feathered and driven out of town.*

tear down *v.* **1.** To take all down in pieces; destroy. *The workmen tore down the old house and built a new house in its place.* **2.** To take to pieces or parts. *The mechanics had to tear down the engine, and fix it, and put it together again.* **3.** To say bad things about; criticize. *"Why do you always tear people down? Why don't you try to say nice things about them?" Dorothy doesn't like Sandra, and at the class meeting she tore down every idea Sandra suggested.*

tell it like it is *v. phr., slang, informal* To be honest, sincere; to tell the truth. *Joe is the leader of our commune; he tells it like it is.*

tell it to the marines *or* **tell it to Sweeney** *slang* I don't believe you; stop trying to fool me. *John said, "My father knows the President of the United States." Dick answered, "Tell it to the marines."*

tell off *v.* **1.** To name or count one by one and give some special duty to; give a share to. *Five boy scouts were told off to clean the camp.* **2.** *informal* To speak to angrily or sharply; attack with words; scold. *Mr. Black got angry and told off the boss. Bobby kept pulling Sally's hair; finally she got angry and told him where to get off.*

tell on *v.* **1.** To tire; wear out; make weak. *The ten-mile hike told on Bill.* **2.** *informal* To tell someone about another's wrong or naughty acts.—Used mainly by children. *Andy hit a little girl and John told the teacher on Andy. If you hit me, I'll tell Mother on you.*

tempest in a teapot *n. phr.* Great excitement about something not important. *Bess tore her skirt a little and made a tempest in a teapot.*

that'll be the day *informal* That will never happen. *Joe wanted me to lend him money to take my girl to the movies. That'll be the day! "Wouldn't it be nice if we had to go to school only one day a week?" "That'll be the day!"*

the creeps *n., informal* **1.** An uncomfortable tightening of the skin caused by fear or shock. *Reading the story of a ghost gave Joe the creeps. The queer noises in the old house gave Mary the creeps.* **2.** A strong feeling of fear or disgust. *The cold, damp, lonely swamp gave John the creeps. The dog was so ugly it gave Mary the creeps.*

the lid *n., slang* Something that holds back or holds out of sight. *The police blew the lid off the gambling operations. John kept the lid on his plans until he was ready to run for class president. The chief of police placed the lid on gambling in the town.*

the pits *n., slang* **1.** A low class, blighted and ill-maintained place, motel room or apartment. *Max, this motel is the pits, I will not sleep here!* **2.**

he end of the road, the point
f no return, the point of total
uin of one's health (from the
rug anticulture referring to
he arm-pits as the only place
hat had veins for injections).
*John flunked high school this
ear for the third time; he will
ever get to college; it's the pits
or him.* **3.** A very depressed
tate of mind. *Poor Marcy is
own in the pits over her recent
ivorce.*

e ropes n. plural, informal
Thorough or special knowl-
dge of a job; how to do some-
hing; the ways of people or
he world. *On a newspaper a
ub reporter learns his job from
n older reporter who knows
he ropes. When you go to a
ew school it takes a while to
earn the ropes. Betty showed
ane the ropes when she was
earning to make a dress. Mr.
ones was an orphan and he
ad to learn the ropes when he
as young to make his way in
he world.*

e score n., slang The truth;
he real story or information;
what is really happening; the
vay people and the world re-
lly are. *Very few people know
he score in politics. You are
oo young to know the score
et. What's the score anyhow?
When will the program begin?*

e tracks n. The line between
he rich or fashionable part of
own and the poor or unfash-
onable part of town. *The poor
hildren knew they would not
e welcome on the other side of
he tracks. Mary's mother did
ot want her to date Jack, be-
ause he came from across the
racks.*—Often used in the ex-

pression *the wrong side of the
tracks. The mayor was born on
the wrong side of the tracks, but
he worked hard and became
successful.*

the works n., plural, slang **1.**
Everything that can be had or
that you have; everything of
this kind, all that goes with it.
*When the tramp found $100, he
went into a fine restaurant and
ordered the works with a steak
dinner.* **2.** Rough handling or
treatment; a bad beating or
scolding; killing; murder.—
Usually used with *get* or *give.
The boy said that Joe was going
to get the works if he ever came
back to that neighborhood
again. The newspaper gave the
police department the works
when they let the burglars get
away. The gangster told his
friend he would give him the
works if he double-crossed him.*

think aloud or **think out loud** v.
To say what you are thinking.
*"I wish I had more money for
Christmas presents," Father
thought aloud. "What did you
say?" said Mother. Father answered, "I'm sorry. I wasn't
talking to you. I was thinking
out loud."*

think better of v. To change
your mind about; to consider
again and make a better decision about. *John told his
mother he wanted to leave
school, but later he thought better of it.*

think little of v. phr. Think
that (something or someone) is
not important or valuable.
*John thought little of Ted's plan
for the party. Joan thought little
of walking two miles to school.*

think nothing of v. phr. To

think or consider easy, simple, or usual. *Jim thinks nothing of hiking ten miles in one day.*

think out *v.* **1.** To find out or discover by thinking; study and understand. *Andy thought out a way of climbing to the top of the pole.* **2.** To think through to the end; to understand what would come at last. *Bill wanted to quit school, but he thought out the matter and decided not to.*

think over *v.* To think carefully about; consider; study. *When Charles asked Betty to marry him, she asked him for time to think it over. Think over what we studied in history this year and write a lesson on the thing that interested you most.*

think piece *n., slang* **1.** The human brain. *Lou's got one powerful think piece, man.* **2.** Any provocative essay or article that, by stating a strong opinion, arouses the reader to think about it and react to it by agreeing or disagreeing. *That article by Charles Fenyvesi on Vietnamese refugees in the Washington Post sure was a think piece!*

think twice *v.* To think again carefully; reconsider; hesitate. *The teacher advised Lou to think twice before deciding to quit school.*

think up *v.* To invent or discover by thinking; have a new idea of. *Mary thought up a funny game for the children to play.*

third world *n.* **1.** The countries not aligned with either the former U.S.S.R.-dominated Communist bloc or the U.S.A.-dominated capitalist countries. *New Zealand made a move toward third country status when it disallowed American nuclear submarines in its harbors.* **2.** The developing nations of the world where the industrial revolution has not yet been completed. *Africa and the rest of the third world must be freed from starvation and illiteracy.*

three sheets in the wind *or* **three sheets to the wind** *adj. phr. informal* Unsteady from too much liquor; drunk. *The sailor came down the street, three sheets in the wind.*

through the mill *adv. phr.* **1.** Experienced. *You could tell immediately that the new employee had been through the mill.* **2.** Through real experience of the difficulties of a certain way of life. *Poor Jerry had had three operations in one year, and now he's back in the hospital. He's really gone through the mill.*

through thick and thin *adv. phr.* Through all difficulties and troubles; through good times and bad times. *The friends were faithful through thick and thin. George stayed in college through thick and thin because he wanted an education.*

throw a curve *v. phr., slang, informal* **1.** To mislead or deceive someone; to lie. *John threw me a curve about the hiring.* **2.** To take someone by surprise in an unpleasant way. *Mr. Weiner's announcement threw the whole company a curve.*

throw a monkey wrench *or* **throw a wrench** *v. phr., infor-*

mal To cause something that is going smoothly to stop. *The game was going smoothly until you threw a monkey wrench into the works by fussing about the rules. The Michigan tacklers threw a wrench into the Wisconsin team's offense. He hoped to see the class plan fail and looked for a chance to throw a wrench in the machinery.*

throw away v. **1.** To get rid of as unwanted or not needed; junk. *Before they moved they threw away everything they didn't want to take with them. I never save those coupons; I just throw them away.* **2.** To waste. *The senator criticized the government for throwing away billions on the space program.* **3.** To fail to make use of. *She threw away a good chance for a better job.*

throw down the gauntlet v. phr. To challenge, especially to a fight. *Another candidate for the presidency has thrown down the gauntlet.*

throw in v. To give or put in as an addition; to give to or with something else. *John threw in a couple of tires when he sold Bill his bicycle. Mary and Tess were talking about the prom, and Joan threw in that she was going with Fred.*

throw in one's lot with or literary **cast in one's lot with** v. phr. To decide to share or take part in anything that happens to; join. *The thief decided to throw in his lot with the gang when he heard their plans. Washington was rich, but he decided to cast in his lot with the colonies against Britain. When Carl was old enough to vote, he threw in his lot with the Democrats.*

throw in the sponge or **throw up the sponge** or **throw in the towel** v. phr., informal To admit defeat; accept loss. *After taking a beating for five rounds, the fighter's seconds threw in the sponge. When Harold saw his arguments were not being accepted, he threw in the towel and left.*

throw off v. **1.** To get free from. *He was healthy enough to throw off his cold easily.* **2.** To mislead; confuse; fool. *They went by a different route to throw the hostile bandits off their track.* **3.** To produce easily or as if without effort. *She could throw off a dozen poems in a night.*

throw one's weight around v. phr., informal To use one's influence or position in a showy or noisy manner. *John was the star of the class play, and he was throwing his weight around telling the director how the scene should be played. Bob was stronger than the other boys, and he threw his weight around.*

throw out or **toss out** v. **1.** To put somewhere to be destroyed because not wanted. *He didn't need the brush anymore so he threw it out.* **2.** To refuse to accept. *The inspector tossed out all the parts that didn't work.* **3.** To force to leave; dismiss. *When the employees complained too loudly, the owner threw them out.* **4.** To cause to be out in baseball by throwing the ball. *The shortstop tossed the runner out.*

throw the baby out with the bath (bathwater) *v. phr.* To reject all of something because part is faulty. *God knows that there are weaknesses in the program, but if they act too hastily they may cause the baby to be thrown out with the bathwater.*

throw the book at *v. phr., informal* To give the most severe penalty to (someone) for breaking the law or rules. *Because it was the third time he had been caught speeding that month, the judge threw the book at him.*

throw together *v.* **1.** *also* **slap together** To make in a hurry and without care. *Bill and Bob threw together a cabin out of old lumber. The party was planned suddenly, and Mary threw together a meal out of leftovers.* **2.** To put in with other people by chance. *The group of strangers was thrown together when the storm trapped them on the highway. Bill and Tom became friends when they were thrown together in the same cabin at camp.*

throw up *v.* **1.** *informal or slang* **heave up.** To vomit. *The heat made him feel sick and he thought he would throw up. He took the medicine but threw it up a minute later.* **2.** *informal* To quit; leave; let go; give up. *When she broke their engagement he threw up his job and left town.* **3.** To build in a hurry. *The contractor threw up some temporary sheds to hold the new equipment.* **4.** To mention often as an insult. *His*

father threw up John's wastefulness to him.

throw up one's hands *v. phr.* To give up trying; admit that you cannot succeed. *Mrs. Jones threw up her hands when the children messed up the living room for the third time. When Mary saw the number of dishes to be washed, she threw up her hands in dismay.*

thumb a ride *v. phr., informal* To get a ride by hitchhiking; hitchhike. *Not having much money, Carl decided to thumb a ride to New York.*

thumb one's nose *v. phr.* **1** To hold one's open hand in front of one's face with one's thumb pointed at one's nose as a sign of scorn or dislike. *After Bob ran into the house he thumbed his nose at Tom through the window.* **2.** *informal* To look with disfavor or dislike; regard with scorn; refuse to obey.—Used with *at.* *Betty thumbed her nose at her mother's command to stay home. Mary thumbed her nose at convention by wearing odd clothes.*

thus and so *also* **thus and thus** *adv. phr.* In a particular way; according to directions that have been given. *The teacher is very fussy about the way you write your report. If you don't do it thus and so, she gives you a lower mark.*

tickle pink *v. phr., informal* To please very much; thrill; delight. Usually used in the passive participle. *Nancy was tickled pink with her new dress.*

tick off *v.* **1.** To mention one after the other; list. *The teacher ticked off the assignments that*

ne had to do. **2.** To scold; re-
ake. *The boss ticked off the
aitress for dropping her tray.*
To anger or upset. Usually
ed as *ticked off. She was
ked off at him for breaking
eir dinner date again.*

over *v.* To carry past a
fficulty or danger; help in
d times or in trouble. *He was
t of work last winter but he
d saved enough money to
e him over until spring. An
cream cone in the afternoon
ed her over until supper.*

down *v.* To keep (some-
e) from going somewhere or
ing something; prevent from
aving; keep in. *Mrs. Brown
n't come to the party. She's
d down at home with the chil-
en sick. The navy tied the en-
y down with big gunfire
ile the marines landed on the
ach. I can't help you with his-
y now! I'm tied down with
se algebra problems.*

**to one's mother's apron
ings** Not independent of
ur mother; not able to do
ything without asking your
ther. *Even after he grew up
was still tied to his mother's
on strings.*

in *v.* To connect with
nething else; make a con-
ction for.—Often used with
h. *The teacher tied in what
said with last week's lesson.
e English teacher sometimes
es compositions that tie in
h things we are studying in
er classes. The detectives tied
the fingerprints on the man's
with those found on the
e, so they knew that he was
thief.*

n. A connection; a point

of meeting. *John's essay on
World War II provides a perfect tie-in with his earlier work
on World War I.*

tie in knots *v. phr.* To make
(someone) very nervous or
worried. *The thought of having
her tooth pulled tied Joan in
knots. The little boy's experience with the kidnapper tied
him in knots and it was hard
for him to sleep well for a long
time.*

tie one's hands *v. phr.* To
make (a person) unable to do
anything.—Usually used in the
passive. *Since Mary would not
tell her mother what was bothering her, her mother's hands
were tied. Charles wanted to
help John get elected president
of the class, but his promise to
another boy tied his hands. Father hoped Jim would not quit
school, but his hands were tied;
Jim was old enough to quit if he
wanted to.*

tie the knot *v. phr., informal*
To get married; also to perform a wedding ceremony.
*Diane and Bill tied the knot
yesterday. The minister tied
the knot for Diane and Bill
yesterday.*

tie up *v. phr.* **1.** To show or
stop the movement or action
of; hinder; tangle. *The crash of
the two trucks tied up all traffic
in the center of town. The strike
tied up the factory.* **2.** To take
all the time of. *The meeting will
tie the President up until noon.
The Senate didn't vote because
a debate on a small point kept it
tied up all week. He can't see
you now. He's tied up on the
telephone.* **3.** To limit or prevent the use of. *His money is*

tied up in a trust fund and he can't take it out. Susan tied up the bathroom for an hour. **4.** To enter into an association or partnership; join. *Our company has tied up with another firm to support the show.* **5.** To dock. *The ships tied up at New York.* **6.** *slang* To finish; complete. *We've talked long enough; let's tie up these plans and start doing things.*

tie-up *n.* A congestion; a stoppage of the normal flow of traffic, business or correspondence. *There was a two-hour traffic tie-up on the highway. No pay checks were delivered because of the mail service tie-up.*

tight end *n.* An end in football who plays close to the tackle in the line. *The tight end is used to catch passes but most often to block.*

tighten one's belt *v. phr.* To live on less money than usual; use less food and other things. *When father lost his job we had to tighten our belts.* Often used in the expression *tighten one's belt another notch. When the husband lost his job, the Smiths had to do without many things, but when their savings were all spent, they had to tighten their belts another notch.*

tighten the screws *v. phr.* To try to make someone do something by making it more and more difficult not to do it; apply pressure. *When many students still missed class after he began giving daily quizzes, the teacher tightened the screws by failing anyone absent four times.*

tilt at windmills *v. phr., literary*

To do battle with an imagina foe (after Cervantes' D Quixote). *John is a nice g but when it comes to depa mental meetings he wastes e rybody's time by constan tilting at windmills.*

time and again *or* **time and ti again** *adv.* Many times; peatedly; very often. *I've t you time and again not to to the vase! Children are forge and must be told time and ti again how to behave.*

time and a half *n. phr.* F given to a worker at a rate h again as much as he usua gets. *John got time and a h when he worked beyond usual quitting time. Tom g one dollar for regular pay an dollar and a half for time an half.*

time is ripe The best time I come for doing something. 7 *Prime Minister will hold ea tions when the time is ripe. I saw his mother was upset, so decided the time was not ripe tell her about the broken w dow.*

time of one's life *n. phr.* very happy or wonderful tir *John had the time of his life the party. I could see that was having the time of her lif*

time out *n. phr.* Time dur which a game, a lecture, a cussion or other activity stopped for a while for sor extra questions or informal cussion, or some other reas *He took a time out from stu ing to go to a movie. The pla called time out so he could his shoe. "Time out!"—The dents said, "Could you expl that again?"*

off v., *informal* To tell something not generally known; tell secret facts to; warn. *The class president tipped off the class that it was the superintendent's birthday. The thieves did not rob the bank as planned because someone tipped them off that it was being watched by the police.*

the scales v. phr., *informal* 1. To weigh. *Martin tips the scales at 180 pounds.* 2. *or* tip **the balance** To have important or decisive influence; make a decision go for or against you; decide. *John's vote tipped the scales in our favor, and we won the election.*

for tat n. phr. Equal treatment in return; a fair exchange. *Billy hit me, so I gave him tit for tat. I told him if he did me any harm I would return tit for tat. They had a warm debate and the two boys gave each other tit for tat.*

a fault adv. phr. So very well that it is in a way bad; to the point of being rather foolish; too well; too much. *Aunt May wants everything in her house to be exactly right; she is neat to a fault. Mary acts her part to a fault. John carries thoroughness to a fault; he spends many hours writing his reports.*

all intents and purposes adv. phr. In most ways; in fact. *The President is called the head of state, but the prime minister, to all intents and purposes, is the chief executive.*

a man adv. phr. Without exception; with all agreeing. *The workers voted to a man to go on strike. To a man John's*

friends stood by him in his trouble.

to and fro adv. phr. Forward and back again and again. *Father pushed Judy in the swing, and she went to and fro. Busses go to and fro between the center of the city and the city limits. The man walked to and fro while he waited for his phone call.*

to a T or **to a turn** adv. phr. Just right; to perfection; exactly. *The roast was done to a turn. His nickname, Tiny, suited him to a T.*

to-be adj. That is going to be; about to become.—Used after the noun it modifies. *Bob kissed his bride-to-be. The principal of the high school greeted the high school students-to-be on their last day in junior high.*

to be sure adv. phr. Without a doubt; certainly; surely. *"Didn't you say Mr. Smith would take us home?" "Oh, yes. To be sure, I did."*—Often used before a clause beginning with but. *He works slowly, to be sure, but he does a good job. To be sure, Jim is a fast skater, but he is not good at doing figures.*

to blame adj. phr. Having done something wrong; to be blamed; responsible. *John was to blame for the broken window. The teacher tried to find out who was to blame in the fight.*

to boot adv. phr. In addition; besides; as something extra. *He not only got fifty dollars, but they bought him dinner to boot.*

to date adv. or adj. phr. Up to the present time; until now. *To* *date twenty students have been accepted into the school. The police have not found the runaway to date. Jim is shoveling snow to earn money, but his earnings to date are small.*

to death *adv. phr., informal* To the limit; to the greatest degree possible.—Used for emphasis with verbs such as *scare, frighten, bore. Cowboy stories bore me to death, but I like mysteries. Sara is scared to death of snakes. John is tickled to death with his new bike.*

toe the line *or* **toe the mark** *v. phr.* To be very careful to do just what you are supposed to do; obey the rules and do your duties. *The new teacher will make Joe toe the line. Bill's father is strict with him and he has to toe the mark.*

Tom, Dick, and Harry *n. phr.* People in general; anyone; everyone.—Usually preceded by *every* and used to show scorn or disrespect. *The drunk told his troubles to every Tom, Dick and Harry who passed by.*

tone down *v.* To make softer or quieter; make less harsh or strong; moderate. *He toned down the sound of the TV. She wanted the bright colors in her house toned down. When the ladies arrived, he toned down his language. The strikers were asked to tone down their demands for higher pay so that there might be a quicker agreement and an end to the strike.*

tongue-lashing *n.* A sharp scolding or criticism. *Jim's mother gave him a tongue-lashing for telling family secrets.*

to no avail *or* **of no avail** *adj. phr., formal* Having no effec useless, unsuccessful. *Tom practicing was of no avail. F was sick on the day of th game. Mary's attempts learn embroidering were to n avail.*

too bad *adj.* To be regrette worthy of sorrow or regret; r grettable.—Used as a pred cate. *It is too bad that we are s often lazy. It was too bad B had measles when the circ came to town.*

too many cooks spoil the bro *or* **stew** A project is likely go bad if managed by a mul plicity of primary movers.— proverb. *When several peop acted all at once in trying reshape the company's inves ment policy, Tom spoke u and said, "Let me do this myself! Don't you know th too many cooks spoil th broth?"*

to one's face *adv. phr.* D rectly to you; in your presenc *I told him to his face that didn't like the idea. I called hi a coward to his face.*

to one's heart's content *ad phr.* To the extent of one wishes; one's complete satisfa tion. *There is a wonderful sma restaurant nearby where yo can eat to your heart's content.*

to order *adv. phr.* Accordi to directions given in an ord in the way and size wante The manufacturer built th machine to order. A very b man often has his suits ma to order.*

tooth and nail *adv. phr.* Wi all weapons or ways of fightin

as hard as possible; fiercely.—
Used after *fight* or a similar
word. *When the Indian girl
was captured, she fought tooth
and nail to get away. The
farmers fought tooth and nail
to save their crops from the
grasshoppers. His friends
fought tooth and nail to elect
him to Congress.*

op-drawer *adj.*, *informal* Of
the best; or most important
kind. *Mary's art work was top-
drawer material. Mr. Rogers is
a top-drawer executive and gets
a very high salary.*

o pieces *adv. phr.* **1.** Into broken pieces or fragments; destroyed. *The cannon shot the
town to pieces. The vase fell to
pieces in Mary's hand.* **2.** *informal* So as not to work; into a
state of not operating. *After
100,000 miles the car went to
pieces. When Mary heard of
her mother's death, she went
to pieces.* **3.** *informal* Very
much; greatly; exceedingly.
*Joan was thrilled to pieces to
see Mary. The noise scared Bob
to pieces.*

op off *v.* To come or bring to
a special or unexpected ending;
climax. *John batted three runs
and topped off the game with
a home run. Mary hadn't finished her homework, she was
late to school, and to top it all
off she missed a surprise test.
George had steak for dinner
and topped it off with a fudge
sundae.*

o speak of *adj. phr.*, *informal*
Important; worth talking
about; worth noticing.—Usually used in negative sentences.
Did it rain yesterday? Not to
speak of. What happened at the
meeting? Nothing to speak of.
Judy's injuries were nothing to
speak of; just a few scratches.*

to the best of one's knowledge
As far as you know; to the extent of your knowledge. *He has
never won a game, to the best of
my knowledge. To the best of
my knowledge he is a college
man, but I may be mistaken.*

to the bitter end *adv. phr.* To
the point of completion or conclusion.—Used especially of a
very painful or unpleasant task
or experience. *Although Mrs.
Smith was bored by the lecture,
she stayed to the bitter end.
They knew the war would be
lost, but the men fought to the
bitter end.*

to the contrary *adv. or adj. phr.*
With an opposite result or
effect; just the opposite; in disagreement; saying the opposite. *Although Bill was going to
the movies, he told Joe to the
contrary. We will expect you for
dinner unless we get word to the
contrary. School gossip to the
contrary, Mary is not engaged
to be married.*

to the full *adv. phr.* Very
much; fully. *The campers enjoyed their trip to the full. We
appreciated to the full the
teacher's help.*

to the good *adv. phr.* On the
side of profit or advantage; in
one's favor; to one's benefit;
ahead. *After I sold my stamp
collection, I was ten dollars to
the good. The teacher did not
see him come in late, which was
all to the good.*

to the hilt *or* **up to the hilt** *adv.
phr.* To the limit; as far as

possible; completely. *The other boys on the team told Tom he couldn't quit. They said, "You're in this to the hilt." The Smith's house is mortgaged up to the hilt.*

to the manner born *adj. phr.* At ease with something because of lifelong familiarity with it. *She says her English is the best because she is to the manner born.*

to the nth degree *adv. phr.* To the greatest degree possible; extremely; very much so. *Scales must be accurate to the nth degree. His choice of words was exactly to the nth degree.*

to the tune of *adv. phr., informal* To the amount or extent of; in the amount of. *He had to pay to the tune of fifty dollars for seeing how fast the car would go. When she left the race track she had profited to the tune of ten dollars.*

to the wall *adv. phr.* Into a place from which there is no escape; into a trap or corner.— Usually used after *drive* or a similar word. *John's failing the last test drove him to the wall. The score was 12–12 in the last minute of play, but a touchdown forced the visitors to the wall. Bill had to sell his five Great Danes. The high cost of feeding them was driving him to the wall.*

touch and go *adj. phr.* Very dangerous or uncertain in situation. *Our team won the game, all right, but it was touch and go for a while. At one time while they were climbing the cliff it was touch and go whether they could do it.*

touch off *v.* **1.** To cause to fir or explode by lighting th priming or the fuse. *The bo touched off a firecracker.* **2** To start something as if b lighting a fuse. *The coach's res ignation touched off a quarrel.*

touch on *or* **touch upon** *v.* T speak of or write of briefl *The speaker touched on severa other subjects in the course o his talk but mostly kept himsel to the main topic.*

touchup *n.* **1.** A small repair; small amount of paint. *Just small touchup here and ther and your novel may be publish able.* **2.** Redoing the color o one's hair. *My roots are show ing; I need a touchup.*

touch up *v.* **1.** To paint ove (small imperfections.) *I want t touch up that scratch on th fender. The woodwork is done but there are a few places h has to touch up.* **2.** To improv with small additions o changes. *He touched up th photographic negative to mak a sharper print. It's a goo speech, but it needs a littl touching up.* **3.** *slang* To tak into lending; wheedle from. *H touched George up for fiv bucks.*

tough act to follow *n. phr.* speech, performance, or activ ity of such superior quality tha the person next in line feel and thinks that it would b very difficult to match it i quality. *Sir Lawrence Olivier performance of* Hamlet *was tough act to follow in ever sense.*

tough cat *n., slang* A man wh is very individualistic and, as result, highly successful with women. *Joe is a real tough cat, man.*

tough cookie *n. phr.* An extremely determined, hard-headed person, or someone with whom it is unusually difficult to deal. *Marjorie is a very pretty girl, but when it comes to business she sure is one tough cookie.*

track down *v.* To find by or as if by following tracks or a trail. *The hunters tracked down game in the forest. She spent weeks in the library tracking the reference down in all their books on the subject.*

trade in *v.* To give something to a seller as part payment for another thing of greater value. *The Browns traded their old car in on a new one.*

trade-in *n.* Something given as part payment on something better. *The dealer took our old car as a trade-in.*—Often used like an adjective. *We cleaned up the car at trade-in time.*

trade on *v.* To use as a way of helping yourself. *The coach traded on the pitcher's weakness for left-handed batters by using all his southpaws. The senator's son traded on his father's name when he ran for mayor.*

tread water *v. phr.* To keep the head above water with the body in an upright position by moving the feet as if walking. *He kept afloat by treading water.*

trial and error *n.* A way of solving problems by trying different possible solutions until you find one that works. *John*

found the short circuit by trial and error. The only way Tom could solve the algebra problem was by the method of trial and error.*

trial balloon *n.* A hint about a plan of action that is given out to find out what people will say. *John mentioned the class presidency to Bill as a trial balloon to see if Bill might be interested in running. The editorial was a trial balloon to test the public's reaction to a change in the school day.*

trick of the trade *n. phr.,* usually in plural, *informal* 1. A piece of expert knowledge; a smart, quick, or skillful way of working at a trade or job. *Mr. Olson spent years learning the tricks of the trade as a carpenter. Anyone can learn how to hang wallpaper, but only an expert can show you the tricks of the trade.* 2. A smart and sometimes tricky or dishonest way of doing something in order to succeed or win. *The champion knows all the tricks of the boxing trade; he knows many ways to hurt his opponent and to get him mixed up.*

trick or treat *n.* The custom of going from house to house on Halloween asking for small gifts and playing tricks on people who refuse to give. *When Mrs. Jones answered the doorbell, the children yelled "Trick or treat." Mrs. Jones gave them all some candy. On Halloween Bill and Tom went out playing trick or treat.*

tripped out *adj., slang, informal* Incoherent, confused, faulty of speech, illogical; as if under the influence of drugs or alcohol. *It was hard to make sense of anything Fred said yesterday, he sounded so tripped out.*

trip up *v.* **1.** To make (someone) unsteady on the feet; cause to miss a step, stumble, or fall. *A root tripped Billy up while he was running in the woods, and he fell and hurt his ankle.* **2.** To cause (someone) to make a mistake. *The teacher asked tricky questions in the test to trip up students who were not alert.*

trump card *n.* Something kept back to be used to win success if nothing else works. *The coach saved his star pitcher for a trump card. Mary had several ways to get Joan to come to her party. Her trump card was that the football captain would be there.*

trump up *v.* To make up (something untrue); invent in the mind. *Every time Tom is late getting home he trumps up some new excuse. The Russians were afraid he was a spy, so they arrested him on a trumped-up charge and made him leave the country.*

try on *v.* To put (clothing) on to see if it fits. *She tried on several pairs of shoes before she found one she liked. The clerk told him to try the coat on.*

try one's hand *v. phr.* To make an inexperienced attempt (at something unfamiliar.) *I thought I would try my hand at bowling, although I had never bowled before.*

tryout *n.* An audience at a theater or opera for would-be actors and singers. *The Civic Opera is holding tryouts throughout all of next week. Maybe I'll go and see if I can sing in the chorus.*

try out *v. phr.* **1.** To test by trial or by experimenting. *He tried golf out to see if he would like it. The scientists tried out thousands of chemicals before they found the right one. The coach wants to try the new play out in the first game.* **2.** To try for a place on a team or in a group. *Tom tried out for the basketball team. Shirley will try out for the lead in the play.*

tug-of-war *n.* **1.** A game in which two teams pull on opposite ends of a rope, trying to pull the other team over a line marked on the ground. *The tug-of-war ended when both teams tumbled in a heap.* **2.** A contest in which two sides try to defeat each other; struggle. *A tug-of-war developed between the boys who wanted to go fishing and those who wanted to go hiking. Betty felt a tug-of-war between her wish to go to the movies and her realizing she had to do her homework. The tug of war between the union men and management ended in a long strike.*

tune in To adjust a radio or television set to pick up a certain station. *Bob tuned in his portable radio to a record show. Tom tuned in to Channel 11 to hear the news.*

tune out *v. phr.* To not listen to something. *"How can you work in such a noisy environment?" Jane asked Sue. "Well, I simply tune it out," she answered.*

tune up *v.* **1a.** To adjust (a musical instrument) to make

e right sound. *Before he bean to play, Harry tuned up his
anjo.* **1b.** To adjust a musical
astrument or a group of musi-
al instruments to the right
ound. *The orchestra came in
nd began to tune up for the
oncert.* **2.** To adjust many
arts of (car engine) which
ust work together so that it
ill run properly. *He took his
r to the garage to have the en-
ne tuned up.*

e-up *n.* **1.** The adjusting or
xing of something (as a mo-
r) to make it work safely and
ell. *Father says the car needs a
ne-up before winter begins.* **2.**
xercise or practicing for the
urpose of getting ready; a
ial before something. *The
am went to the practice field
r their last tune-up before the
me tomorrow.*

n a blind eye *v. phr.* To
retend not to see; not pay at-
ntion. *The corrupt police
ief turned a blind eye to the
en gambling in the town.
ob turned a blind eye to the
No Fishing" sign.*

n a deaf ear to *v. phr.* To
retend not to hear; refuse to
ear; not pay attention. *Mary
rned a deaf ear to Lois's ask-
g to ride her bicycle. The
acher turned a deaf ear to
ob's excuse.*

n color *v. phr.* To become
different color. *In the fall the
aves turn color. When the dye
as added the solution turned
lor.*

n down *v.* **1.** To reduce the
udness, brightness, or force
. *The theater lights were
rned down. Turn down that
dio, will you? The hose was*

throwing too much water so I
turned down the water a little
bit. **2.** To refuse to accept; reject. *His request for a raise was
turned down. If she offers to
help, I'll turn her down. Many
boys courted Lynn, but she
turned them all down.*

turn in *v.* **1.** *or* **hand in** To
give to someone; deliver to
someone. *I want you to turn in
a good history paper. When the
football season was over, we
turned in our uniforms.* **2.** To
inform on; report. *She turned
them in to the police for breaking the street light.* **3.** To give in
return for something. *They
turned in their old money for
new. We turned our car in on a
new model.* **4.** *informal* To go
to bed. *We were tired, so we
turned in about nine o'clock.*

turn in one's grave *or* **turn over
in one's grave** *v. phr.* To be
so grieved or angry that you
would not rest quietly in your
grave. *If your grandfather
could see what you're doing
now, he would turn over in his
grave.*

turn off *v.* **1.** To stop by turning
a knob or handle or by work-
ing a switch; to cause to be off.
*He turned the water off. He
turned off the light.* **2.** To leave
by turning right or left onto another way. *Turn off the highway at exit 5. The car turned off
on Bridge Street. slang* **3.** To
disgust, bore, or repel (someone) by being intellectually,
emotionally, socially, or sexually unattractive. *I won't date
Linda Bell anymore—she just
turns me off.*

turn on *v.* **1.** To start by turning
a knob or handle or working a

switch; cause to be on. *Jack turned on the water. Who turned the lights on?* **2.** *informal* To put forth or succeed with as easily as turning on water. *She really turns on the charm when that new boy is around.* **3.** To attack. *The lion tamer was afraid the lions would turn on him. After Joe fumbled the ball and lost the big game, his friends turned on him.* **4.** *slang* The opposite of turning someone off; to become greatly interested in an idea, person, or undertaking; to arouse the senses pleasantly. *Mozart's music always turns me on.* **5.** Introducing someone to a new experience, or set of values. *Benjamin turned me on to transcendental meditation, and ever since I've been feeling great!*

turn one's back on *v. phr.* To refuse to help (someone in trouble or need.) *He turned his back on his own family when they needed help. The poorer nations are often not grateful for our help, but still we can not turn our back on them.*

turn one's head *v. phr., informal* To make you lose your good judgment. *The first pretty girl he saw turned his head. Winning the class election turned his head.*

turn one's nose up at *v. phr.* To scorn; snub; look down at somebody or something. *I don't understand why Sue has to turn her nose up at everyone who didn't go to an Ivy League college.*

turn one's stomach *v. phr., informal* To make you feel sick. *The smell of that cigar was*

enough to turn your stomach. The sight of blood turns my stomach.

turn on one's heel *v. phr.* To turn around suddenly. *When John saw Fred approaching him, he turned on his heel. When little Tommy's brother showed up, the bully turned on his heel.*

turnout *n.* The number of people in attendance at a gathering. *This is a terrific turnout for Tim's poetry reading.*

turn out *v.* **1.** To make leave or go away. *His father turned him out of the house. If you don't behave, you will be turned out.* **2.** To turn inside out; empty. *He turned out his pockets looking for the money. Robbers turned out all the drawers in the house in a search for jewels.* To make; produce. *The printing press turns out a thousand books an hour. Sally can turn out a cake in no time. Mary turns out a poem each week for the school paper.* **4.** *informal* To get out of bed. *At camp the boys had to turn out early and go to bed early too.* **5.** *informal* To come or go out to see or do something. *Everybody turned out for the big parade. Many boys turned out for football practice.* **6.** To prove to be; in the end; be found to be. *The noise turned out to be just a dog scratching at the door. His guess turned out to be right. Everything turned out all right.* **7.** To make (a light) go off. *Please turn out the lights.*

turnover *n.* **1.** The proportion of expenditure and income realized in a business; the volume of traffic in a business. *C-*

urnover is so great that in two hort years we tripled our riginal investment and are ex- anding at a great rate. **2.** Tri- ngular baked pastry filled vith some fruit. *John's favorite dessert is apple turnovers.* **3.** The number of employees oming and going in a com- any. *The boss is so strict in ur office that the turnover in ersonnel is very large.*

rn over *v.* **1.** To roll, tip, or urn from one side to the ther; overturn; upset. *He's go- ng to turn over the page. The ike hit a rock and turned over.* **.** To think about carefully; to onsider. *He turned the prob- em over in his mind for three days before he did anything bout it.* **3.** To give to someone or use or care. *I turned my ibrary books over to the li- rarian. Mrs. Jackson brought er boy to the school and urned him over to the house ather. Bob turns over most of he money he earns to his nother.* **4.** Of an engine or mo- or; to start. *The battery is dead nd the motor won't turn over.* **a.** To buy and then sell to cus- omers. *The store turned over 5,000 worth of skiing equip- ent in January.* **5b.** To be ought in large enough mounts; sell. *In a shoe store, hoes of medium width turn ver quickly, because many eople wear that size, but a pair f narrow shoes may not be old for years.*

rn over a new leaf *v. phr.* To start afresh; to have a new eginning. *"Don't be sad, ane,"* Sue said. *"A divorce is ot the end of the world. Just*

turn over a new leaf and you will soon be happy again."

turn tail *v. phr., informal* To run away from trouble or dan- ger. *When the bully saw my big brother, he turned tail and ran.*

turn the clock back *v. phr.* To return to an earlier period. *Mother wished she could turn the clock back to the days be- fore the children grew up and left home. Will repealing the minimum wage for workers un- der age eighteen turn the clock back to the abuses of the last century?*

turn the other cheek *v. phr.* To let someone do something to you and not to do it in re- turn; not hit back when hit; be patient when injured or in- sulted by someone; not try to get even. *Joe turned the other cheek when he was hit with a snowball.*

turn the tables *v. phr.* To make something happen just the opposite of how it is sup- posed to happen. *The boys turned the tables on John when they took his squirt gun away and squirted him.*

turn the tide *v. phr.* To change what looks like defeat into victory. *We were losing the game until Jack got there. His coming turned the tide for us, and we won.*

turn the trick *v. phr., informal* To bring about the result you want; succeed in what you plan to do. *Jerry wanted to win both the swimming and diving con- tests, but he couldn't quite turn the trick.*

turn thumbs down *v. phr.* To disapprove or reject; say no.— Usually used with *on. The com-*

pany turned thumbs down on Mr. Smith's sales plan. The men turned thumbs down on a strike at that time.

turn up v. **1.** To find; discover. The police searched the house hoping to turn up more clues. **2.** To appear or be found suddenly or unexpectedly. The missing boy turned up an hour later. A man without training works at whatever jobs turn up.

turn up one's nose at v. phr. To refuse as not being good enough for you. He thinks he should only get steak, and he turns up his nose at hamburger.

twiddle one's thumbs v. phr. To do nothing; be idle. I'd rather work than stand around here twiddling my thumbs.

twist one around one's little finger also **turn one around one's little finger** or **wrap one around one's finger** v. phr. To have complete control over; to be able to make (someone) do anything you want. Sue can twist any of the boys around her little finger.

twist one's arm v. phr., informal To force someone; threaten someone to make him do something.—Usually used jokingly. Will you dance with the prettiest girl in school? Stop, you're twisting my arm! I had to twist Tom's arm to make him eat the candy!

two bits n., slang Twenty-five cents; a quarter of a dollar. A haircut only cost two bits when Grandfather was young.

two cents n. informal **1.** Something not important or very small; almost nothing. Paul was so angry that he said for two cents he would quit the team. When John saw that the girl he was scolding was lame, he felt like two cents. **2.** or **two cents worth** Something you want to say; opinion.—Used with possessive. The boys were talking about baseball, and Harry put in his two cents worth, even though he didn't know much about baseball. If we want your two cents, we'll ask for it.

two-faced adj. Insincere; disloyal; deceitful. Don't confide too much in him as he has the reputation of being two-faced.

two strikes against one n. phr.—From baseball. Two opportunities wasted in some undertaking, so that only one chance is left. Poor John has two strikes against him when it comes to his love for Frances: first, he is too fat, and, second he is bald.

two-time v., slang To go out with a second boy or girlfriend and keep it a secret from the first. Joan was two-timing Jim with Fred. Mary cried when she found that Joe was two-timing her.

U.F.O. n. phr. Unidentified Flying Object. *Some people think that the U.F.O.s are extraterrestrial beings of higher than human development who pay periodic visits to earth to warn us of our self-destructive tendencies.*

ugly duckling n. An ugly or plain child who grows up to be pretty and attractive. *Mary was the ugly duckling in her family, until she grew up.*

under a cloud adj. phr. **1.** Under suspicion; not trusted. *Joyce has been under a cloud since her roommate's bracelet disappeared. The butcher is under a cloud because the inspectors found his scales were not honest.* **2.** Depressed, sad, discouraged. *Joe has been under a cloud since his dog died.*

under age adj. phr. Too young; not old enough; below legal age. *He could not enlist in the army because he was under age. Rose was not allowed to enroll in the Life Saving Course because she was under age.*

under arrest adj. phr. Held by the police. *The man believed to have robbed the bank was placed under arrest. The three boys were seen breaking into the school building and soon found themselves under arrest.*

under cover adv. or adj. phr. Hidden; concealed. *The prisoners escaped under cover of darkness. He kept his invention under cover until it was patented.*

under fire adv. phr. Being shot at or being attacked; hit by attacks or accusations; under attack. *The soldiers stood firm under fire of the enemy. The principal was under fire for not sending the boys home who stole the car.*

under one's belt adv. phr., informal **1.** In your stomach; eaten; or absorbed. *Once he had a good meal under his belt, the man loosened his tie and fell asleep. Jones is talkative when he has a few drinks under his belt.* **2.** In your experience, memory or possession; learned or gotten successfully; gained by effort and skill. *Jim has to get a lot of algebra under his belt before the examination. With three straight victories under their belts, the team went on to win the championship.*

under one's breath adv. phr. In a whisper; with a low voice. *The teacher heard the boy say something under his breath and she asked him to repeat it aloud. I told Lucy the news under my breath, but Joyce overheard me.*

under one's nose or **under the nose of** adv. phr., informal In sight of; in an easily seen or noticeable place. *The thief walked out of the museum with the painting, right under the nose of the guards. When Jim gave up trying to find a pen, he* saw three right under his nose on the desk.

under one's own steam *adv. phr., informal* By one's own efforts; without help. *The boys got to Boston under their own steam and took a bus the rest of the way. We didn't think he could do it, but Bobby finished his homework under his own steam.*

under one's thumb *or* **under the thumb** *adj. or adv. phr.* Obedient to you; controlled by you; under your power. *The Jones family is under the thumb of the mother. Jack is a bully. He keeps all the younger children under his thumb. The mayor is so popular that he has the whole town under his thumb.*

under one's wing *adv. phr.* Under the care or protection of. *Helen took the new puppy under her wing. The boys stopped teasing the new student when Bill took him under his wing.*

under the circumstances *also in the circumstances* *adv. phr.* In the existing situation; in the present condition; as things are. *In the circumstances, Father couldn't risk giving up his job.*

under the counter *adv. phr., informal* Secretly (bought or sold). *That book has been banned, but there is one place you can get it under the counter. The liquor dealer was arrested for selling beer under the counter to teenagers.*—Also used like an adjective, with hyphens. *During World War II, some stores kept scarce things hidden for* under-the-counter-sales *to good customers.*

under the hammer *adv. phr.* Up for sale at auction *The Brights auctioned off the entire contents of their home. Mrs. Bright cried when her pewter collection went under the hammer. The picture I wanted to bid on came under the hammer soon after I arrived.*

under the sun *adj. or adv. phr.* On earth; in the world.—Used for emphasis. *The President's assassination shocked everyone under the sun. Where under the sun could I have put my purse?*

under wraps *adv. or adj. phr.* Not allowed to be seen until the right time; not allowed to act or speak freely; in secrecy; hidden.—Usually used with *keep*. *We have a new player, but we are keeping him under wraps until the game. What the President is planning will be kept under wraps until tomorrow. The spy was kept under wraps and not allowed to talk to newspapermen.*

until hell freezes over *adv. phr., slang* Forever, for an eternity. *He can argue until hell freezes over; nobody will believe him.*

up against *prep. phr.* Blocked or threatened by. *When she applied to medical school, the black woman wondered whether she was up against barriers of sex and race prejudice.*

up against it *adj. phr., informal* Faced with a great difficulty or problem; badly in need. *The Smith family is up against it be-*

cause Mr. Smith cannot find a job. You will be up against it if you don't pass the test. You will probably fail arithmetic.

up a tree adv. or adj. phr. **1.** Hunted or chased into a tree; treed. *The dog drove the coon up a tree so the hunter could shoot him.* **2.** informal in trouble; having problems; in a difficulty that it is hard to escape or think of a way out of. *John's father has him up a tree in the checker game.*

up for grabs adj. phr., informal Available for anyone to try to get; ready to be competed for; there for the taking. *When the captain of the football team moved out of town, his place was up for grabs.*

up front[1] n., slang, informal The managerial section of a corporation or firm. *Joe Catwallender finally made it (with the) up front.*

up front[2] adj., slang, informal Open, sincere, hiding nothing. *Sue was completely up front about why she didn't want to see him anymore.*

up in arms adj. phr. **1.** Equipped with guns or weapons and ready to fight. *All of the colonies were up in arms against the Redcoats.* **2.** Very angry and wanting to fight. *Robert is up in arms because John said he was stupid. The students were up in arms over the new rule against food in the dormitory.*

up in the air adj. or adv. phr. **1.** informal In great anger or excitement. *My father went straight up in the air when he heard I damaged the car. The*

Jones family are all up in the air because they are taking a trip around the world. **2.** also **in midair** Not settled; uncertain; undecided. *Plans for the next meeting have been left up in the air until Jane gets better. The result of the game was left hanging in midair because it rained before the finish.*

up one's sleeve or **in one's sleeve** adv. phr. **1.** Hidden in the sleeve of one's shirt or coat and ready for secret or wrongful use. *The crooked gambler hid aces up his sleeve during the card game so that he would win.* **2.** informal Kept secretly ready for the right time or for a time when needed. *Jimmy knew that his father had some trick up his sleeve because he was smiling to himself during the checker game.*

upper hand or **whip hand** n. Controlling power; advantage. *In the third round the champion got the upper hand over his opponent and knocked him out. The cowboy trained the wild horse so that he finally got the whip hand and tamed the horse.*

Upsadaisy! or **Upsee-daisy!** or **Upsy-daisy!** adv. phr. A popular exclamation used when just about anything is lifted, particularly a small child raised to his or her highchair or bed. *"Upsee-daisy!" the nurse said with a smile on her face, as she lifted the baby from its bed.*

ups and downs n. phr. Vicissitudes; alternating periods between good and bad times; changes in fortune. *He is now a* *wealthy stock trader, but at the beginning of his career he, too, had many ups and downs.*

upset the applecart *or* **upset one's applecart** *v. phr., informal* To ruin a plan or what is being done, often by surprise or accident; change how things are or are being done, often unexpectedly; ruin or mix up another person's success or plan for success. *John upset the other team's applecart by hitting a home run in the last inning and we won the game. We are planning a surprise party for Bill, so don't let Mary upset the applecart by telling him before the party. Frank thinks he is going to be the boss, but I'll upset his applecart the first chance I get.*

upside down *adv. phr.* Overturned so that the bottom is up and the top is down. *The ladybug lay upside down in the sand and was unable to take off. The problem with this company is that everything is upside down; we need a new C.E.O.*

up the creek *or* **up the creek without a paddle** *adj. phr., informal* In trouble or difficulty and unable to do anything about it; stuck. *Father said that if the car ran out of gas in the middle of the desert, we would be up the creek without a paddle. I'll be up the creek if I don't pass this history test.*

up tight *or* **uptight** *adj., slang, informal* Worried, irritated, excessively eager or anxious. *Why are you so uptight about getting that job? The more you worry, the less you'll succeed.*

up to *prep.* **1.** As far, as deep, or as high as. *The water in the pond was only up to John's knees. Mary is small and just comes up to Bill's chest. The shovel sank in the soft mud all the way up to the handle.* **2.** Close to; approaching. *The team did not play up to its best today. Because of the rain, the number of people at the party didn't come up to the number we expected.* **3.** As high as; not more than; as much or as many as. *Pick any number up to ten. There were up to eight fire engines at the fire.* **4.** *or* **up till** *or* **up until**—Until; till. *Up to her fourth birthday, the baby slept in a crib. Up to now I always thought John was honest. We went swimming up till breakfast time. Up until last summer we always went to the beach for our vacation.* **5.** Capable of; fit for; equal to; strong or well enough for. *We chose Harry to be captain because we thought he was up to the job. Mother is sick and not up to going out to the store.* **6.** Doing or planning secretly; ready for mischief. *What are you up to with the matches, John? Mrs. Watson was sure that the boys were up to no good, because they ran when they saw her coming.* **7.** Facing as a duty; to be chosen or decided by; depending on. *It's up to you to get to school on time.—I don't care when you cut the grass. When you do it is up to you.*

up-to-date *adj.* Modern; contemporary; the latest that technology can offer. *"I want an up-to-date dictionary of Ameri-*

an idioms," Mr. Lee said, "that has all the latest Americanisms in it."

to no good *adv. phr.* Intending to do something bad; perpetrating an illicit act. *We could tell from the look on Dennis the Menace's face that he was once again up to no good.*

to par *or informal* **up to scratch** *or informal* **up to snuff** 1. In good or normal health or physical condition. *I have a cold and don't feel up to par. The boxer is training for the fight but he isn't up to scratch yet.* 2. *or* **up to the mark** As good as usual; up to the usual level or quality. *The TV program was not up to par tonight. John will have to work hard to bring his grades up to snuff.*

to the chin in *or* **in up to the chin** *adj. phr., informal* Used also with *ears, elbows, eyes* or *knees* instead of *chin,* and with a possessive instead of *the.* 1. Having a big or important part in; guilty of; not innocent of; deeply in. *Was Tom mixed up in that trouble last night? He was up to his ears in it. Mr. Johnson is up to the eyes in debt. Mrs. Smith is in debt up to her chin.* 2. Very busy with; working hard at. *Bob is up to his neck in homework. They are up to their elbows in business before Christmas.* 3. Having very much or many of; flooded with. *Mary was up to her knees in invitations to go to parties.*

ed to[1] *adj. phr.* In the habit of or familiar with. *People get*

used to smoking and it is hard for them to stop. *Farmers are used to working outdoors in the winter. After my eyes became used to the dim light in the cave, I saw an old shovel on the ground. On the hike Bob soon got tired, but Dick did not because he was used to walking.*

used to[2] *or* **did use to** *v. phr.* Did formerly; did in the past.— Usually used with an infinitive to tell about something past. *Uncle Henry used to have a beard, but he shaved it off. Did your father use to work at the bank? People used to say that tomatoes were poison.*—Sometimes used without the infinitive. *I don't go to that school any more, but I used to. We don't visit Helen as much as we used to. I used to go to the movies often. Did you use to?*

used to be *or* **did use to be** *v. phr.* Formerly or once was. *Mary used to be small; but she has grown up. Dick used to be the best pitcher on the team last year; now two other pitchers are better than he is.*

use every trick in the book *v. phr., informal* To avail oneself of any means at all in order to achieve one's goal, not exclusive of possibly immoral or illegal acts. *Algernon used every trick in the book to get Maxine to go out with him, but she kept refusing.*

use one's head *or slang* **use one's bean** *or slang* **use one's noodle** *or slang* **use one's noggin** *v. phr.* To use your brain or mind; think; have common sense.—Often used as a command. *If you used your bean you wouldn't be in trouble now. Never point a gun at anybody, John. Use your head!*

use up *v. phr.* **1.** To use until nothing is left; spend or consume completely. *Don't use up all the soap. Leave me some to wash with. Jack used up his last dollar to see the movies.* **2.** *informal* To tire completely; make very tired; exhaust; leave no strength or force in.—Usually used in the passive. *After rowing the boat across the lake Robert was used up.*

vanishing cream n. A cosmetic cream for the skin that is used chiefly before face powder. *Mrs. Jones spread vanishing cream on her face before applying her face powder.*

vanity case n. **1.** A small case containing face powder, lipstick, and other things and usually carried in a woman's handbag; a compact. *She took out her vanity case and put lipstick on.* **2.** A handbag or a small bag carried by a woman and holding various toilet articles. *She had the porter carry her big bags and she herself carried her vanity case.*

variety show n. A program that includes several different kinds of entertainment (as songs, dances, comic skits and little dramas). *Jane's father was the master of ceremonies of a variety show on TV.*

variety store n. A store that sells many different kinds of things, especially items that are fairly small and in everyday use. *I went into a variety store and bought some paint. Five-and-ten cent stores are a kind of variety store.*

very well interj., formal Agreed; all right.—Used to show agreement or approval. *Very well. You may go. Very well, I will do as you say.*

vibrations or **vibes** n. Psychic emanations radiating from an object, situation, or person. *I don't think this relationship will*

work out—this guy has given me bad vibes.

vicious circle n. phr. A kind of circular or chain reaction in which one negative thing leads to another. *Some people take so many different kinds of medicine to cure an illness that they develop other illnesses from the medicine and are thus caught in a vicious circle.*

Vietnam syndrome n., informal An attitude in government circles that diplomacy may be more effective in solving local political problems in other countries than the use of military force, stemming from the failure of the U.S. military intervention in Vietnam. *The pundits of Foggy Bottom display the Vietnam syndrome these days when it comes to Iran.*

voice box n. The part of the throat where the sound of your voice is made; the larynx. *Mr. Smith's voice box was taken out in an operation, and he could not talk after that.*

voiceprint n., technological, colloquial The graphic pattern derived from converting an individual's voice into a visible graph used by the police for identification purposes, much as fingerprints. *They have succeeded in identifying the murderer by using a voiceprint.*

vote a straight ticket v. phr.

To not differentiate one's ballot according to individual names and posts, but to vote for all candidates for all positions of the same party. *"I never have time to study the ballot in detail,"* Marie said, *"and so I tend to vote a straight Republican ticket."*

vote in *v. phr.* To elevate to the status of "Law of the Land" by special or general ballot. *Congress has finally voted in the Brady Law that re-quires that prospective gun owners wait a special period of time before making their purchase.*

vote one out *v. phr.* To terminate one's elected office by casting a negative vote about that person (judge, congressman, etc.), mostly so that someone else might occupy the same position. *Congressman Smith was voted out last November in favor of Congresswoman Bradley.*

wade in or **wade into** v., *informal* **1.** To go busily to work. *The house was a mess after the party, but Mother waded in and soon had it clean again.* **2.** To attack. *When Bill had heard Jim's argument, he waded in and took it apart. Jack waded into the boys with his fists flying.*

wait at table or **wait on table** or **wait table** v. phr. To serve food. *Mrs. Lake had to teach her new maid to wait on table properly. The girls earn spending money by waiting at table in the school dining rooms.*

waiting list n. A list of persons waiting to get into something (as a school). *The nursery school enrollment was complete, so the director put our child's name on the waiting list. The landlord said there were no vacant apartments available, but that he would put the Rogers' name on the waiting list.*

waiting room n. phr. The sitting area in a doctor's, lawyer's, accountant's, etc. office, or in a hospital, or other workplace, where people wait their turn. *Some doctor's offices have elegantly furnished waiting rooms with magazines, newspapers, and coffee for the patients.*

wait on or **wait upon** v. **1.** To serve. *Sue has a summer job waiting on an invalid. The clerk in the store asked if we had*
been waited upon. **2.** *formal* To visit as a courtesy or for business. *We waited upon the widow out of respect for her husband. John waited upon the President with a letter of introduction.* **3.** To follow. *Success waits on hard work.*

wait on hand and foot v. phr. To serve in every possible way; do everything for (someone). *Sally is spoiled because her mother waits on her hand and foot. The gentlemen had a valet to wait on him hand and foot.*

wait up v. phr. To not go to bed until a person one is worried about comes home (said by parents and marriage partners). *My mother always waited up for me when I went out as a young student. She always waits up for her husband when he's out late.*

walk a tightrope v. phr. To be in a dangerous or awkward situation where one cannot afford to make a single mistake. *"When we landed on the moon in 1969," Armstrong explained, "we were walking a tightrope till the very end."*

walk away with or **walk off with** v. **1.** To take and go away with; take away; often: steal. *When Father went to work, he accidentally walked off with Mother's umbrella. How can a thief walk off with a safe in broad daylight?* **2.** To take, get, or win easily. *Jim walked away with all the honors on Class*

Night. Our team walked off with the championship.

walking papers *or* **walking orders** *also* **walking ticket** *n., informal* A statement that you are fired from your job; dismissal. *The boss was not satisfied with Paul's work and gave him his walking papers. George is out of work. He picked up his walking ticket last Friday.*

walk of life *n. phr.* Way of living; manner in which people live. *Many rich people have yachts; people in their walk of life can afford them. The banker did not want his son to marry a girl in a different walk of life. People from every walk of life enjoy television.*

walk on air *v. phr., informal* To feel happy and excited. *Sue has been walking on air since she won the prize. His father's compliment left Jed walking on air.*

walk out *v.* **1.** To go on strike. *When the company would not give them higher pay, the workers walked out.* **2.** To leave suddenly; especially to desert. *He didn't say he wasn't coming back; he just walked out.*—Often used informally with *on. The man walked out on his wife and children.*

walk over *or* **walk all over** *or* **step all over** *v. phr,* To make (someone) do whatever you wish; make selfish use of; treat like a slave; impose upon. *Jill is so friendly and helpful that people walk all over her. We wanted the man's business, so we let him step all over us.*

walk the plank *v. phr.* **1.** To walk off a board extended over the side of a ship and be drowned. *The pirates captured the ship and forced the crew to walk the plank.* **2.** *informal* To resign from a job because someone makes you do it. *When a new owner bought the store, the manager had to walk the plank.*

wallflower *n.* A girl who has to sit out dances because nobody is asking her to dance. *"I used to be a wallflower during my high school days," Valerie complained, "but my luck changed for better once I got into college."*

war baby *n., informal* A person born during a war. *War babies began to increase college enrollments early in the 1960s. The war babies forced many towns to build new schools.*

warm one's blood *v. phr.* To make you feel warm or excited. *When the Bakers came to visit on a cold night, Mr. Harmon offered them a drink to warm their blood.*

warm the bench *v. phr., informal* To act as a substitute on an athletic team. *Bill has been warming the bench for three football seasons; he hopes that the coach will let him play this year.*—**bench warmer** *n., informal* A substitute player. *Last year Ted was only a bench warmer, but this year he is the team's star pitcher.*

warm up *v.* **1.** To reheat cooked food. *Mr. Jones was so late that his dinner got cold; his wife had to warm it up. When the children had left for school, their mother warmed up the breakfast coffee.* **2.** To become friendly or interested. *It takes* *an hour or so for some children to warm up to strangers. As he warmed up to his subject, Tom forgot his bashfulness.* **3.** To get ready for a game or other event by exercising or practicing. *The dancers began to warm up fifteen minutes before the performance. The coach told us to warm up before entering the pool.*

warm-up *n.* A period of exercise or practice in preparation for a game or other event. *During the warm-up the baseball players were throwing the ball around and running up and down the side of the field. Before the television quiz program, there was a warm-up to prepare the contestants.*

wash and wear *adj.* Not needing to be ironed.—Refers especially to synthetic and synthetic blend fabrics. *Dick bought three wash and wear shirts to take on his trip. Sally's dress is made of a wash and wear fabric.*

wash one's hands of *v. phr.* To withdraw from or refuse to be responsible for. *We washed our hands of politics long ago. The school washed its hands of the students' behavior during spring recess.*

waste away *v.* To become more thin and weak every day. *Jane is wasting away with tuberculosis. After Mrs. Barnes died, her husband wasted away with grief.*

waste one's breath *v. phr.* To speak or to argue with no result; do nothing by talking. *The teacher saw that she was wasting her breath; the children re-* *fused to believe her. I know what I want. You're wasting your breath.*

watch it *v. phr. informal* To be careful.—Usually used as a command. *You'd better watch it. If you get into trouble again, you'll be expelled. Watch it— the bottom stair is loose!*

watch one's language *v. phr.* To be careful of how one speaks; avoid saying impolite or vulgar things. *"You boys watch your language," Mother said, "or you won't be watching television for a whole week!"*

watch one's step *v. phr.* To mend one's ways; exercise prudence, tact, and care. *I have to watch my step with the new boss as he is a very proud and sensitive individual.*

water down *v.* To change and make weaker; weaken. *The Senator argued that the House should water down the bill before passing it. The African American did not accept watered down Civil Rights legislation. After talking with the management about their demands, the workers agreed to water them down. The teacher had to water down the course for a slow-learning class.*

water over the dam *or* **water under the bridge** *n. phr.* Something that happened in the past and cannot be changed. *Since the sweater is too small already, don't worry about its shrinking; that's water over the dam.*

way the wind blows *or* **how the wind blows** *n. phr.* The direction or course something may go; how things are; what may happen. *Most senators find out which way the wind* *blows in their home state before voting on bills in Congress.*

ways and means *n. plural* Methods of getting something done or getting money; how something can be done and paid for. *The boys were trying to think of ways and means to go camping for the weekend. The United States Senate has a committee on ways and means.*

wear down, wear off or **wear away** *v.* **1.** To remove or disappear little by little through use, time, or the action of weather. *Time and weather have worn off the name on the gravestone. The eraser has worn off my pencil. The grass has worn away from the path near the house.* **2.** To lessen; become less little by little. *The people went home as the excitement of the fire wore off. John could feel the pain again as the dentist's medicine wore away.* **3.** To exhaust; tire out, win over or persuade by making tired. *Mary wore her mother down by begging so that she let Mary go to the movies.*

wear on *v.* **1.** To anger or annoy; tire. *Having to stay indoors all day long is tiresome for the children and wears on their mother's nerves.* **2.** To drag on; pass gradually or slowly; continue in the same old way. *Johnny tried to wait up for Santa Claus but as the night wore on, he couldn't keep his eyes open. As the years wore on, the man in prison grew old. The boys' quarrel wore on all afternoon.*

wear one's heart on one's sleeve also **pin one's heart on one's sleeve** *v. phr.* To show your

feelings openly; show everyone how you feel; not hide your feelings. *She wears her heart on her sleeve. It's easy to see if she is sad or happy. Sometimes it is better not to pin your heart on your sleeve.*

wear out *v.* **1a.** To use or wear until useless. *Bobby got a toy truck that would run on a battery, and he used it so much that he soon wore it out. The stockings are so worn out that they can't be mended any more.* **1b.** To become useless from use or wear. *The old clock finally wore out. One shoe wore out before the other.* **2.** or **tire out** To make very tired; weaken. *The children played inside when it rained, and they soon wore out their mother. When Dick got home from the long walk, he was all worn out.*—Often used with oneself. *Don't wear yourself out by playing too hard.* **3.** To make by rubbing, scraping, or washing. *The waterfall has worn out a hole in the stone beneath it.*

wear out one's welcome *v. phr., informal* To visit somewhere too long or come back too often so that you are not welcome any more. *The Smith children have worn out their welcome at our house because they never want to go home. This hot weather has worn out its welcome with us.*

wear the trousers or **wear the pants** *v. phr., informal* To have a man's authority; be the boss of a family or household. *Mr. Wilson is henpecked by his wife; she wears the trousers in that family. Mrs. Jones talks a* *lot but Mr. Jones wears the pants in their house.*

wear thin *v.* **1.** To become thin from use, wearing, or the passing of time. *My old pair of pants has worn thin at the knees. This old dime has worn very thin.* **2.** To grow less, or less interesting; decrease. *The joke began to wear thin when you heard it too many times. The teacher's patience began to wear thin when he saw that no one knew the lesson.*

wear well *v.* **1.** To continue to be satisfactory, useful, or liked for a long time. *My old overcoat has worn very well. Their marriage has worn well. That author wears well.* **2.** To carry, accept, or treat properly or well. *Grandfather wears his years well. Tommy has won many honors but he wears them well.*

weasel out *v. phr.* To renege on a previous promise; not keep an obligation for some not always straight reason. *I'm so tired I think I am going to weasel my way out of going to that meeting this afternoon.*

weasel word *n.*, *informal* A word which has more than one meaning and may be used to deceive others. *When the thief was being questioned by the police, he tried to fool them with weasel words.*

weed out *v.* **1.** To remove what is unwanted, harmful, or not good enough from. *Mother weeded out the library because there were too many books. Many colleges and universities weed out their freshman classes to make room for better students.* **2.** To take (what is not

wanted) from a collection or group; remove (a part) for the purpose of improving a collection or group; get rid of. *The coach is weeding out the weak players this week. The teacher told Elizabeth to read over her English composition and weed out every sentence that was not about the subject.*

weigh down *also* **weight down** **1.** To make heavy; cause to go down or bend with weight; overload. *The evergreens are weighed down by the deep snow.*—Often used with *with* or *by. There are so many children in the back seat that they are weighing down the back of the car.* **2a.** To overload with care or worry; make sad or low in spirits.—Usually used in the passive. *The family is weighed down by sorrow. The company is weighed down by debt.* **2b.** To make heavy, hard, or slow; make dull or uninteresting.—Often in the passive used with *by* or *with. The book is weighted down with footnotes. The TV program is weighed down by commercials.*

weigh in *v.* **1a.** To take the weight of; weigh. *The man at the airport counter weighed in our bags and took our plane tickets. A doctor weighed in the wrestlers.* **1b.** To have yourself or something that you own weighed.—Often used with *at. I weighed in at 100 pounds on the scale today. We took our bags to the airport counter to weigh in.* **1c.** To have yourself weighed as a boxer or wrestler by a doctor before a match.—Often used with *at. The champion didn't want to weigh in at* more than 160 pounds. **2.** *slang* To join or interfere in a fight, argument, or discussion. *We told Jack that if we wanted him to weigh in with his opinion we would ask him.*

weigh on *or* **weigh upon** *v.* **1.** To be a weight or pressure on; be heavy on. *The pack weighed heavily on the soldier's back.* **2.** To make sad or worried; trouble; disturb; upset. *Sadness weighed on Mary's heart when her kitten died. John's wrongdoing weighed upon his conscience. The teacher's advice weighed upon Tom's mind.* **3.** To be a burden to. *His guilt weighed heavily upon him.*

weigh one's words *v. phr.* To choose your words carefully; be careful to use the right words. *When a teacher explains about religion, he must weigh his words because his pupils may be of several different faiths. When old Mr. Jones talked to the students about becoming teachers, he spoke slowly, weighing his words. In a debate, a political candidate has little time to weigh his words, and may say something foolish.*

weight of the world on one's shoulders *or* **world on one's shoulders** *or* **world on one's back** *n. phr.* A very heavy load of worry or responsibility; very tired or worried behavior, as if carrying the world; behavior as if you are very important. *Don't look as if you had the weight of the world on your shoulders, Henry, just because you have to mow the lawn. John acts as if he were carrying the world on*

his back because he has a paper route.

welcome mat *n.* **1.** A mat for wiping your shoes on, often with the word welcome on it, that is placed in front of a door. *Mother bought a welcome mat for our new house.* **2.** *informal* A warm welcome; a friendly greeting.—Used in such phrases as *the welcome mat is out* and *put out the welcome mat. Our welcome mat is always out to our friends. Spread out the welcome mat, children, because Uncle Bill is visiting us tonight.*

well and good *adj. phr.* Good; satisfactory. *If my daughter finishes high school, I will call that well and good.*—Often used without a verb to show agreement or understanding. *Well and good; I will come to your house tomorrow.*

well-to-do *adj.* Having or making enough money to live comfortably; prosperous. *John's father owns a company and his family is well-to-do.*—Often used with *the* like a plural noun. *This is the part of town where the well-to-do live.*

wet behind the ears *adj. phr., informal* Not experienced; not knowing how to do something; new in a job or place. *The new student is still wet behind the ears; he has not yet learned the tricks that the boys play on each other.*

wet blanket *n. informal* A person or thing that keeps others from enjoying life. *The teenagers don't invite Bob to their parties because he is a wet blanket. The weatherman* *throws a wet blanket on picnic plans when he forecasts rain.*

wet one's whistle *v. phr., slang* To have a drink, especially of liquor. *Uncle Willie told John to wait outside for a minute while he went in to the cafe to wet his whistle.*

what about *interrog.* About or concerning what; in connection with what.—Often used alone as a question. *"I want to talk to you." "What about?"*

what for¹ *interrog.* For what reason; why? *I told Mary what I was going to town for. What are you running for?*—Often used alone as a question. *Billy's mother told him to wear his hat. "What for?" he asked.*

what for² *n. phr., informal* A scolding, or other punishment.—Usually used with *get* or *give. Tom got what for from his father for answering him rudely, and I heard him crying in the house. The teacher gave me what for because I was late.*

what have you *or* **what not** *n. phr., informal* Whatever you like or want; anything else like that. *The store sells big ones, small ones, medium ones, or what have you. We found suits, coats, hats and what not in the closet.*

what if What would, or will, happen if; what is the difference if; suppose that. *What if you go instead of me? What if we paint it red. How will it look? "You can't go now" said mother. "What if I do?" Dick asked. What if Jack scores a touchdown?*

what of it *or* **what about it** *interj., informal* What is wrong with it; what do you care.

Martha said "That boy is wearing a green coat." Jan answered, "What of it?" "John missed the bus." "What of it?"

what's up *or* **what's cooking** *also* **what's doing** *slang* What is happening or planned; what is wrong.—Often used as a greeting. *"What's up?" asked Bob as he joined his friends. "Are you going to the movies?" What's cooking? Why is the crowd in the street? What's doing tonight at the club? Hello Bob, what's up?*

what's with *or* **what's up with** *also* **what's by** *slang* What is happening to; what is wrong; how is everything; what can you tell me about. *Mary looks worried. What's with her? What's with our old friends? I'm fine. What's with you?*

what with *prep.* Because; as a result of. *I couldn't visit you, what with the snowstorm and the cold I had. What with dishes to wash and children to put to bed, Mother was late to the meeting.*

wheel and deal *v. phr., slang* To make many big plans or schemes; especially with important people in government and business; in matters of money and influence; handle money or power for your own advantage; plan important matters in a smart or skillful way and sometimes in a tricky, or not strictly honest way. *Mr. Smith made a fortune by wheeling and dealing on the stock market. The senator got this law passed by wheeling and dealing in Congress.*—**wheeler-dealer** *n. phr., slang* A person with power and control.

The biggest wheeler-dealer in the state has many friends in high places in business and government and is a rich man himself.

when hell freezes over *adv. phr.*, *slang* Never. *I'll believe you when hell freezes over.*

when push comes to shove *adv. phr.* A time when a touchy situation becomes actively hostile or a quarrel turns into a fight. *Can we count on the boss' goodwill, when push comes to shove?*

when the chips are down *adv. cl.*, *informal* When the winner and loser of a bet or a game are decided; at the most important or dangerous time. *Tom hit a home run in the last inning of the game when the chips were down. When the chips were down, the two countries decided not to have war.* [From the fact that in gambling games, a person puts chips or money down in front of him to show that he is willing to risk an amount in a bet.]

where it's at *adv. phr.*, *informal* That which is important; that which is at the forefront of ongoing social, personal, or scientific undertakings. *Young, talented and black, that's where it's at. We send sophisticated machines to Mars instead of people, that's where it's at.*

where the shoe pinches *n. phr.*, *informal* Where or what the discomfort or trouble is. *Johnny thinks the job is easy, but he will find out where the shoe pinches when he tries it. The coach said he wasn't worried about any position except quarterback; that was where the shoe pinched.*

while ago *adv.* At a time several minutes in the past; a few minutes ago; a short time ago.—Used with *a*. *I laid my glasses on this table a while ago; and now they're gone. A while ago, Mary was tired and wanted to go home; now she's dancing with Bob as if she could dance all night.*

while away *v.* To make time go by pleasantly or without being bored; pass or spend. *We whiled away the time that we were waiting by talking and playing cards. We whiled away the summer swimming and fishing.*

while back *adv.* At a time several weeks or months in the past.—Used with *a*. *We had a good rain a while back, but we need more now. Grandfather is well now, but a while back he was in the hospital for three weeks.*

whipping boy *n. phr.* The person who gets punished for someone else's mistake. *"I used to be the whipping boy during my early days at the company," he musingly remembered.*

whip up *v.*, *informal* **1.** To make or do quickly or easily. *Mary whipped up a lunch for the picnic. The reporter whipped up a story about the fire for his paper.* **2.** To make active; stir to action; excite. *The girls are trying to whip up interest for a dance Saturday night.*

whispering campaign *n.* The

preading of false rumors, or aying bad things, about a person or group, especially in politics or public life. *A bad man as started a whispering campaign against the mayor, saying at he isn't honest.*

istle in the dark *v. phr., informal* To try to stay brave nd forget your fear. *Tom said e could fight the bully with ne hand, but we knew that he as just whistling in the dark. rom the fact that people ometimes whistle when walking in a dark, scary place to eep up their courage.]*

ite elephant *n. phr.* Unanted property, such as real state, that is hard to sell. *That ig house of theirs on the corer sure is a white elephant.*

ite lie *n. phr.* An innocent ocial excuse. *I am too busy to o to their house for dinner night. I will call them and tell little white lie about having e flu.*

itewash *n., informal* A oothing official report that atmpts to tranquilize the pubc. *Some people believe that the arren Commission's report the Kennedy assassination as a whitewash.*

itewash something *v., inforal* To explain a major, naonal scandal in soothing fficial terms so as to assure e public that things are under ontrol and there is no need to anic. *Many people in the nited States believe that Presint Kennedy's assassination as whitewashed by the Warren ommission.*

ole cheese *slang or informal*

whole show *n., informal* The only important person; big boss. *Joe thought he was the whole cheese in the game because he owned the ball. You're not the whole show just because you got all A's.*

whoop it up *v. phr., slang* **1.** To make a loud noise; have a noisy celebration; enjoy yourself noisily. *The team whooped it up after winning the game.* **2.** To praise something enthusiastically; encourage enthusiasm or support—Often used with *for. Father wanted to go to the country, but the children whooped it up for the beach.*

who's who *or* **who is who** *informal* **1.** Who this one is and who that one is; who the different ones in a group of people are or what their names or positions are. *It is hard to tell who is who in the parade because everyone in the band looks alike. It took the new teacher a few days to remember who was who in the class.* **2.** Who the important people are. *John didn't recognize the champion on television. He doesn't know who is who in boxing. After about a year, Mr. Thompson had lived in this town long enough to know who was who.*

why and wherefore *n.* The answer to a question or problem. Usually used in the plural. *Father told him not to always ask the whys and wherefores when he was told to do something.*

wide of the mark *adv. or adj. phr.* **1.** Far from the target or the thing aimed at. *James threw a stone at the cat but it went wide of the mark.* **2.** Far from the truth; incorrect. *You were wide of the mark when you said I did it, because Bill did it.*

wildcat strike *n. informal* A strike not ordered by a labor union; a strike spontaneously arranged by a group of workers. *The garbage collectors have gone on a wildcat strike, but the union is going to stop it.*

wild goose chase *n. phr.* An absurd and completely futile errand. *I was on a wild goose chase when I was sent to find a man who never really existed.*

window dressing *n. phr.* An elaborate exterior, sometimes designed to conceal one's real motives. *All those fancy invitations turned out to be nothing but window dressing. All he really wanted was to be introduced to my influential father-in-law.*

wind up *v.* **1.** To tighten the spring of a machine; to make it work or run. *Mary wound up the toy car and let it run across the room. He doesn't have to wind up his watch because it is run by a battery.* **2.** To make very excited, nervous, upset.— Usually used in the past participle. *The excitement of her birthday party got Jane all wound up so she could not sleep.* **3.** *informal* To bring or come to an end; finish; stop. *John got two hits and wound his afternoon up with a home run. Before Jim knew it, he had spent all his money and he wound up broke. The boys followed the path to the left and wound up where they started.* **4.** To put (your business or personal affairs) in order; arrange; settle. *Fred wound up his business and personal affairs before joining the Navy.* **5.** To swing your arm with the ball just before pitching to a batter. *The pitcher wound up quickly and then threw a curve.*

win hands down *v. phr.* To win conclusively and without external help. *The opposition was so weak that Dan won the election hands down.*

winning streak *n.* A series of several wins one after the other. *The team extended their winning streak to ten.*

win over *v. phr.* To convert to one's position or point of view. *The Democrats offered him a high-level executive position and thus won him over to their side.*

wipeout *n.* A total failure. *The guy is so bad at his job that he is a total wipeout.*

wipe out *v.* **1.** To remove or erase by wiping or rubbing. *The teacher wiped out with an eraser what she had written on the board.* **2.** *informal* To remove, kill, or destroy completely. *The earthquake wiped out the town. Doctors are searching for a cure that will wipe out cancer. The Indians wiped out the soldiers who were sent to stop their attacks.*

wisecrack *n.* A joke or witty remark usually made at someone else's expense. *The comedians kept up a steady stream of wisecracks.*

wise guy *n. phr., informal* A person who acts as if he were smarter than other people; a person who jokes or shows off too much. *Bill is a wise guy and displeases others by what he says.*

wise up to *v. phr., slang* To finally understand what is really going on after a period of ignorance. *Joe immediately quit his job when he wised up to what was really going on.*

wish on *v.* **1.** To use as a lucky charm while making a wish. *Mary wished on a star that she could go to the dance. Bob wished on his lucky rabbit's foot that he could pass the test.* **2.** *or* **wish off on** *informal* To get rid of (something unwanted) by passing it on to someone else. *Martha did not like to do the dishes and wished the job on to her little sister. Tom got a very ugly tie for his birthday and when Billy's birthday came, Tom wished the tie off on Billy.*

witch-hunt *n. phr.* A hysterical movement during which people are persecuted for having views (political or religious) considered different or unpopular. *During the McCarthy era many innocent Americans were accused of being Communists, as Republican patriotism deteriorated into a witch-hunt.*

with bells on *adv. phr., informal* With enthusiasm; eager or ready and in the best of spirits for an event. *"Will you come to the farewell party I'm giving for Billy?" asked Jerry. "I'll be there with bells on," replied Ed.*

with child *adv. phr., literary* Going to have a baby; pregnant. *The angel told Mary she was with child.*

with flying colors *adv. phr.* With great or total success; victoriously. *Tom finished the race with flying colors. Mary came through the examination with flying colors.*

within an inch of one's life *adv. phr.* Until you are almost dead; near to dying. *The bear clawed the hunter within an inch of his life.* Often used after *to*. *The prize fighter was beaten to within an inch of his life.*

within reason *adv. or adj. phr.* Within the limits of good sense; in reasonable control or check; moderate. *I want you to have a good time tonight, within reason. If Tom wants to go to the fair, he must keep his expenses within reason. Jean's plans are quite within reason.*

with open arms *adv. phr.* **1.** With the arms spread wide for hugging or catching. *When Father came home from work, little Sally ran out to meet him with open arms. Dick stood under the window with open arms, and Jean dropped the bag of laundry down to him.* **2.** With words or actions showing that you are glad to see someone; gladly, warmly, eagerly. *When Grandmother came to visit us at Christmas, we welcomed her with open arms. After his pioneering flight in the Friendship VII, Col. John Glenn was welcomed with open arms by the people of his hometown.*

without fail *adv. phr.* Without failing to do it or failing in the doing of it; certainly, surely. *Be* *here at 8 o'clock sharp, without fail. Ben promised to return the bike at a certain time without fail.*

with the best *or* **with the best of them** *adv. phr.* As well as anyone. *Bob could horseback ride with the best of them, but he never boasted about it. John can bowl with the best of them.*

wolf in sheep's clothing *n. phr.* A person who pretends to be good but really is bad. *Mrs. Martin trusted the lawyer until she realized that he was a wolf in sheep's clothing. Mr. Black was fooled by the salesman's manners until he showed that he was really a wolf in sheep's clothing by selling Mr. Black a car that was falling apart.*

word for word *adv. phr.* In exactly the same words. *Mary copied Sally's composition word for word. Joan repeated the conversation word for word. She learned the poem many years ago but she recited it word for word.*

word of mouth *n. phr.* Communication by oral rather than written means. *The merchant told us that the best customers he had were recommended to him by word of mouth.*

worked up *also* **wrought up** *adj., literary* Feeling strongly; excited; angry; worried. *Mary was all worked up about the exam. John got worked up when they blamed him for losing the game.*

work in *v.* **1.** To rub in. *The nurse told Mary to put some cream on her skin and to work it in gently with her fingers.* **2.** To slip in; mix in; put in; *When*

Mary was planning the show she worked a part in for he friend Susan.

working girl *n., slang* **1.** *(vu gar, avoidable)* A prostitute. *didn't know Roxanne was working girl.* **2.** A girl, usuall single, who supports herself b working in an honest job, suc as in an office, etc. *The averag working girl can't afford such fancy car.*

work into *v.* **1.** Force into littl by little. *John worked his foo into the boot by pushing an pulling.* **2.** Put into; mix intc *Mary worked some blue int the rug she was weaving.*

work off *v.* To make (some thing) go away, especially b working. *John worked off th fat around his waist by doin, exercise every morning. M Smith worked off his anger b chopping wood.*

work on *also* **work upon** *v.* Have an effect on; influence *Some pills work on the nerve and make people feel mor relaxed.* **2.** To try to influenc or convince. *Senator Smit worked on the other committe members to vote for the bill.*

work one's fingers to the bon *v. phr.* To work very hard. " have to work my fingers to th bone for a measly pittance of salary," Fred complained.*

workout *n.* A physical exer cise session. *My morning work out consists of sit-ups an push-ups.*

work out *v. phr.* **1.** To find a answer to. *John worked out hi math problems all by himself Mary had trouble getting alon, with her roommate, but the* orked it out. **2.** To plan; develop. *Mary worked out a beautiful design for a sweater. Alice worked out a new hairdo.* **3.** To accomplish; arrange. *The engineers worked out a system for getting electricity to the factory.* **4.** To be efficient; get results. *If the traffic plan works out, it will be used in other cities too.* **5.** To exercise. *John works out in the gym two hours every day.*

work over *v. phr., slang* To beat someone up very roughly in order to intimidate him or extort payment, etc. *Matthew was worked over by the hoodlums in the park right after midnight.*

work up *v.* **1.** To stir up; arouse; excite. *I can't work up any interest in this book. He worked up a sweat weeding the garden.* **2.** To develop; originate. *He worked up an interesting plot for a play.*

world is one's oyster Everything is possible for you; the world belongs to you; you can get anything you want. *When John won the scholarship, he felt as though the world was his oyster. The rich girl acts as though the world is her oyster.*

world without end *adv. phr., literary* Endlessly; forever; eternally. *Each human being has to die, but mankind goes on world without end.*

worse for wear *adj. phr.* Not as good as new; worn out; damaged by use.—Used with *the*. *Her favorite tablecloth was beginning to look the worse for wear.*—Often used with *none* to mean: as good as new. *The*

doll was Mary's favorite toy but it was none the worse for wear.

worth a cent *adj. phr.* Worth anything; of any value.—Used in negative, interrogative, and conditional sentences. *The book was old and it was not worth a cent.*

worth one's salt *adj. phr.* Being a good worker, or a productive person; worth what you cost. *Mr. Brown showed that he was worth his salt as a salesman when he got the highest sales record for the year.*—Often used with *not* or *hardly*. *When the basketball team did so poorly, people felt that the coach was hardly worth his salt.*

would that *or* **I would that** *or* **would God** *or* **would heaven** *literary* I wish that.—Used at the beginning of a sentence expressing a wish; followed by a verb in the subjunctive; found mostly in poetry and older literature. *Would that I could only drop everything and join you. Would that my mother were alive to see me married.*

wouldn't put it past one *v. phr.* To think that someone is quite capable or likely to have done something undesirable or illegal. *Congressman Alfonso is insisting that he didn't violate congressional ethics, but knowing both his expensive habits and his amorous escapades, many of us wouldn't put it past him that he might have helped himself to funds illegally.*

wrapped up in *adj. phr.* Thinking only of; interested only in. *John has no time for sports because he is all wrapped up in his work. Mary was so* *wrapped up in her book she didn't hear her mother calling her. Jean is so wrapped up in herself, she never thinks of helping others. Mrs. Brown gave up her career because her life was all wrapped up in her children.*

wrap up *or* **bundle up** *v. phr.* **1.** To put on warm clothes; dress warmly. *Mother told Mary to wrap up before going out into the cold.* **2.** *informal* To finish (a job). *Let's wrap up the job and go home.* **3.** *informal* To win a game. *The Mets wrapped up the baseball game in the seventh inning.*

wreak havoc with *v. phr.* To cause damage; ruin something. *His rebellious attitude is bound to wreak havoc at the company.*

wringing wet *adj.* Wet through and through; soaked; dripping. *He was wringing wet because he was caught in the rain without an umbrella. He was wringing wet after working in the fields in the hot sun.*

write home about *v. phr.* To become especially enthusiastic or excited about; boast about.—Often used after *to. Mary's trip to the World's Fair was something to write home about. Joe did a good enough job of painting but it was nothing to write home about. "That was a dinner worth writing home about!" said Bill coming out of the restaurant.*

write off *v. phr.* **1.** To remove (an amount) from a business record; cancel (a debt); accept as a loss. *If a customer dies when he owes the store money, the store must often write it off.*

2. To accept (a loss or trouble) and not worry anymore about it; forget. *Mr. Brown had so much trouble with the new T set that he finally wrote it of and bought a new one. Jim mistake cost him time an money, but he wrote it off to e perience.* **3.** To say that (something) will fail or not be goo believe worthless. *Just becau the boys on the team are youn don't write the team off.*

write-off *n.* A loss. *This la unfortunate business venture ours is an obvious write-off.*

writer's block *n. phr.* A cond tion of being unable to write; period when the words ju won't come. *One of the mo common problems writers o casionally experience is writer's block that may last shorter or a longer time. The say that the reason for Erne Hemingway's suicide was a s vere and seemingly endle writer's block.*

write-up *n.* A report or stor in a newspaper or magazin *There was a write-up of the a cident in the newspaper. I rea an interesting write-up abo the President in a new mag zine.*

write up *v.* **1.** To write the stor of; describe in writing; give full account of. *Reporters fro many newspapers are here write up the game. The mag zine is writing up the life of th President.* **2.** To put somethin thought or talked about int writing; finish writing (som thing). *John took notes of wh the teacher said in class and wrote them up when he g* *home. The author had an idea for a story when he saw the old house, and he wrote it up later.*

riting *or* **handwriting on the wall** *n. phr., literary* A warning; a message of some urgency. *"This nuclear plant is about to explode, I think," the chief engineer said. "We'd better get out of here in a hurry, the handwriting is on the wall."*

X

x-double minus *adj.*, *slang*, *informal* Extremely poorly done, bad, inferior (said mostly about theatrical or musical performances). *Patsy gave an x-double minus performance at the audition and lost her chance for the lead role.*

X marks the spot. An indication made on maps or documents of importance to call attention to a place or a feature of some importance. *The treasure hunter said to his companion, "Here it is; X marks the spot."*

x-rated *adj.*, *slang informa* Pertaining to movies, maga zines, and literature judgec pornographic and therefore of limits for minors. *My son cele brated his 21st birthday by go ing to an x-rated movie.*

x-raying machine *n.*, *slang citizen's band radio jargon* Speed detection device by radar used by the police. *The smokies are using the x-raying machine under the bridge!*

k-yak or **yakety-yak** or **akib-yak** n., slang Much alk about little things; talking all the time about unimortant things. Tom sat ehind two girls on the bus nd he got tired of their silly ak-yak.

ar-round or **year-around** adj. Jsable, effective, or operating ll the year. Colorado is a yearound resort; there is fishing in he summer and skiing in the inter.

low-bellied adj., slang Exremely timid, cowardly. Joe ennett is a yellow-bellied guy, on't send him on such a tough ssignment!

s-man n., informal A peron who tries to be liked by greeing with everything said; specially, someone who alays agrees with a boss or the ne in charge. John tries to get head on his job by being a yesan.

o-hoo interj. Used as an inormal call or shout to a person o attract his attention. Louise pened the door and called Yoo-hoo, Mother—are you ome?"

u bet or **you bet your boots** or **ou bet your life** informal lost certainly; yes, indeed; ithout any doubt.—Used to eclare with emphasis that a hing is really so. Do I like to ki? You bet your life I do. You et I will be at the party. You an bet your boots that Johnny will come home when his money is gone.

you can't teach an old dog new tricks It is very hard or almost impossible to train an older person to acquire some new skill.—A proverb. You'll never teach your grandfather how to do his income tax on a personal computer. You can't teach an old dog new tricks.

you don't say interj., informal—Used to show surprise at what is said. Your ring is a real diamond? You don't say! "Bill and Jean are going to get married." "You don't say!"

you're telling me interj., informal—Used to show that a thing is so clear that it need not be said, or just to show strong agreement. "You're late." "You're telling me!"

you said it or **you can say that again** interj., slang Used to show strong agreement with what another person has said. "That sure was a good show." "You said it!" "It sure is hot!" "You can say that again!"

you tell 'em interj., slang Used to agree with or encourage someone in what he is saying. The drunk was arguing with the bartenders and a man cried, "You tell 'em!"

yours truly adv. phr. **1.** Signing off at the end of letters. Yours truly, Tom Smith. **2.** I, the first person singular pronoun, frequently abbreviated as t.y. As t.y. has often pointed

out. . .*T.y. is not really inter-*
ested in the offer.
yum-yum *interj., informal—*
Used usually by or to children,
to express great delight, espe
cially in the taste of foo
"Yum-Yum! That pie is good!"

Z

ero hour *n.* **1.** The exact time when an attack or other military action is supposed to start. *Zero hour for the bombers to take off was midnight.* **2.** The time when an important decision or change is supposed to come; the time for a dangerous action. *It was zero hour and the doctor began the operation on the man. On the day of the championship game, as the zero hour came near, the players grew nervous.*

ero in on *v.* **1.** To adjust a gun so that it will exactly hit (a target); aim at. *Big guns were zeroed in on the enemy fort. American missiles have been zeroed in on certain targets, to be fired if necessary.* **2.** *slang* To give your full attention to. *The Senate zeroed in on the Latin-American problems. Let's zero in on grammar tonight.*

zone defense *n.* A defense in a sport (as basketball or football) in which each player has to defend a certain area. *The coach taught his team a zone defense because he thought his players weren't fast enough to defend against individual opponents.*

zonk out *v. phr., slang* **1.** To fall asleep very quickly. *Can I talk to Joe?—Call back tomorrow, he zonked out.* **2.** To pass out from fatigue, or alcohol. *You won't get a coherent word out of Joe, he has zonked out.*

zoom in *v. phr.* **1.** To rapidly close in on (said of airplanes and birds of prey). *The fighter planes zoomed in on the enemy target.* **2.** To make a closeup of someone or something with a camera. *The photographer zoomed in on the tiny colibri as it hovered over a lovely tropical flower.*

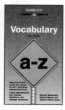